DYNAMICS OF NEW PANCHAYATI RAJ SYSTEM IN INDIA

Volume V : PANCHAYATI RAJ AND MULTI-LEVEL PLANNING

Dynamics of New Panchayati Raj System in India

Vol.	I	:	Select States
Vol.	II	:	Select States
Vol.	III	:	Select States
Vol.	IV	:	Empowering Women
Vol.	V	:	Panchayati Raj and Multi-level Planning
Vol.	VI	:	Panchayati Raj and Empowerment of Dalits
Vol.	VII	:	Finance in Panchayati Raj System
Vol.	VIII	:	Panchayati Raj and Common Property Resource Management
Vol.	IX	:	Participatory and Direct Democracy : Gram Sabha
Vol.	X	:	Capacity Building for Panchayati Raj Leaders and Functionaries
Vol.	XI	:	State-Local Body Relationship
Vol.	XII	:	Panchayati Raj and Socio-Political and Economic Transformation
Vol.	XIII	:	Leadership in Panchayati Raj Institution
Vol.	XIV	:	Thinkers Framework on Panchayati Raj
Vol.	XV	:	Theoretical Nuances of Local Bodies

About the Editor

Prof. Ganapathi Palanithurai, Coordinator in Rajiv Gandhi Chair, Gandhigram Rural Institute is an academic activist working with the people in rural areas for building the capacity of the leaders and people to reinvent sustainable grassroots democracy. He is heading the Department of Political Science and Development Administration, in Gandhigram Rural University, Tamil Nadu. His policy advocacy role at the governmental level is increasingly felt at present in all the three levels, namely sub-regional, regional and national as he does more field work than theorisation. He has been associating himself with Centre Planning Commission, State Planning Commission of Tamil Nadu, Population Foundation of India, Ford Foundation, UNICEF, Rajiv Gandhi Foundation, CAPART, Ministry of Rural Areas and Employment and DANIDA (Danish-Indo Development Agency) in specific areas of activities in connection with empowerment of people. He is in the network of the Non-Governmental Organisations for Panchayat activities. He involves himself in capacity building exercise for local body leaders. He has to his credit twenty-nine books, seventy-five articles on three major areas, namely, Legislative Behaviour, Ethnicity and Panchayati Raj System. He was a recipient of Fellowship from Sastri Indo-Canadian Institute, New Delhi and World Academy of Art and Science, USA. He is the Chairman of the Tamil Nadu Council for Sustainable Livelihoods. He has visited the US and Canada, on academic assignments. He was a visiting fellow in the McGill University, Canada in 1989. He is a life member of Indian Institute of Public Administration, Indian Association of Public Administration, Indian Association of Political Science, Indian Association of American Studies and Indian Association of Canadian Studies. He is a member of the expert committee constituted by the Government of Tamil Nadu to monitor the training programme for local body leaders.

DYNAMICS OF NEW PANCHAYATI RAJ SYSTEM IN INDIA

VOLUME V

Panchayati Raj and Multi-level Planning

Edited by
G. PALANITHURAI

CONCEPT PUBLISHING COMPANY, NEW DELHI-110059

Cataloging in Publication Data—DK
Courtesy: D.K. Agencies (P) Ltd. <docinfo@dkagencies.com>

Dynamics of new panchayati raj system in India / edited by
G. Palanithurai.
v. 5 cm.
Contributed articles.
Includes bibliographical references.
Includes indexes.
Contents: v. 5. Panchayati raj and multi-level planning
ISBN 8170229103 (set)
ISBN 8180692442 (v. 5)

1. Panchayat—India. 2. Local government—India.
I. Palanithurai, G. (Ganapathy), 1953-

DDC 320.840 954 21

ISBN 81-8069-244-2 (Vol. V)
ISBN 81-7022-910-3 (Series)

First Published **2006**

Published and Printed by

Ashok Kumar Mittal
Concept Publishing Company
A/15-16, Commercial Block, Mohan Garden
New Delhi-110059 (India)

Phones: 25351460, 25351794
Fax: 091-11-25357103
E-mail: publishing@conceptpub.com

TO

THE DIVINE MOTHER

(In India) one should begin with the old panchayat system in the villages and the work upto the top. The panchayat system and the guilds are more representative and they have a living contact with people, they are thc parts of the people's ideas.

– Sri Aurobindo

The village Republic will be managed by a panchayat which will be living political force and entity. Panchayats will be united in a free and voluntary association by "ever widening circle of village republics". It will not be an "apex sustained by the bottom", but an oceanic circle where centre will be the individual always ready to perish for the village, the latter ready to perish for the circle of villages and so on, sharing the majesty of the oceanic circle which they are parts.

– Mahatma Gandhi

We trust the people

We have faith in the people

It is the people who must

determine their own destinies

and the destiny of the Nation

To the people of India, let us

ensure maximum democracy and

maximum devolution. Let the

people be empowered.

– Rajiv Gandhi

PREFACE

Planning was considered a serious exercise which needed experts and which was done at the central level. Down below that nobody thought about it and it took near about two and a half decades to convince the policy makers that planning could be done at the provincial level. Around the middle of the 70s planning at the provincial level was concretized however imperfect it was. Still it took another two decades to convince the administrators and policy makers to have such planning exercise below the state level. There were stray experiences of such planning at the district level but not as a system. It was only through the 73rd and the 74th Amendments to the Constitution of India that planning at the grassroots took concrete shape. Yet, it has failed to gain momentum as the belief system and the thought process of policy makers and administrators have not changed.

Attempts have been made at different levels in different historic contexts to plan for development at the grassroots. Nomenclatures such as Decentralized Planning, District Planning, Multi Level Planning and Micro Level Planning have been used and different connotations have been attributed. Why micro level planning at the grassroots is a major question. A very simple answer is that despite the rigorous planning efforts by the Central and State Governments, many of the basic facilities and services to ensure livelihood security have not been provided to the people to their satisfaction. The amount spent on those activities is not small. Yet people's needs could not be met. A cursory analysis of the spending in a district for rural development activities and the basic needs projected by the people through the Gram Sabha works out to the ratio 10:1. Because all development activities are in the supply driven mode and not in the demand driven mode, basic needs are unmet. As allocated money is available at difficult levels through the schemes and programmes of the governments whether they are required by the community or not, it is being spent. Sometimes, the money is being wasted. To avoid wastages and to meet the requirements of the communities, planning at grassroots is considered an imperative. Further it helps the people to participate in the development process. Against this background micro level planning is considered essential.

At present, barring West Bengal and Kerala, exercises have been undertaken in different places because of the initiative of development organizations in planning for development at the grassroots. In Kerala and West Bengal planning initiatives were undertaken by the State Government itself. In other states only development organizations took the initiative. These initiatives are attempts to break the myth that planning cannot be done at the micro level as experts are available only at a higher level. Further, planning was considered a highly technical exercise which requires the support of technocracy. This myth has also been broken. These new initiatives and exercises are considered innovations as they are being attempted with the participation of the people. Recording these new initiatives is considered an imperative and hence this study. No officer is willing to work with the people as they consider this process meaningless. Hence, a large number of barriers hinder the process of involving people in development activities.

The purpose of this volume is to bring to light the activities generated from the people by development organizations to decide their destiny. In the Indian context volumes of literature are available on planning at the Centre and in the States. Development activities are carried out down below the State level. But these activities are planned only at the top. For the first time in India planning is now done at the ground level with the participation of the people. But it faces varied bottlenecks, which are highlighted in this work. It is not the aim to theorize the planning process at the micro level. The main objective is to analyze the process and to identify the advantages and weaknesses in the whole process and thereby find ways and means to remove the weaknesses in the whole process and to spread these practices to other areas for replication. Academics are far away from the grassroots. Many researchers find a paucity of literature in this area and hence this study.

My research and field teams working in the projects, helped me in completing this assignment. Our aim is to democratize society, empower the people and specifically empowering women and other marginalized groups for which we have built a grassroots movement through our Rajiv Gandhi Chair for Panchayati Raj Studies. To build a movement varied activities are essential. They are creating awareness among the people, building the capacity of the leaders at the grassroots, building alliance among academics, media and development organizations, sensitizing academics, building rapport with bureaucrats, and policy lobbying with political party leaders. These are the activities of the Rajiv Gandhi Chair for Panchayati Raj Studies. In all these activities Dr.V. Ragupathy, Mr. M.A. Thirunavukkarasu, Mr. S. Devaraj, Mr. M. Gurusamy, Ms. G. Uma, Mr. A. Thangathurai, Mr.K. Tamilarasan, Ms. Rekha, Ms. B. Jeyashri, Mr. S.P. Ramesh, Mr. Karthik, Ms. J.Vanishree are the partners and stakeholders. I express my gratitude to them. My family members are always cooperative and supportive to all my academic endeavours. My wife Mrs. Mala, my kids P. Senthil Vadivu and P. Aurobindh spare me from family calls and social calls and hence I am able to devote myself fully to academic assignments and extension activities. I express my gratitude to them.

Gandhigram Rural Institute has been devoted, right from the days of its formation, to rural development activities and to empowering women. It spearheads a movement for village democracy, appropriate technology, sustainable development and women empowerment.

Gandhigram June 2004 **G. PALANITHURAI**

CONTENTS

LIST OF CONTRIBUTORS

Mahi Pal
Associate Professor
Haryana Institute of Rural Development
Nilokheri
Haryana

Regi Thomas
C/o Rajiv Gandhi Chair
Gandhigram Rural Institute
Gandhigram - 624 302

Binu Paul G.D.
C/o Rajiv Gandhi Chair
Gandhigram Rural Institute-Deemed University
Gandhigram - 624 302

Rakesh Hooja
Joint Secretary (K-1)
Ministry of Home Affairs
Government of India
New Delhi.

N.D. Mani
Head
Department of Rural Development
Gandhigram Rural Institute-Deemed University
Gandhigram - 624 302

P. Kanniappan
Director
Rural Energy Centre
Gandhigram Rural Institute-Deemed University
Gandhigram - 624 302

T. Ramachandran
Department of Mathematics
R.V.S. College of Engineering and Technology
Dindigul

K. Narayana Rao
Senior Economist
Management Services Department
Indian Overseas Bank
Central Office
763, Anna Salai
Chennai - 600 002

M. Devandra Babu
Faculty Member
Institute for Social and Economic Change
Nagarbhavi (Post)
Bangalore

G. Palanithurai
Dean
Faculty of Rural Social Sciences
Rural University
Gandhigram

The Hunger Project
3-3/18, Vasant Vihar
New Delhi - 110 057

PRIA-Participatory Research in Asia
42, Tughlakabad
Institutional Area
New Delhi - 110 062

INTRODUCTION

Four decades of central planning and the implications of central planning could not generate a positive note about the major achievements in terms of providing basic services to the people to lead a decent human life in both rural and urban areas. It has been questioned for long whether centralized governance and centralized planning would be able to meet the basic needs of the communities at the grassroots and if the answer is no, what is the alternative? This question gained momentum in the 1970s and vigorously drew the attention of many of the policy making sections in the 1980s. Proposals for state level and sub-state level planning were considered. Sporadic attempts were made here and there and positive results were shown to the effect that local needs and problems could be attended to. Discussions were open among the academics, policy makers and administrators about the planning at the sub-state level and finally it has taken a concrete shape through the 73rd and 74th Amendments to the Constitution of India. For development of any family, community organization, association, institution, planning and management are essential. The entire Indian society has been oriented to receive benefits from above and all development activities are always in the supply driven mode and not in the demand driven mode. In terms of meeting the basic needs, our institutions have not fared well. Governments are spending continuously for implementing programmes. People's demand for basic services continue to increase. To bridge the gap between the demands of the people and the spending of government, micro level planning is considered vital. Micro level planning is not intended to provide basic facilities but also to generate employment opportunities for the skilled and unskilled manpower available in the rural and urban areas, protect the natural resources and to involve the people in the planning process. It makes the people partners in the development process.

But planning was considered a serious exercise which needed a large number of experts and which could be done only at the central and state levels. The belief still exists. The 73rd and 74th

Amendments to the Constitution of India made it mandatory that planning should be done at the sub-state level in an integral way. Every Gram Panchayat, every Block Panchayat, every Town Panchayat, every Municipality, every Corporation should have a perspective plan document prepared with the participation of the people. For the entire district the District Planning Committee should prepare a development plan. A District Planning Committee has been duly and legitimately constituted to prepare the plan for the whole district. As per the new dispensation, Kerala and West Bengal have shown the way. But other states have not shown such interest in the new exercise which needs political will, a new mindset, a new culture among the political class, bureaucrats and the people. There are a large number of development organizations involved in the process of planning at the micro level as they work with the communities to achieve development and social justice.

The new exercises are pilot attempts and are not spread throughout the state. Bilateral and multi lateral funding agencies are also interested in such micro experiments as constitutional provisions are available. These exercises are bringing out a variety of postulates, information and insights into the development initiatives. When the above exercises are visualized from the perspective of the background of poor devolution of powers, functions, functionaries and finances, it can be observed that they are mere wish lists and not the plans of the people. Further, participatory planning at the grassroots is a romantic idea in a context wherein the government pervades everywhere and people are relegated to the background as beneficiaries. The new proposal needs an array of activities at different levels from the State Government to the community at the grassroots. The government machinery has to be geared to understand the new context and the people and their representatives have to be sensitized on the steps to be taken at their level to plan for development at the grassroots. In the absence of the above, it is imperative on the part of the development organizations to initiate the process with the objective of sensitizing both the government and the elected representatives to local bodies on the task of planning at the micro level with the participation of the people. Against the above backdrop, it is envisaged that all the experiences have to be documented and hence this volume. Scholars from various states have contributed to this volume. Barring a few, all the articles narrate field based experiences.

Mahi Pal, viewing the Panchayati Raj system by his continuous observation in the field, takes stock of the constitutional initiative for planning at the micro level and assesses the steps taken by the State Governments in his article entitled "Decentralized Planning and Panchayati Raj in India: Provisions and Practice—Some Evidences". While analyzing the planning at the grassroots, he touches upon the basics of devolution, namely transfer of powers, functions, finance and functionaries in the states, and the bottlenecks involved in the process. Finally he brings to light the perspectives of the State Government in constituting the District Planning Committee and entrusting the responsibilities to the District Planning Committee to prepare a plan for the integrated development of the whole district. He identifies the gap between the intention and the reality. He presents the all India scenario of planning at the grassroots.

"Regional Information System and Development Indices: Relevance in Panchayati Raj" by Regi Thomas and Bino Paul is a basic paper dealing with the database and the methodology of using the same for planning. They commence their article with the experience of Kerala. The article presents a strong argument for maintaining an information system for planning from below at different levels. While developing the scientific device the authors have not forgotten the aim of achieving sustainable development. While planning at the micro level, it is necessary to understand how to measure the impact of planning and its activities. Constructing development indices on different aspects is an imperative. The article extensively analyses the data collection process, data analysis, benchmarking index computation, evolving Panchayat development index, Panchayat product index, resource index, financial resources index, industrial development index, human resource index, biodiversity index, welfare index, physical quality of life index, participation index, health index and privilege index. They provide the needed wherewithal for scientific planning. The question is do we have such mechanism at the grassroots to adopt such a rigorous exercise? The article provides basic inputs for planning at the micro level on a scientific basis.

A civil servant with academic thirst, Rakesh Hooja in his article entitled, "District Planning Practice and Theory with Special Reference to 'How to' Aspects" brings to light the gap between the theoretical assumptions and the practice in India, especially in relation to district planning. Even before the enactment of the amendments (73rd and 74th) to the Constitution of India the concept of District Planning was in practice. He captures the present scenario in the light of the Constitutional Amendment with regard to planning at the grassroots. Based on the experience in many countries he highlights the major risks involved in the process of planning in the Indian context. He indicates the policy issues regarding decentralized planning that are envisaged in India. While discussing the practical aspect of planning at the district level and below, he recollects the dominant thought process on decentralized planning in India from the perspective of economic and development thinkers. He indicates the needed skills and techniques at the district level, block level and village level for planning exercises. Incidentally explaining the Hanumantha Rao model of District Planning he discusses the models and modalities followed in the states during pre-73rd and 74th Amendments period. Finally, he suggests an organizational model for planning. He also underlines a few cautions.

N.D. Mani's article "Information System for Panchayat Planning" deals with data collection and management for Panchayat level planning. He indicates the requirements of data for all the subjects indicated in the 11th Schedule. His analysis is based on the studies conducted by him at district and block level in a project. He works out a detailed chart of the micro aspects in each and every subject indicated in the 11th Schedule. The Panchayat information system plays a crucial role in the planning process. He codifies the tasks to be performed by the functionaries. He puts forth the key assignments which are to be completed before the preparation of the plan documents.

P. Kanniappan and T. Ramachandran's article entitled "Bio-Mass Assessment and Optimization Model for Energy Planning in Rural Areas" gives the details of sectoral planning with the aim of providing an alternative approach. Energy crisis is a major crisis in rural areas. To overcome the energy crisis, a number of steps have to be taken, of which converting bio mass into energy is a viable solution. Kanniappan and Ramachandran, being experts in energy audit, have conducted several studies in Tamil Nadu to assess the biomass in the rural areas. Based on their experiences through their studies, they have suggested ways and means to develop a plan for energy management. For any comprehensive planning at the district level or block level energy management it would be much helpful to the planners. This article is drawn from a project which had carried out for the Government of Tamil Nadu.

"Issues and Problems in Implementation of Decentralized Planning: A Case Study of Tamil Nadu" by K. Narayana Rao analyses the linkages between the powers devolved and the planning exercise undertaken against the backdrop of the new political and economic dispensation. Further he evaluates the environment in which the planning exercise is being undertaken at the grassroots in Tamil Nadu. The whole discussion is on planning and participation of people in the centralization and decentralization continuum. Being a banker, he finally concludes, based on his analysis, that a fine balance has to be arrived at between centralization and decentralization. Over centralization and over decentralization never delivered goods and services in the past. A fine balancing of activities of development should be maintained in a continuum of decentralization and centralization at an optimum level.

M. Devendra Babu in his article entitled "Decentralized Planning in Karnataka" analyses the decentralization process in Karnataka and, keeping it in the backdrop, analyses the decentralized planning in Karnataka in the post-73rd Amendment era. He evaluates the plans of the three-tier structure and the implementation of the same. He identifies the gap between the needs and the available resources. He looks into the plan process against the backdrop of the environment and the capacity of the institutions. He brings out the advantages, implications and weaknesses of the plan initiatives of the grassroots institutions in Karnataka.

"Micro Level Plan in Rajasthan" by The Hunger Project is a field based study. The Hunger Project is helping the Panchayats to plan for development at the micro level. The Hunger Project has initiated planning through Panchayats with the participation of the community. The entire planning exercise has been documented. It is more of a process than achieving physical targets. It records the steps and the sequence of activities carried out in the planning process. The Hunger Project has been carried out in different regions of Rajasthan and all these activities are covered in this article. This article covers the preparatory exercises, plan preparation, training conducted, mass mobilization for participation and prioritizing the needs of the people and implementation. The strengths and weaknesses in the whole exercise have been discussed in this article.

PRIA's "Micro Planning and Panchayats" is yet another experience in carrying out the micro plan exercise at the grassroots with the active support of a development organization. PRIA initiated this work in Madhya Pradesh, Bihar, Haryana, Himachal Pradesh, Kerala, Rajasthan and Uttar Pradesh. In the above mentioned states, PRIA selected Gram Panchayats and in all the selected Gram Panchayats it operated the project. Each and every case has been documented, in which explanations are offered to cover how the process was started, how the plan was prepared, how activities were been prioritized, how the activities were carried out, who were all the prime movers in this exercise, what are the learnings in this exercise and what are the implications of the planning at the bottom. Each and every case is reported individually. Even variations have been highlighted.

"Planning for Development at Grassroots in Tamil Nadu" by G. Palanithurai is the experience of a project work carried out in two districts in Tamil Nadu. Through The Hunger Project initiative planning was initiated at the Gram Panchayat level. A very simple device was used whereby the interested leaders could be motivated to plan for development at the grassroots. In the first phase ten Gram Panchayats in Sivagangai District were selected and planning was done with the help of a development organization. It was supported by the district administration. In the planning social development was given thrust. It was learnt that it is very difficult to shift the emphasis to social development. In the second phase thirteen Gram Panchayats in Pudukkottai District were selected with the support of the district administration. Gandhigram Rural

Institute was directly involved in the planning process. A series of activities were carried out by Gandhigram Rural Institute to prepare a plan document. The whole process and the steps taken were analysed and reported. The variations between the two districts were analyzed. The problems involved, the weaknesses identified and the advantages gained are elaborately explained in the article. The major points that emerged from the project for replicability have been analyzed and reported.

1

DECENTRALISED PLANNING AND PANCHAYATI RAJ IN INDIA

Provisions and Practice—Some Evidences

MAHI PAL

Introduction

The large size of the country, uneven distribution of resources in different regions, socio-cultural conditions with the existence of multi-ethnic, multi-lingustic and multi-cultural society have made a strong case for decentralized planning in India. Of course, the need for decentralized planning for economic reconstruction of rural India was emphasized even before Independence. After Independence no doubt, several attempts were made in 1950s, 1960s, 1970s and 1980s to operationalise decentralized planning across the country. Although in some States model district plans were formulated, they could not be operationalised due to non-existence of people's institutions at district or sub-district levels on sustainable basis. Various Expert Committees and Working Groups on the subject had also been constituted at the national level to give impetus to local planning with people's participation. The Constitution (73rd and 74th Amendment) Acts 1992 have not only given sustained base to the people's institutions in the forms of the Panchayats and Municipalities but also made provisions for the constitution of the District Planning Committee (DPC) at district level. This Committee is expected to prepare a draft district plan after integrating rural and urban plans prepared by the Zilla Panchayat (ZP) and the Municipalities and forward the same to the State Government. We have by now a decade of experience of the functioning of decentralized planning and Panchayati Raj Institutions (PRIs). In this context, it is proper time to assess and evaluate as to what extent provisions of the decentralized planning and Panchayati Raj Institutions contained in the Constitutional Amendment Acts have been put into practice.

Hence, the present paper focuses on as what was expected by the Constitution from Panchayats towards formulation and implementation of decentralized planning at their levels and what has been practiced form Gram Sabha to DPC.

Constitutional Provisions for Decentralized Planning

Article 243G of the Constitution which contains the powers, authority and responsibilities of Panchayat says "Subject to the provisions of this Constitution, the Legislature of a State may, by law, endow the Panchayats with such powers and authority as may be necessary to enable them to function as institutions of self-government and such law may contain provisions for the devolution of powers and responsibilities upon Panchayats at the appropriate level, subject to such conditions as may be specified therein, with respect to—(a) the preparation of plans for economic development and social justice, (b) the implementation of schemes for economic development and social justice as may be entrusted to them including those in relation to the matter listed in the Eleventh Schedule".

Article 243W of the Constitution contains similar provisions for urban local bodies.

Article 243ZD of the Constitution says that:

(1) There shall be constituted in every State at the district level a District Planning Committee to consolidate the plans prepared by the Panchayats and the Municipalities in the district and to prepare a draft development plan for the district as a whole.

(2) The Legislature of a State may, by law, make provision with respect to—

(a) the composition of the District Planning Committee
(b) the manner in which the seats in such Committees shall be filled:
Provided that not less than four-fifth of the total number of members of such Committee shall be elected by, and from amongst, the elected members of the Panchayat at the district level and of the Municipalities in the district in proportion to the ratio between the population of the rural areas and of the urban areas in the district;
(c) the functions relating to district planning which may be assigned to such Committees; and
(d) the matter in which the Chairpersons of such Committee shall be chosen.

(3) Every District Planning Committee shall, in preparing the draft development plan have regard to—

(i) matters of common interest between the Panchayats and the Municipalities including spatial planning, sharing of water and other physical and natural resources, the integrated development of infrastructure and environmental conservation; and
(ii) the extent and type of available resource whether financial or otherwise.

(4) The Chairperson of every District Planning Committee shall forward the development plan, as recommended by such Committee, to the Government of the State.

Above mentioned constitutional provisions enabled the State Governments to make the Panchayats viable and vibrant institutions so that they could prepare economic and social planning with people's participation emerging from Gram Sabha at village level to DPC at district level. It was also expected from the States that they not only devolve adequate functions, funds and functionaries to the Panchayats but also strengthen the planning machinery at different levels. Let us see as to what extent these enabling provisions have been grounded at the grassroots level.

Level of the Implementation of the Provisions

In above context, it was expected that for the purpose of formulation of the decentralized plan the first step which was to be taken up was that the needs of the local community should have been identified in the Gram Sabha (GS) for the consideration and approval of the same by the Gram Panchayat. The plans prepared by all GPs falling under the jurisdiction of the Panchayat Samiti/Mandal Panchayats/ Taluk Panchayats/Panchayat Union/Block Panchayats/Kesthrea Panchayat were to be assembled at this level with the purpose to have detailed discussion on the plan proposals received form GPs and if there were some gaps or lacunae in the plans prepared by them, the same should have been sorted out with the participation of the members of this tier of Panchayati Raj System.

The plans prepared by all the Panchayat Samities of a district should have been forwarded to the Zilla Parishad (ZP). The ZP at its level might have had detailed discussion on the proposals received from the Panchayat Samities and forwarded the same after making necessary changes if required to the DPC for its necessary action. In a similar fashion plans of the urban areas were also expected to be forwarded to the DPC. This Committee was expected to prepare the draft development plan for the entire district and forwarded the same to the State Government. These are the constitutional provisions which were to be practiced by the State Governments, Panchayats, Municipalities and DPC for practicing the decentralized planning across the country. But with some exception like Kerala state, above indicated procedure was rarely put into practice at the ground level. Now, let us comment on the strength of PRIs in term of their powers and authority endowed with them to discharge their constitutional responsibilities.

Status of the Powers and Authorities of the Panchayats

The plans for economic development and social justice could be prepared by the Panchayats on the basis of the functions, finances and functionaries (hereafter referred as Triple F) devolved to them by the State Governments. Let us analyze the status of the Triple Fs across the country in the following part of the paper.

Transfer of Functions

The State Governments were supposed to transfer the functions and powers pertaining to 29 subjects listed in the Eleventh Schedule of the Constitution to the Panchayats. As per information on functional devolution given in the Agenda Paper of the First Meeting of the Empowered Sub-Committee on Financial and Administrative Empowerment of Panchayati Raj Institutions held on June 26, 2003, out of the total States and UTs only Assam, Karnataka, Chattisgarh, Tamil Nadu, West Bengal have transferred 29 subjects to the Panchayats. The States and UTs of Arunachal Pradesh, Jharkhand, Chandigarh and Pondicherry have not devolved some functions to the Panchayats. The rest of the States UTs have transferred only some functions to them (Table 1.1) ranging from 3 in D&N Haveli to 26 functions in Kerala. As evident from this Table although several States have given a number of responsibilities to the Panchayats, these have not been put into practice. This, in turn, has not adversely affected the efficiency and effectiveness of the Panchayats but also not enabled them to prepare plan for economic development and social justice as envisaged by the Constitution. The Working Groups on Decentralized Planning rightly observed".... Items listed as responsibilities in the States are couched in vague terms. A glance of the variety of these items reveals that they are a shopping list of sectors and sub-sector, broad activities in a sub-sector and activities in a sub activities/specific responsibilities under a broad activity, with no role clarity..... In some States the line departments still exercise the powers of supervision and control over the schemes of subjects transferred to the Panchayats" (Working Groups 2001).

Transfer of Finance

Giving functions to Panchayats without matching funds is irrelevant. This, in fact happened with the State Panchayat Acts. Before listing the functions to be performed by the Panchayats, the number of States have introduced certain qualifying clauses such as 'within the limit of its funds', 'to the extent its funds allow to perform', 'as far as the Gram Panchayat funds at its disposal', etc. This presents a hazy picture about finances of the Panchayats because it is the resources at their disposal that determine their roles in formulating and implementing plans at their levels.

One the issue of the role of the State Finance Commission in financially empowering Panchayats, the Mid-Term Appraisal of the 9th Plan observed that: "More buoyant taxes like sales tax excise are kept out of the purview of PRIs. All SFCs have put great emphasis on internal revenue mobilization but non has suggested any effective mechanism for PRIs to generate their own revenue... The SFCs reports have paid less attention to issue of autonomy, financial management and auditing procedures. The main deficiency of the report lies in the fact that the recommendations are not based on clear statement of the spending responsibilities of local bodies. Indeed the absence of attention to the elementary principle, the expenditure assignment must precede any tax or revenue assignment, has made most of the SFCs recommendations suspect". (Mid Term Appraisal: 2000). The Working Groups on the State Resources also commented in the same manner as "The suggestions of the first generation SFCs if fully implemented will go a long way in improving the revenue generation capacity of the local bodies. However, the SFCs have failed to take a comprehensive view of the resource sharing between the State and local bodies still remains limited and unsettled. The State Governments have also been slow and hesitant in accepting the recommendations of the SFCs". (Working Group: 2002).

The extent of devolution of financial powers to the Panchayats may be seen in Table 1.1. This table shows that except Karnataka none of the States and UTs has transferred the funds to the Panchayats pertaining to 29 subjects listed in the 11th Schedule of the Constitution. The States/UTs of Arunachal Pradesh, Assam, Bihar, Jharkhand, Haryana, Manipur, Punjab, Rajasthan, Tamil Nadu, Tripura, Uttranchal, Chandigarh, D&N Haveli, Pondicherry and Lakshadweep have not transferred none of the functions from the list of 29 subjects of the 11th Schedule of the Constitution to the Panchayats. In rest of the States/UTs the functions transferred to the Panchayats ranged between 2 in Himachal Pradesh and 24 in Sikkim.

Table 1.1: Status of Devolution of Department/Subjects with Funds, Functions and Functionaries to Panchayati Raj Institutions (as on 29.05.2003)

Sl. No.	*States/UTs*	*No. of Departments/Subjects Transferred to Panchayats with*			*No. of Depat./Subjects yet to be Transferred to Panchayats with*		
		Funds	*Functions*	*Functi-onaries*	*Funds*	*Functi-ons*	*Functi-onaries*
1	2	3	4	5	6	7	8
1.	Andhra Pradesh	05	17	02	24	12	27
2.	Arunachal Pradesh	—	—	—	29	29	29
3.	Assam	—	29	—	29	—	29
4.	Bihar	—	20	—	29	9	29
5.	Jharkhand	—	—	—	29	29	29
6.	Goa	6	6	—	23	23	29
7.	Gujarat	15	15	15	14	14	14
8.	Haryana	—	Almost all 29 subjects	—	29	—	29
9.	Himachal Pradesh	02	26	*	27	3	22
10.	Karnataka	29	29	29	—	—	—
11.	Kerala	15	26	15	14	3	14
12.	Madhya Pradesh	10	23	09	19	06	20
13.	Chattisgarh	10	29	09	19	—	20
14.	Maharashtra	18	18	18	11	11	11
15.	Manipur	—	22	04	29	07	25
16.	Orissa	05	25	21	24	04	8
17.	Punjab	—	07	—	29	22	29
18.	Rajasthan	—	16	—	29	13	29
19.	Sikkim	24	24	24	5	5	5
20.	Tamil Nadu	—	29	—	29	—	29
21.	Tripura	—	12	—	29	17	29
22.	Uttar Pradesh	12	13	09	17	16	20
23.	Uttranchal	—	11	11	29	18	18
24.	West Bengal	12	29	12	17	—	17
25.	A&N Islands	6	6	6	23	23	23
26.	Chandigarh	—	—	—	29	29	29
27.	D&N Haveli	—	03	03	29	26	26
28.	Daman & Diu	5	9	3	24	20	26
29.	NCT Delhi	Panchayati Raj system is yet to be revived					
30.	Lakshadweep	—	06	—	29	23	29
31.	Pondichery	—	—	—	29	29	29

* No functionary has been transferred. However, GPs and IPs have been made the appointing authorities with regard to 9 functions on contract basis.

Note: The provisions of the Constitution (73rd Amendment) Act 1992 are not applicable to the States of J&K, Mizoram and Nagaland.

Source: Agenda Paper: 1st Meeting of the Empowered Sub-Committee on Financial and Administrative Empowerment of Panchayati Raj Institutions held on 26.6.2003, Ministry of Rural Development, Department of Rural Development.

The Report of the Task Force of Devolution of Powers and Functions to the PRIs brought out by the Ministry of Rural Development worked out total annual plan outlay of the State plans partly or wholly pertained to 29 subjects indicated in 11th Schedule of the Constitution. An amount of Rs. 40,818.65 crores was calculated as plan outlay for annual plan 2000-2001 for the schemes/ programmes of the State Governments under the subject listed in the Eleventh Schedule of the Constitution. Similarly, an amount of Rs. 31,575.87 crores plan outlay has been earmarked for the annual plan 2000-2001 for the schemes/programmes of the Central Ministries under the subjects listed in the Eleventh Schedule of the Constitution. It may be noted that an amount of Rs. 72,394.52 crores, which legitimately belongs to the Panchayats has been under the domain either by the Central Government or by the State Governments.

The Working Group on State Resource observed that "simple reluctance to mobilize, lack of role clarity as between tiers, lack of staff support, unviable administrative area, creation of parallel channels of flow of funds like MP funds, MLA funds, state sponsored schemes independent of PRIs like Janmabhoomi in Andhra Pradesh are among the major factors explaining low revenue levels of local bodies. There are State like Bihar and Tripura which have not collected any money from PRIs" (Working Group: 2002).

It is clear from the above analysis that a large amount of funds pertaining to 29 subjects listed in the 11th Schedule of the Constitution is still under the control of the Central and State Governments. Hence, without rationalizing fiscal federalism the task of preparing plans for economic and social justice by the rural and urban local bodies with people's participation will remain a distant dream. This requires an urge from the grassroots in the form of movement for making local bodies as autonomous institutions in the areas of their jurisdictions.

Transfer of Functionaries

Putting personnel under the control of the Panchayats pertaining to 29 subjects of the 11th Schedule is no less important than the transferring the functions and finances to them. In this context also, status is not better than that of financial devolution as the Table 1.1 shows. This Table depicts that except Karnataka none of the State/ UTs has transferred personnel pertaining to the 29 subjects listed in the 11th Schedule of the Constitution. The States/UTs of Arunachal Pradesh, Assam, Bihar, Jharkhand, Goa, Haryana, Punjab, Rajasthan, Tamil Nadu, Tripura, Chandigarh, Pondicherry and Lakshadweep have not transferred none of the functionaries of 29 subjects to the Panchayats. In rest of the States/UTs transferred ranged between 2 in Andhra Pradesh and 24 in Sikkim.

Above discussion on the status of the devolution of Triple Fs on the Panchayats gives adequate evidence that with some exceptions (like States of Karnataka and Kerala), status of the Panchayati Raj Institutions in term of making them autonomous in preparing decentralized plans at their levels is the same as it was before the enactment of the Amendment to the Constitution.

On the gloomy picture on devolution from the Central and State Governments to the Panchayats that emerged from above discussion what was observed by the Task Force on PRIs is worthwhile to quote here. "Though some steps have been taken by the MORD to goad the State Governments to strengthen and deepen the process of democratic decentralization, it has not yielded the desired results. Most Central Ministries have not yet internalized the PRIs role in the delivery of services handled by the Ministry. What is true of the Central Government is also true of the State Governments. Leaving aside one or two States such as Kerala, which have taken active steps for substantially empowering PRIs in planning and development, there is little by way of operationalising models of such empowerment. Even State like Kerala feel handicapped in regard to Central schemes since the guidelines for implementation are drawn by the concerned agency of Central Government". (Task Force on PRIs: 2001).

It is clear from above discussion that the Panchayats have not emerged as institutions of self governance at their respective levels due to non devolving desired power and authority to them. In such a situation, the fate of the local planning, these institutions are expected to prepare at their levels is obvious.

Table 1.2: State wise Status of District Planning Committees

Sl. No.	States/UTs	Status of Constitution of DPCs
1.	Andhra Pradesh	Not Constituted
2.	Arunachal Pradesh	Not Constituted
3.	Assam	Not Constituted
4.	Bihar	Not Constituted
5.	Chattisgarh	Constituted Minister if Chairperson of DPC
6.	Goa	Not Constituted
7.	Gujarat	Not Constituted
8.	Haryana	Only in 16 Districts, rest under consideration
9.	Himachal Pradesh	Only in 6 Districts out of 12 Minister is Chairperson of DPC
10.	J & K	Yet to adopt the provisions of 73rd Amendment Act
11.	Jharkhand	Not Constituted
12.	Karnataka	Yes in all Districts, Presidents, ZP is Chairperson of DPC
13.	Kerala	Yes, Chairperson of DP is Chairperson of DPC
14.	Madhya Pradesh	Yes, District in charge Ministers are Chairpersons
15.	Maharashtra	Not Constituted
16.	Manipur	Yes in 2 Districts out of 4, Adhyksha, District Panchayat is Chairperson
17.	Meghalaya	Not Applicable
18.	Mizoram	Not Applicable
19.	Nagaland	Not Applicable
20.	Orissa	25 Districts, Minister is Chairperson of DPC
21.	Punjab	Not yet but is constitution is under active consideration
22.	Rajasthan	Yes Chairperson of DP is Chairman of DPC
23.	Sikkim	Yes
24.	Tamil Nadu	Yes Chairperson of DP is Chairman
25.	Tripura	Not Constituted
26.	Uttar Pradesh	Yes, Ministers are Chairpersons
27.	West Bengal	Yes, Chairperson of DP is Chairperson of DPC
28.	A & N Islands	Yes Chairman of DP is Chairman of DPC
29.	Chandigarh	Not Constituted
30.	D&N Haveli	Yes Chairman, DP is Chairman of DPC
31.	Daman & Diu	Yes Chairman, DP is Chairman of DPC
32.	NCT Delhi	Not Constituted
33.	Lakshadweep	Yes Collector cum Dev. Commissioner is Chairperson
34.	Pondicherry	Not Constituted Panchayat Election not held so far.

Source: Agenda Paper: 1st Meeting of the Empowered Sub-Committee on Financial and Administrative Empowerment of Panchayati Raj Institutions held on 26.06.2003, Ministry of Rural Development, Department of Rural Development.

Status of the Constitution of District Planning Committees

Let us throw some light on the status of the District Planning Committee (DPCs) across the country. This Committee which was to be constituted as per Article 243ZD of the Constitution is expected to integrate rural and urban plans prepared by Panchayats and Municipalities and also to take into consideration spatial planning, sharing of water and other physical and natural resources, integrated development of infrastructure and environment conservation in the district. These important functions of the Committee are aimed at to facilitate interface between Panchayats and their counterparts. This Committee attempts to integrate rural and urban areas which is essential for preparing and executing a meaningful plan of the district as a whole for its economic development with social justice. But even after the passing of a decade of the conformity legislation by the States, as many as 12 States/UTs yet to constitute these Committees. Table 1.2 depicts the progress made towards constituting DPCs across the States. It is clear from this table that only 18 States/UTs, namely Chattisgarh, Haryana (only in 16 districts out of 19 districts), Himachal Pradesh (only in 6 districts out of 12 districts), Karnataka, Kerala, Madhya Pradesh, Manipur (only 2 districts out of 4 districts) Orissa, Rajasthan, Sikkim, Tamil Nadu, Uttar Pradesh and West Bengal and four Union Territories namely Andaman & Nicobar Islands, Daman&Diu, D&N Haveli and Lakshadweep have taken action to constitute DPCs. Out of 18 States/UTs where this Committee has been constituted only in 9 States/UTs the Chairpersons of the Zilla Parishad has been made the Chairperson of this Committee. In rest of the States/UTs where these Committees have been constituted either Minister or Bureaucrat has been made the chairperson of these bodies.

The Tenth Plan document on the progress made by the States towards operationalizing DPC lamented that "State Governments have not given adequate attention to the DPCs and the Government of India's guidelines on district planning have not been fully operationalized". The document expected from the States that "DPCs should be set up and its functionaries must be trained in the basics of planning. The Gram Sabha/Panchayat should be associated with the preparation of village development plans based on the felt needs of the people. These plans should be integrated with the Panchayat Samiti and district level plans to make the grassroots planning process a reality in the Tenth Plan period" (Five Year Plan, Vol. II).

But as saying goes 'proof of the pudding is in eating'. What will the status of the decentralized planning in future the time will tell. But the progress made in this direction so far which has already been depicted in Table 1.2 shows the poor progress towards the formation of DPC itself leave aside its functions, powers and authority of it and even its functioning. On the gloomy picture emerged across the States about the formation of DPCs, Oommen rightly commented "Looking back, one can firmly maintain that decentralized planning has been virtually abandoned by the majority of the states with impunity... Although all states have constituted State Finance Commissions, the Commission's task will remain incomplete without reference to the DPCs. In fact, DPCs are alive and kicking only in Kerala" (Oommen, 2002). Kerala's experiences in decentralized planning is innovative in many way. Besides devolving united funds to the Panchayats in lock stock and barrel, creation of Voluntary Technical Corps comprising technical, experienced people to assist the Panchayats in need identification, situational analysis, strategy setting, projectisation, plan finalization and plan vetting at local was found very useful by the rural people. The efforts made by Kerala in enabling Panchayats to prepare local plans with people's participation should be emulated by other States if provisions of the Constitution are to be put into practice.

Conclusion

The evolution process of decentralized planning in India had started even before Independence in this regard has taken place except in few States. One of the important factors for this dismal picture has been initiated by the democratic institutions at the district levels. Instead of constituting people's institutions, i.e., PRIs, the Central and State level political leaders have created parallel institutions dominated by the officials and nominees.

A major breakthrough in the field of decentralized planning

has been achieved with the Panchayats and the urban local bodies as well as District Planning Committee becoming a constitutional entities. Adequate space has also been given to the marginalized groups to express their felt needs in these bodies. However, the balance sheet of the functioning of the decentralized planning with PRIs depicts more liabilities and very less assets after a decade of its functioning. The Tenth Plan Document indicated some measures which will be taken during the Plan period to strengthen grassroots planning. But these are not new which are included in this plan only. In fact, decentralized planning has been emphasized in all the Plan Documents. But what is the fate of the decentralized planning everybody knows. The Tenth Plan Document may not be proved as the tenth draft of the First Plan. Thus people's campaign for strengthening PRIs is needed to put the provisions of the Constitution into practice.

NOTES AND REFERENCES

Government of India, Mid Term Appraisal of the Ninth Five Year Plan (1997-2002), New Delhi: Centre Planning Commission, 2000.

Government of India, The Report of the Working Group on Decentralized Planning and Panchayati Raj Institutions for the Tenth Five Year Plan (2002-07), New Delhi: Centre Planning Commission, 2001.

Government of India, Report of the Task Force on Panchayati Raj Institutions (PRIs), New Delhi: Centre Planning Commission, 2001.

Government of India, Report of the Task Force on Devolution of Powers and Functions Upon Panchayati Raj Institutions, New Delhi: Ministry of Rural Development, 2001.

Government of India, Report of the Working Group on States' Resources for the Tenth Five Year Plan (2002-2007), Volume-II, Government of India, New Delhi: Centre Planning Commission, 2002.

Government of India, Agenda Paper for the Ist meeting of the Empowered Sub-Committee on Financial Administrative Empowerment of the Panchayati Raj Institutions, held on June 26, 2003, New Delhi: Ministry of Rural Development, 2003.

Government of India, Five Year Plan, Volume-II, Sectoral Policies and Programmes, New Delhi: Centre Planning Commission, 2002.

Mahi Pal, "Decentralized Planning and Panchayati Raj: Report of the Working Group in Tamil Nadu", *Economic and Political Weekly,* (March 24, 2001).

Mahi Pal, "Evolution of Decentralized Planning in India", *Kurukshetra,* (June 1997).

Oommen, M.A., "Rationalizing fiscal federalism vis-à-vis rural local governments", Panchayati Raj Update, (September, 2002).

2

REGIONAL INFORMATION SYSTEM (RIS) AND DEVELOPMENT INDICES

Relevance in Panchayati Raj

REGI THOMAS AND BINO PAUL G.D.

Introduction

An information system like RIS supplies adequate information needed for implementation of Panchayati Raj. Also, it makes resource allocation exercises more transparent. The present paper explores the potential of RIS as a tool for micro-level planning.

Peoples Plan: The Kerala Experience

The introduction of the Panchayati Raj System of decentralized planning is a step towards the realization of the Gandhian vision of *Gram-swaraj*. The 9th Plan in Kerala, popularly known as the 'peoples plan' has gone a step further in bringing down the process of planning to the people, to the beneficiaries. Within a short span of time, commendable progress is made in the process of decentralizing the power to the people. All the 900 plus Panchayats came up with project reports and development reports which were prepared in consultation with the people and with the help of them. Another significant achievement is the resource mapping done in different panchayats, again with the participation of people. A visiting world bank team has remarked "Three million people (10% of the states population) take part in Gram Sabhas and other rural development and local governance" (*Indian Express,* 3/1/1999). However, people plan faced scathing attack, and opposition criticized lack of effective monitoring and lack of transparency in project implementation due to lack of information. Despite divergent perspectives, most critics pointed out the essentiality of social auditing, based on comprehensive data base. Supply of reliable information is essential for achieving the objectives of democratic decentralized planning. The paper attempts to formulate a Regional Information System which consists of development indicators which can be used for monitoring and evaluation of micro-level planning.

Kerala: Achievements and Constraints

Kerala has made long strides in development, and has achieved a relatively high standard in Physical Quality of Life Index as well as Human Development Indices. Kerala has achieved a PQLI comparable with the developed world. The state also has achieved almost cent percent literacy, and has a very low birth rate and infant mortality rate. The state also has the highest number of educated unemployed people. There is a large number of people working outside the state, including a large percentage of it working abroad, primarily in the Persian Gulf countries. In 1994, the amount of remittance from the NRIs in the middle-east alone came to 27 per cent of the state domestic product. The state also happens to be one of the most densely populated regions in the world, with a population density of 746 people per square kilometer, where most of the population is living in rural areas. The state falls into the pre-humid to humid agro-eco-system and is endowed with more than 300 cms of rain spread over two monsoons in 7 months. The major challenge of Kerala model of development emerges from the fact that inequality between resource endowment and its utilisation. Information is one of the major determinants of resource utilisation and sustainable development. Within the constraint of a high population density, to ensure a equitable and sustainable utilization of resource requires, planning is needed at the grassroots with the peoples participation. This can result in investment for sustainable economic development and employment generation with due consideration on eco-system.

Regional Information System (RIS)

Sustainability and social relevance of an objective function seems to be directly related to supply of information on constraints and its inter-dependence among them. Therefore, optimality of objective function of regional planning is dependent on supply of information. For a information. For a sustainable development of a region, one has to integrate the spatial, socio-economic and resource information. This involves the information about the natural divisions in the region including watersheds and agro-geo-political boundaries. Though these information are available in various levels, this is rarely integrated, and there are no tools available to integrated them. A regional information system proposed in this paper tries to integrate information for planning, especially in the micro-level. The spatial information are those about the natural division, like coastal land, mid land, high land etc., agro-climatic zones, soil types and land capitability, political/revenue/in development divisions and over and above the watersheds, which is crucial in sustainable development. The social information consists of demographic profile, including vital rates, caste and religious composition, age and sex composition, education and employment information. It can also map the social support systems and development initiatives existing. The economic/ resource information consists of details land, cropping pattern, land utilization, livestock, water bodies, rainfall, humidity, income, savings, capital formation, development aid and its development, plan allocation and expenditure. As the part of people's plan, most of the panchayats have carried out the exercise of data collection.

A typical panchayat database consists of following information areas:

1. Agriculture and irrigation
2. Animal husbandry and fisheries
3. Industries
4. Education
5. Drinking water, public health, sanitation
6. Transport and communication, energy and market information
7. Housing and social welfare

8. Cultural
9. Women
10. Co-operation
11. SC/ST welfare
12. Resource mapping at the panchayat level, including land classification
13. Banking and Co-operation
14. Employment

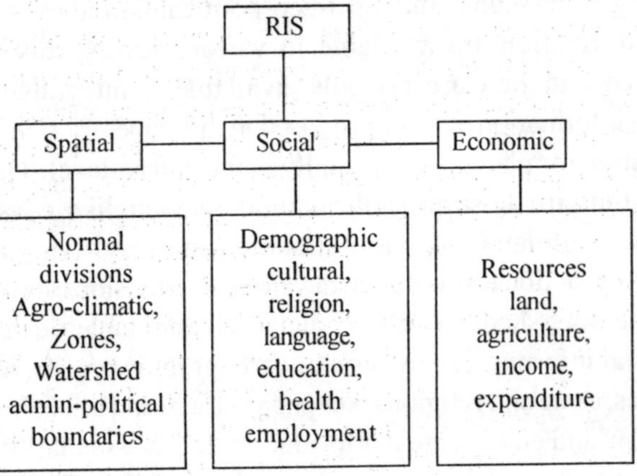

Fig. 2.1: Reword Information System

Sustainable Development

Optimum development of resources adequate information about resources in the state. Ideally sustainable means self-reliance and self-sufficiency at the micro-level. This is possible only with self-reliance in the panchayat level, to the extend possible. Optimum resource utilization within the carrying capacity of the eco-system ensures long-term sustainability. This also calls for maintaining the quality of physical environment. There are cases when production for lively hood may critically degrade the whole eco-system, posing serious threat for quality of life for the future generations. For instance the coin-rotting in the coastal areas, when operated at large scale can pollute the air and water sources. Intensive aqua culture, and even chemical intensive agriculture can also pollute water bodies to critical levels. Unfit for human or animal use. Watershed is the most viable unit for optimizing the use of resources in Kerala micro, macro and meso watersheds have been identified and the information is already available. Despite a high rainfall spread over more than half of the year, many panchayats in the state runs into severe water shortages in peak summer, and this call for a special attention. The majority of the population in the state is dependent on open wells for drinking water, and with a rising population density the problems are likely to become acute in the near future. This calls for greater attention planning at the watershed level. The political boundaries of the panchayats or other administrative units often overlaps with different watersheds and different natural divisions. It is not unlikely to find a variety of agro-eco-system in a panchayat. The problem of water and soil conservation will be acute (may not be addressed properly) when the planning is done within the political or administrative boundaries ignoring the natural divisions. Most of the land in Kerala falls into mid and high ranges where the terrain is mostly undulating. Soil and water conservation, deciding the right kind of cropping pattern etc., becomes important.

These issues call for a planning in micro-level, but with integrating information from higher levels, wherever the unit is viable. With the help of a regional information system one can integrate the different types of information available in different levels. For example, the natural divisions or the geographical divisions in the state can be broadly divided into three (even four; if we divide the high lands into two), the agro-climatic zones into 13, watersheds into mere than couple of hundreds. Around 44 rivers are flowing across these divisions, there will be a number of tributaries contributing to the rivers. There are vast water bodies in the coastal region. There are long tracts of forests and interface areas, where a lot of people are linked to them directly or indirectly for their livelihood. Further there are revenue/political/administrative divisions cutting across these natural division like, 14 revenue districts, 151 development blocks, 61 taluks, 990 panchayats, 1452 revenue villages, 140 assembly constituencies and 20 parliamentary constituencies. All these divisions are in some way or other are related to administrative or development of local population.

If the available information is integrated at apex levels, and is made available to the units in micro-level like district panchayats, block-panchayats and grama panchayats, planning can be done effectively, by taking into account all the available resources, and constraints and deploying it to meet local needs in priority. This can ensure a sustainable development at the macro-level and ensure optimum utilization of resources with equity.

The resource-flows, market linkages, water catchments etc., also often cut across the boundaries of panchayats. In a number of cases the water catchment of a panchayat may lie in one or two of the neighbouring panchayats. Some particular cropping pattern in the neighbouring panchayat may cause severe water shortage, or silting up of the water bodies in the locality. Much of these problems can be tackled by information system, where the naturally viable units are taken as units of planning. Based on that information, panchayats or other local-administrative units can go ahead with planning. Geographical Information Systems (GIS) available in the market can be used for integrating information for planning. The regional information system based on a GIS can be programmed as a planning-tool incorporating all the incorporating all the economic and other variables currently used in panchayat level planning.

Measuring Development

The Regional Information System can be used as a tool for evaluating development at the micro-level. There are no appropriate indices available currently for measuring determinants of development or even the economic-product in micro level. The lowest level in which the economic product is calculated at present is in the state level. It is required to measure the variables and quality them in some way to study the development for further planning. Development indices are explained elsewhere in the paper.

In the panchayat level an RIS can provide spatial information, giving details of natural geographical divisions, agro-climatic zones in the panchayat, micro-watersheds, including the location of the panchayat in the macro and meso watersheds, and land capabilities, particularly the slope of the land. Also the data on wind, rainfall, humidity, soil types, climate and vegetation. In the social information, detailed demographic profile can be stored and retrieved in the ward (for even in smaller levels). In the economic information, household level saving, income , expenditure resource information including cropping pattern, livestock statistics, grant in aids, plan allocations, development aid through NGOs, local charity missions, industrial spread, employment and other details can be collected and used for planning.

Development Indices

Indices are supposed to simplify complex data without losing comprehensiveness. A set of social and economic indices are proposed to quantify and measure development. A single index is not sufficient to understand or explain complex economic or social phenomenon. Indices are designed to absorb information on both economic and non-economic activities having economic value which can be quantifiable or imputable.

The concept stock and flow classification of variables may be relevant in the estimation of net economic product, resource endowment, resource utilisation and welfare at the panchayat level. The data on stock can be collected or updated in five years, generally before the Five Year Plans, and this information can be used for computing various indices. The data on flow have to be collected annually, and net economic product can be derived out of this information. To get more realistic picture of development, appropriate indices should be formulated to absorb changes in different sectors like education, health, transport and communication, industries, agriculture, social welfare (with special reference to weaker sections in the society), banking/cooperation, energy and participation. An over all development can be computed on the basis of data provided by RIS.

Data Collection

Calculation of the economic product at the panchayat level requires collection of details of flow annually, with the help of a well structured questionnaire. During the first stage of the peoples plan, data on different heads were collected with the help of participatory action. The same method can be extended for annual data collection. If the annual data collection is proving to be difficult, the economic product can be calculated once in two years or in three in years. Some of the data are available with the local administrative bodies and Banking institutions. If made mandatory, such data can be made available to the panchayat in annual internals without much additional burden. Details of stock, can be collected once in five years, preferably before the Five Years Plans. Local recreational clubs, reading rooms, co-operative societies, planning forums (if available) can also be trained to collect the information, without much economic burden. Yet another possibility is to train the high school students in data collection through science clubs other cultural activity units, and do the processing in the school as an educational programme. Junior P.H.Cs or P.H.Cs invariably present in the panchayat can maintain the details of health care, provided a well structured information system is made available to them. Similarly, Krishi Bhavans in all the panchayats also can maintain most of the agricultural information and update it annually. Co-operative milk producting units in the panchayats, with the help of Gram Sabha or the elected ward representative can maintain the live stock statistics and productivity figures. Active development organizations, including religious bodies can take an active role in data collection.

Methodology for Determining the Indices

An index is an average score/ratio computed on the basis of an empirically supported bench mark. For example, to find out the health index, take a dozen or two of the panchayats, where the over all health standards are good, find out the variables which are causing the better health and take it as benchmarks in calculating the relative health standards in the other regions. The indicators of better health care, which is used in conventional economics, such as doctors or other medical personnel to the population, number of beds available, access to higher institutions of medical sciences, morbidity rates, infant mortally rates, death rates, access to safe drinking water etc., can be used to calculate the health index. But other than the conventional indicators, a number of traditions embedded in the social system including locally available herbs and medicinal plants, special diets, eating habits, also may have a bearing in the health care status of a panchayat.This has to be verified empirically.

Benchmarking

Benchmarking can be done based on norms (set by competent bodies in the national or state levels) or on performance. The former method is likely to have a problem since much of the calculation are done in the national level. Performance based benchmarking will be a better option, because it can better accommodate the local issues and diversity. The panchayats, where significant achievements in participatory developments are made, can be taken as samples, one each from a District. The average or best performance in each of the sectors can be taken as benchmarks for comparison. If the development in these panchayats are not well balanced, Benchmarking has to be done sector wise, taking panchayats which has shown significant development in particular sector.

Norm-based benchmarking can be adopted as short-run methodology, if performance-based benchmarks require time and resources.

Index Computation: Ration Method *vs* Ranks

Indicators used in the computation of various development indices are of three types:

1. Integers
2. Percentages/Ratios
3. Figures in physical units

To compute an index, indicators are to be under standardised. The standardisation can be done by Ratio method or rank method. The former method will convert all indicators into ratios (independent of units). This information is done by dividing p3rticular indicator by norm or performance based benchmarks. According to the second method, indicators of various panchayats will be ranked, and ranks will be used for constructing indices. However, this method presumes an integrated database and advanced software support. Resource and infrastructure are major constraints to the application of Rank method. Ratio method can be a long term method.

All indicators (referred in this paper) will be transformed, by ratio method, into scores. A score can be defined as the ratio of indicator to benchmark indicator multiplied by 100.

Score i = (Indicator i/Benchmark Indicator) * 100

An index can be defined as simple average indices or average scores, can be called primary index.

Primary Index (Average Score) =∑i= 1 tn Score i/n

An index, which is the simple average of primary indices or average scores, can be called secondary index

Secondary Index =∑i =1 tn Primary Index/n

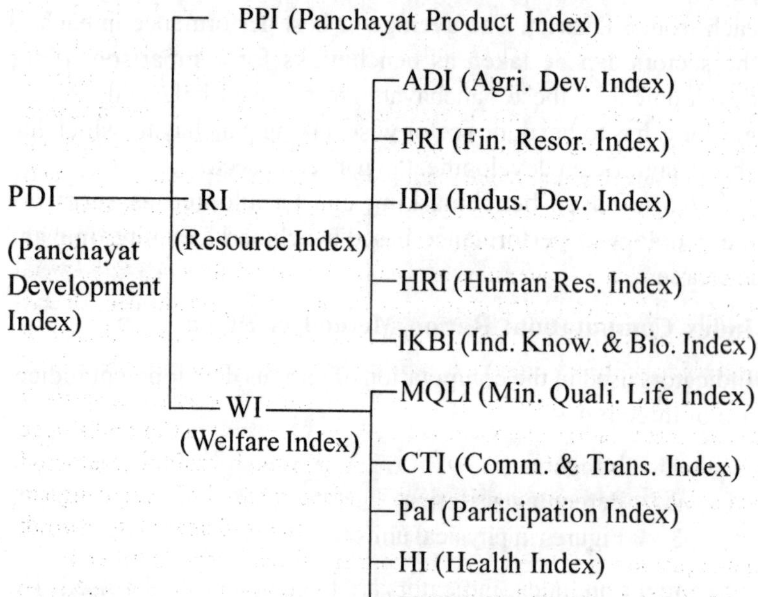

Fig. 2.2: Regional Information System (RIS): System of Development Indices

Panchayat Development Index (PDI)

The prime objective of these arguments is to derive at single development index which encompasses fourteen information areas can be operationalised at panchayat level with minimum infrastructure support. Also, there is scope for the information and empirical verification of indices using trained manpower and computers at district level.

The proposed index is Panchayat Development Index (PDI) which is the simple average of per capita product index (PPI), Resource Index (RI), Welfare Index (WI)
Symbolically

PDI = (PPI+RI+WI)/3 ----------------(1)

Each of the Indices is explained below

Panchayat Product Index (PPI)

Panchayat product can be defined as the annual value of goods and services produced in a panchayat. This is the sum of external and internal income, and welfare cost. This is necessarily a flow variable. Following identities would explain the index.

Panchayat Product = (Internal Income + External Income) - Welfare cost --------- (2.1)

Internal income = Rewards paid to internal (within panchayat) factors of production, (land, labour, capital and any entrepreneurial activity) + income of local administration including taxes grant in aid and development aid ------(2.2)

Net External Income = Remittance from internal factors of production employed out side the panchayat-rewards paid for services by non-residents ------------(2.3)

[this is applicable only to the panchayats where large number of well paid employees are working in the panchayat. In other case this can be ignored].

Welfare cost - Expenses incurred by the local administrative body ---------- (2.4)

The possible sources of income are : Salaries/wage, transfer payments, external remittances, income from homesteads, local taxes, grants in aid, development aid bought in by NGOs and charitable institutions. Welfare cost includes the maintenance of local roads, ponds, expenses in running welfare institutions. Data are currently available in most of the heads mentioned above. Data where it is not available can be generated with the help of participatory surveys conducted by Gram Sabha, as mentioned earlier.

The ratio of Panchayat Product of panchayat will give the per capita income panchayat. Panchayat Product index (PPI) will be a relative score based bench mark per capita product.

Resource Index (RI)

RI is an indicator of natural resources, human resources, capital, heritage and externalities. Heritage, here, means local traditions and information which has commercial significance. Externalities can be both negative and positive. Examples of negative externalise are issues like loss of diversity, environmental hazards, resource depletion etc. Positive externalities include the ecological pay-offs, extrinsic value addition to the individual properties arising out of infrastructure/ capital formation. The basic objective of RI is to measure the resource endowment and its utilisation.

Resource Index (RI), a secondary index, is the simple average of primary indices like Agricultural Development Index (ADI), Financial Resource Index (FRI), Industrial Development Index (IDI), Human Resource Index (HRI) and Indigenous Knowledge and Bio-diversity Index (IKBI).

Symbolically

$$RI = (ADI+FRI+IDI+HRI+IKBI)/5 \quad \text{---------} \quad (3)$$

Each of these indices are explained below

Agricultural Development Index (ADI)

For the computation of the ADI, following information constitute database:

1. Operational holding (average and numbers)
2. Productivity
3. Cropping intensity
4. Cropping pattern (contribution to food security)
5. Inputs (purchased externally, internally generated, organic, inorganic)
6. Linkage (contribution to fuel, contribution to industry)
7. Live stock population, productivity
8. Access to agricultural institutions, agricultural credit
9. Land capacity, soil type, depth
10. Irrigation
11. Mechanization

12. Indigenous knowledge system - role in agricultural production
13. Employment generation (employment, wage)
14. Access to market
15. Fishing, income from (marine as well as from local water sources)

Most of the information is available in the panchayat level at present. These data can be brought under four major heads. There are as follows: (1) Land availability, utilisation and productivity (2) Self Sufficiency (Production of foodgrain) (3) Inputs (Irrigation, credit, homestead-generated inputs like organic manure, labour) (4) Agriculture allied activities.

Ideal surrogates, for above areas, absorb agricultural development. For example, Average size of operational holding (AI), Productivity Index (A2) and cropping intensity (A3) may represent first information area. The ratio of foodgrain production to food consumption (A4) shows extent of self sufficiency in food production achieved by panchayat or if information is not available, change in cropping pattern would indicated the self sufficiency (A5). Information on water table (A6) and water shed (A7) indicates the irrigation potential. Per capita agricultural availability (A8) and per hectare consumption of organic manure (A9) would be better surrogates for credit and internally generated inputs. Rate of change in wage (A10) and proportion of population (A11) engaged in allied activities like fishing would represent labour and allied activities. All indicators are expressed in scores (A1 to A11).

Ideally, ADI would absorb all information. However, more representative scores can be short listed depending upon the availability of data.

$$ADI = (A1+A2+A4+A6+A9+A10)/6 \quad \text{---------}(3.1)$$

Appropriateness of the ADI (equation 3.1) can be challenged from the angle of geographical diversity. For example, the panchayats in the coastal region are equally dependent own sea for their survival. Their access to the continental shelf is almost equal to having land for cultivation. Also the Kaipadu lands in the northern Kerala, Pockali lands in Central Kerala, Paddy lands in Kuttuanandu and Kole lands and the back waters stretching from one end of Kerala to other etc., has a significant inland fishing potential. Quality of land, bio-diversity, availability of water etc., has a nearing on future production of land. This calls for weighting of indicators which constitute ADI. Discussion on weighting is beyond the scope of this paper.

Financial Resources Index (FRI)

The FRI absorbs information on uses and sources of finance in a Panchayat. The index summaries following indicators:

1. Saving mobilization: Commercial banks, co-operative banks, post office saving banks-percentage distribution.
2. Credit sources (banks, money lenders, local self-help groups, development Agencies, charities percentage distribution) (% of institutional lending, F1).
3. Access to banking [physical access (population coverage), F2]
4. Cost of finance (interest rates - official, market)
5. Access to development fund (per capita availability of development capital, F3)
6. Uses (construction, agriculture, business, marriage, education - percentage distribution). Productive Use of Credit (Agricultural + Small Scale Ind + Education + Infrastructure/Capital Formation)/Total Credit, (F4)
7. Ratio of NRI/NRE deposits to total deposit, (F5)
8. Ratio of NRE/NRI deposit to panchayat product, (F6)
9. Credit deposit ratio, (F7)
10. Ratio of credit to NRE/NRI deposit, (F8)
11. Ratio of credit to panchayat product
12. Deployment or credit for NRE rehabilitation
13. Per capita development capital availability for SC/ST
14. Per capita development capital availability for women and marginalised
15. Transfer Earnings/Resource transfer like Dowry (Approximate value) (F9).

FRI is the simple average of more representative scores (F1

to F9) like proportion of institutional credit (F1), Population covered by banks (F2), per capita availability of Development Fund (F3), Productive use of credit (F4), Credit deposit ratio (F7), or ratio of credit to NRE/NRI deposit (F8) and Resource transfer like dowry (F9).

FRI (1) = (F1+F2+F3+F4+F7+F9)/6 ----------(3.2.1)

The NRI/NRE deposits has a significant bearing in the economy of Kerala. The total NRE deposits was more than 30 per cent of the state domestic product of Kerala during 1996. More than 8 per cent of the total NRE deposit came from middle east alone. This deposit is fairly distributed in most of the panchayats in Kerala, baring a few exceptions. This capital has not been productively deployed so far, as it is reflected from the credit deposit ratio of 44.2. Taking into account the significance of NRE/NRI deposits, FRI can be reformulated by incorporating F7 instead of F6.

FRI (2) = (F1+F2+F3+F4+F8+F9)/5 ---------(3.2.2)

It is to be noted that F8 is the ratio of F7 to F5

F8 = F7/F5 -----------(3.2.2.1)

The statistics reveals that the states financial resources are highly sensitive to external factors, including the political stability of the middle eastern countries and foreign trade.

Deployment of NRE investment along with providing rehabilitation opportunities is going to be one of the priority areas, considering the number of people returning after employment abroad. This can also create employment opportunities in the panchayat. With adequate incentives, a lot of deposit can be mobilized at the panchayat level. Co-operative banks so far has served as credit source for marginal farmers, agricultural labourers and agriculturists. Their CDR, in 1996 was 135.5 that too with negligible NRE deposit base. In the mean time the CDR of the public sector was 42.4 and their NRE deposit constituted 43.7 per cent of total deposit. For private sector banks, 44.24 and NRE deposit was 33.3 per cent.

Per capita development capital availability from financial institutions like IDBI, IFCI, UTI, GIC, LIC, NABARD, NCDC was

Rs. 49, one of the lowest compared against the national average of Rs. 305 and Gujarat, Rs. 876, which is highest.

Industrial Development Index (IDI)

The IDI summaries information on industrial development of Panchayat. The scope of the index is broad; the industry covers Small Scale Industries (SSI), Khadi and Village Industries (KVI), other cottage industries, house hold level industrial production destined for market and Large Scale Industries. The index would absorb following data:

1. Employment Generation: Proportion (%) of working population of panchayat employed in industrial sector (IDI),
2. Industrial wages (ID2),
3. Entrepreneurship (local entrepreneurs, micro-enterprises, handicrafts),
4. Access to Industrial Finance (Linkage with local resources (agri, produces, natural resources etc.),
5. Positive Externalities/negative externality (ID 3),
6. Resource availability for industries [raw materials; (Linkage with local resources agri produces, natural resources etc., Ratio of economic value of locally available raw material to total value of raw material)] (ID 4).

All indicators (ID 1.......ID 4) are expressed in sectors
IDI can be computed by using above listed scores

IDI = (ID1+ID2+ID3+ID4)/4 -----------(3.3)

Human Resource Index (HRI)

High educated unemployment and large scale manpower are salient features on an economy like Kerala. The prime objective of the HRI is to absorb vital information on Human Resource Potential, its exports and private and social investment on human resource development literacy and basic education, being more or less universal, are not considered for the computation of index.

Computation of HRI is based on following information:

1. People employed within the state (as % of labour force in the panchayat),

2. Skilled/semi skilled labour employed abroad and other states of the country (as % of labour force in the panchayat), (Hr 1);
3. Technical manpower, Professionals, Research degree holders (as % of labour force in panchayat) {including students} (Hr2);
4. Investment for Human resources (Fees, Capitation Fees, Endowments, Scholarships), (Hr3);
5. Rehabilitation possibilities for repatriates; and
6. Geographical proximity to higher educational institutions (Hr4)

HRI is the simple average of scores Hr1, Hr2, Hr3 and Hr 4

HRI = (HR1+HR2+HR3+HR4)/4 -----------(3.4)

Indigenous Knowledge and Bio-Diversity Index (IKBI)

The IKBI intends to absorb economic value of traditional knowledge, tradition and heritage and bio-diversity of the panchayat. The index is based on following information:

1. Historical monuments, shrines, festivals and other heritages (revenue generated)(IK1),
2. Performing/Fine arts/Sports: Artists and Institutions (approximate income) (IK2),
3. Application of traditional knowledge (Health+primary education + organic agriculture inputs +water harvesting systems + organic products (eg. honey) + handicrafts etc., + local cuisine (diversity: e.g. variety of curries, pickles etc) {approximate value} (IK3)
4. Flora-Fauna diversity (no. of species) : (IK4)IKBI can be computed from above scores

IKBI = (IK1+IK2+IK3+IK4)/4 ---------(3.5)

Welfare Index (WI)

Welfare Index summaries information on minimum quality of life, infrastructure, participation, health and less privileged society. WI is secondary index (simple average) of Minimum Quality of Life Index (MQLI), Communication and Transportation Index (CTI), Participation Index (PI), Health Index (HI), Private Index (PI)

WI = (MQLI+CTI+PAI+HI+PI)/5 ----------(4)

Minimum Quality of Life Index (MQLI)

MQLI absorbs information on food, nutrition, housing, energy, safe drinking water and basic education. The index is computed on the basis of following information:

1. Per capita Availability of Food (M1)
2. Per capita Availability of Protein—rich food (M2)
3. Per capita Consumption Expenditure (approximate):(M3)
4. House Hold size
5. Categories of houses (based on energy use, consumer goods, houses within homesteads..): per cent of pucca houses (M4)
6. Power consumption (house hold, industry, agriculture, street lights....)
7. Sources of Power (% share): per cent of electrified houses (M5)
8. Sources of Fuel (% internally generated) (M6)
9. Proportion of population having Access to Safe Drinking Water (M7)
10. Enrollment, drop-out, teacher student ratio, success rate of SSLC (SSLC pass % would be more representative surrogate: M8)
11. Literacy and elementary education (more relevant for states other than Kerala)

The index can be computed with more representative scores.

MQLI = (M3+M4+M5+M6+M7+M8)/6 ----------(4.1)

The score M6 is important because Kerala faces critical shortage in power supply through out the year. Local level initiatives can solve a lot of the energy crisis by demand side management possibilities for stand alone systems (micro-hydel, wind, bio-gas), where ever possible can be explored. Providing energy efficient devices such as CFL lamps can reduce a lot of power consumption in the local level. Homestead farming system in Kerala supplies most of the fuel for cooking, and this renewable source of energy can be produced sustainable with adequate planning.

Communication and Transportation Index (CTI)

The CTI is based on following data,

1. Modes of transport (percentage distribution of road, rail and water)
2. Roads (panchayat, state, NH) (Length of all weather - Pucca Road in km) C1
3. Number of vehicles, average daily commuters
4. Media subscription, readership, access to libraries (Ratio of Newspaper subscribers to total households) C2
5. Access to post office (Population Coverage) C3
6. Telephones per 1000 people C4
7. Access to other modes of communication (Fax, Telex, Speed post, Telecom centers)
8. Ratio of No. of Television sets to total house holds C5
9. Personnel Computer (PC) per 1000 people.

CTI is defined as simple average of C1, C2, C3, C4 and C5

$$CTI = (C1+C2+C3+C4+C5)/5 \text{ -------- } (4.2)$$

Participation Index (Pa 1)

Quantifying peoples participation in development activities is not an easy task. One of the possible ways of doing this is to take the ratio of actual cost of development projects in year (Pa 1) to the spending from the panchayat (Pa 2). This will give the share of peoples contribution in development activities. It is to be noted that Pa 1 and Pa 2 are scores

$$PaI = Pa1/Pa2 \text{ ------- } (4.3)$$

Health Index (HI)

Data are available or can be obtained in the following areas:

1. Morbidity rate (HI)
2. Death rate
3. Birth rate
4. No.of suicides (H2)
5. Doctor population ratio (to other medical personnel) (H3)
6. Ratio of population to hospital beds (access, since medical

facilities are available across the boundaries of panchayat, and centers of specialization are generally concentrated in District headquarters, or in urban centers) (H4)

7. Indigenous medical traditions, knowledge available and access to such systems (no.of Registered Medical Practioners (RMPL) and non RMPL: M5)
8. Infant Mortality Rate (Relevant for state other than Kerala) (H6).

In the existing health care structure, primary health care facilities are available in all the panchayats. These institutions can maintain and update most of the health related information. Specialized health care institutions are generally located in urban centers, and what matters in the panchayat level is the access to them. If mandated, panchayat wise registration of treatments can be maintained at these institutions, both private and public. Panchayats where local knowledge traditions and informal health care traditions are active, they have to be assessed, and information can be collected by participatory action. Scores - H2, H3, H4, and H5 - would constitute an H1 which is more appropriate to states like Kerala.

$$HI = (H2+H3+H4+H5)/4 \text{ ----------}(4.5)$$

Privilege Index (PI)

The PI absorbs information on women, SC/ST, marginal, landless and unemployed:

1. Share of SC/ST population—their employment opportunities, enrolment rate, dropout rate, housing standard, coverage of development schemes, (Pi 1)
2. Recreation, cultural activities (Pi 2)
3. Land less, marginal and unemployed people (% in total working population (Pi 3)
4. Women work participation rate (Pi 4)

The index is simple average of representative scores Pi 3 and Pi 4

$$PI = (Pi\ 3 + Pi\ 4)/2 \text{ --------}(4.5)$$

A Summary

The main objective of RIS is to provide and co-ordinate information for Panchayat level planning. The system, explained here, persumes more advanced panchayat base like Kerala. However, the application is not strictly confined to Kerala; it can be extended to other states with some modification. RIS may be useful for various institutions - NGOs/Development Agencies/Monitoring institutions/Financial Institutions— who are involved in Micro-level planning.

NOTES AND REFERENCES

1. Development Plan Documents (prepared as the part of people's plan) of Karukutti (Central Kerala), Erumeli (South Kerala), and Pathuvam, Kalyasseri (North Kerala), Panchayats.

2. *Manorama Year Book* (Malayalam Version), 1998.

3. Bureau of Economics and Statistics, Statistics for Planning, 1996.

4. Government of Kerala, *Economic Review,* 1996.

3

DISTRICT PLANNING PRACTICE AND THEORY WITH SPECIAL REFERENCE TO 'HOW TO' ASPECTS

RAKESH HOOJA

DECENTRALIZED PLANNING IN INDIA: OBJECTIVES, HANDICAPS AND HOPES

With the passing of the 73rd Constitutional Amendment Act the legislatures of various States in India have been empowered to devolve powers and responsibilities, subject to such conditions as the legislature may specify, regarding the preparation of plans for economic development and social justice, upon panchayat bodies at the district, intermediate and village levels. The 74th Constitutional Amendment Act provides for the setting up at the district level of a District Planning Committee to consolidate the plans prepared by the panchayats and the municipalities in the district and to prepare a draft district development plan for the district as a whole. Thus district planning which has been talked about, and tried out in various ways to a lesser or larger extent, from at least the Second Five Year Plan Period, is now getting better institutionalized.

This has imparted an urgency to the need for better understanding of ideas and issues such as the relationship between national and state level plans and the district plans; planning structures at central, state and district levels, funding arrangements; planning and for planning for infrastructure development, provision of services and production and income generation using resources optimally and how to integrate these with techniques for participative planning; training of state and district level personnel; the various experiments and experiences over time in different parts of the country at district, block or micro-area planning; the various government reports and related literature on the issues; and the like.

Accordingly, there is a need to figure out what sort of exposure, orientation and training needs to be provided to concerned functionaries and even to people's representatives at the district and lower levels, so that objectives of decentralized planning can be achieved. Such objectives include:

(a) increased people's participation;
(b) improved quality of development efforts and improved management of programmes;
(c) the provision of resources and programmes for each area and for different groups inhabiting the area on the basis of an assessment of the specific area's problems, resources and potentialities;
(d) spatial planning (including considering the need for relaxation of uniform norms related to distance or population thresholds) for provision of services and facilities in specific areas;
(e) use of locational theory and rural growth centre or central place planning and centrality scoring techniques;
(f) greater feeling of involvement in the planning effort on the part of both of lower level functionaries and the local people;
(g) strengthening of local government bodies;
(h) locally optimal arrangement for each cluster of villages, or people within a village, to meet their own perceptions of their needs rather than through uniform standards prescribed in a uniform manner for the entire country or state as a whole;
(i) better consideration of available local level resources or of the lack of and need for the same, and or local problems, than would be possible through planning at higher levels;

(j) greater mobilization of resources at the local level;

(k) evolution of participatory mechanisms to promote local level leadership, habits of self-help, motivation and willingness to undertake local plan formulation and implementation;

(l) creating a psychology for development and change at local levels;

(m) reduction in regional disparities;

(n) meeting of basic needs of the people in a better manner which could help to bring into the mainstream peripheral groups and the poor deprived;

(o) better partnership may be achieved between the people and development agencies;

(p) small mini-projects may be individually planned for using project approach-based analysis at the local or district level which may not be possible at higher levels where only generalized guidelines can be framed for particular types of small schemes;

(q) successful marriage of project planning and participatory planning may prove easier at levels closer to the grassroots;

(r) local social or physical barriers not always apparent on maps can only be considered while planning locally and not during state or higher level plan exercise; and

(s) integrated and comprehensive multi-sector planning may prove easier at lower levels, while at higher levels mono-sector planning or sectorally segmented planning subsequently complied, as is being done at present, may have to be resorted to.

International development experts and aid donors appear to have some additional expectation from decentralization. However, following a cross country study[1], Crook and Manor (1994) have indicated that many of these expectation are misplaced and unlikely to be achieved. They indicate that not much can be expected in terms of planning form below or by grassroots peoples councils through elected local councils, like panchayats because of (a) lack of administrative and of trained manpower, (b) lack of information base (no inventory of capital resources, no assessment of local economy, inadequate statistical base), (c) a short-term outlook and the liking of local politicians for keeping their wish list projects open-ended and flexible at all times leading to ad-hoc decisions and ad-hoc processes being followed, (d) grants from higher authorities are heavily earmarked, (e) decentralized planners have no control over resources and (f) higher authorities have little interest in decentralized planning. Similarly, not much local mobilisation of resources is likely because (a) in impoverished areas the amount of mobilizable resources may be limited, (b) elected councillors hesitate to impose taxes-local elites are reluctant to task themselves, (c) local people are cynical about what local councils may do with locally raised resources and the existence of under-resource local authorities may deepen the popular cynicism, (d) locally raised resources are inadequate for any but the most modest development or service provision hence unless major Central/State Government financial support flows in on a continuous basis, local persons may not be inclined to add their merge locally raised resources to the available pool. Decentralization is unlikely to reduce Central/State Government expenditure because (a) decentralization is bound to entail significant starting up costs, (b) decentralization by definition involves larger number of staff and more costs on travel and honoraria etc., (c) decentralized bodies need to be provided with large amounts of resources to take up activities which would win them the confidence of the people, (d) to monitor adequately decentralized system requires a large monitoring bureaucracy.

Further, Crook and Manor suggest that tasks which Central/State Government try to get rid of by devolving responsibility for them upon local councils are not likely to be performed adequately because of (a) insufficient resources, (b) incapacity of the local bureaucracy, (c) disinclination of elected local bodies to tackle many of tasks especially if they do not entail construction of physical assets. Decentralization will do little or nothing directly to benefit vulnerable groups or to alleviate poverty because (a) elites exercise dominance, or national level elites build local power bases, (b) the personalization of power relations is more intense at intermediate or local levels. Accordingly governments may be well advised to insulate programmes aimed at aiding the vulnerable or at alleviating poverty from decentralized planning and implementation. Democratic because (a) the local councils are supra-local in character and have quite distinct interests from those of village communities and attempts at mobilization map cause these differing interests to come into conflict, (b) elections to local bodies tend to create divisions within or between local communities, (c) local socio-economic structures permit inequalities which allow elites to dominate and this weighs against community participation, (d) it is extremely difficult to combine the role of community delegate/development animator with that of District level political and manager of District resources. Decentralization cannot be expected to reduce absenteeism among public employees or to increase their work rate when they are on the job. Crook and Manor also indicate that decentralization inflates popular expectations much beyond what can be satisfied by local councils; that people fail to understand the limitation of what decentralized or local bodies, or even local government can achieve; and that greater transparency made possible by decentralization makes corruption more visible (and there may also occur decentralization of corruption)—leading to a mood of popular exasperation even when corruption may actually have declined.

Despite highlighting many problem areas regarding decentralization, Crook and Manor feel that decentralization has, especially in their Indian case study area (the State of Karnataka), positively influenced the way that State and Society interact and the popular experience of one Indian State (Rajasthan), is similar, i.e., that despite there being a large element of truth in the points made by Crook and Manor, the various possible advantages of decentralization are likely to be achieved atleast to a significant extent, and thus, on balance there is need to make district planning a major thrust area.

It should, however, be clarified that district planning is much broader than only the planning of governmental programmes, but involves the planning for both governmental and private activities for the local area and its development so as to lead to the achievement of national, state level and local areas goals in an integrated manner. What is needed is a two way approach; the process of planning from below lending realism and concreteness of content and being sensitive to regional variations, with the downward movement of planning from above setting broad macro-priorities, lending coherency and ensuring flow of national resources and funds to various regions and areas as well as to framework to ensure maximum results. At all but the highest and lowest levels, planning impulses would emanate not only within the level itself but also from the higher and lower levels.

POLICY ISSUES FOR OPERATIONALIZING DECENTRALIZED PLANNING

Before the reader turns ensuring narration about district and decentralized planning in the multi-level planning framework, we would also like to list some policy issues regarding decentralized planning that we consider relevant in today's Indian context. These include:

1. What should be the main level of decentralized plannings; should it be state, region, district, block or mandal, growth centre, cluster of villages, or a single village?
2. What should be the machinery set up to operationalise decentralized planning?
3. What challenges would be required at the state level?
4. What strategy and time frame would be appropriate— if the Hanumantha Rao Report is to be followed, then would only the first or second stages mentioned therein be appropriate rather than the third or full decentralization state?
5. What functions would be most appropriate at which level in the multi-level framework?
6. Are safeguards or mechanisms necessary, or feasible, to keep local elites or vested interests from capturing or distorting the decentralized planning process? Similarly, what mechanisms can be evolved to keep an individual expert or administrator or politician from forcing his professional or personal bias to be adopted as planning decisions due to his personality or status while interacting at lower levels of planning?
7. Would pulls from certain parts of the plannings region (say an electoral constituency or the member of

Parliament's home village) compromise efficiency criteria in allocating funds and resources?

8. Could the transitional costs involved (financial or otherwise) be reduced if the movement towards decentralization is kept gradual and would a gradual movement lead to greater stability and sustainability of the procedures of planning and decision-making structures that are being established?
9. How would decentralized planning fit in which the needs of indicative planning or facilitative planning to influence the behaviour or private entities and individuals in ways that are considered conducive to development and are expected to reinforce and integrate with planned governmental activity?
10. With the existing limitation of skills and data at lower levels how can the need for methodological rigour and correctness be balanced with practical considerations to decide the extent of analysis necessary before proper planning decisions are taken without unnecessary delay and excessive cost being expended on the planning activities? Can partial application of techniques or use of simplified methodology or ready reckoners and some sort or rapid appraisal suffice?
11. When the planning and implementing body becomes the one and the same as is inevitable when the planning function is decentralized to lower levels, how can it be ensured that the planner does not fix for himself as targets easy to perform tasks rather than more vital or important tasks, or that the planner/implementor is not overly influenced by immediate short-term problems and goals rather than being able to take a broad long term perspective?
12. How can possible conflicts and differences between district and state level planners be minimized or kept to a minimum level and what would be the position of national planners in view of such conflicts of interests?
13. How can genuine local participation, mobilization and raising of resources be ensured?

14. How to integrate plans and avoid inconsistencies, duplication and even working at cross purposes, between different sub-sectors and different projects in the same area?
15. In view of the above, what advantages can accrue from decentralized planning in the immediate short run, and it the long run?

APPROPRIATE AREAL UNIT

As regards the appropriate areal unit for decentralized plannings, the possible planning units below the state level could be: (i) Intermediate region between state and district, (ii) The District, (iii) The block or Mandal Panchayat, (iv) A growth centre (v) A cluster of villages or (vi) A cluster of watersheds.

Historical and administrative reasons point towards the district as a major unit of decentralized planning. The intermediate region state and district does not exist today except for specific purposes like Command or Hill or Tribal Area Development and the block or Mandal Panchayat may prove to be too small to be a fully viable unit, while growth centre planning may prove too costly, time consuming and cumbersome to be taken up on a mass scale. The same may hold true for trying to plan separately for each cluster of five to ten villages or watersheds.

The comparative advantages of preferring the district as the major planning unit below the state level are given below:

1. It is large enough to serve as a viable planning unit.
2. It has a settled pattern of administration with a high degree of internal consistency and well established administrative relationships.
3. The long history of district administration has ensured that citizens' awareness of administrative processes in a district is adequate, implying that a new or different administrative or planning unit would need major reorientation as regards the perceptions, on the part of the masses, of new administrative boundaries and of procedures.
4. People living in an established district have a sense of belonging to the entity; of pride and loyalty a community

feeling that takes years to build up.

5. Panchayat bodies are district based.
6. Several central, state and quasi-governmental agencies have set up area or sub-area headquarters at the district level.
7. Assembly and parliamentary constituencies are moulded as per district boundaries.
8. Most of the records and information pertaining to land records development loaning, housing, roads, electrification, irrigation, agriculture, schools and the like, in fact all government departments data, is district based. Computerised data systems like DISNIC and CRISP have also been built up on a district basis.
9. Livestocks, human, agricultural, economic and industrial census provide district level data.
10. District level credit planning, DRDA (District Rural Development Agency) planning and even embryonic district developmental planning is already being done (the first two in every and the last in many states).
11. Major operations like relief and employment generation have always been planned and carried out at district level, the relief plan and its implementation involves a number of department and agencies at the district level.
12. Most districts are manageable in terms of size, enabling local initiative and involvement, and yet not too small to pursue meaningful and viable planning.
13. Coordinating mechanisms already exists at the district level.
14. Sample data, e.g., of crop cutting, is statistically significant only at the district level and not for lower levels.
15. Since the district already exists as an administrative unit, to take up planning at the district level would ensure that evaluating the overall impact on the people and the area of the local administrative and planning effort in an area would become feasible.

EVOLUTION OF THINKING ABOUT DISTRICT PLANNING

Now to turn to a brief, almost telegraphic overview of decentralized planning. Despite its advocacy earlier also, we can start out story with the mention of panchayats in independent India's Constitution and subsequently the advent of the Five Year Plans. The second plan spoke of decentralized planning, but the Community Development era did not see much movement in this direction. The Balwant Rai Committee Report 1958 gave life to Panchayati Raj and to initial efforts at block and district planning.

In the Third and Fourth Five Year Plan periods, along with Community Development, Panchayati Raj based district planning with the help of district level officers was attempted. It petered out into mere paper exercises as lists of demands from below and directions from above could not mesh in the prevailing ethos of ad-hoc coordination of panchayat planning (Mathur 1966, Mathur and Narain 1969).

Gadgil Kale's Lecture on District Development Planning, 1966, had a significant impact on the thinking of planners, administrators, scholars etc.

The Government of India's Ford Foundation—assisted pilot project on rural growth centres which led to the Roy and Patil Manual for Block Level Planning (1977) proved too cumbersome, costly and time consuming for operationalization and replication and failed to achieve an interdisciplinary focus (Fisher 1979) though attempts at some sort of growth centre planning were made from time to time and the subsequent Hanumantha Rao Report (1984) also advocates growth centre approach.

The Planning Commission issued guidelines for district planning in 1969, which were later reported in Hanumantha Rao Report (1984).

District Planning was formally adopted in a limited way by some states such as Maharashtra from 1972 onwards when district planning boards were set up (Inamdar and Kshire 1986).

Throughout the early 1970s, academic debates on decentralized district planning went on; for example, special numbers issued by

Indian Journal of Public Administration 1973 and *Journal of LBS National Academy of Administration,* 1975. V.K.R.V. Rao's articles and talks in the early 1970s commanded respect and the introduction of Integrated Rural Development (IRD) led to block level credit planning. In the late 1970s the Ashoka Mehta Committee 1978 gave a boost to panchayat based development.

It was also in 1978 that a Planning Commission Committee, set up under Professor Dantwala to consider the question of block level planning in the context of IRD, presented its report and a possible methodology for block level planning was worked out, recognizing that the block would be one level in a multi-level framework including the Centre, States and Districts. However, except for the preparation of IRD Action plans for each block, what little decentralized planning was attempted was at the district level. The National Institute of Rural Development (formerly NICD) Hyderabad from the early 1970s and Lal Bahadur Shastri National Academy of Administration from the late 1980s have continued working on the methodology of micro-level and decentralized planning; holding seminars, preparing model plans, writing reports suggesting methodologies etc., In the late 1990s Karnataka, Andhra Pradesh and West Bengal experimented with their own models of decentralized planning.

The report of the working group on District Planning Commission; (Hanumantha Rao Report) was issued in 1984 and adopted as part of Seventh Five Year Plan, though only a few State could make actual progress. The 1992 Constitutional Amendment is the latest milestone which has been achieved after renewed political, bureaucratic and academic interest starting with the organizing of District Collectors workshops attended by the then Prime Minister in 1987-88 and cumulating in three separate Amendment Bill on Panchayati Raj being introduced in Parliament and the passage of the 73rd and 74th Amendments relating to Panchayats and Municipalities in 1992.

We may also at this point highlight some publications which could work as a good introduction for persons new to the tissues related to the evolution of district planning including the related themes of decentralized and panchayat planning.

For a brief introduction to Panchayati Raj, Sweta Mishra (1994) is adequate as in Inamdar (1992) regarding the developmental delivery system which includes panchayat institutions and governmental and non-governmental bodies. Similarly, if only one or two references are to be considered on the concept and issues of district and multi-level planning then the F.A.O. Social and Development paper 52 (1985) followed by the Hanumantha Rao Report and Hooja (1986—District Planning) or Mathur and Hooja (1996) could serve the purpose. For the period when Panchayati Raj was initially Vibrant Jacob (1967) and Ram Reddy (1977) are useful and for a focus on decentralized planning in the same period Mathur and Narain (1969) is a must. Kamta Prasad Planning and its Implementation (1984) while covering the same period provides a link to some issues of administrative planning as does Venugopal Reddy (1979). Inamdar and Kshire (1986) is recommended because in the mid-1980s Maharashtra's experience was amongst the most commented upon and also seems to have influenced the Hanumantha Rao Report. For those more interested in the methodological details Lalit Sen (1972) in the earlier period and the volumes by Amitav Mukherjee in the 1990s are indicated are Misra, Urs and Nataraj (1978), R.P. Misra (1992) and especially Misra and Achyuta (1990). For a historical overview we would like to suggest Joshi (1989) and our paper in Hooja and Mathur.

Among recent collections of articles, through in the immediate pre constitution Amendment era, Yugandhar and Mukherjee (1991), Hooja and Raju (1993) and the special number of The Administrator (1991) or even Hooja and Mathur (1991), concentrate on the district planning focus. For recent developments from the Panchayati Raj focus the special numbers of Journal of Rural Development (1991 & 1997) and Institute of Social Science (1994) are relevant. For an earlier review of various Panchayat Acts see Sudesh K. Sharma (1976). For those already having exposure to an understanding to the problems, processes and implications of Panchayati Raj the more complex analysis of P.C.Mathur (1990) though focussed more on Rajasthan may prove interesting. For a more simple overview of Panchayati Raj in Rajasthan from 1959 to 1999 Hooja and Hooja 1999 may satisfy the reader.

Though not directly with the subject we also recommended Cernea (1991) to the reader in view of the people-centered approach to development advocated by it. For project analysis despite some of its chapters being too complex for use by decentralized planners Gittinger (1982) is still a good introduction to the concepts and approach.

DECENTRALIZED PROJECT PLANNING ANALYTICAL SKILLS AND TECHNIQUES

Now to turn to the question regarding what skills and knowledge are likely to prove relevant for decentralized planning. What is required is:

(a) Knowledge of the areas needs, potentials, resources and resource gaps,
(b) Knowledge of state and national level goals, plans, schemes and resource flows,
(c) Responsiveness to peoples needs and knowledge of their aspirations,
(d) Knowledge of participatory planning and local mobilization techniques,
(e) Knowledge of how the government administrative system and the existing market system works in the regions/area,
(f) Planning and project-planning expertise,
(g) Area and spatial plannings knowledge and concepts,
(h) Some knowledge of various disciplines and technical subjects having a bearing on development (i.e., basic knowledge regarding agriculture, animal husbandry, civil engineering, rural industries, health and education management and similar subjects), and
(i) Ability to combine the above and prepare integrated and comprehensive plans based on a broad vision.

Such knowledge would not be available with any one single individual even at the highest policy level in the country. However, teams of local administrators; peoples representatives etc. could be built up gradually to develop a feel and understanding for each of the above points. For that atleast initially attempts should be made to impart training not only to district and block level planners but also to state level planners in:

1. Identifying locally felt needs (as well as aspirations; which may match neither the needs not the available resources) and mobilising the local populace to ensure peoples participation and participatory planning.
2. Project/Scheme identification.
3. The project approach and basics of project planning.
4. Area planning and concepts like growth centre planning.
5. Integrating and compiling different aspects of plan proposals and proposals regarding various schemes/projects into a coherent district or local area plan.
6. Interacting with the state government planning cells and planning departments and their district level staff.
7. Interacting with the large sized panchayat bodies that have come into existence as a result of the recent constitutional amendments.
8. National and state level planning goals.
9. Sources of, and ways to gain access to, data available at national and state levels which could prove useful for decentralized plannings.
10. Nowadays some knowledge in the use of computers could also be imparted as their use could make planning exercises that much easier.

For identification of the local needs and aspirations like problem tree analysis, or problem-matrix analysis on the one hand and rapid Rural Appraisal (RRA) and Participatory Rural Appraisal (PRA) on the other which need to be taught. Of course as regards motivation of the populace there is no simple formula or technique that could be taught.

As regards project identification it could be suggested to the potential planners that project/scheme ideas can come to them from either analytical or non analytical sources like the following:

Analytical Sources	Non-Analytical Sources
1. Resource Analysis of areas and households	1. Political Directions
2. Needs Analysis	2. Political Pressures
3. Demands Analysis	3. Declared Government Policies and objectives
4. Market Analysis	4. Formal (and even informal) interaction amongst officers or between officials and non-officials.
5. Rapid Rural Appraisal	5. Guidelines of Aid giving Agencies/ National Programmes etc.
6. Social Mapping/Cultural inventories	6. Replication of inventories existing project ideas
7. Diagnostic and Strategy exercises	7. Feedback from exercises failed projects
8. Brain storming	8. Touring in Area
9. Surveys of literature	9. Common sense administrative or political experience
10. Project identification Missions or Groups	10. Bargaining between sanctioning and implementing agencies/departments
11. The population, agriculture, animal husbandry, industry, etc., census conducted at regular intervals	11. Casual Reading of Newspapers, Magazines, Books.
	12. Meetings of Villages and Panchayats bodies or citizens
	13. Citizens' petitions and applications.

Cruits and Watson have suggested that analytical sources of project ideas can be further divided into the sub categories of administrative search and intellectual search. Some possible methods of the two types of search are given below.

Administrative Search	**Intellectual (Academic) Search**
Consult Populations, (surveys, local committees, discussions, villagers meetings)	Analyze Economy
Consult local leaders and other key informants formally or informally (even in a seminar)	Analyze Society
Consult Government Departments through routine meetings and special working groups	Special problem oriented analytical studies
Consult Research organizations/ consultants through planning studies	Diagnostic and Strategy Exercises

Roberts Chambers has indicated the following criteria for simple project selection: Cost effectiveness, decision matrices, priority ranking, check-listing and preparation of lists of costs and benefits.

Just as for purposes of decentralized planning the project identification needs to be kept simple, similarly project planning also need not entail full and detailed project analysis with New Present Value (NPV), Internal Rate of Return (IRR) and Cost Benefit (CB) rations in detail required for each and every project appraisal.

Infact for many small projects even rough use of the project approach with a rough comparison of Costs Benefits may prove adequate and would also be an improvement over the scheme budget exercises presently most often done in government. Not every project needs to have exact values assigned to the costs, benefits and rates of returns and in some cases mere qualification, and in others even identification may be enough.

Of course the project approach needs to be properly understood at the district and lower levels, both among administrators and amongst panchayat leaders, not only for project formulation purposes, but also for project implementation since it would help avoidance of blind application of norms worked out by some other agency without trying to see if any special local conditions exist that would lead to unintended latent impacts of implementation which had not been anticipated by the project formulator.

Similarly if the project approach is understood at the local planning level, then better sensitivity analysis is possible since instead of abstract generalized eventualities like percentage cost on time over run and its impact on cost and benefit flows being considered at sate or regional level, at the local level locally specific likely eventualities can be better identified and quantified for sensitivity analysis with respect to each such specific eventuality.

Local planners mistakenly think of project life as only covering the period up to benefit delivery or completion of construction, and have to be reminded that the period in which the impact of a project is being felt has to be considered part of project life for pre project appraisal purposes and that intangible benefits and costs both have to be considered, as have possible negative impact of projects.

It also needs to be explained to local planners as to how project analysis needs to include technical appraisal, institutional—organisational—managerial appraisal, commercial appraisal, financial appraisal, economic appraisal, sustainability appraisal (with its sub-categories of social appraisal and environmental appraisal) and what this writer likes to refer as acceptability appraisal (involving acceptability on the part of the beneficiaries, the non-beneficiaries in the area, and the lower, middle and senior level implementors, as well as concerned officials and non-officials including peoples representatives) since in case acceptability is not forthcoming then either the project objectives may need to be modified (the second best may be better than the optimal of the 'best') or special acceptability—including mechanisms may need to be built into the project at a cost. Only after the above can decisions about accepting/ rejecting, projects or regarding ranking of projects be undertaken.

Most district and block level functionaries have never really thought in terms of locational and area planning or of growth centre concepts. However, once exposed to basic area based concepts, most are quick to understand issues of both geographic and social distance and of physical and social barriers as also how to fit their projects/scheme into a framework of spatial planning that would prove most beneficial for the area they are to plan for and implement in. They also start appreciating how sectoral plans and growth/service centre plans can each lead to modifications in the other so that an integrated area development plan catering to sectoral needs and central-place based planning can evolve. Use of methodological devices like Gutmans Scalogram for growth centres and for facilities provided at such centres are also easily understood by them. Experiences of the Government of India—Ford Foundation Pilot Project on Rural Growth Centres may however caution planners that the growth centre approach has to be integrated with other approaches and cannot be the sole criteria for preparing plans.

As regards preparing holistic district plans, many writers have set forth their views (see Mukherjee 1991, for summaries) over the last few decades and numerous model district plans (e.g. Mushari, Rayalseema, Dharmapur, Wardha, NIRD, Plans) have also been prepared. However, this writer feels that, if Gadgils views from the 1960s, V.K.R.V. Rao's from the 1970s and those of the Hanumanantha Rao (Group) Report of 1984 are put across to potential planners at the district or block levels, then many of the issues that run through most writing on district planning would get properly discussed.

Gadgil (1966) had suggested that each district be divided into mandi areas each of which would have a market centre as its nucleus. He suggested (as their reader has understood him) that the district planning exercise start with the preparation of a Physio-geographic plan of socio-economic overheads so as to direct the activities of producers and consumers. This would involve the provision of basic services and amenities to be spread throughout the area. The next aspect to be considered is the conservation, proper exploitation and development of natural resources. Then one needs to plan for production through a system of incentives and disincentives for individual workers, managers and entrepreneurs and the use of encouragement, regulation and prohibition. Also required is planning for unemployment involving the choice of the type and volume of projects which provide employment. The plan would also have to be dovetailed. This would involve questions of balances and availabilities, of priorities and of financial resources available—all to be considered within the framework of national objectives, policies and plans. Also to be considered would be questions regarding the need for setting up new organisations, or re-allocating functions amongst various existing institutions. Finally, according to Gadgil, the district planner would have to ensure coordination, synchronization and 'proportionality' of the various parts of the plan.

According to V.K.R.V. Rao (1973) the district planner has to work at two levels: the District and the Economic Area. (Here again the summary that follows reflects the way this authors has understood Rao's views). He has to look to speedy economic growth, integrated and elective utilization of resources (both human and natural), increase in employment, increase in social services and social consumption, redressal of regional imbalances, improving the lot of socially and economically backward sections of the population, and speedy abolition of poverty. While details of plans for conservation of natural resources and for production etc., need to be worked out at the Economic Area level, areawise and sectoral financial allocation, distribution of employment oriented schemes and solving of organisational problems, and best done at the district level with coordination and synchronization efforts being done at both levels and overall integration with state and natural plans being done at the district level. The district planner must identify his district's resources and the extent of their utilization, the nature and extent of infrastructural development required, the district socio-cultural profile, the nature and extent of the existing social infrastructure and facilities, the consumption requirements, existing social satisfaction, the position of the deprived wage levels, unemployment and under-employment and the prevailing income distribution. He has also to learn to anticipate local reactions.

The District Plan should not be a mere collection of various departments or sub-departments proposals, nor a mere spelling out of targets and financial allocations, but a much more comprehensive document, which, keeping in mind financial constraints, spells out logical relations between sectoral and the department plans and between various Economic Areas in a district and which determines the chronological order in which schemes are to be started and implemented. It is to be based on calculations of demand and supply where the need for equipment, trained personnel, buildings, raw material, skilled and unskilled labour etc. have been checked against available supply and an attempt made to improve the internal organization of the implementing agencies.

The planner, according to V.K.R.V. Rao, must combine knowledge of local and district conditions with that of plan formulation techniques. He has to be able to anticipate crisis situations so as to avoid emergencies and crash programmes and to replace them by consist and routinized efforts. Given the knowledge of Central and State Projects in the district, and the corresponding inflow of outlays, of local natural resources, production, land uses, credit supply, infrastructure and social service facilities, etc., the district planner should give priority to the development of socio-economic overheads and to resource development, rather than to the social services that local pressures demand.

THE MAINSTREAM OR HANUMANTHA RAO REPORT MODEL OF DISTRICT PLANNING

The Planning Commission had constituted a Working Group on District Planning under Dr. Hanumantha Rao whose recommendations were accepted by Government of India as part of the Seventh Plan. The functions of the district planning body as suggested by the Group are: (a) crystallization of local needs and objectives within the broad framework of national and state level objectives, (b) taking stock of the natural and human endowments of the district and the regions within the district as well as the level and pattern of development attained so far, (c) listing and mapping of amenities at the village, block and district levels, (d) formulation of district plans in their socio-economic, temporal and spatial dimensions programmes and priorities relevant for the district, (f) coordination and implementation of the district plan, (g) monitoring and review of implementation of the district plan and programmes with due regard to their linkages and dependencies.

The Group suggested the following steps for the planning exercise

(i) Formulation of the major objectives of district planning, (ii) Compilation of data, (iii) Bringing out the profile of the district in relation to the basic objectives, (iv) Formulating the main strategy and thrust, (v) Analysing existing programmes and projects regarding. (a) modifications of ongoing schemes/projects, (b) removal of inter block disparities, (c) assessment of unemployment/underemployment and proposals regarding manpower planning/budgeting, (d) inclusion of new projects and plans, (e) inter linkages between various projects/ programmes, (f) organisation and management to eliminate gaps in implementation, (g) the relationship and links between the district plan and the state development plan, (vi) Assessment of resources for allocation to various programmes/projects, (vii) Preparing a statement of physical components of the plan.

For each local level scheme the minimum details required are: (a) description of the scheme and its significance to the area, (b) location, (c) raw material and inputs requirement and linkages, (d) volume and value of likely resultant output, (e) number of beneficiaries, (f) likely employment generation, (g) (for some select schemes only) simple cost-benefit calculation. The district planner would also have dovetail in an integrated manner, resources available from—(a) State Plan for particular projects, (b) State plan for schemes of general nature not tied to specific projects, (c) local bodies, (d) from credit institutions, and (e) raised by voluntary agencies and other local sources.

The Working Group also emphasised, manpower planning, spatial planning, implementational coordination, plan integration, and public participation. Since, the Hanumantha Rao report was adopted by the Government of India, and many state governments had also professed to have adopted its broad approach, we reproduce below the three stages towards decentralization set forth in the report, as well as the main features, in the form of summarized points.

In fact the Hanumananth a Rao report and the FAO's Economic and Social Development Paper 52 have used almost identical language about the stages through which are to move gradually towards "full" decentralized planning.

***STAGE-I:* Initiation—Establishing Prerequisites**

(i) Define scope of district planning and district sector schemes;
(ii) Disaggregate plan funds to district level;
(iii) Formulate criteria for inter district allocation of plan funds;
(iv) Strengthen planning capability at district level;
(v) Establish horizontal machinery at district level and link it vertically with monitoring mechanisms at the higher level;
(vi) Establish district planning board/council/committee with representation form the public;
(vii) Establish planning procedures for five year plan and annual plan budget.

***STAGE-II:* Limited Decentralization (or Embryonic District Planning)**

(i) Bring limited sectors of activity, e.g. Minimum Needs Programme agriculture and allied activities, within the purview of planning at the district level;
(ii) Introduce the concept of free fund (united funds) and encourage limited localism in district planning;
(iii) Improve multi-level resource allocation for development budgeting;
(iv) Provide extensive delegation of powers to district level, including powers of re-appropriation;
(v) Streamline procedures for dovetailing district plans into the state plan and for deriving annual plan budget from five year plan.

***STAGE-III:* Final or Full Decentralisation**

(i) Enlarge localism to cover decision-making in all district sector activities;
(ii) Introduce administrative reforms to delegate all decision-making powers to districts level;
(iii) Encourage and provide for high level of popular participation;
(iv) Adopt budgetary practice that encourages local initiative;
(v) Render functionaries of development departments accountable to district planning body;

(vi) Prepare perspective plans for the district to guide five year plans and annual plan budgets;

(vii) Improve and strengthen local government;

(viii) Evolve healthy relationship between the political executive and normal government bureaucratic.

While the above give a reasonably good idea of the approach followed by the Hanumantha Rao working group, it would be worthwhile at this juncture to briefly set forth the salient features of the report as this author has understood them (more details are available in Hooja 1986 or Hooja 1994 a).

Main Features of the Hanumanatha Rao

1. Treat district as part of multi-level planning framework.
2. Divide state government funds into state sector funds and district sector funds rationally to each district.
3. Differentiate between district sector funds commited to state department schemes in the district and those available for the district level to utilize at its own discretion.
4. Encourage the raising of funds locally for use in the district.
5. Have single planning, coordinating and monitoring bodies at the district level.
6. Have district planning cells in the state planning department to co-ordinate and guide the district bodies.
7. Plan jointly for both rural and urban areas.
8. Integrate DRDA planning, sectoral departmental planning and famine relief works planning into decentralized planning.
9. The collector should be the coordinator at the district level of all developmental and planning activities and play an important role in the district planning body.

Methodology (to be deliberately kept simple, as the report emphasises, for easy application in the field).

1. Take stock of natural and human endowments and level of development so far achieved in the district.
2. Prepare a district profile.
3. Analyse existing programmes.
4. Work out the needs of the inhabitations.

5. Integrate local needs with local resources and national/state plans.
6. Examine existing organizational structure.
7. Formulate strategy or main developmental thrust for the district.
8. Prepare physical and financial components of district plan which is multi-disciplinary and comprehensive or integrated and areas specific, growth and people's need-oriented, poverty alleviating and linked to (or integrated with) state department plan schemes.
9. Undertake manpower planning for the district, identifying skills locally available as well as the lack of skills required for local activities and to plan for employment generation especially for unskilled, unemployed poor.
10. Spatial planning especially to: (i) relax existing state level norms based on distance or population thresholds for providing services at specific centres as per growth centre analysis, (ii) point out functional gaps in different parts of the district, and (iii) help reduce inter-block and inter locality disparities within the district.
11. Institutional credit planning especially, for the rural poor.
12. Use of the recommendations of the 1969 District Planning Guidelines of the Planning Commission regarding consultation with state departments, district level officers, panchayat elected non-officials and progressive people in the district before submitting plan proposals to the state planning department for approval. (For a summary of the Guidelines see Hooja 1986).

As the last point in the proceeding list, which mentions the 1969 guidelines, itself emphasises, the Hanumanatha Rao report was not drafted in a Vacuum, but built upon previous experience and intellectual debate.

MODELS AND MODALITIES FOLLOWED IN THE STATES: AN OVERVIEW OF THE PRE-CONSTITUTION AMENDMENT PERIOD

The Pre-Constitutional Amendment status of district planning has been paraphrased below:

At the state level, most was done in a sectorally segmented manner. Some decentralisation has been achieved through DRDA planning and some states had also embarked on embryonic or limited district planning (See Table 3.1).

While the general approach advocated in the Hanumantha Rao report and especially its first two stages has been followed by many states, not all have adopted uniform practices. Even the report itself had suggested that each state should be free to take its own decision about an appropriate interdependency mix between devolution of authority *vis-a-vis* centralized coordination-cum-financial allocation authority. However, the common features to be found in many states are as follows:

(a) The Plan funds are clearly divided between state and district sectors.

(b) Norms for allocation of funds from the sate level based on objective indicators and criteria (like total population of Scheduled Castes/Scheduled Tribes/Small farmers, agriculture backwardness, irrigation backwardness, industrial backwardness, drinking water problem, other special problems, ability to raise local funds etc.) for each district have been worked out and the principle of weightages applied. Raising of funds at the district level is encouraged.

(c) Most states have categorized district sector schemes, primarily on the basis of the schemes' benefits being confined to the district.

(d) Some united or discretionary funds have been provided at the district level (while many states have a district sector which also includes united funds, others have only provided united funds as a first step towards decentralization).

Table 3.1: Comparison of Sectoral, Rural Development and Regional Planning Efforts in India

Sectoral Planning (Department by Department Plans compiled into state plans)	Rural Development Planning (DRDA Planning)	Regional Planning (Area and Project Planning or embryonic District Planning)
(1)	(2)	(3)
MERITS 1. Technical proposals can be better prepared on basis of functionally specialized projects.	1. Focus on special activities e.g. poverty alleviation, employment generation, diffusion of innovations and technology utilization of local resources, diversification of rural economy	1. Sectoral, special equity-based, rural development, and spatial as well as social and welfare planning all integrated into a comprehensive multi-disciplinary, multi-level framework.
2. It is the existing planning practice the people, the administrators and the politicions have got used of operating it	2. Greater focus on people as beneficiary	2. Decentralization of proposal and decision making possible and some slight devolution of powers may also occur, thus greater possibility of integration of peoples participation and heirarchial administrative functioning.
3. Easier to integrate plan preparation and implementation on sectoral department basis and to obtain feedback for future planning.	3. Element of peoples participation often involved	3. Caters in a better manner to area needs, provision of basic services, and integration of different sectors.
4. Easier to monitor progress on department by department basis for State Planning Department or National Planning Commission.	4. Better Planning / projectization of local level projects.	4. Integration of rural and urban planning (to reflect actual links) possible.
	5. Some consideration of spatial aspects, attempt to understand organizational characteristics of local production activities and social structures	5. Both department by department and area by area monitoring facilitated.
	6. Setting up of special agencies for implementation within sector/department based framework.	6. Intra-regional and Inter-regional agroclimatic and cultural etc. differences better catered for.

Contd.....

DEMERITS		
1. Duplication of efforts by various departments possible. 2. One department's activities may have learnt dysfunctional effects on another department's efforts 3. Real life is not sectorally segmented but integrated, hence departmental functioning may not properly comprehend or reflect developmental needs nor lead to appropriate and optimal development. 4. Special equity and locational aspects may get neglected	1. Has to be attempted within sectoral department based framework. 2. Inter-departmental coordina-tion of integration difficult to achieve leading to sectorally segmented or monosector activities. 3. Less emphasis on normal growth, production and infrastructure activities. 4. DRDA Planning becoming a more 'glamorous' activity may harm normal departmental staff. 5. May be resented by local elites. 6. Upsets interia of existing administrative system accustomed to sectoral departments planning and thus DRDA planning may not get fully integrated into the regular administr-ative system and even special agency administrators may be half hearted due to prevailing administrative culture. 7. Clash possible between peoples participation and hierarchical administration. 8. Urban areas and urban poor neglected 9. The DRDA or special agency, the regular departmental staff, and bankers, local panchayat leaders etc. can each blame the other for non achievement of targets thus providing each implementor with what E.J. Clay and BB. Schaffer (ed) Room for Manoeuvre, (Heineman Educational Books, 1984) refers to as escape hatches'.	1. Established funct-ional departments may not be willing to shed their autonomy. 2. Local elites may capture the district sector fund planning process to the detriment of others. 3. Regional/national leaders and or bureau-crats may not want local political initiative to develop. 4. New system needs time, effort, organiza-tional restructuring, special training etc. so as to evolve properly. 5. Local implementers may want only easy to achieve rather than more vital targets to be assigned to them. 6. Local planners may merely set forth a shopping list of dema-nds without considering existing resource or other constraints.

Source: This table has developed by the author from one originally prepared by him for a seminar presentation during his stay at School of Development Studies, University of East Angila, United Kingdom in 1986-87. It was originally used in Rakesh Hooja "Regional and District Planning: Why and How" in Hoshair Singh and D.P. Singh (ed) *Indian Administration: Current Issues and Problems,* Aalekh, Jaipur 1991 and has been slightly modified since then and used in various earlier forms in some of my subsequent publications.

(e) Maneuverability has been allowed in some states to the District Planning Body and a certain percentage of total district outlay may be re-appropriated by it.

(f) The District Planning Body may be headed by a Minister or the Divisional Commissioner or the Collector, who, if not the Chairman may be the Vice Chairman and may also head the Executive Committee of the District Planning Body.

(g) The District Planning Body consists of members from Parliament, State Legislature, Municipal and Panchayati Raj Institutions, Banks and also district level officers.

(h) A small district planning cell has been set-up in every district.

(i) In most states, only annual plans of district sector schemes are prepared at the district level and that too by sectoral officers and these may be scrutinized by the executive committee and by the District Planning Body.

(j) In most cases, the plans approved at the district level are forwarded to the state government for final approval.

(k) The heads of various departments are required to perform more of an advisory than a controlling role for district sector schemes.

(l) Implementation in invariably undertaken by the district level officers though monitoring is undertaken through periodic review meetings of the District Planning Body or its executive.

(m) The project approach and an in-built system for periodical monitoring and applying corrective measures are both lacking in the micro level plans formulated by most states.

(n) In most states, committee liabilities of on-going schemes use up most of the funds earmarked for the district sector, leaving the little money for fresh district level planning.

(o) Most states have set-up district planning cells at the state level to guide the District Planning Bodies.

There have also been reports of slight reversal of decentralization in some states, even though most states appear to be moving at least to the stage of limited decentralization or the second stage set forth in the Hanumantha Rao report. Karnataka,

West Bengal and Andhra Pradesh have tried to evolve somewhat different models then the one described above.

As a supplement to my above list it would be relevant to paraphrase B.M. Joshi's 1989 description of the then existing status of decentralized planning in the pre constitution amendment era. Joshi states (summary by this writer):

1. Though the need for decentralization has been successively stressed in the Five Year Plans, only a few states have actually tried to operationalize it and here also the process has only gone to one level below i.e district level.
2. After publishing of Balwantrai Mehta Report most of the State introduced Panchayati Raj Institutions. However, after the initial enthusiasm had died down, these institutions lost their importance and basic function. They have normally not exercised any control over district plan funds.
3. New planning bodies have been created at the district level for decentralized planning work. In most states Panchayati Raj Bodies have not been associated in any manner with the formulation and monitoring of the district plan. In some others Zila Parishads have become subordinates to the district planning bodies or at times mere implementing agencies. There have been only few exceptions.
4. During the years, many new autonomous and semi-autonomous bodies have mushroomed at the district level. They have their district level functionaries and they work independently of each other and are not part of the district planning bodies.
5. A demarcation of activities between the State and the District has been done on the basis of twin norms of location and coverage of benefit. But the classification is not very accurate and scientific and many of the activities which ought to have been done by the districts have been retained at the State level.
6. Plans are prepared at the district level strictly according to guidelines fixed at the State headquarters. The results in disaggregation of State Plan into district plans and not on proposals based on local needs coming up in the district

plan. The devolution of funds based on area, population, and level of development does not give sufficient elbow room to district authorities to prepare new schemes. The funds are hardly sufficient to carry on continuing schemes. In a few states incentive money or united funds are allotted to the district level.

7. Not much headway has been made at administrative and financial delegation. The old system of centralized accounting and budgeting is still being followed.
8. In almost all State the technical planning machinery at the district level is extremely inadequate both quantitatively and qualitatively. The district plans prepared now are simply a collection of sectoral plans prepared by different departmental heads at the district level.

TOWARDS THE FUTURE—AN ORGANIZATIONAL MODEL

It is my belief that the current practice of planning in isolation of individual sectoral programmes and projects would have to be discarded as far as planning at the district level is concerned. District Planning has to be a single wholistic operation like an area plan wherein different activities (including activities in the private sector) are harmonised into an integrated plan.

The 74th Amendment Act 1992 has provided for a district planning committee to consolidate the panchayat (rural) plans of the district. 80 per cent of its membership has to be from Panchayat and Municipal bodies. However, in addition to the feedback that elected representatives of local bodies can provide and the detailed discussions that can be held in their forums, district planning would also need detailed analysis and studies and inputs from experts and government servants. Further, due to the overlap of functions already mentioned (also see Table 3.2), there is need for a body with functionaries from the state and district levels to work with the state panchayat/municipality non-officials to minimize the differences and strains between the state and district levels. In this context and keeping in view the fact that the new post-constitution Amendment Panchayat Bodies are mostly very large and somewhat unwidely (perhaps functioning and behaving like mini-legislative assemblies) and that the same may be the case with the district planning committee as per the 74th Constitutional Amendment, a recommendation of the NDC Committee on Micro Level Planning and Involvement of People at Grass Root Level (Chimanbhai Patel Committee 1993) that the District Rural Development Agency (DRDA) and the District Planning Board (DPB) be merged into District Planning and Development Board and that the Zila Parishads continue to exist as a separate agency becomes significant because the Parishads would definitely be too large to themselves undertake a meaningful plan exercise. The Chimanbhai Patel Committee has also emphasised training and making available Central Assistance for providing district planning staff at district block levels. In fact what would be required would be compact and competent planning teams in each district and block. Hence I feel that, in addition to the Constitutional Body a prescribed in the 74th Amendment, we should have a District Planning Council to smoothen the process of multi-level planning and better results.

The District Planning Council could be the apex body at the district level with a Cabinet Minister not belonging to the district as chairman and consisting of both official and non-official members. Of course having the Divisional Commissioner or Collector at the chairman may also be considered as an alternative. The composition of this council may vary from state to state, but an illustrative possible model has been worked out as follows:

Minister	*Chairman*
Divisional Commissioner	Co-Chairman
Collector	Vice Chairman
Zila Pramukh	Vice Chairman
MPs(all) & MLAs (3)	Members
Nominees from Members of Zila Parishad/Panchayat Samities (3)	Members
Two Pradhans (3 if total Pradhans in district are more than 8)	Members

Five main district level officers-	Members
Chairman Urban Improvement Trust/Municipal Council (2)	Members
Representative of Commissioner - Command Area Development/Tribal Area Development	Member
Lead Bank Officer	Member
Chief Executive Officer of Zila Parishad	Member
Representative of State Planning Department	Member
Nominated Planning Experts	Members
Additional Collector Development and Project Director D.R.D.A	Member Secretary
Chief Planning Officer	Co-Secretary

The District Planning Executive Committee could be the main executive body at the district level responsible for formulation of plan and the monitoring of its implementation subject to guidance and supervision by the District Planning Council as well as by the much larger constitutionally created District Planning Committee. The Collector would be the chairman of this committee. The other members may include Zila Pramukh, two district level officers, two planning experts, two non-official members of the District Planning Council, Lead Bank officer, Additional Collector Development in charge of the DRDA, and Chief Planning Officer.

A district planning cell, headed by the Chief Planning Officer, would assist the Collector and District Planning Executive Committee for plan formulation and its implementation. The Collector would need to be vested with sufficient coordinational authority to ensure integrated plans can be prepared with the help of departmental officers.

At the State level also the State Planning Department should set-up a district planning cell and many other departments may have to follow suit since the departments at the State level and their officers levels would have to play an advisory role in the district planning process.

The district planners would also have to sensitise themselves to and yet keep themselves has removed from and above the differing perceptions about the needs and objectives of their area and its people that members and Chairman of the Gram Sabha, Panchayat Samiti and Zila Parishads as also members of the State legislature have. This can lead to inter-level conflicts. In fact since in the post-Constitution Amendment Panchayati Raj, direct elections to various levels have been provided for instead of the earlier practice of indirect elections, the Chairman Gram Panchayat and member on behalf of the Gram Panchayat in the Panchayati Samiti no more being the same person, could have very different objectives and interests. Similar could be the position between the Chairman Panchayat Samiti and the Panchayat Samiti representative in the Zila Parishad who would also in the new dispensation cease to be the same person. Similarly, even amongst administrators the perceptions about appropriate goals and objectives are likely to differ from department to department and level to level. Thus many conflicts of interest exist which the planner would have to sort out while his proposals. Hence, the district planner would need to develop great inter-personal dealing skills.

FEW WORDS OF CAUTION

Thus the reality in decentralized planning under the new Panchayati Raj would prove to be very different what many district and block level functionaries and panchayat leaders had been excepting. It does not imply merely the delegation of powers to sanction certain types of government works within certain limits level bodies. Not is it likely to mean that State and Central Governments would merely passion some of the resources raised by them to Panchayati bodies to spend as they like thereby enabling panchayat leaders to distribute more largesse.

Instead as had been indicated above throughout this paper the nature of planning functions change from level to level. Accordingly a table of level wise planning functions originally prepared by Kuklinsky and modified twice by this paper writer (the last time for a Bibliography on Multi Level and District Planning brought out in 1995 by Madhya Pradesh Institute of Social Science Research as a monograph) is being reproduced here:

Table 3.2: Types of Planning In Multi Level Framework (In the Indian Context)

1. National Planning	(a) Global or Macro Level Planning (b) Inter Sectoral Planning (c) Inter Regional Planning (d) Planning for Special Target Groups and Special Areas (e) Integrating with State Plans (f) Planning to facilitate and Catalyze private activity.
2. Regional Planning (done at State Level):	
(a) Inter Local Planning	1. Macro Planning for region 2. Inter-school planning for region 3. Functional-spatial-equity integration
(b) Local Planning	1. Macro Planning for local areas 2. Inter school planning for local area 3. Spatial Planning 4. Planning for the provision of services and facilities 5. Planning for special target groups and areas 6. Planning to catalyze and facilitate private activity.
(c) Planning region specific details of national programmes	
(d) Integrating with national plans and micro level plans	
3. Micro Level Planning (done at District level):	
(a) Inter Local Planning	1. Macro Planning for district 2. Inter Sectoral planning for district 3. Functional-spatial-equity integration 4. Spatial planning 5. Planning for the provision of services and facilities 6. Planning for special target groups and areas 7. Participative planning

Contd......

(b) Local planning for needs of localities (cluster of villages, or even a single village).
(c) Planning details of national and state programmes for the district.
(d) Integrating with State plans.

Source: This table has been further adapted and modified from Rakesh Hooja, "District and Regional Planning—Why and How" in Hosiar and D.P.Singh (ed) *Indian Administration—Current Issues and Problems* (1990), where it has been originally adapted from A.R. Kuklinsky "some basic issues in Regional Planning" in R.P. Misra, D.V. Urs and V.K. Nataraj (ed) *Regional Planning and National Development* (1978). It is being reproduced from the authors monograph published by MPISSR, Ujjain (1995).

Thus a good local plan would be one which would be partly sanctioned at the local level and partly a State or intermediate levels and partly left to private agencies and individuals to undertake after an integrated view of various activities desirable for the local area has been taken.

It is to be hoped that after proper orientation and training the district and block level functionaries and panchayat leaders shall bring about not only better planning aimed at the prioritization of goals and at such resource mobilization and use which is closer to the optimal than is being achieved at present, but would also enable multi-level interaction in the planning process which is based on greater knowledge, understanding and trust than at present.

Accordingly the various States that are now busy working out how to ensure the conditions necessary to facilitate decentralized and multi-level planning as well as how to solve the operational problems, involved in the renewed endeavour at decentralized planning that has been reinforced by the Amendments to the Constitution and the subsequent changes each of the State has effected in their Panchayat and Municipal legislations, would do well to remember that decentralized planning is not going to be easy and that a long drawn out and steady-in fact perhaps slow and steady-effort would be required to achieve the results of genuine decentralized district planning. Policy makers in such states and at the national level would also do well to remember what FAOs Social and Economic Report No.52 had pointed out way back in 1985 that there are certain pre-requisites in whose absence decentralized planning may not succeed. These include political and official willingness to operate multi-level planning, appropriate politico-administrative structures with clearly distinguished roles for the participating partners, clear definition of function sharing between various levels, provision of adequate financing at all levels to match the functions to be preformed along with rational allocation criteria for such finances, the power and authority at lower levels to mobilise funds to augment transfers from higher levels, the autonomy to plan for decentralized sector in line with national and state priorities and objectives, a properly equipped planning machinery with adequate capabilities to plan, programme, analyse and translate projects into action, and adequate powers and authorities at sub national and district levels as well as the freedom within reasonable limits of control.

NOTES AND REFERENCES

Arora, R.K. and Rakesh Hooja (ed) 1996 *Administration of Rural Development,* Arihant, Jaipur.

Aziz, *Decentralized Planning: The Karnataka Experiment,* New Delhi: Sage, 1994.

Bendavid-Val, A. and P.Waller (ed), *Action Oriented Approaches to Regional Development Planning,* New York: Preager, 1975.

Benjamin Fisher, H. "Growth Centre Planning in India" in R.P. Misra and K.V. Sundaram (ed) *Rural Area Development,* New Delhi: Sterling, 1979.

Cernea, Michael (ed.) *Putting People First,* London: Oxford University Press, 1991.

Chambers, R., '*Project Selection for Poverty Focussed Rural Development World Development*' Vol. 6, 1978.

Chambers, R. *Rural Appraisal-Rapid, Relaxed and Participatory,* Discussion paper 3, I.D.S. Sussex 1992.

Clay, E.J. and Schaffer, B.B. (ed.), *Room for Maneuver*, London: Heineman, 1984.

Coork, R. and Manor, J. *Enhancing and Institutional Performance and Democratic Decentralization in South Africa, O.D.A.*, New Delhi: Report, copy circulated at a British Council Seminar, 1994.

Cruits, D. and Waston, J.R. "Planning That Non Planners Can Do", *Journal of Rural Development,* 1987.

F.A.O. *Towards improved Multi Level Planning for Agriculture and Rural Development,* F.A.O. Economic and Social Development paper No.52, 1985.

Gadgil, D.R. *District Development Planning,* Poona: (Gokhale Institute of Politics and Economics), 1966.

Gittinger, J.P. *Economic Analysis Agriculture Projects,* New York: John Hopkins, 1982.

Hanumantha Rao, C.H. "Decentralized Planning: Overview of Experience and Prospects" *Economic and Political Weekly,* Vol. 24, No.8, (25 Feb 1989).

Hooja, Rakesh. "District as a Planning Unit - Style and Locus" *Indian Journal of Public Administration,* Vol. 19, No. 2, 1973.

Hooja, Rakesh. (a) "Project Approach and Development Administration in India", *Prashasnika,* Vol. 9, 1980.

Hooja, Rakesh. (b) "Planning for Rural Development by Field Staff, *Indian Journal of Public Administration*", Vol. 26, 1980.

Hooja, Rakesh. "Project Formulation for Rural Development Administration - A Rajasthan Viewpoint", *Administrative Change,* Vol. 9, 1981.

Hooja, Rakesh. "Project Formulation and Planning : Special Problems of Rural Projects and Some Examples of Rajasthan Responses", *Prashasnika,* Vol. 12, 1983.

Hooja, Rakesh. *District Planning-Concept Setting and State Level Applications,* Jaipur: Aalekh, 1986.

Hooja, Rakesh. *Administrative Interventions in Rural Development,* Jaipur: Rawat, 1987.

Hooja, Rakesh. "District and Regional Planning Why and How", in Hoshiar Singh and D.P.Dingh (eds) *Indian Administration: Current Issues and Problems,* Jaipur: Aalekh, 1991.

Hooja, Rakesh. "Decentralized Planning and the Hanumantha Rao Report" in Asha Kaushik (ed.), *Democratic Concerns: The Indian Experience,* Jaipur: Aalekh, 1994.

Hooja, Rakesh. "Three Disparate Book on Panchayati Raj Past and Present", *Indian Book Chronicle,* Vol. 19, No. 8 (1994).

Hooja, Rakesh. "Issues in Preparing Manpower for Effective Decentralized Planning", *Political Economy Journal of India,* Vol. 3, No. 2 (1994).

Hooja, Rakesh *Bibliography On Multilevel and District Planning,* Ujjain: (Madhya Pradesh Institute of Social Science Research), 1995.

Hooja, Rakesh "Training of Panchayat Raj Functionaries - Some issues" in *Journal of Rural Development,* Vol. 16. No. 4 (1997).

Hooja, R. and Hooja, M. "Continuity and Changes in Rajasthans Panchayati Raj" paper presented at Government of Karnataka and Institute of Social Sciences Delhi National Seminar at Bangalore in January, 1999.

Hooja, R. and Raju, B.Y., (ed.), *Decentralized Planning in Multi Level Framework*, Jaipur: Rawat, 1993.

Inamdar, N.R. and Kshire, K.V. *District Planning in India,* New Delhi: Oxford, 1986.

Institute of Social Sciences, *The Status of Panchayati Raj in the States of India,* New Delhi: Concept, 1994.

Jacob, George (ed.), *Readings in Panchayati Raj,* Hyderabad: NIRD, 1967

Jain, R.B. (ed.) *Panchayati Raj,* New Delhi: IIPA, 1981.

Joshi, B.M. "Evolution and Practice of Decentralized Planning in India", *Indian Journal of Public Administration,* Vol. 35, No. 1 (1989).

Kamath, A.R. *Selected Writings and Speeches of D.R. Gadgil on Planning and Development,* New Delhi: Orient, Longmans, 1973.

Mathew, George. *Panchayati Raj - from Legislation to Movement,* New Delhi: Concept, 1994.

Mathur, Kuldeep. "Promise of Local level Planning" *Indian Journal of Public Administration.* Vol. 26, No. 3 (1980).

Mathur, Kuldeep (ed.), *Panchayati Raj Planning and Democracy,* Bombay: Asia Publishing House, 1996.

Mathur, P.C. *The Political Dynamics of Panchayati Raj,* New Delhi: Konark, 1990.

Mathur, P.C. and Hooja, Rakesh *Projects, Planning and Development Administration,* Jaipur: Rawat, 1996.

Misra, R.P. (ed.), *Regional Planning Concepts Techniques, Policies, Case Studies,* New Delhi: Concept, 1992.

Misra R.P., and Achyuta, R.N. *Micro Level Rural Planning,* New Delhi: Concept, 1990.

Misra, R.P. and Sundaram, K.V. *Multi-Level Planning and Integrated Rural Development,* New Delhi: Heritage, 1980.

Misra, R.P. and Urs, D.V. and Nataraj, V.K. (ed.), *Regional Planning and National Development,* New Delhi: Vikas, 1978.

Mishra and Swetha, *Democratic Decentralization in India,* New Delhi: Mittal Publications, 1994.

Mukherjee, Amitabh (ed), *Participatory Rural Appraisal Methods and Applications in Rural Planning,* New Delhi: Vikas, 1995.

Mundle, S. *District Planning in India,* New Delhi: IIPA, 1977.

Planning Commission, *Guidelines for the Formulation of District Plan,* New Delhi: Planning Commission, 1969.

Prasad, Kamta (ed), *Planning and its Implementation,* New Delhi: IIPA, 1984.

Prasad, Kamta (ed), *Planning at the Grassroots,* New Delhi: Sterling, 1994.

Prodipto Roy and B.P.Patil, *Manual for Block Level Planning,* New Delhi: MacMillan, 1977.

Raghavaiah, V., "District Planning and Administration—The Case for a Inified and Integrated Approach" *Indian Journal of Public Administration,* Vol. 23, No. 4 (1991).

Raghuvilu, C.V., and Narayana, E.A., "Reforms in Panchayati Raj—A comparative Analysis of Andhra Pradesh, Karnataka and West Bengal", *Indian Journal of Public Administration,* Vol. 37, No. 1 (1991).

Rao, V.K.R.V., "District Planning Concept" in V.L.S. Prakasa Rao *et.al; Working Paper on District Planning Officers Programme,* Bangalore: Institute of Social and Economic Change, 1973.

Rao, V.M. "Decentralized Planning - Priority Issues", *Economic and Political Weekly,* Vol. XXIV, No. 25, June 24, (1989).

Reddy, G. Ram (ed), *Patterns of Panchayati Raj in India,* New Delhi: MacMillan, 1977.

Report of the Team for the study of Community Projects and National Extension Service (chairman Balwantrai Mehta). 1958 Government of India.

Report of the Committee on Panchayati Raj Institutions (Chairman Ashok Metha) 1978 Government of India.

Report of Planning Commission's Working Group on District Planning (Chairman C.H. Hanumantha Rao) 1984 Government of India.

Report of Planning Commission's Working Group on Block Level Planning (Chairman M.L. Dantwala) 1978 Government of India.

Report of the National Development Council Committee on Micro Level Planning and Involvement of People at the Grassroot Level (Chairman Chimanbhai Patel) 1993 Government of India.

Sen, L.K. *Integrated Area Development,* New Delhi: Department of Personnel Government of India, 1972.

Sen, L.K. (ed), *Readings in Micro Level Planning and Rural Growth Centers,* Hyderabad: NICD, 1972.

Sharma, K. Sudesh. *Panchayati Raj in India,* New Delhi: Trimurti, 1976.

Singh, S.S. and S.Mishra, *Legislative Framework of Panchayati Raj in India,* New Delhi: Intellectual Publishing House, 1993.

Smith, Peter (ed), *Project Identification in Developing Countries, Institute of Development Policy & Management,* U.K: University of Manchester, 1978.

Sundaram, K.V. *District Planning in India,* Delhi: Daya, 1979.

Special No. on Multi Level Planning, *Indian Journal of Public Administration,* 1973 Vol. 19, No.3.

Special No. on District Planning, *Journal of L.B.S. National Academy of Administration,* 1975, Vol.20. No.1.

Special No.on Decentralization, *Indian Journal of Public Administration,* 1978, Vol. 24. No. 3.

Special No. on Panchayati Raj, *Journal of Rural Development,* 1991, Vol.36.No.3.

Special No.on Decentralized Planning, *The Administrator,* 1991, Vol.36, No.3.

Special No. on Panchayati Raj, *Journal of Rural Development,* 1997, Vol.16, No.4.

Venugopal Reddy, Y. *Multi-Level Planning in India,* New Delhi: Vikas, 1979.

Yugandhar, B.N. and A. Mukherjee (ed), *Readings in Decentralized Planning,* New Delhi: Concept, 1991.

4

INFORMATION SYSTEM FOR PANCHAYAT PLANNING

N.D. MANI

In India, the need for data has increased manifold in terms of amount, type, reliability, accuracy, level and periodicity of updation. After the introduction of 73rd Constitutional Amendment three tiers of planning viz., village panchayat, panchayat union and district have become reality. They are the important sub-district levels of planning. The new Panchayat Raj System of planning, has further increased the need for data on various sectors of economy particularly, rural economy down to the village panchayats.

The data required for planning would vary according to the scope of planning at different levels. Further, the data on different sectors of planning, may have to be processed for obtaining useful information to assist planning. By way of implementation of programmes, large volume of data are generated and they have to be used for updating of data. The task of updating the already available data bases at regular intervals has to be undertaken. The dynamic nature of data sets will decide the period of updation. The data available in different government departments at District and Block levels at present bristle with inherent problems.

Problems in Data Collection

Major part of data, derived from different sources, are collected for different purposes and thus they are incompatible. Lacking consistency, they are often unsuitable for sharing and re-using. There are also intractable problems of classification and codification of data and even legibility[1]. The data at district level offices are being collected at different levels. However, majority of the data are gathered at block level. Data at panchayat/hamlet levels are rarely available. The process of collection, consolidation and supply of data is a time drawn one. Hence the required data are rarely available when it is needed. Departments functioning at district level, collect and publish the data for other users. Due to delay in the entire operation from data collection to publication, the published data are outdated in most of the cases.

Responsibility of collection of data often rests with people at the bottom of hierarchy, who are neither provided with appropriate training nor monetary incentives. And they are flooded with many other additional responsibilities. With their heavy work load, naturally the quality of data collected by them poor obviously. Now a days the process of planning is complex, requiring more data particularly relevant data. The data are not available at one place. In most of the cases, the users have to visit more than one office as the required data are not available at one source. This is another reason for the delay in collection of data. Primary data are collected by the departments for different purposes. Sometimes same data is collected for the same area by more than one department. This shows that there is lack of coordination among these departments. This leads to wastage of time, men and material resources. The question of integrity of data supplied by the departments is frequently raised by the users. Because the soundness of decisions is entirely governed by the quality of data. Due to above mentioned reasons, the data supplied by the departments are not fully reliable. Majority of the departments collect data only for their use. However, other departments also use a portion of this data. To make out the portion of data, the secondary user has to do lot of editing and processing. The departments generate data while implementing programmes. They collect and collate these data for preparing fortnightly, monthly, quarterly, half yearly and yearly reports. However, they fail to update their existing data bases. Panchayat Raj Institutions do not have technical and professional experts for planning and execution of activities.[2] Keeping in view, the timely collection, compilation, dissemination and online accessibility of data on different sectors at various levels, National Informatics Centre (NIC), was conceived and started in 1976. NIC, now has computer centres at all district headquarters. The departments working at district level are welcome to feed, store and transmit the data to their state headquarters. Existing computer facilities at district level, have not been decentralised to block level. Available computer facilities can process numerical data in tabular form and not the maps and satellite data.

Data Required for Panchayat Planning

For furnishing information for planning purposes at District and block levels not many attempts have been made. A small beginning was made by Afsal Mohamed[3] by preparing an atlas with the objective of using it not only for preparing the Annual and Five Year Plans but also for adopting a long range strategy for its development. Similar studies were conducted by Mani at District[4] and Block[5] levels. While NIC allows user departments feed and use numerical data. In the decentralised planning system, the elected representatives require data on all aspects covering 29 subjects stipulated in 11th schedule (article 243 G) of 73 Constitutional Amendment for making sound decisions. Further, they will have to take location/area specific decisions. Therefore, the data as required for planning in the 29 subjects are furnished below:

Activities proposed in 11th schedule data required

Activities proposed in 11th schedule	Data required
1. Agriculture including agricultural extension	Soil Relief Slope Landuse Area under different crops Season-wise Cropping pattern

Season-wise
Yield season-wise
Consumption of
Fertilizers,
pesticides, insecticides
Landholdings number/size
Sources of water
River network
Ground water potential
Depth of ground water table
Agro-service centre
  Implements
  Repair
  Servicing
Depots
Government
Seed
Fertiliser
Pesticide
Private
Seed
Fertiliser
Pesticide
Godowns
Private mandies
Regulated markets
  Location
  Commodity dealt
Market
  Location
Implements
  Tractor
  Oil engines
  Electric pumps
  Sprayers
  Sugarcane crushers
  Oil ghanies

	Threshers
	Farmers cooperatives
2. Land development, land reforms, land integration and soil resource	Land use and land cover Soil, texture, depth, porosity, chemical properties etc. Land capability Land suitability
3. Minor irrigation, water management, watershed development	Irrigated area source-wise Flow Wells Number Yield Energised Irrigated area season-wise Gross irrigated area Net irrigated area Annual rainfall Normal rainfall Watershed details Land use/land cover Soil Slope Geology Hydro geomorphology River network Watershed programmes Minor irrigation works completed with location
4. Livestock, dairy and poultry	Cows Exotic- She/he Native- She/he Buffaloes Exotic- She/he Native- She/he Draught animal Goats/sheep

	Poultry farms
	Broiler
	layer
	Pig farms
	Production of
	Meat
	Egg
	Broiler
	Milk
	Milk products etc.
	Milk collection centres
	Milk route
	Milk chilling plants
	Cold storage
	Fodder
	Cattle feed centre
	Poultry feed centre
	Veterinary facilities
	Incidence of diseases
	Prevalence of diseases
	Market for livestock and products
	Milk cooperatives
5. Fisheries	Location of tanks
	Ownership of tanks
	Spread of water
	Duration of availability of water
	Production and sales
	Prawn farm
	Fish hatcheries
	Fish feed
	Fishermen cooperatives
	Market for fish
6. Social forestry and farm forestry	Area covered under
	Social forestry
	Farm forestry

	Area suitable for social forestry Area suitable for farm forestry Degraded forest land Road and rail margins Waste lands Government lands
7. Minor forest produce	Type of Minor Forest Produce (MFP) Quantity of MFP Quality of MFP Number of units Total investment Number of male/ female employed
8. Raw material for small/ food processing units	Industrial cooperatives Credit facilities Marketing facilities Training facilities
9. Khadi and village handicraft industries	Type of Khadi and villages industries Handicraft units Number of units Total investment number of male/female employed
10. Village habitat or settlement	Families without house sites and house, caste wise Families without house sites caste wise Families with house site but without house Caste wise Income and consumption levels Migration of labourers

	Telephone
	Private
	STD booths
	Post office
	Post and telegraph office
	Police station
	Area covered
	Street lights
	Drainage facilities
11. Drinking water	Problem villages
	Sources of drinking water
	Villages yet to get drinking water facilities break up of SC, ST and total
	Over head tanks
	Pressure pumps
	Ground level reservoirs
	Drinking water schemes
	- existing
	- proposed
12. Fuel and fodder	Fodder availability
	Type
	Quantity
	Requirement
	Deficit
13. Roads, small bridges, water ways and other link roads	Road network
	Status
	Type
	Present condition
	Bridges, culverts
	Bus route
	Bus traffic flow
	Traffic census
	Commodity flow by road
	Accident prone area
	Navigable rivers

14. Electrification of villages and distribution of electricity	Electrified villages Power grid Villages to be electrified Distance from nearest transformer
15. Non-conventional energy sources	Wind speed, direction, duration Availability of wind mills Capacity Bio gas/gobar gas Ownership Availability Capacity Solar energy Ownership Availability Capacity Bio mass Type Quantity
16. Poverty alleviation programmes	Distribution of beneficiaries- Scheme wise Achievements - Physical - Financial Unemployment Caste wise Sex wise educated uneducated under employed Small and marginal farmers Caste wise population below poverty line Caste wise

	Physically handicapped
	Widow
17. Education, primary and middle schools	Balwadi
	Primary school
	Middle school
	Boys
	Girls
	Co-education
	Secondary school
	Boys
	Girls
	Co-education
	Arts and Science Colleges
	Single teacher school
	Professional colleges
	Facilities available
	Building
	Laboratory
	Library
	Facilities required
	Building
	Laboratory
	Library
	Distance between schools and village
	School going age group children 5 to 14 years
	Private schools
	Aided
	Unaided
	Matriculation schools
	Distance between school and village
18. Technical education and training	Location of technical institutions/training centres
	Facilities available

	Facilities required
	Distance between institutions and villages
	Hostel
	School
	College
	For boys
	For girls
19. Adult and non-formal education	Location of adult and other non-formal education centres
	Programme implementing agencies
	Adult illiterates
20. Libraries	Libraries
	Facilities available
	Facilities required
	Problems faced
21. Cultural activities	Location of Cinema theaters
	Temporary tents
	Fairs
	Festivals
22. Weekly markets and shops	Location weekly markets
	permanent markets
	cattle shandies
23. Health, sanitation, hospitals, primary health centres and dispensaries	Location of Hospitals
	Primary health centres
	sub-centres
	Dispensaries
	Facilities available
	Number of beds
	X- ray
	Clinical lab
	ECG etc.

	Private practitioners
	Homeopathy
	Siddha
	Unani
	Medical shops
	24 hours
	Villages with proper drainage facilities
	Disease prone area
	Season wise Frequency of occurrence
24. Family welfare	Maternity centres
	facilities available
	facilities required
	Eligible couples
	Couple Protection Ratio
	Family planning methods adopted
	Infant deaths < 1 year
25. Women and children development	Centres of ICDS/TINP
	DWCRA
	Women groups
	Women headed families
	Women population
	age wise
	caste wise
	education wise
	Noon meal centres
	number
	location
	children fed
26. Social welfare, welfare of mentally retarded and physically handicapped	Location of centres for the welfare of physically handicapped mentally retarded mentally retarded population

	Physically handicapped population
27. Welfare of weaker sections particularly SC and ST.	SC and ST population Living below poverty line Mentally retarded Physically handicapped Unemployed educated uneducated sex wise
28. Public distribution system	Fair price shops area covered population served Villages without fair price shops distance from the nearest shop
29. Maintenance of community assets	Community centre Library Community TV Tanks Temples Community well Pasture lands Social forestry area

Panchayat Information System

Panchayat Information System (PIS) will use data bases created for different sectors of rural economy, for generating reports/ information as required for planning purposes. One of the pre-requisites of this system is scientific collection, storing, processing and dissemination of data. There are important activities in the establishment of PIS. viz., data collection, collation, compilation, data entry, data processing, reporting, updating and transmitting.

Tasks Ahead

Collection, collation, compilation and dissemination of data at different levels is a stupendous task. At present, a number of departments collect data at village level by utilising the services of lower level functionaries of respective departments. They use the data, when they prepare and submit progress reports to their higher officials at district and state level and they rarely use this data for updation. And they have no time to spare for doing activities such as collection, compilation and updating of data. Therefore, there is an urgent need for a suitable agency to assist these departments in collection, compilation and sending of data. As the task is voluminous one, computers will be of great help in this endeavour. The computers can handle large volume of data and processing and updating is easier. There is also an added advantage in using computers for data handling i.e., data base management system.

Coordinating Departments

At the district level, there are two departments directly involved in data collection, processing and dissemination viz., District Statistical Office (DSO) and National Informatics Centre (NIC).[6] DSO has their officials at taluk and block levels to collect and document data in a systematic way. This department is a state government department. NIC was launched at district level, with the aim of computerising data of all government departments by storing, processing, updating and disseminating their data. Facilities at the district centre of NIC are being used by some of the government departments. PC based terminals are expected to be installed in the third phase of NIC at the block level covering more than 5100 blocks[6]. And they also have a proposal to start computer cell at Block levels. It is a central government organisation. Though there is a difference in the governing body of these two departments, they work complementary to each other. Therefore, the above mentioned work of assisting other departments in data collection and compilation can be assigned to these two departments.

Data Collection and Verification

NIC in consultation with DSO may prepare formats for collection of data. This will enable the NIC in writing programs for creating data bases, processing and generation of reports. The responsibility of data collection will rest with respective line departments. The data collected (in the formats supplied by DSO) by them should be handed over to DSO. The Statistical Inspectors will check the data for completeness and correctness.

Training

DSO and NIC will train the data collecting personnel drawn from different departments in the use of formats for collection of data and compilation and coding of data. They may also be motivated by giving some monetary incentives.

Creation of Database

NIC will create data bases and also write programs for generating reports from the information system. The design of the format of the reports will be decided by NIC in accordance with the requirement and also based on available formats in data collecting departments.

Feeding of Data

The middle level officials of various government departments will feed the data in the computer of NIC after getting the clearance from DSO. Thus, the responsibility of data collection, feeding of data will rest with different government departments. Training, supervising all data collecting phase of establishing PIS and checking of the data for completeness will be the duty of DSO. Providing training computer facilities, creating data entry forms, reports, etc. will be the activities of NIC.

Nature of Software

The type of data required for panchayat planning are in different formats i.e., government offices supply data in tabular form, Survey of India furnishes data in map form, while satellite data are available in digital form. At the village panchayat level, the area/location specific decisions will have to be taken. This requires maps as they provide locations along with spatial information. Therefore, proposed information system should be capable of handling all these different data sets and also provide the information as desired by planner either in tabular statement or map form.

The proposed information system should be capable of doing all the above activities. The data base management system should be used in conjunction with Geographical Information System (GIS). It is a computerised information system and it offers the capability of storing, retrieving, analysing, manipulating, displaying and integrating environmental, economic and social data in a single system[7]. It is now possible, not only to integrate graphically displayed information precisely, tied to its geographical location on the surface of the earth, but also statistical or socio-economic information, to simulate alternative planning data and use it for more realistic development activities[8].

The officials of NIC will have to be trained in the proposed information system with GIS capabilities or a person may be appointed with experience in GIS. The computer facilities available in NIC district centre will have to be upgraded with A0 digitizer, A0 plotter and a sophisticated GIS software.

Merits of Panchayat Information System (PIS)

The above process of establishing Panchayat Information System (PIS) will significantly help all Panchayati Raj Institutions. PIS to be managed by NIC will provide data/ information quickly as required by the elected representatives. Since the data is collected at village panchayat level, aggregating them for a cluster of villages, panchayat union or district will not be a problem.

The entire process is computerised and hence, delay in updation is ruled out.

The question of compatibility with regard to village panchayat and revenue village can be resolved with the use of Geographic Information System. As the data collected by various departments are stored in the computers of NIC, the secondary users need not go to different departments. The data stored in the computers of NIC should be made available to all needy secondary users. There should be no restrictions on the use of data. In addition, the departments can also disseminate data by availability NICMAIL facilities of NIC District Centres to their higher officials. The data are collected in the format furnished by the DSO, therefore there will be no duplication of data collection. No two departments should be permitted to collect similar data from the same area. The proposed PIS will greatly assist and guide the elected Panchayat Members and Presidents in decision making by furnishing information as required by them. The output of the PIS will definitely revolutionise the operation of New Panchayat Raj System.

NOTES AND REFERENCES

1. INDO-US Workshop on Geographic Information System, Background Papers, Government of India, New Delhi: Ministry of Environment and Forests, 1992, p. 2
2. B.M.Chitlangi, Environment protection in Rural India through Panchayati Raj, *Kurukshetra,* Jan-Feb (1997), p. 70
3. Afsal Mohamed, *Planning Atlas of Medak District, Andhra Pradesh, India,* Hyderabad: The Centre for Economic and Social Studies, 1998.
4. N.D. Mani, *Resource Atlas of Dindigul District, Tamil Nadu,* New Delhi: National Informatics Centre, Planning Commission, 1997.
5. N.D. Mani, *Watershed Maps of Athoor Block, Dindigul District,* Dindigul: District Rural Development Agency, Dindigul District, 1998.
6. National Informatics Network–"Globalization of Computer Communication", *The Hindu,* (December 15, 1993).
7. G. Palanithurai, *Empowering People–Issues and Solution,* New Delhi: Kanishka Publishers Distributors, 1996.
8. An Application of Geo Technology, *The Hindu,* (October 4, 1998), p VIII.
9. A paper on "Remote Sensing and GIS" presented at the workshop on Introductory Remote Sensing and Geographical Information System, Dept. of Geography, University of Madras, Madras, 1992.

5

BIOMASS ASSESSMENT AND OPTIMIZATION MODEL FOR ENERGY PLANNING IN RURAL AREAS

P. KANNIAPPAN AND T. RAMACHANDRAN

In this paper, we have developed an optimization model (Linear Programming Model) in order to minimize total cost of consumption of commercial energy sources such as electricity, kerosene, diesel and fertilizer by way of generating electricity from the surplus Biomass by suitably allocating the land area for cultivation of various crops, subject to meeting the food requirements of the block under consideration with regard to cereals, pulses, oil seeds, sugar and vegetables as well as energy requirement for household sector, industrial sector, agricultural sector and the fodder requirements of the animal population. Further, the model takes care of utilising the available sources such as land, human labour, animal pair hours in this block.

This model included two groups of linear constraints. The first group of constraints is designed for the minimum production requirements for food, fodder, electricity for cooking, lighting and other activities. The second set of constraints is built for the availability of resources with regard to land, human labour, animal power, tractor power in this book. The model takes care of the energy requirements of the block, by way of producing electricity from surplus biomass for various activities and thus making the block self-sufficient in the consumption of energy so as to make the block to have sustainable development. The model solution shows that the electrical energy generated from the surplus biomass can meet the electrical energy requirement for various activities in this block through proper allocation of land for various crops. That is, by installing a biomass based power plant in this block, we can make this block self sufficient with reagard to electrical energy requirement.

Introduction

Energy is the key for the economic development of any country. As world population is growing at an exponential rate, the per capita energy consumption is increasing at an alarming rate. Hence, the future demand for energy is going, on increasing on account of population growth and owing to gradual but steady improvement in the standard of living people in the world. In agricultural sector, power consumption in India was increased from 14bkWh in 1980-81 to 70bkWh in 1993-94. Top priority was given to rural electrification programme, as a result, out of 5,79,132 villages (1981 Census), 4,95,508 villages (85%) were electrified by March 1994. The transmission and distribution losses in India increased from 17.6 per cent in 1970-71 to 22.8 per cent of generation by 1994-95.

The declining reserves, escalating costs and the population effect of conventional fossilfuels have necessiated sound energy sources. The search for new energy sources is a major concern of today's economics and industry. Among the possible solutions, agricultural and forestry residues or generally Biomass residues can be used as raw materials to generate energy. Biomass is one such alternative, which efficiently harnessed, would reduce the "Rural Energy Crisis" prevalent particularly in developing countries like India. Biomass is the fourth largest source of energy in the world, supplying about 14 per cent of primary energy. India alone has a surplus of about 300 million tonnes of agricultural residues every year comprising mainly ricehusk, paddy straw, sugarcane leaves and wheat residues. These are, presently often, disposed of by burning in fields. Apart from the resulting extensive smoke and fly ash problems in the environment, this also represents a large loss of energy. Thus Biomass based decentralised energy generation technologies offer an attractive solution to the Rural energy crisis.

At present, Biomass is converted into electricity, most often by direct combusion, followed by steam cycle. Large scale power plants are in operation mainly in countries such as the U.S. Denmark, Sweden and Finland. Since India is an agro-based economy, considerable quantum of energy can be generated by combustion process from any agricultural residue, wood, bagasse, sugarcane trash, ricehusk, deoliedbran, paddy straw etc.

Understanding the importance and availability of Biomass in India, the Ministry of Non-conventional Energy Sources (MNES), Government of India and Tamil Nadu Energy Development Agency (TEDA), Government of Tamil Nadu have framed comprehensive policies in respect of Biomass based power generation at taluk level. MNES and TEDA have developed Biomass based power project proposals so as to attract entrepreneurs to come to start power projects at the taluka level by providing enough financial incentives and soft loan facilities.

Energy is an important resource for agriculture and at the same time agriculture is a resource for energy. There is a interaction between energy and agriculture in villages. The requirements for food, fuel and fodder in villages are interrelated in a variety of ways. The interplay is influenced by the availability of resources such as land, water, livestock, commercial energy and labour. Hence, agricultural activities consume energy and the agricultural residues can be used to generate electricity. This kind of interaction has been used by many Operations Research Scientists to develop optimization models for energy planning. In this direction, several authors have developed energy models with different objectives and with many constraints. R.P. Singh *et al.* (1992) and Raja *et. al.* (1997) have developed energy mix models for increasing the total revenue of the block. Shasi Bala Malik *et al.* (1994) have described an integrated energy system planning approach for Waradha district in Maharashtra state, India for the year 2000 AD and suggested optimal mix of new/conventional energy technologies using the computer based mixed integer programming model. K.C. Dhawan *et al.* (1993) described a model for Energy demand and supply in Indian Agriculture and established the future energy requirements. Ghosh *et al.* (1995) have developed a large scale MCDM (Multi-Criterion Decision Making) model for optimal allocation of land under cultivation for various crops in different seasons using Goal programming C.S. Sinha *et al.* (1991) developed a framework for evaluating the relative economics of some common lighting technologies, and this is incorporated into linear programming frame work to obtain the best option for satisfying the lighting demand of a village subject to various constraints. S. Singh and L. Marsh (1994) developed a model for maximising the energy production from both yield and residue, by proper allocation of lands.

Kanniappan, P. *et al.* (1998) developed a linear programming model to maximize the output of surplus biomass, by suitably allocating, the irrigated land and un-irrigated land for various crops in the block in two seasons namely Karif and Rabi. Kanniappan, P. *et. al.* (World Renewable Energy Congress V, Florence, Italy 1998) developed a Taluk level linear programming model to maximize the surplus biomass in order to meet the power demand of the taluka, by suitably allocating land area for different crops using crop intensity and we have included two more constraints viz, fertilizer and pesticides in addition to the previous model. In this paper, we have assessed the availability of various energy resources and requirements of energy for various sectors, in a typical Indian block (Nilakkottai) and also we have developed a linear programming model to minimize the consumption of commercial energy sources by way of generating electricity from surplus biomass, through optimal allocation of land area for different crops subject to the available energy sources and meeting the energy demand of the block. From this Linear Programming model solution, by changing cultivation pattern, we can minimize the consumption of commercial energy sources by way of consuming power that can be generated from the surplus biomass for various agricultural, household and other activities of the block. This linear programming be extended to taluka/state/national level energy planning in order to obtain self sufficiency in energy consumption.

Block Profile

The study area, Nilakkottai block is located between 10°47″N Latitutde and 77° 75″ E longitude and situated in Nilakkottai Taluk of Dindigul District, Tamil Nadu, India. The Block consists of 28 Revenue villages with 188 Hamlets. There are 28,005 households with a population of 1,31,630 according to 1991 census with a projected population of 1,55,336 for the year 2000 AD. Geographical area of the Block is 250.17 sq.kms, of which 56 per cent covers agricultural land and the remaining 44 per cent covers barren land, uncultivable land, cultivable waste land, land under miscellaneous tree crops and land put to non-agricultural purposes.

The available cultivable land of 13,882 ha includes 7,832 ha of irrigated land and 6,050 ha of non-irrigated land. In this block, about 2,442 ha of land is used for cultivation in Karif season and 11,951 ha of land is used in Rabi season in a year. The reason for this trend is attributed to non-availability of sufficient water sources, labour forces and the financial problems faced by the framers in this block. In addition to the ground water, Vaigai river water is utilised for cultivation areas of the block. This river maintains the water level in wells to some extent in summer season. The major crops grown in this block are paddy, sorghum, sugarcane, pulses, groundnut, cotton and flowers. The average rainfall in the block is 1428.3 mm per year.

Methodology

The data pertaining to house holds were collected from each village of the block. The criteria used for the selection of household were primarily land holding pattern and the socio-economic status. Household data is primary in nature whereas and block level data are secondary.

The essential data like land area, types of crops grown and population for each village of the block were collected from the government departments like Statistical Office, Agricultural Department, National Informatic Centre and Block Development Office etc., The collected data were used to compute average yield of various crops, annual production of crop, energy expenditure, and total annual utilization of various sources. The crop related data pertaining to yield per ha of various were collected from the Agriculture Department, Dindigul and the Yield to residue ratio for various crops are obtained from Tamil Nadu Agriculture University (TNAU), Coimbatore, India and possible power generation from the agricultural residue obtained from a hectare of land area for each crop (MNES—TEDA Project) are presented in Table 5.1.

Annual food requirement of Human population of the block for different food items are given in Table 5.2. Nutrient of various crops (ton/ha), Nutrient content of the crop residue of various crops (kg/ton), feed coefficient of crop residue (ton/ton) and Electrical and diesel energy required for irrigation (kwh/ha and lit/ha respectively) are presented in Table 5.3. Human, Animal and Tractor power required for various operations of cultivation of land different crops are summarised from the primary data and are given in Table 5.4. Sector wise energy requirement of the block are given in Table 5.5. Livestock related data of the study area such as population, dung output, fodder requirements are presented in Table 5.6. Cost of Commercial Energy per unit and energy content in mwh are presented in Table 5.7.

Table 5.1: Crop Related Data

Sl No.	*Name of Crop*	*Yield (ton/ha)*	*Yield to Residue ratio (ton/ha)*	*Residue production (ton/ha)*	*Possible power Mwh/ha of Residue Cc=(Ycxrc)*1.5*
c	*yc*	*rc*	*YcXrc*		
1	Paddy	4.53	1.30	5.89	3.90
2	Sorghum	2.75	2.00	5.50	3.67
3	Cumbu	2.50	1.70	4.25	2.83
4	Gram	0.99	0.67	0.66	0.44
5	Groundnut	2.45	0.33	0.80	0.53
6	Gingilly	0.80	1.70	1.36	0.91
7	Sunflower	1.30	1.46	1.90	1.27
8	Sugarcane	110.00	0.58	63.80	42.50
9	Vegetables	15.50	1.10	1.70	1.13
10	Cotton	4.00	3.00	12.00	8.00
11	Flower	0.50	1.50	0.75	0.50

* 1.5 tons of crop residue = 1 Mwh electrical energy

Sources : Agricultural Department, Dindigul, Tamil Nadu, India
Tamil Nadu Agricultural University, Coimbatore, Tamil Nadu, India
MNES - TEDA Project—Nilakkottai Taluk, Tamil Nadu, India.

Table 5.2: Annual Food requirement

Name of Food items	*Food requirement gm/day/head*	*Annual Food Requirement*	
		kg/head	*tonnes (for the block)*
Cereal - c	460	167.9	26081
Pulses - p	40	14.6	2268
Vegetables - v	100	36.6	5685
Oil & Fat - o	40	14.6	2268
Sugar - s	30	11.0	1709

Source : A Text book of foods, nutrition and diebetics

Table 5.3: Nutrients and Energy content related data

Particulars	*Required Nutrients (ton/ha)*			*Nutrients content in Residue (kg/ton)*			*Energy for irrigation Electricity*	*Diesel*
	N	*P*	*K*	*N*	*P*	*K*	*(Kwh/hac.)*	*(lit/hac)*
Paddy	0.181	0.125	0.058	16.200	4.200	11.20	827	720
Sorghum	0.091	0.047	0.030	5.300	1.000	11.00	217	190
Cumbu	0.055	0.034	0.034	5.300	1.000	11.00	128	120
Gram	—	—	—	0.000	0.000	0.00	70	60
Groundnut	0.023	0.032	0.049	17.000	4.000	14.00	102	95
Gingilly	0.023	0.032	0.049	16.000	3.100	11.10	102	95
Sunflower	0.023	0.032	0.049	16.000	3.100	11.10	102	95
Sugarcane	0.245	0.272	0.110	3.500	1.000	6.00	336	302
Vegetables	0.028	0.025	0.016	4.400	1.000	7.00	98	88
Cotton	0.103	0.076	0.076	4.400	1.000	7.00	186	190
Flower	0.028	0.025	0.016	4.400	1.000	7.00	52	41
Dung cake	—	—	—	15.000	7.500	10.00	—	—
Biogas Sludge (kg/m3	—	—	—	0.016	0.014	0.01	—	—

Source : Energy models for 2000 and beyond.

Table 5.4: Production activities (crops) along with their budgets per hectare as used in linear programming model fcr optimization

Production	*Pruduction activities*										
Resources	*pad-dy*	*Sorg-hum*	*Cum-bu*	*Gram*	*Grou-ndnut*	*Ging-illy*	*Sun-flower*	*Suga-rcane*	*Vege-tables*	*Cott-on*	*Flo-wer*
Land (hac.)	*1*	*1*	*1*	*1*	*1*	*1*	*1*	*1*	*1*	*1*	*1*
Human Labour (hrs)											
Irrigation											
Electricity	700	176	84	56	90	90	90	360	70	208	68
Bullock	1200	320	170	110	150	150	150	480	182	420	132
Diesel	700	176	84	56	90	90	90	360	70	208	68
Ploughing											
Bullock	320	320	320	320	320	320	320	320	320	320	320
Tractor	12	12	24	12	12	12	12	12	12	12	12
Transport											
Bullock	200	200	200	200	200	200	200	200	200	200	200
Tractor	51	51	51	51	51	51	51	51	51	51	51
Harvesting & other operations	706	1012	809	896	733	733	733	1058	616	2258	848
Animal labour (pair hrs)											
Ploughing	320	320	320	320	320	320	320	320	320	320	320
Irrigation	1440	380	240	140	190	190	190	604	210	380	70
Transport	200	200	200	200	200	200	200	200	200	200	200
Tractor (hrs)											
Ploughing	10	10	10	10	10	10	10	10	10	10	10
Tractor	51	51	51	51	51	51	51	51	51	51	51

Source : Primary data

Table 5.5: Sectorwise Annual Energy Consumption

No.	*Sector*	*Per capita energy consumption ('000 kcal)*	*Annual energy consumption*	
			('000 kcal)	*(mwh)*
1.	Cooking	2968.75	461153750	536225
2.	Lighting	126.86	19705924	22914
3.	Industry	17.20	2671779	3107
4.	Commercial	25.83	4012329	4665
5.	Public utilities	4.76	739399	860

Source : Primary data

Table 5.6: Live Stock related data

Animal Type b	*Population ab*	*Dung kg/day/ animal*	*Total Dung ton/year*	*Gas yield m³/kg*	*Total Fodder Requirement*	
					kg/animal/y	*tons/y*
Bullock	6683	10.40	25369	0.036	2409	16099
Cow	16305	9.00	53562	0.036	2168	35351
Buffalo	6626	13.40	32408	0.036	3373	22347
Sheep	15975	0.80	4665	0.036	228	3644
Goat	16020	0.80	4678	0.036	136	2192
Pig	461	0.80	135	0.036	776	358
Poultry	61109	0.04	892	0.062	49	2979
Others	4366	2.54	4048	0.036	319	1394
Total			125757			84364

Note : Quantity of dung required to produce 100 m^3 of biogas = 28 tons
Source : Khandwal, K.C. *et al.* (1989); Maheswari, R.C. *et al.* (1981); Singh *et al.* (1992)

Table 5.7: Cost of Commercial Energy/Unit

Energy Sources	*Unit*	*Cost (Rs. '000)*	*Primary Energy (Mwh)*
Electricity	Mwh	1.25	1.00
Diesel	1000 lit	8.00	10.50
Kerosene	1000 lit	6.00	10.06
Fodder	ton	0.50	0.66
Fertilizer			
N	ton	5.20	—
P	ton	5.27	—
K	ton	2.83	—
Dung cake	ton	—	3.84
Biogas	1000m^3	—	5.00
Fire wood	ton	—	5.47

Source : Primary data

Model Formulation

In this paper, we have developed a Linear Programming model to minimize consumption of commercial energy sources by way of generating power from the surplus biomass through the optimal allocation of land area for different crops and the choice of the energy mix. Optimal allocations are made subject to the condition that the food, fuel and feed requirement of the block are satisfied and by using the available land and other energy sources.

In developing this model, we have taken into consideration the various operations involved in agricultural activities. Some earlier models by Parikh (1985), Singh *et al.* (1992) and Painuly *et. al.* (1992) did not take into consideration of certain constraints on irrigation, labour and ploughing. The model in this paper is developed in such a way that if the solutions of the model are implemented, then the economic conditions and local energy utilisation of the block can be improved by consuming the energy generated from surplus biomass and thereby we can avoid importation of energy which will ultimately lead to energy self-sufficiency in energy consumption.

Objective Function

The objective function seeks to minimize the total cost of commercial or purchased energy items.

Total cost of consumption of commercial energy

Grid electricity + Diesel + Kerosene + Fertilizer + Fodder

$$\text{Min } Z = \sum c^{el} \times G^{e}_{i} + \sum c^{d} \times D_{i} + \sum c^{k} x k_{i} + \sum c_{n}^{fe} \times f_{n} + c^{fo} \times B^{fo}$$

Z - Total cost of commercial energy consumption in Rs `000 where i =1,2,....,6 and n=N,P,K

Set of Constraints

Demand Constraints

Cereal Constraints

Total quantity of cereal yield obtained from allocated land area	Total quantity of cereal requirement
$\sum Y_{c} \times L_{c}$	c
	Where c = 1,2,3

Pulse Constraints

Total quantity of pulses yield obtained from allocated land area	Total quantity of pulses requirement
$\Sigma Y_c \times L_c$	p
	Where c = 4

Oil Seed Constraints

Total quantity of oil seed yield obtained from allocated land area	Total quantity of oilseed requirement
$\Sigma Y_c \times L_c$	o
	Where c = 5,6,7

Sugar Constraints

Total quantity of sugarcane yield obtained from allocated land area	Total quantity of pulses requirement
$\Sigma Y_c \times L_c$	s
	Where c = 8

Vegetable Constraints

Total quantity of vegetable yield obtained from allocated land area	Total quantity of vegetable requirement
$\Sigma Y_c \times L_c$	v
	Where c = 9

Cooking Constraints

Electrical energy equivalant of (biomass + kerosene + grid electricity	Total electrical energy requirement
$+Q\,(e_c \times r_c \times y_c)\,L^{ff}_c + K^e \times K_i + G_i^e +$ wood + bio electricity + biogas + dung cake) = ff used as a fuel)	ff
$w^e \times w^i + B^{el}_i + (db)^e \times Q_i^{db} + (dg)^e \times Q^d$	Where c=6,10,11and i = 1

In this constraint, bio electricity means electricity generated from surplus biomass

Wood Constraints

Quantity of wood used for cooking and others	Total quantity of wood available
ΣW_i	Σw where i = 1,4

Lighting Constraints

Electrical energy equivalant of Kerosene + grid electricity + + bioelectricity + biogas	Total lighting energy requirement
$k^e \times k_i + G_i^e + B^{el}_i + (db)^e \times Q_i^{db}$	l where i = 2

Biogas Constraints

Volume of biogas used for cooking + biogas used for lighting	Total volume of biogas generated
ΣQ_i^{db}	Σ^{db} where i = 1,2

Other Operations

Electrical energy equivalant of wood + grid electricity + + bioelectricity + diesel	Total energy required for other operations
$w^e \times W_i + G_i^e + B^{el}_i + d^e \times D_i$	oo where i = 4

Fertilizer Constraints

Quantity of nutrient of type n in allocated biomas + both fertilizer +	Total required quantity of nutrient type n
$\Sigma(f_{c,n}{}^e \times r_c \times y_c)L_c{}^{fe} + F_n$ +	$\Sigma(f_{c,n} \times L_c)$
dung + biogas slurry	
$f^d{}_n \times N^d + f^{db}{}_n \times s \times Q^d$	where n = N,P,K and c = 1,2,...11

Electricity Constratints

Electricity required gride electricity allocated + bioelectricity allocated
for irrigation for irrigation for irrigation
$\Sigma(i^e_c \times L^{ei}_c)$ ΣG^e_i $+ B^{el}_i$
where i = 3 and c = 1,2,....,11

Diesel Constraints

diesel required diesel allocated
for irrigation for irrigation
$\Sigma(i^d_c \times L^{di}_c)$ D_i
where i=3 and 1,2,...,11

diesel required diesel allocated
for ploughing for ploughing
$\Sigma(p^d \times L^{tp}_c)$ D_i
where i=5 and 1,2,...,11

diesel required diesel allocated
for Transport for irrigation
$t^d \times (Tkm)^{tt})$ D_i
where i = 6

Animal Feed Constraints

residue used as + bought fodder Total fodder requirement
fodder
$\Sigma(r_c \times y_c)\, L_c^{fo} + B^{fo}$ f
where c = 1,2,3,4,5

Supply Constraints

Dung Balance

quantity of dung used as quantity of dung available
fertilizer + dung cake + biogas
$N^d + Q^d + (e)^{db} \times Q^{db}$ = $\Sigma(d_b \times a_b)$

Human Labour Constraint

Total labour hours utilized for Tractor ploughing + Bullock ploughing + Other perations + $\Sigma(h_c^{tp} \times L_c^{bp} \times L_c^{bp} + h^o_c \times L_c$ +	Available human labour hours
Total human labour hours utilized for electrical irrigation + diesel irrigation + bullock irrigation $h^{ei}_c \times L_c^{ei} + h^{di}_c \times L^{di}_c + h^{bi}_c \times L^{bi}_c) +$	h
Total human labour hours utilized for Tractor transport + Bullock transport + animal maintenance $h^{tt} x(Tkm)^{tt} + h^{bt} x(Tkm)^{bt} + \Sigma(h_b^{am} xa_b)$ where c = 1,2,....,11	

Tractor Ploughing Constraint

Tractor hours utilized for land ploughing + transport	Available tractor hours
$Q(t_c^{tp} \times L_c^{tp}) + t^{tt} \times (Tkm)^{tt}$	t
	where c = 1,2,....,11

Bullock Ploughing Constraint

bullock pair hours utilized for land ploughing + transport + irrigation	Available bullock pair hours
$\Sigma Q\ (b_c^{bp} \times L_c^{bp}) + b^{bt} \times (Tkm)^{bt}$	a
$+ \Sigma(b_c^{bi} \times L_c^{bi})$	where c = 1,2,....,11

Bio Electricity Constraint

Total electrical energy of equivalant of (biomass - biomass used as fuel)	total bio electricity consumption
$\Sigma(r_c \times y_c \times e_c)L_c - \Sigma(e_c \times r_c \times y_c)L_c^{ff}$ biomass used as fodder - biomass as fertilizer	
$\Sigma(e_c \times r_c \times y_c)L_c^{fo} - \Sigma(e_c \times r_c \times y_c)L_c^{fe}$	B^{el}_i
	where c = 1,2,....,11

Land Constraint

land area under crop using bullock ploughing + tractor ploughing	= Allocated land area under crop c
$(L_c^{bp} + L_c^{tp})$	L_c
	= where c = 1,2,....,11

Total land area under crop c for irrigation (Electricity + Diesel + Bullock) under crop c	= Allocated land area
$(L_c^{ei} + L_c^{di} + L_c^{bi})$	L_c
	where c = 1,2,...,11

Total land area under crop c for	Allocated land area under crop c
(Fuel + Fodder)	
$(L_c^{fo} + L_c^{ff} + L_c^{fe})$	= L_c
	where c = 1,2,...,11

Total allocated land area for different crops	= Available land area
ΣL_c	= 1
	where c = 1,2,...,11

Available Human Hours	(h)	=	320350×10^2
Available Bullock Pair House	(a)	=	36082×10^2
Available Tractor hours	(t)	=	770×10^2
Available Fire Wood	(w)	=	6500 tons
Diesel required for transport	(td)	=	20 lit/100km
Diesel required for transport	(pd)	=	30 lit/ha

Interpretation of Model Solutions

The newly developed model is solved by HYPER LINDO software package in a Pentium, computer system. The optional land allocation for different crops, total biomass generation, quantity of biomass allocated for fodder (cropwise) and surplus biomass utilised for power generation are presented in Table 5.8. Optimum allocation of energy sources such as biomass, dung, kerosine, diesel, biogas etc., for different activities like cooking , lighting other operations, fodder etc., in this block are shown in Table 5.9. The optional allocation of bioelectricity generated from the surplus biomass for cooking, lighting, irrigation, other operations are also given in Table 5.9.

A special feature of this model is that it gives the optimal land area for cultivation of different crops as well as the land area from which the biomass generated is exclusively used for fodder. Further from the model solution we are able to arrive at the quantity of biomass that could be generated from the allocated land area under different crops, and the part of which used for the generation of electrical power for local consumption. From the optimal solution of the model presented in the Table 5.8, we can clearly conclude that if the crops are grown in the allocated area mentioned in the second column of the Table, then electrical energy produced from the surplus biomass will meet the electrical energy requirement of the block. That is the block need not purchase (consume) electrical energy from the grid, kerosine, fodder and also food stuffs from out side the block, the block is able to achieve hundred per cent self sufficiency in respect of electrical requirement of various activities like cooking, lighting, irrigation and other operations. This means that the electrical energy generated from the surplus biomass will be able to meet the complete electricity demand of this block for various activities.

Scope of the Model

The model can be run under different scenarios of increasing cost of fertilizer, increasing the consumption of cooking and lighting energy and decreasing the availability of wood in future as a mark of development of the block. This model can be implemented for energy planning activities at the taluka/district/state/national level by suitable changing and incorporating the relevant data and be performing post optimal anlysis.

Table 5.8: Optimum Land Allocation Details

Name of Crops	*optimum are allocated in hec.*	*biomass generation in tons*	*biomass utilised for*		*irrigation using*			*ploughing using*	
			fodder in in tons.	*power gene in Mwh*	*elec. in hec*	*bull. in hec*	*dies. in hec*	*tractor in hec*	*bullock in hec*
Paddy	924.193	5443.49	5443.49	—	924.193	—	—	924.193	—
Sorghum	—	—	—	—	—	—	—	—	—
Cumbu	8757.763	37220.49	31688.93	5531.56	8757.763	—	—	2246.661	6511.102
Gram	2290.909	1511.99	—	1511.99	2290.909	—	—	—	2290.909
Groundnut	925.714	740.57	740.57	—	925.714	—	—	925.714	—
Gingilly	—	—	—	—	—	—	—	—	—
Sunflower	—	—	—	—	—	—	—	—	—
Sugarcane	1107.647	70667.87	—	70667.87	1107.647	—	—	—	1107.647
Vegetables	366.774	623.51	—	623.51	366.774	—	—	—	366.774
Cotton	—	—	—	—	—	—	—	—	—
Flower	—	—	—	—	—	—	—	—	—
Total	14373.000	16207.92	37872.99	78334.93	4373.000	—	—	4095.967	10272.432

Table 5.9: Optimum Energy Distribution for Different Activities

Sources/Activities	*Cooking*	*Lighting*	*Irrigation*	*Other Opes*	*Fertili-zer*	*Fodder*	*Plough-ing*
Bio electricity (Mwh)	17763.13	22914.00	2891.69	8632.00	—	—	—
Electricity (Mwh)	0.00	0.00	0.00	0.00	—	—	—
Dung (tons)	125757.00	—	—	—	0.00	—	—
Wood (tons)	6500.00	—	—	0.00	—	—	—
Kerosene('000 lit)	0.00	0.00	—	0.00	—	—	—
Biogas ('000 lit)	0.00	0.00	—	0.00	—	—	—
Diesel ('000 lit)	—	—	—	—	—	—	95.171
Bought Fertilizer							
N (tons)	—	—	—	—	951.89	—	—
P (tons)	—	—	—	—	753.36	—	—
K (tons)	—	—	—	—	524.44	—	—
Crop residue (tons)	0.00	—	—	—	—	37873	—
Bought Fodder (tons)	—	—	—	—	—	—	—
Grazing (tons)	—	—	—	—	—	46491	—

Notations Used in this Model

1. Variables are in capital letters
2. Coefficient are in small letters
3. Superscript indicates the identification index
4. Subscript indicates the running index

Nomenclature of Sets and Parameters

Variables

G^e_i — Grid electricity assigned for purpose i in Mwh

D_i — Diesel assigned for purpose i in '000 lit

K_i — Kerosene assigned for purpose i in '000 lit

F_n — Fertilizer type n assigned for agriculture activities in tonnes

B^{fo} — Bought feed in tonnes

L_e — Allocated land area for crop c in hectares

L_e^{ff} — Residue obtained from this land area under crop c used as fuel in hec.

L_e^{fo} — Residue obtained from this land area under crop c used as fodder in hec.

L_e^{fe} — Residue obtained from this land area under crop c used as fertilizer in hec.

W_i — Wood used as fuel for purpose i

B_i^e — Electricity generated from surplus biomass (bioelectricity) used for the purpose i in Mwh

Q_i^{db} — Quantity of biogas used for purpose i in '000 m^3

Q^{db} — Quantity of biogas produced in '000 m^3

Q^d — Quantity of dung used for purpose i in tonnes

N^d — Quantity of dung used as fertilizer in tonnes

L_e^{tp} — Land area under tractor ploughing in hec (under crop c)

L_e^{bp} — Land area under bullock ploughing in hec (under crop c)

L_e^{ei} — Land area under electrical irrigation in hec (under crop c)

L_e^{di} — Land area under diesel irrigation in hec (under crop c)

L_e^{bi} — Land area under bullock irrigation in hec (under crop c)

$(TKM)^{tt}$ — Distance travelled by tractor in '00 kms

$(TKM)^{bt}$ — Distance travelled by bullock in '00 kms

Co-efficients

c^{el} — Cost of 1 Mwh electricity in Rs. '000

c^d — Cost of 1 Mwh electricity in Rs. '000

c^k — Cost of 1000 lit. kerosene in Rs. '000

c^{fo} — Cost of 1 tonne of bought fodder in Rs. '000

c_n^{fe} — Cost of 1 tonne of bought fertilizer type n in Rs. '000

Y_e — Yield of crop c per hectare

c — Required quantity of cereal yield in tonnes per year

p — Required quantity of pulses yield in tonnes per year

v — Required quantity of vegetables yield in tonned per year
o — Required quanitity of oilseeds in tonnes per year
s — Required quantity of sugarcane yield in tonnes per year
r_c — Yield to residue ration per hectare of crops
e_c — Energy equivalant of crop residue under crop c per hectare in Mwh
k^e — Energy equivalant of 1000 lit of kerosene in Mwh
w^e — Energy equivalant of 1 tonne of firewood in Mwh
db^e — Energy equivalant of '000m^3 of biogas in Mwh
dg^e — Energy equivalant of 1 tonne of firewood in Mwh
w — Available firewood
d^e — Energy equivalant of 1000 lit of diesel in Mwh
ff — Required quantity of fuel for cooking in Mwh
l — Required quantity of fuel for lighting in Mwh
oo — Required quantity of fuel for other operations in Mwh
f — Required quantity of fodder in tonnes
e^{db} — Dung required to generate 1000m^3 of biogas in tonnes
a_b — Number of animal type b
d_b — Quantity of dung output from animal type b in tonnes per year
h_c^{tp} — Human hours required for tractor ploughing in '00 hours
h_c^{bp} — Human hours required for other activites in '00 hours
h_c^{o} — Human hours required for other activities in '00 hours
h_c^{ei} — Human hours required for electricity irrigation in '00 hours
h_c^{di} — Human hours required for diesel irrigation in '00 hours
h_c^{bi} — Human hours required for bullock irrigation in '00 hours
h^{tt} — Human hours required for tractor transport in '00 hours
h^{bt} — Human hours required for bullock transport in '00 hours
h_b^{am} — Human hours required for animal maintenance in '00 hours
h — Available labour hours in '00 hours

t_c^{tp} — Tractor hours required for ploughing 1 hectare of land under crop c in '00 hours

t^{tt} — Tractor hours required for travelling in '00 hours

t — Available tractor hours in '00 hours

b_c^{bp} — Bullock pair hours required for ploughing 1 hectare 9under crop c0 in '00 hours

b^{bt} — Bullock pair hours required for travelling in '00 kms in '00 hours

b_c^{bi} — Bullock pair hours required for travelling '00 kms in '00 hours

a — Available bullock pair hours in '00 hours

l — Available land area in hectares

$f_{c,n}^{c}$ — Quantity of fertilizer content of type n in crop residue in tonne/tonne

f_n^{d} — Quantity of fertilizer content of type n in dung tonne/tonne

f_n^{db} — Quantity of fertilizer content of type n in biogas slurry tonne/tonne

s — Biogas slurry output in tonnes/'000 m^3 of biogas

$f_{c,n}$ — Requires quantity of fertilizer type n per hectare of land area under crop c in tonnes

i^e — Electricity required for irrigation of land under crop c in Mwh/hcc

i^d — Diesel required for irrigation of land under crop c in '000 lit

p^d — Diesel required for ploughing 1 hectare of land under crop c in '000 lit

f^d — Diesel required for travelling '00 kms in '000 lit

Running Index

i = Consumption of energy for purpose

i = 1. Cooking 2. Lighting 3. Irrigation 4. Other operations 5. Ploughing 6. Transport

n = Fertilizer type

c = types of crops

c = 1. Paddy 2. Sorghum 3. Cumbu 4. Gram 5. Groundnut 6. Gingilly 7. Sunflower 8. Sugarcane 9.Vegetables 10. Cotton 11. Flower

Identification Index

el = Electricity d = diesel k = kerosene

fo = Fodder fe = fertilizer e = energy in Mwh

ff = fuel d = dung db = biogas

c = crop tp = tractor ploughing bp = bullock ploughing

o = other activites di = diesel irrigation

ei = electricity irrigation bi = bullock irrigation

bt = bullock transport tt = tractor transport

am = animal maintenance

NOTES AND REFERENCES

Begum Raheena, M. *A Text Book of foods, Nutrition and Dieties,* New Delhi: Sterling Publishers Private Limited, 1988, p 188.

Biomass Assessment Study in Nilakkottai Taluk - Report, (1997) - sponsored by Ministry of Non - conventional Energy Sources, co-sponsored by Tamil Nadu Energy Development Agency (MNES - TEDA), conducted by Department of Mathematics, Gandhigram Rural Institute, Gandhigram, Tamil Nadu.

Dhawan, K.C. J.P.Mittal and B.S. Bhullar, Energy Scenario of Indian Agriculture and its Future Requirements, *Energy,* vol 18, 657-664, (1993).

Jyotiparikh, *Energy Models for 2000 and Beyond,* New Delhi: Tata McGraw Hill Publishing Company Limited, 1997.

Kanniappan, P. and T. Tamilchelvam, Proceedings of the Lecture-Cum-Seminar on Energy from Agricultural Residue, *International Journal of Energy Research* (accepted for publication), 1993.

Khandelwal, K.C. and S.S. Mahdi, *Biogas Manual,* 1989.

Maheswari, R.C. P.K. Srivastava, S. Tomar and B.P. Nema, Energy cences and Resource Assessment of village Islamnagar in the district of Bhopal-Bhopal, Central Institute of Agricultural Engineering - Bhopal, 1981.

Malik, Shashi Bala, P.S. Satsangi, S.C. Tripathy and R. Balasubramanian, Mathematical Model for Energy Planning of Rural India, *International Journal of Energy Research,* Vol. 18, (1994) 469-482

Raja, C.E. Sooriamoorthi, P. Kanniappan and T. Ramachandran, Energy Planning and Optimization Model for Rural Development—A case of Sustainable Agriculture, *International Journal of Energy Research,* Vol. 21, (1997) 527-548.

Sinha, C.S., and T.C.Kandpal, Optimal Mix of Technologies for Rural India: The Lighting Sector, *International Journal of Energy Research,* Vol. 15, (1991) 653-665.

Singh, R.P., J.P. Painly, J.Parikh and Chandra Sen, Rural Energy and Agricultural Interaction in 2000 AD—A Study of Uttar Pradesh, *Indian Journal of Agricultural Economics,* Vol. 1992, 601 - 617.

Singh, S. and L. Morsh, Optimization of Biomas Production in a Village, *Biomas and Bio Energy,* Vol. 6, (1994) 287-295.

Teddy, TERI Energy Data Directory and Yearbook, New Delhi: Tata Energy Research Institute, New Delhi 1997.

6

ISSUES AND PROBLEMS IN IMPLEMENTATION OF DECENTRALISED PLANNING

A Case Study of Tamil Nadu

K. NARAYANA RAO

The 73rd Constitutional Amendment Act 1992 has given Constitutional recognition to rural local self-governing institutions enabling decentralized governance through Panchayati Raj Institutions. Following this, many States in the country have adopted a three-tier system of Panchayat Governance at the village, intermediate Taluk/Block and District level. The powers and resources of the Institutions at each level. The decision-making process, their inter linkages differ from State to State. Experience indicates that a strong commitment to Rural Development is necessary if the impact is to be effective and broad-based. Coordination at the local level is emphasized in view of the growing evidence that Multi-sectoral Programmes can be implemented more effectively through increased decentralized planning.

Panchayat Act came into force in Tamil Nadu in 1994. After two years, in 1996, 1.17 lakh persons were elected in the State to run 13,000 Institutions of the three-tier Panchayati Raj System. Thirty per cent of the posts were reserved for women in addition to those reserved for the members of the SC/ST. Gram Sabha meetings are to be convened at least four times a year as per the Government directive. Tamil Nadu did not have elected Panchayat bodies for over ten years before the elections were held in 1996.

The following objectives are examined in the Present Paper in functioning of Panchayati Raj Institution in Tamil Nadu in relation to decentralized planning:

1. The level of success of Gram Sabha as instrument of participatory democracy.
2. The adequacy of existing powers of Panchayats to carry out the role functions assigned to them.
3. The impact of control exercised by the Government over Local bodies in its planning/ Governance.

Suggestions for overcoming the difficulties/deficiencies are made the broad structure of Panchayati Raj System in Tamil Nadu Constituting Village Panchayat, Panchayat Union and District Panchayat is described hereunder.

Village Panchayat

A Village Panchayat is constituted for a minimum of 500 population. A Village Panchayat would have members ranging from a minimum of 5 to a maximum of 15. The ward members and the president are to be elected directly by the voters. The vice president of the village Panchayat is elected indirectly among the elected members of the village Panchayat. All village Panchayats will get their financial resources from the government directly without any intermediary. The Panchayat union will not interfere in the process. The Gram Panchayat presidents have been designated as executive heads and they have been entrusted with powers and responsibilities. The beneficiaries for the Central Government schemes and programmes have to be selected by the Gram Panchayats in the Gram Sabha. Provisions have been made for convening gram sabha meetings in each Village Panchayat (VP) under the 1994 Act. Originally Gram Sabha will meet at least thrice in a year and if VP failed to convene it, the inspector of Panchayats (the district collector) is authorized to do so.

Panchayat Union

For each development block a Panchayat union is formed. Each Panchayat union has a chairperson and a vice chairperson elected indirectly by the members of the Panchayat council. Union council members are elected directly by the people. For every 5000 population one union council member will be elected by the people. Members of the parliament and legislative assembly elected from that area are ex-officio members of the Panchayat union council. The Panchayat union construction and maintaining roads, irrigation tanks and lakes, initiating family welfare activities, executing noon meal schemes and implementing schemes for *Adi Dravidas* are some of the activities carried out by the Panchayat Council.

District Panchayat

The District Panchayat is constituted with the directly elected members for every 50,000 population and indirectly elected chairperson and vice chairperson among the council members. Members of the parliament and state legislative assembly of that area are ex-officio members of the District Panchayat council. The District Panchayat can advise the government on all matters concerning Panchayati Raj Institutions particularly on services and development programmes; supervising the progress of works undertaken by the government, village Panchayat and Panchayat council in the districts and also collecting data and information regarding the district. To enable the district Panchayat to perform the assigned functions, an administrative change has been effected and by which the Divisional Development office which is nearer to the district headquarters will supervise the district Panchayat activities. Yet another office which is away from the headquarters will look after the auditing of the District Panchayat activities and the third one will be attached to the district Panchayat.

The State Government appointed a commission under the aegis of the State Planning Commission (SPC) with Shri L.C. Jain as Chairman and five other members to provide the guidelines for entrustment of powers and responsibilities to the Panchayats. The Commission submitted its report in April 1997. It suggested various measures to provide meaning and substance to the devolution of powers and functions to Panchayat institutions in the State with regard to the 29 items listed in Schedule IV of the 1994 Act. Some efforts have been made by the State Government to clearly assign functional responsibilities among the three-tiers, particularly, in view of the SPC recommendations. So far, about 27 Government orders have been passed which entrust powers to Panchayats in 26 subjects. In terms of the activities under each of these 26 subjects, the Village Panchayats have been conferred powers totally in 147 items, Panchayat Union Council with 152 items and District Panchayats with 154 items. Powers of the Panchayats as delineated in 1994 Act to various Panchayat tiers are given in the Annexure.

Elected Membership in the Panchayats (1996 Election)

Panchayat Tier	*Total No. of Panchayats*	*Total Ward Member-ship*	*No. of SC Members*	*No. of ST Members*	*General Category*	*Women Members*
Village Panchayat	12,584	40,734	7,808 (19.17)	415 (1.02)	19,927	13,578 (33.33)
Panchayat Union Council	384	6,497	1,357 (20.88)	43 (0.66)	5,099	2,424 (36.1)
District Panchayat	28	648	137 (21.14)	3 (0.46)	508	234 (36.1)
Total	12,996	47,87	9302 (19.43)	461 (0.96)	25,534	16,236 (33.91)

Note : (a) Total ward membership of VPs indicated here is excluding the 12,584 VP presidents who are also elected directly.

(b) Figures in parenthesis indicates percentages.

Source: State Election Commission, Government of Tamil Nadu.

Recently in February 1999, a new Panchayat union in Salem district was notified (Yercaud Panchayat Union) with 9 village Panchayats. The request of 23 town Panchayats has also been accepted and the State Government notified these to become village Panchayats in April 1999 Another new village Panchayat, namely "Perumathur" was also notified in Cuddalore district in January 1999. Thus, the total number of village Panchayats in the state has now increased to 12, 617, while PUCs have increased to 385.

Decentralised Planning

Experience indicates that the planning and implementation of rural development calls for a substantial measure of decentralization involving the strengthening of local government and other development institutions. Community involvement in the selection of schemes and implementation is very crucial in decentralized planning exercise. To quote World Bank Report on Rural Development, 1975 "In the people's Republic of China reliance on decentralized local level management is a corner stone of the economic system. There is a clear trend in the same direction in a number other countries—Algeria, Tanzania, Kenya and India for example. However, apart from use of special project authority—often separate from the existing local authority progress towards decentralization is generally still modest". We have since made a good progress in this direction beginning with remarkable contribution to decentralized planning by D.R. Gadgil's District Development Planning.

The rationale for decentralized planning arises from the inability of the existing arrangements whereby schemes for local development are decided, implemented and managed by departments of the State Government. The local communities are rarely consulted or involved in the process. The perception of the people at local level on the requirements for local development are generally different from those of "rational" officials. The right balance in this relationship is difficult to strike. The lack of congruence between the two can be overcome, to a great extent, through education, participatory modes of governance. The issue of decentralization in the Planning process was also emphasized in the Shukla Committee Report. The Committee has also suggested a number of measures aimed at developing more power for utilizing plan funds. The Planning Commission accepted that the "decentralization of planning process" would be thrust area in the formulation of Ninth Plan.

It is imperative that the decentralized administrative structure has to formulate and implement local level plans keeping in view the felt needs of the people. In the implementation of development programmes, local interest and initiative are to be encouraged. What can be planned/done at a lower level should not be passed on to the higher level. There is reluctance on the part of many State Governments to devolve power and finance to lower levels. One is also confronted with the meaningful assignment of functions among various tiers and matching them with the powers. It has been observed that in a large number of cases decentralized planning has degenerated into a compilation of district level schemes (Thomas Issac and Richard Franke, *Local Democracy and Local Development,* March 2000).

Review of Past Efforts Towards Decentralized Planning

In retrospect, the various attempts made by the State towards decentralized planning were halting, desultory, and lacking in consistent policies and political will. The first attempt initiated in 1971 as a perspective planning exercise turned out to be non-starter. The second one attempted in the 80's as some pilot project exercise was externally induced (at the instance of Union Planning Commission) and did not have a lasting impact. The third attempt of a State sponsored scheme of Decentralized District planning started in 1993-94 and has made some dent and is being continued. Now it is expected to merge into the PRI-based multilevel planning process being initiated in the current Ninth Plan.

Besides the statutory and constitutional package the Planning Commission has also underlined the need for taking up preparation from the village level in its Approach paper to the Ninth Five Year Plan. The relevant excerpts from this paper are given below:

* The District Planning Committee will provide the umbrella for the preparation of integrated district development plan.
* The Gram Sabha would list out priorities and assist in the selection of beneficiaries for various programmes and schemes. In this way the aspirations of the people would be articulated. Thereafter, the planning process would begin from below with the preparation of village plans, which would be incorporated into the intermediate level plans and finally merged into a district plan.
* A Core Planning Team, comprising of experts from various disciplines should be formed. The team should obtain inputs from the Remote Sensing Centres, ARPU and other

organizations on the physical and natural resource endowments of the area and assist in formulation of the plans.

* Keeping in view the resources available at each level, programmes/schemes should be taken up on the basis of identified priorities.
* In so far as earmarking of resources for decentralized planning is concerned the recommendation of NDC Committee is that 41 per cent of plan resources be set apart for this. This could include a proportion as untied funds and as incentive grants to match the contribution raised by Panchayati Raj Institutions. Thereafter, sectoral allocations at the State level should be on the basis of demands made from below by the district and in keeping with national priorities. In this way, it would be possible to bring about both a vertical and a horizontals integration of resources and services.

The District Planning Committee, a contribution of the 74th amendment, can hardly be expected to perform the tasks assigned to it. Despite the all hopes expressed in favour of decentralized planning in many states there is lack of skilled personnel who are familiar with its essentials. It continues to be seen as a mechanical disintegration of state level plans (V.K. Natraj, MIDS Madras, "Non finance factors impinging on devolution of finances".)

The district Panchayat, like its predecessor, the District Development council is vested with purely advisory role with the Panchayat union council being the main executive body within the three tier system of decentralization adopted in the State. The 1994 Act assigns one important function to the Panchayats is with regard to the preparation of a development plan. It was expected that every village Panchayat should prepare annually a development plan for the village and submit to the PUC. Similarly, the PUC has to prepare a development plan for the Panchayat union after incorporating the plans of the village Panchayat and submit to the District Panchayat (DP). The DPs, on their part have to incorporate the development plan of the PUC and prepare a development plan for the district. This is to be submitted to the District Planning Committee constituted in every district by the government comprising MPs and MLAs representing the district, the chairman of the district Panchayat, Chairman of the Municipal Councils. All the district level officers are ex-officio members of the DPC and they do not have voting rights. Not less than 4/5 of the members are elected from among the elected members of the Panchayat at the district level and municipalities in the district in proportion to the ratio between rural population and urban population in the district. The DPC has to meet at least once in 3 months. Earlier DPC was headed by the district collector and the State Government recently issued orders making presidents of District Panchayat as chairman of DPC.

An important parameter of decentralization relates to the decision-making process, that of people as part of the electorate and of the people's representatives as elected members of the system. The policy of reservation of seats in the local bodies to the disadvantaged sections of the society viz, SC/ST and women enables them to take part in the planning process. While there has been democratic decentralization in principle, in practice the effectiveness of these groups in decision-making is very limited due to political influences and lack of awareness of their rights.

Gram Sabha and its Effectiveness as Participatory Democracy

The Gram Sabha is the pivot of functional participatory democracy in its most direct and authentic form. Article 243-B of the Constitution defines the Gram Sabha as a body consisting of persons registered in the electoral rolls relating to a village, which forms the territorial area of a Panchayat, an institution of local self-government. The Constitution leaves to the state legislatures to define the powers and functions of gram sabha. The Tamil Nadu Panchayat Act, 1994 stipulates that subject to the orders of the government the gram sabha shall meet at least thrice in a year. There should not be more than six months gap between the two meetings. The act also provides that if the village Panchayat fails to convene the Gram Sabha, the Inspector will convene it. Gram Sabhas major functions are: (1) to approve the village plan as also the annual budget of the Panchayat and (2) review the progress of work on the schemes entrusted to the Panchayat. The quorum for a Gram Sabha meeting is one-third of total number of its members. Subsequently, it was modified to 10 per cent of the total membership.

In November 1998, the government directed that Gram Sabha meetings be convened at least four times in a year on January 26, May 1, August 15, and October 2. Though these meetings, have been held on the specified dates since 1998 but the people's response has been not enthusiastic in most places, according to Panchayat movement activists and political leaders. Any significant rise in public awareness about the importance of gram sabha is not shared by knowledgeable persons in the field. There are many reasons for people in not taking active part in the meetings. Most of them are wage earners and can not afford to go without wages by attending the meeting. They feel that the government instead of insisting on convening meetings on specific days, flexibility in fixing the date and time in convening the meetings to suit the local conditions could have been given to Panchayat presidents. The concept of Gram Sabha is being new, people need time to familiarize with the new political entry. The reluctance of most bureaucrats and MLAs, and MPs to share power and involve people in gram sabha meetings made people to be indifferent.

Tamil Nadu did not have elected Panchayat bodies for nearly 10 years before elections were held in 1996. During this period, people were totally dependent on bureaucrats and MPs and MLAs to take care of their local needs. In some cases, Gram Sabhas are treated to settle scores. In the process, the purpose of Gram Sabha as an instrument of participatory democracy is forgotten. People in villages near Chennai seemed to show little interest in the meetings. Several of them confessed that they signed the minutes of the meeting, which were circulated to them at their homes or workplaces, without bothering to find out whether such meetings were actually held (S.Viswanathan "Limiting peoples power" *Front Line,* July 21, 2000.)

Accordingly to E.K.Santha, Institute of Social Sciences, Chennai chapter, there is a need to bring about a more favourable atmosphere for grassroots level democratic institutions to flourish. There has to be a consistent campaign to create awareness among the people about their own empowerment and they must have a say at least in matters relating to their own locality. "There should therefore, be a deliberate attempt from the state to spread awareness about the importance of Gram Sabha meetings" says Santha. While the people look at the Gram Sabha as a forum to harass the Panchayat chief, the latter treats it as a holistic gathering.

Under the existing frame work, the powers of Panchayats which are accountable to Gram Sabhas are limited. They could not deal with several major issues like education health, nutrition, agriculture which are touching the rural people directly. If the Gram Sabha and other Panchayati Raj Institutions were to function as instruments of social transformation as originally envisaged, Panchayat institutions should be given more powers to deal with subjects which have relevance on the people's actual needs. Decentralization requires a number of changes in administrative structure, allocations of functions and powers and control of resources. All three are interrelated and to an extent, would have to be introduced simultaneously. Democratic decentralization of planning implies that people can be involved not merely in making the demands but also in making the decisions about how to improve the economic conditions and welfare of the communities. For democratic decentralization to succeed, literacy plays a dominant role and enlightened political leadership hastens the process.

R. Illango, a technocrat turned Panchayat president of Kuthampakkam village in Tiruvallur district agrees that there is a need to create greater awareness among the people about the Gram Sabha. In four years Mr. Illango developed Kuthampakkam village with the full co-operation of the villages. The Panchayat annual income recorded an increase from Rs. 3.7 lakhs in 94.95 when there was no elected Panchayat to Rs. 12.4 lakhs in 1997-98 a year after he took over as president. The value of works executed increased from Rs. 40,000 to Rs. 4.8 lakhs. He succeeded in mobilizing local resources and talent and ensuring people participation through contribution in the form of labour. By employing innovative methods he cut down expenditure on several projects. He feels that Panchayat presidents have to be motivated by the state and non-government organizations. It is learnt that the government has decided to pick up 112 honest Panchayat presidents in the next four years at the rate of one from each of the 28 districts a year and help development their villages on the Kuthapakkam pattern. There are a few success stories like Cheyyum Panchayat president in Kanchepuram district, Vallimalai Panchayat in Vellore district. As the saying goes one swallow does not make a summer. Persuasion and involvement of government to popularize the Panchayat experiment are urgently required as the system is yet to capture the imagination of the people.

Resources of Local Bodies—Devolution of Resources

The State Finance Commission has suggested the following criteria for distribution of funds amongst the Panchayat bodies:

1. Weightage for population 50 per cent (Last census)
2. Weightage for SC/ST population 15 per cent (Last census)
3. Per capita house tax collected 15 per cent
4. Core civil services/Infrastructural deficiencies 20 per cent

The first State Finance Commission made 413 recommendations on various issues broadly confined to four subjects:

(1) Devolution of funds by Government.
(2) Improvement of local resources like taxation and other related items.
(3) Core civic services of local bodies and the requirement of funds for maintenance.
(4) Devolution of functions and powers restructuring of organization and staffing with better control system.

So far, the government have accepted 115 recommendations in full and 129 in principle. In respect of 98 recommendations the government have found them not acceptable. With respect to 69 recommendations, orders are yet to be issued and 2 are said to be under examination.

Devolution of funds by Government

The first State Finance Commission recommended a global sharing of the state government tax revenues to the local bodies to be utilized only for maintenance of core services and salary component. It also recommended the sharing of individual taxes to the local bodies for adoption, in the event of global sharing was not accepted by the government. The Government have accepted the principle of global sharing and consequently 20 recommendations relating to individual tax sharing have therefore become Infructuous out of 98 recommendations shown as unacceptable.

The State Finance Commission recommended a package of sharing from 8 to 12 per cent of the tax revenue of the State excluding the taxes collected on behalf of the local bodies, commencing from 1997-98 with increase of 1 per cent each year till 2000-2001. Though the government have accepted the global sharing in principle the sharing formula has been frozen at 8 per cent for all the five years perhaps due to financial constraints of the State Government. The formula recommended by the commission for allocating the revenue between rural and urban local bodies has also been slightly modified as 55: 45 as against 60 : 40 recommended.

The distribution formula in between the various tiers and also inter-se distribution among the institutions under each tier by the government have been accepted and implemented by government. However, on the Rural side the norms for distribution based on tax performance and performance on core services have not been given effect to and the distribution is still based on SC/ST Population only. On the urban side all the suggestions contained in the formula have been adopted. The Government have also accepted the recommendation to have two pools for transfer of funds, viz, pool "A" and Pool "B". Pool "A" consists of taxes intended for local bodies and collected by the government on behalf of local bodies and pool "B" consists of total tax revenues, excluding pool "A". The government have also accepted to keep a reserve of 15 per cent towards Equalization and Incentive fund. The intention of the SFC was that this equalization fund should be utilized for rectifying deficiencies arising out of the sharing pattern proposed by SFC in the case of any individual local body. While implementing this, the government have chosen to treat it as a discretionary fund on the rural side for distribution to the weaker local bodies for creation of infrastructure as a step to equalize the infrastructure facility.

Out of the incentive fund, the urban bodies are given incentives for initiatives in tax efforts, etc. In the case of Rural local bodies it is found that the incentive grants already in force as statutory grants have been deleted from the Tamil Nadu Panchayat Act and one of the incentive grants namely local cess surcharge matching grant has been totally dispensed with. In the case of house tax matching grant, village Panchayats are given grants every year with reference to government orders. This has adverse effect on the rural local bodies. The commission computed the income from these sources for the purpose of total resource availability for working out the deficit in each tier. The State Finance Commission anticipated that there will be a flow of funds from pool "A" to the extent of Rs. 380 crores per year and under pool "B" Rs. 620 crores for the year 1997-98 and there will be gradual projection in the subsequent years. But on the perusal of the data from government budget documents it is seen that the out flow in pool "A" has been as follows:

1997-1998	Rs. 302 crores
1998-1999	Rs. 351 crores
1999-2000	Rs. 287 crores
2000-2001	Rs. 290 crores

It is clear form the above that the earmarked funds under pool "A" are gradually declining rather item going up, as expected. The major components involved in pool "A" are local cess, local cess surcharge stamp duty surcharge and the entertainment tax. It is observed that there is a gradual decline in the stamp duty surcharge and the entertainment tax released to local bodies. This is a major revenue for rural local bodies and any deficiencies will affect the financial position for normal functioning.

Devolution of funds is done scheme wise and with different conditionalities. This restricts the autonomy of the local bodies to spend the funds in the light of local circumstances. Though much effort has been spent in clarifying the issues of financial devolution to local bodies, it was not so with regard to the responsibilities of local bodies and their autonomy to dispose of the devolved funds. It should be recognized that financial devolution by itself will not accomplish much unless it is accompanied by transfer of functions and the effective authority to plan and implement their own programmes. L.C. Jain Committee report on decentralization can provide the broad framework this. (Recommendations of the seminar on "Devolution of finances to local bodies" held at MIDS, Chennai on September 22—23, 2000). The resources available to Panchayati Raj Institutions are grossly inadequate for the discharge of functions assigned to them. Their scope and authority for deciding the content of programmes is severely circumscribed. Determining the magnitude and distribution of devolution is the main task of State Financial Commissions. One may emphasize the importance of SFCs viewing financial devolution in a broader perspective of the rationale and aims of decentralization. The recommendations of the SFCs are to be treated as mandatory by the State Governments and implemented.

While Karnataka and West Bengal allotted local bodies 40 per cent and 50 per cent respectively of their plan funds, the Tamil Nadu Government allotted only 8 per cent of its total annual income. Although it promised to increase this allotment progressively to 9,10,11 and 12 per cent in the second, third, fourth and fifth year of the Panchayat, it gave only 8 per cent even after 3 years. This amount is very meagre to meet their expenses. Besides, most of the funds realized were tied up under specific schemes.

The State Government has appointed in 1999 the second State Finance Commission to recommend for devolution of resources to local bodies for 2000-2005. The Commission is in the process of collecting and analyzing the data/information. The Department of Evaluation and applied research of the State Government on behalf of the SFC, has completed a study on 1000 Village Panchayats and 50 Panchayat unions and Gram Sabha. It is leant that the May 1st, 2000 meeting of Gram Sabha in the 28 districts were covered for the purpose of the study. The feed back is being processed by the State Finance Commission. It is hoped that the Second Finance Commission would come out with suitable recommendations to further strengthen the financial support to the local bodies and the State Government would seriously address to the recommendations of the SFC.

Government Control Over Local Bodies and Coordination in its Planning/Governance

In the scheme of democratic decentralization, decentralized planning is an integral part. Though for the past two decades efforts are being made to implement decentralized planning, not much success has been achieved. It is slow and uneven across the States. Some measure of success is achieved in a few states like, Gujarat, Maharashtra, Karnataka, West Bengal, Kerala. The State Planning Commission constituted a working group under the chairmanship of L.C. Jain, member State Planning Commission to the entrustment of functions and responsibilities to the rural and urban local bodies and the group submitted its report. The group adopted the following approach for making its recommendations:

(1) The Principle to be applied for bifurcation of functions between State Departments and Panchayats should be that what can be done by the Panchayats and where the Panchayats have greater stake and better access to requisite local information and knowledge necessary for development, that matter be assigned to the Panchayats. Similarly, as between the three tiers of the Panchayati Raj Institutions, the functions to be allocated to each tier should be assigned on the basis of. What it can best do and where it is better placed and only that which it cannot do be assigned to the higher tier, i.e., Panchayat union and/or District Panchayat.

(2) The scheme of devolution should avoid dual control and result in streamlining and hastening of decision-making in respect of development planning and implementation. It should also empower/enable local representative bodies to determine priorities and integrate schemes at the operational level and accordingly deploy / redeploys available resources.

(3) Given a wide range of subjects to be assigned to the Panchayats, to recommend a phased programme of decentralization to ensure its success, the group recommended to identify activities which could be entrusted to the Panchayats immediately, that is, within the first year,

activities, which may be entrusted to the Panchayat in the next to three years. This, while placing more responsibilities on the Panchayats, would lighten the burden on the government.

The Following are Some of the Other Major Recommendations:

1. Merger of District Rural Development Agencies with District Panchayats.
2. Constitution of an empowered committee at State level with Chief Secretary as chairman to provide clarifications and directions for speedy implementation of the committee's recommendations.
3. Granting permission to local bodies to engage professionals/ consultant/chartered Engineer for specific programmes/ projects and for specified periods.
4. Arrangements for technical audit, concurrent audit and strengthening of local fund audit department.
5. Strengthening of Gram Sabha to ensure people's participation.

The recommendations of the L.C. Jain Committee were considered by the cabinet and a number of them were accepted.

The State Planning Commission has initiated actions for operatationlising the district planning based on the recommendation of the Dr. K.V. Sundaram Committee. As a first step, a small district planning cell has been set up in the district in 1999. The State Planning Commission has prepared detailed guidelines for planning at village, block and district levels as also for urban local bodies. Training programmes on decentralized planning have been organised for the district level officials through institutions such as Gandhigram Rural Institute, Institute of Urban Studies, Avinashilingam Institute of Home Science and State institute of Rural development. Training to elected non-official members are also on the anvil. With the above actions initiated in the recent past it is hoped that the planning from below would gain momentum soon.

The elected representatives were voicing criticism that it is incompatible with democratic decentralization for the district collector to act as chairman of district planning committee. Recently, the State

Government has issued orders enabling the chairman of district Panchayats to be chairman of District Planning Committee. It may also be mentioned that district planning officer acts as secretary of the district Panchayat and also as secretary to District Planning Committee. It is obvious that he cannot do justice to the multiple roles he is asked to perform. The government should exclusively entrust the district planning officer with the sole responsibility of assisting the District Planning Committee supported by a few technical personal trained in planning.

Lack of trust, lack of information and loss of power and influence are some of the factors hindering further decentralization of powers to the local bodies. However, the government has been taking steps. Earlier the maintenance of street lights was controlled by the state government. Now, village Panchayats are permitted to undertake this work, which on average works out Rs. 14,000. Similarly, drinking water supply repair/maintenance up to Rs. 7000 is decentralized at village Panchayat level with out estimate. It is increasingly realized by the government that "Social Audit" is more effective then bureaucratic control. With gram sabha functioning more effectively more transparency can be brought out in the functioning of local bodies.

In a recent meeting of the village Panchayat chiefs of Madurai, Theni and Virudunagar districts they have urged the government to repeal section 205 of Tamil Nadu Panchayat Act, dealing with removal of Panchayat chiefs by District collectors. They felt that this provision is an aberration of the tenets of local governance. They also demanded that the parallel chapter 10 of Tamil Nadu Panchayat Act be repealed as these provisions were being used by bureaucracy to control and on most occasions victimize the elected representatives of the Panchayat. All related government departments, now overseeing the activities must be decentralized and the state officials should be made to work as public servants of the Panchayat government. They also urged that the present reserved constituencies for women should be retained for next election also without resorting to rotation of reserved constituencies. Allocation of 8 per cent states revenues to local government bodies was felt inadequate by them and requested that the government should

ANNEXURE - 1

POWERS OF THE PANCHAYATS AS DELINEATED IN THE 1994 STATE ACT

Panchayat Tier	*Types of Responsibilities*		
	Mandatory	*Discretionary*	*Entrusted*
(1)	(2)	(3)	(4)
(a) Village Panchayat	Discharge of municipal services like construction, repair and maintenance of village roads, bridges, drainages, public toilets, burial grounds, wells etc., and providing street lighting on public roads (Sec.110)	Public utility activities like plantation on road sides, opening and maintaining public markets, parks and social educational centres (Section 111)	Any duty which the government may be notification impose (Section 110h)
(b) Panchayat Union	1. Construction and maintenance works pertaining to PU roads, bridges etc.	Managing common works taken up by two or more village Panchayats. Particularly measures of public utility (Sec.115)	1. Execution of the National Extension Service scheme of community development and promoting development of agriculture, animal husbandry and village industries (Sec.113)
	2. Establishment and maintenance of social amenities like dispensaries maternity and child welfare centres, mid-wife services orphanages and elementary schools.		2. The execution of implementation of all or any of the scheme and activities for economic development implemented by government or any other agency [Sec.114(1)]
	3. Training and employment of vaccinators, providing subsidies to rural medical practitioners and grants to private elementary		3. Reviewing schemes and other activities executed by the government or any other agency within its jurisdiction

(Contd.)

Annexure 1: *Contd.*

	schools promotion and encouragement of cottage industries, checking population congestion and providing house sites		
			4. Any other duty which the government may by modification impose [Sec.112 (o)]
(c) Zilla Panchayat	1. Advising the government on all development schemes undertaken by all the VPs, PUCs and all government agencies in the district [(Sec.163(2-a)]		1. A watch-dog role, having to keep account of the progress of measures undertaken by the lower and intermediate Panchayat tiers and government departments [(Sec.163 (2-b)]
			2. Any powers and functions of the VP or PUC, or the Government, which may be given to it by a government notification

ANNEXURE - 2

PANCHAYATI RAJ ADMINISTRATIVE SET-UP, 1994 ACT

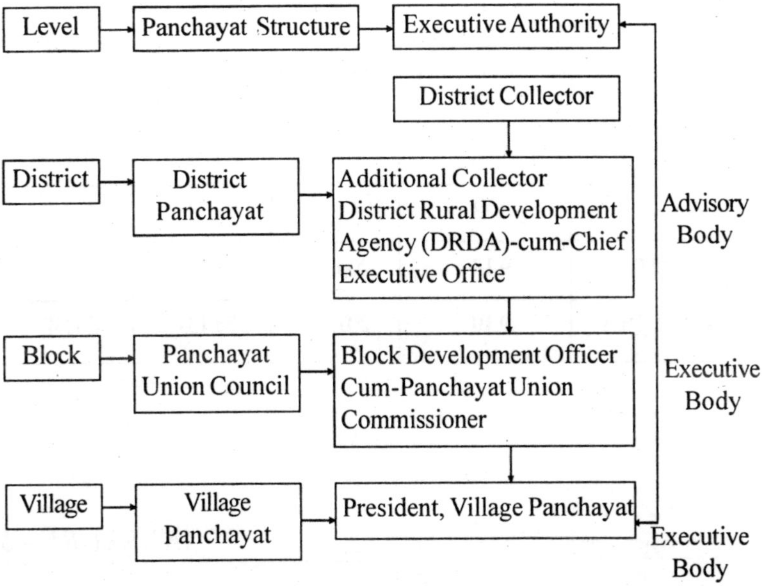

Note: The Government has issued orders recently making the chairman of the district Panchayat as chairman of District Planning Committee.

ANNEXURE - 3

DEVOLUTION OF FUNDS PRIOR TO DEVOLUTION BY ISFC (1996-97)

(Rs. in Crores)

	Grants	Assigned Revenues	Total
Rural	105.87	57.99	163.86
Urban	40.11	235.03	275.14
	145.98	293.02	439.00 (**)

(**) This does not include Commitment of Government on Local Body Pension.

ANNEXURE - 4

STATEMENT SHOWING THE ASSIGNED REVENUE IN POOL-A

Year	*LC & LCS*	*SDC*	*E.T.*	*Total*
1996-97	12.99	213.67	66.35	293.01
1997-98	3.96	223.66	64.26	301.18
1998-99	8.28	251.14	91.78	351.20
1999-2000	9.18	200.17	78.13	287.48
2000-01 (RE)	9.19	207.15	78.13	294.47

ANNEXURE - 5

STATEMENT SHOWING DEVOLUTION OF FUNDS UNDER POOL 'A' AND POOL 'B'

(*Source* - Budget Documents)

(Rs. in crores)

Year	*Pool - A*	*Pool - B*	*Total*
1997-1998 (Actual)	301.88	612.56	914.44
1998-99 (Actual)	351.20	792.91	1144.11
1999-2000 (Revised Budget)	287.48	816.25	1103.73
2000-2001 (Budget Estimate)	294.47	1036.41	1330.88

(** This includes commitment of Government of Local Body Pension).

ANNEXURE - 6

DISTRIBUTION OF POOL 'B' BETWEN RURAL AND URBAN

(Rs. in Crores)

YEAR	*Rural*	*Urban*	*TOTAL*
1997-1998 (Actual)	357.08	255.48	612.56
1998-1999 (Actual)	499.00	283.91	792.91
1999-2000 (Revised Budget)	455.06	361.19	816.25
2000-2001 (Budget Estimate)	577.80	458.61	1036.41

devolve 50 per cent of its total revenue expenditure to local bodies. It is opt to conclude the paper with the quote of Alfred Slow, C.E.O. of General Motors--"All Managements/Organizations ultimately boils to one thing. To find the right balance between centralization and decentralization".

NOTES AND REFERENCES

Bohra, O.P. "Decentralization and Devolution of Powers and Functions to Panchayats" *Journal of Rural Development,* Volume 19, 2000, Hyderabad: NIRD.

Chaudhuri, Saumetra, "Devolution and the Message" *Economic Times,* (8 August, 2000).

Choudhury, R.C., and P.S.Rajakutty, (ed), *Fifty Years of Rural Development in India: Retrospect and Prospect,* Volume II, Hyderabad: NIRD, 2002.

Government of Tamil Nadu, *Report of the Working Group on Decentralized Planning and Panchayati Raj,* Chennai: State Planning Commission, 1997.

Natraj, V.K., MIDS, Chennai "Non-Finance Factors Impinging on Devolution of Finances".

Palanidurai, K.V., Full Time Member State Planning Commission, Chennai, "Democratic Decentralization in Tamil Nadu- A Status Paper" Paper presented in the International Conference on Democratic Decentralization held at Thiruvanthapuram on May 24-28.

Recommendations/Proceedings of the Seminar on Devolution of finances to local bodies-September 22-23, 2000 held at MIDS, Chennai.

Santha, E.K., Women's Participation in Gram Sabhas in Tamil Nadu Institute of Social Science, Chennai chapter.

Sekhar, Medhushree, and Charles Nelson "Panchayat Reforms in Tamil Nadu A perspective" *Journal of Rural Development,* Volume 17, 1998, Hyderabad: NIRD.

Viswanathan, S. "Limiting Peoples Power" in *Front line,* (July 21, 2000).

World Bank Report on Rural Development, Sector policy paper - 1975.

7

DECENTRALISED PLANNING
Status in Karnataka

M. DEVANDRA BABU

Introduction

An upsurge of interest is witnessed towards decentralisation in the last one and half decade in the third world countries. The shift in favour of decentralisation is not only due to the disillusionment with the centralised planning and the emphasis on growth-with-equity policies, but also to the realisation that development is a complex and long term process that cannot be easily planned and controlled from the Centre (Cheema and Rondinelli, 1983:14). Similarly, Harris (1983) came out with the opinion that the national governments are likely to be ineffective and inefficient in the matters of provision of local services. Stiefel and Pearse (1982:146) furthering the cause of decentralization, argued that it would help redress the existing regional disparities and the popular participation would lead to increased control over resources and regulative institutions in a given social situation; and also groups and movements of those hitherto excluded from such control. Not only this, the grassroots governance is essential to build genuine self-reliance and sustainability (Parajalu and Kothari, 1998 : 25). Thus, in a nutshell, decentralization promotes efficiency by allowing a close match between public services and the multiplicity of differing individual preferences, besides promoting accountability and equity.

The success of planning under decentralization depends on certain prerequisites. Along with the prerequisites, the elected representatives of decentralized governments have to play a special role in plan formulation and implementation. Their role lies in: (1) Identification of felt needs and aspirations of the people, (2) Identifying and assessing the human and natural resources, (3) Formulation and prioritisation of plan programmes, (4) Effective implementation and monitoring of the programmes, and (5) Treating the people and non-governmental organisations as complementary institutions for the overall development (Babu, 2001: 83).

With the above background, this paper makes an attempt to study the type and method of planning carried out by PRIs in Karnataka State. The aspects analysed here are: (1) the prerequisites required for grassroots planning, (2) the status in Karnataka State with regard to these prerequisites, (3) planning experience as obtained from the field, and (4) the measures needed to make decentralised planning a reality. The analysis made is based on both quantitative and qualitative information. The former is based on the secondary sources of information and the latter on the observations and discussions held with the official and non-official members of panchayats and citizens for larger studies undertaken in Karnataka during different periods (Aziz, 1994; Babu, 1999; Aziz, *et al.* 2000).

PREREQUISITES FOR DECENTRALISED PLANNING

For the success of planning from below certain prerequisites are needed. These are:

- The first and the foremost need is political decentralization. The institutional structures created below the State should be closer to the people which ensure an instituional arragement for articulating people's needs and aspirations. Further, these institutions should have representation from different sections of the society. The representation should not only be for ordinary seats but also for authority positions. This would take care of both spatial and social disparities in the delivery of services. Further, the elected body should have supremacy over that of bureaucracy. Again, the institutional structure should have a space for peoples' participation in the panchayat's decision making, plan formulation and implementation activities.

- The second requirement is that the decentralized governments should have own motivated and capable staff. Such a staff will have affinity to the institutions they serve. Further the problems of coordination, inferior/superior complexities between the peoples' representatives and the bureaucracy should not arise and the decisions/resolutions carried out without hitches.
- The next important need is functional decentralization. In this respect the higher level government should devolve sufficient functions/responsibilities to the local government. The broad principle that should govern in the distribution of functions is that whatever concerns at a particular level should be entrusted to that level of government. The same principle should apply for different levels of panchayats within the PRI structure.
- Above all, there should be real fiscal decentralisztion from State to local governments. This means the local governments should have own resource raising powers and at the same time freedom in spending as per their needs and priorities. The resources available from all sources should be commensurate with the functions entrusted. These institutions should not become merely the spending agencies for the higher level government.

STATUS OF PREREQUISITES IN KARNATAKA

Keeping the above normative requirements for the effective functioning of local governments in general and planning in particular, it is to be seen to what extent these have been met in reality in the State of Karnataka.

Political Decentralisation

In Karnataka, even before effecting 73rd Amendment to the Constitution in the year 1992, political power had been decentralised in the late 1980s itself. A three - tier PRIs was established in the year 1987 under the 1983 Panchayat Raj (PR) Act. Though it was a three-tier structure, executive powers were vested with only two tiers namely, the Zilla Parishad at the district level and Mandal Panchayat at the village level. The middle tier was a nominated body and assigned only advisory and coordination functions. Reservations for ordinary seats were provided for the Scheduled Castes and Scheduled Tribes (SCs/STs) and for women in the institutions. In the post 73rd Amendment period, a three-tier panchayat structure was established at the district, taluk and village level, all being active bodies in the years 1994 and 1995. Unlike, the Mandals in the 1980s, the present Gram Panchayats are smaller in size both population and area-wise and thus very close to the people. In the structure there is a provision for creation of Gram Sabha below the GP. This provides space for peoples' participation. The Chairpersons of these PRIs were accorded executive status. Further, provisions have been made for standing committees at all the three levels of panchayats. At present, provision for five standing committees at ZP, three each at TP and GP have been provided. The committee on planning shoulders the responsibility of plan preparation.

Further, to cater to the needs of different categories of society, the 73rd Amendment had incorporated provisions for reserving seats and authority positions for various deprived communities and sections. The State government has implemented this provision in toto including reservation for backward classes. The position in Karnataka as far as reservations are concerned is given in Table 7.1.

Table 7.1: Tier-wise and Category-wise Elected Members of PRIs in Karnataka State in the 2000 Elections

Panchayat Tier	*Scheduled Caste*	*Scheduled Tribe*	*Backward Classes*	*General Category*	*Total*	*Women Members*
Zilla	158	54	299	379	890	339
Panchayats	(17.75)	(6.02)	(33.60)	(42.58)	(100.00)	(38.09)
Taluk	583	244	1093	1335	3255	1375
Panchayats	(17.91)	(7.50)	(33.58)	(41.01)	(100.00)	(42.24)
Gram	14871	74992	6652	31051	80073	35922
Panchayats	(18.57)	(9.37)	(33.28)	(38.78)	(100.00)	(44.86)
Total of all	15612	77972	8044	32765	84218	37636
Three Tiers	(18.54)	(9.26)	(33.30)	(38.90)	(100.00)	(44.69)

Note: Figures in brackets are percentages to the respective row totals.
Source: Institute of Social Sciences, Bangalore.

Though the State has implemented political decentralization as per the provisions of the 73rd Amendment, the powers bestowed and the changes effected in the system have been diluted leading to their impact on the governance and planning. The main deviations made relate to withdrawal of important powers vested with the chairpersons and the panchayat body, reduction in the number of standing committees at the ZP level, diminished control over the personnel by the executive head, reduction in the tenure of Chairpersons etc.

Administrative Decentralization

For the effective implementation of decisions and plan programmes adequate personnel is needed. Not only this, the PRIs should have personnel from own service cadre so that they have faith and loyalty to the elected body and carry out the resolutions without any problems. To fulfil this the PRIs should have powers to recruit the required personnel, to transfer and to take disciplinary action on the erring ones. In Karnataka, the PRIs, by and large, have adequate personnel. The number of personnel working in PRIs and the expenditure towards their salary and other benefits is presented in Table 7.2. It can be seen from the table that there are 3.43 lakh personnel working in PRIs and the total expenditure towards their salary was Rs. 2,617 crore in the year 1999-2000. The amount spent on salaries and other benefits works out to 62 per cent in the total grants (plan and non-plan) given to PRIs. Thus, the PRIs have personnel but they are all deputed by the State from different departments. These personnel are more loyal to their parent departments than to the panchayats. The Chairperson/body has no independent power to control and discipline these personnel.

Functional Decentralization

The broad principle the State government supposedly followed in the devolution of functions from the State to PRIs and between the tiers within the panchayat system was subsidiarity principle. On this basis, the functions relating to inter district and State character have been retained with the State and the remaining have been transferred to PRIs. Based on the same principle, the schemes with a village

Table 7.2: PRIs Staff and their Emoluments in Karnataka (1999-2000)

Scale-wise Staff Strength (in no.)				*Sector-wise Emoluments*	*Plan*	*Non-Plan*	*Total*
Scale	Plan	Non-Plan	Total	1. Public Works	—	6646.68	6646.68
2500-3850	4290	16482	20772	2. General Education	26196.39	150534.86	176731.25
2600-4350	1023	8585	9608	3. Sports and Youth Services	—	147.21	147.21
2775-4950	650	4353	5003	4. Medical and Public Health	3767.87	24828.29	28596.16
3000-5450	3639	26106	29745	5. Family Welfare	6624.79	538.33	7163.12
3300-6300	35481	85000	120481	6. ZP. Housing	22.04	—	22.04
3850-7050	6534	46944	53478	7. Welfare of SC/STs and BCM	437.08	5308.19	5745.27
4150-7800	2219	44230	46449	8. Social Security and Welfare	5138.75	331.57	5470.32
4575-8400	5974	16300	22274	9. Crop Husbandry	—	7805.80	78.05.80
5200-9580	475	5090	5565	10. Soil and Water Conservation	—	1554.51	1554.51
5575-10620	299	5000	5299	11. Animal Husbandry	1222.31	7048.43	8270.74
6000-11200	989	3000	3989	12. Fisheries	—	554.49	554.49
6300-11840	260	1760	2020	13. Forest and Wild Life	—	1173.36	1173.36
7400-13120	630	3500	4130	14. Special Rural Deve. Progms.	1364.26	—	1364.26
8000-13440	180	200	380	15. Rural employment	1003.71	2985.35	3989.06
9580-14200	120	506	626	16. Other Rural Deve. Progms.	—	3204.79	3204.79
10620-14960	29	36	65	17. Minor Irrigation	—	310.22	310.22
11520-15840	—	20	20	18. Cottage and Small Industries	241.34	2215.25	2456.59
12800-16720	—	1	1	19. Industries	—	200.62	200.62
Others	4729	8382	13111	20. Secretariat Economic Services	—	280.19	280.19
Total	67521	275495	343016	Total	46018.54	215668.14	261686.68

Source : Government Press, 'Provision of Salary Grants to ZPs' for the year 1999-2000. Annexure - B (Staff) (in Kannada), Government of Karnataka.

orientation had been entrusted to GPs; the schemes with an inter-village had been delegated to the TPs and all schemes with an inter-taluk or district orientation were given to ZPs (Government of Karnataka, 1988-89). Thus the State has assigned a large number of functions to the panchayats. The Karnataka Panchayati Raj Act, 1993, specifies functions of three tiers distinctly under three different Schedules. Schedule-I contains 30 subjects and assigned to GPs, Schedule-II with 29 functions assigned to TPs and Schedule-III with 30 functions assigned to ZPs (Government of Karnataka, 1993: 228-42). These functions relate to provision of basic amenities, infrastructure, and development sectors like agriculture, horticulture, fisheries, minor irrigation, health, education etc. The notable feature in Karnataka's functional devolution was that almost all the subjects enumerated under Article 243 (G) of the Eleventh Schedule of the Constitution has been delegated to the PRIs.

The functions entrusted to PRIs contain large number of sub-programmes/schemes of both State and Centre. Presently, the PRIs have been implementing a total of 665 plan and non-plan schemes. The number of schemes implemented by PRIs (sector and tier-wise) is presented in Table 7.3. It may be observed from the table that the ZPs have been implementing large number of schemes (488) followed by TPs with 173 and GPs with just 4. However, coming to the functions enumerated in the PR Act, the functions under Schedule-I pertaining to GPs have not yet been transferred to them. On the other hand, the functions under Schedules-II and III of TPs and ZPs respectively have been transferred to them. In respect of these schemes they are responsible for formulation of plans and also their implementation. Though, the GPs have been entrusted with just 4 schemes as given in the above table, they have been entrusted with large number of other obligatory functions (not concerned with Sectoral programmes) outside the listed functions under Schedule-I.

Fiscal Decentralization

In Karnataka, the GPs have been given some independent powers of taxation and a fixed grant of Rs. 5 lakh per annum (from 2003-04) to each GP. This apart, they also receive grants from the

Table 7.3: Scctor and Tier-wise Schemes Transferred to PRIs in Karnataka (in Nos.)

Sector	*Plan Schemes*				*Non-Plan Schemes*				*Total Plan and Non-Plan Schemes*			
	ZP	TP	GP	Total	ZP	TP	GP	Total	ZP	TP	GP	Total
1. General Education	141	1	. -	251	7	8	0	253	11	9	0	50
2. Adult Education	3	-	-	3	-	-	0	-	3	0	0	3
3. Sports and Youth Services	16	-	-	16	9	1	0	102	5	1	0	26
4. Medical and Public Health	30	6	-	364	3	4	0	477	31	0	0	83
5. Indian System of Medicine	7	1	-	8	-	-	0	-	7	1	0	8
6. Family Welfare	15	-	-	15	1	-	0	1	16	0	0	16
7. Water Supply and Sanitation	23	1	2	26	3	2	0	5	26	3	2	31
8. Social Welfare	272	6	-	533	41	5	0	496	14	1	0	102
9. Special Component Plan	-	18	-	18	-	-	0	-	0	18	0	18
10. Welfare of Backward Classes	121	0	-	22	-	-	0	-	121	0	0	22
11. Welfare of Women and Children	4	5	-	9	3	1	0	4	7	6	0	13
12. Nutrition	-	1	-	1	-	1	0	1	0	2	0	2
13. Agriculture	13	3	-	16	8	4	0	122	1	7	0	28
14. Soil Conservation	-	-	-	-	1	1	0	2	1	1	0	2
15. Horticulture	9	7	-	16	-	-	0	-	9	7	0	16
16. Animal Husbandry	9	6	-	151	5	3	0	182	4	9	0	33
17. Fisheries	22	-	-	22	9	-	0	9	31	0	0	31
18. Forest	9	-	-	9	-	-	0	-	9	0	0	9
19. Cooperation	14	6	-	20	-	-	0	-	14	6	0	20
20. Rural Development programmes	5	3	-	8	-	-	0	-	5	3	0	8
21. Rural Employment	1	1	1	3	-	-	0	-	1	1	1	3
22. Other RD Prog.	5	2	1	8	1	2	0	3	6	4	1	11
23. Minor Irrigation	6	3	-	9	7	-	0	7	13	3	0	16
24. Cottage and Small Scale Industries	15	-	-	151	9	-	0	193	4	0	0	34
25. Sericulture	7	2	-	9	-	-		-	7	2	0	9
26. Roads and Bridges	17	1	-	18	8	-		8	25	1	0	26
27. Tribal Sub-Plan	-	18	-	18	-	-		-	0	18	0	18
28. Handloom and Textiles	16	-	-	16	-	-		-	16	0	0	16
29. Science and Technology	1	-	-	1	-	-		-	1	0	0	1
30. Secretariat Economic Services	-	-	-	-	3	-		3	3	0	0	3
31. Public Works	-	-	-	-	7	-		7	7	0	0	7
Total	300	131	4	435	188	42		230	488	173	4	665

Source: Rural Development and Panchayati Raj Department, Government of Karnataka.

Centre for two purposes - one, for implementing the 'Sampoorna Grameena Rojgar Yojana' (earlier it was called JRY and JGSY) programme and two, grant recommended by Central Finance Commission. On the other hand, the Taluk and Zilla Panchayats have no independent taxation powers. The TPs however get a share in the stamp duty (a surcharge of 3 per cent). The ZPs and TPs largely depend upon the grants from the State for plan and non-plan purposes. A lumpsum allocation is indicated in advance to each ZP as its plan outlay. The ZP in turn makes the allocation to the TPs and GPs under its jurisdiction as per the guidelines and criteria. In respect of non-plan schemes the State government meets fully the requirement under salary component and for maintenance of assets and other essential services transferred to PRIs.

The grants are provided under two broad heads, namely, plan and non-plan. A part of the plan grants is conditional and matching in nature. The grants given to PRIs under the Centrally Sponsored Schemes by the Centre are by and large conditional and matching. The extent of grants provided in the budgets for PRIs by the State is presented in Table 7.4. It can be seen from the table that the total amount of grants (plan and non-plan) allocated to all the three tiers during 1987-88 was Rs. 917 crore and the same has increased to Rs.4,828 crore during 2001-02 - a five fold rise in a matter of fifteen years. Out of the total grants, the share of non-plan grants is more than that of plan grants.

Coming to the plan grants, the share of PRIs in the State's total plan outlay has been increasing in absolute terms but in percentage terms it is declining. For instance, during 1987-88 the share of PRIs in the State's total plan outlay was 32.23 per cent and the same has declined to 19.09 per cent in the year 2001-02. In fact, the share of plan grants of PRIs up to 1991-92 was more than 34 per cent and from 1992-93 onwards there is a decline to the extent of 8 to 10 per cent.

The State provides lumpsum plan grants to Zilla Panchayats as districts' plan outlay. The ZPs in turn make allocations to the TPs and GPs. The extent of shares allocated to each tier under plan grants unfolds the extent of their hold over planning and implementation. The information on tier-wise shares is presented in

Table 7.4: Plan and Non-Plan Grants Transferred to PRIs (all the three-tiers) in Karnataka

(Rs. crore)

Year	*Grants Allocated to PRIs*							
	Plan (Centre & State)	*Non-Plan*	*Total*	*Per cent share of plan grants in the total grants*	*Per cent share of non-plan grants in the total grants*	*State plan outlay (State) & (Central Share)*	*Share of PRIs in the State plan outlay*	*Per cent share of PRIs in the state plan outlay*
1987-88	364.84	551.73	916.57	39.80	60.20	1132	365	32.23
1988-89	392.95	597.12	990.07	39.69	60.31	1152	393	34.11
1989-90	444.82	697.06	1141.88	38.90	61.04	1306	445	34.06
1990-91	545.28	694.22	1239.50	43.99	56.01	1366	645	39.92
1991-92	675.04	837.95	1512.99	44.62	55.38	1937	675	34.85
1992-93	670.08	973.51	1643.59	40.77	59.23	2625	670	25.53
1993-94	739.61	1097.93	1837.54	40.25	58.04	3621	793	21.92
1994-95	972.61	1213.05	2185.66	44.50	55.50	4175	973	23.30
1995-96	1100.31	1354.1	2454.41	44.83	55.17	4648	1100	23.67
1996-97	1272.84	1628.55	2901.39	43.87	56.13	5311	1213	23.97
1997-98	1419.74	2020.98	3440.72	41.26	58.74	5605	1420	25.20
1998-99	1447.03	2357.01	3804.04	38.04	61.96	6513	1447	22.22
1999-00	1527.82	2707.95	4235.77	36.07	63.93	7087	1528	21.56
2000-01	1696.96	2892.47	4589.43	36.90	63.02	8506	1697	19.95
2001-02	1834.30	2993.63	4827.93	37.99	62.01	9605	1834	19.09

Source : 1. '*Economic Survey 1997-98*', Government of Karnataka;
2. Reserve Bank of India, '*RBI Bulletins*' (various issues).

Table 7.5. It can be seen from the table that on an average, the shares of ZPs, TPs and GPs in the PRIs total plan grants are 43, 44 and 13 per cent respectively. From this it is clear that the share of GPs are far lower than the other two higher tiers.

From the point of balanced development and equity it is essential for the government to distribute grants on an objective criteria. We have three-tier PRIs below the State and it is important to see which criteria are followed in the distribution of grants. The State has adopted 12 criteria for allocation of plan grants across the ZPs since

Table 7.5: Tier-wise Share of Plan Grants (State and Centre) in Karnataka Between 1995-96 to 1999-2000

(Rs. lakh)

	1995-96		*1996-971*		*999-2000*			
Panchayat Tier	*Allocation*	*Per-cent to total*	*Allocation*	*Per-cent to total*	*Allocation*	*per-cent to total*	*Total of Three years*	*Per-cent to total*
Zilla Panchayats	46447.55	42.21	50780.99	39.90	69037.85	45.19	166266.39	42.62
Taluk Panchayats	46068.62	41.87	57861.53	45.46	67382.66	44.10	171312.81	43.92
Gram Panchayats	17515.10	15.92	18641.8	14.65	16361.28	10.71	52518.18	13.46
Total of Three Tiers	110031.27	100.00	127284.32	100.00	152781.79	100.00	390097.38	100.00

Source: 1. Rural Development and Panchayati Raj Department, Government of Karnataka.

2. Government of Karnataka, *'Budget Allotment for Zilla Panchayats - Plan and Non-Plan'* (various years).

1987-88. Further a different set of criteria (six) has been introduced for distribution of grants across the TPs in the year 1998 (Babu, 2002). As far as GPs are concerned, the State government is making Rs. 3.5 lakh grant annually to every GP uniformly. From 2003-04 this amount would be Rs. 5 lakh as announced in the current year budget. Sampoorna Grameena Rojgar Yojana grant to GPs is distributed on the basis of SC/ST population of the respective panchayats. Besides, the GPs receive grant from the Centre on the recommendations of the Central Finance Commission based on different criteria.

PLANNING: PROBLEMS AND PROSPECTS

We have observed above the prerequisites required for the effective governance and planning under decentralisation and also the actual status relating to those prerequisites. Keeping the status of decentralisation in view, it is pertinent here to analyse for the way the planning is carried out in the field, the problems encountered and the future prospects. These are discussed in the following paragraphs.

Tier-wise Planning Process

As the State has adopted a three-tier PRI system—village, taluk and district level, it is possible to formulate the district plan from the village level. This is true also in the sense that the State plan is a product of both the PRIs and the State. The annual draft plan preparation below the State level starts from August month every year. The State Planning Department normally indicates the approximate share of Plan grants to each ZP in the months of July-August and the concerned ZP in turn indicates the share of each TP and GP in the district and on this basis all the three tiers start formulating draft plans simultaneously. The GPs prepare their plans and send the same to their respective TPs. Each TP in turn scrutinises and consolidates the plans of GPs under its jurisdiction and builds them into its own plan. The TPs in turn forward their consolidated plans to their respective ZPs. The ZP in turn scrutinises and consolidates all the TP plans under its jurisdiction and integrates them into its own plan. Through this process there emerges one district plan. The ZPs forward their draft plan to the State Planning Department. Finally, the district plans are integrated into the State plan. So far so good, but the question is what methods do the different tiers adopt in formulating their plans? As per the concept of decentralised planning, the PRIs are expected to formulate plans based on the needs and aspirations of the people and the local resource potential (natural, human and animal) and finally integrate the projects/schemes vertically and horizontally. This process calls for the active participation of elected representatives, citizens and coordination and cooperation of different departments.

First, let us study the extent of possibility of each tier formulating plan projects from the grass root level. As brought out earlier, the PR Act clearly demarcates the functions of each tier. A cursory look at the functions entrusted reveals that the GPs have very minimal role in the planning aspect. The State is yet to transfer sectoral programmes to GPs and their main concern is provision of amenities and maintenance and management assets created. The area where the GPs have the scope to prepare plan is for SGRY and beneficiary programmes. They prepare only the action plans.

On the other hand, the TPs and ZPs have been entrusted with sectoral programmes and as such they formulate both draft and action plans as per the time schedule prescribed by the State Planning Department. Thus, in reality the development plans are prepared from taluk and district tiers within the decentralised system.

Functional Freedom

After knowing that the local governments have a role in the local plan formulation, the next question that needs to be answered is whether the PRIs have complete freedom in choosing the projects/schemes on their own based on the local needs and aspirations? The field reality in this respect is that the schemes which the State was implementing before the establishment of PRIs at the district and below were transferred to them for implementation. It is said that full freedom is given to the ZPs to take up programmes according to the local needs. However, in reality it is different. A study on decentralised planning in the State also subscribes to this point. It points out that "the outlay is communicated to the district and the programmes are fitted within this outlay" (Naginahal, 1995: 31). Again, the programmes entrusted to PRIs consist of Central Plan Schemes (CPSs) and Centrally Sponsored Schemes (CSSs). There are altogether 47 of such schemes under PRIs. These schemes are conditional in nature and the PRIs have to implement them irrespective of their need at the local level. Naginahal points out that "the Central sector and CSSs are accepted without carrying out a detailed study about its implications. Whether a particular programme is feasible or not is also not looked into" (Naginahal, 1995: 31). This implies that the local governments have to plan for the already entrusted programmes/schemes and their maneuverability is very limited.

Allocative Freedom

Another important question relates to the area of discretion that is vested with the PRIs in development planning. No doubt the State government is providing lumpsum plan grants to the PRIs, and as such they have been advised to follow certain broad guidelines while allocating money to the sectors/schemes. These guidelines are: (1) provision for committed expenditure on salaries and allowances,

(2) spillover works of previous years, (3) minimum needs programmes (MNPs) (4) ongoing schemes relating to scholarships, farms, hospitals, hostels, schools etc. and (5) matching share for Centrally Sponsored Schemes (Government of Karnataka, 1988). Thus, the PRIs have to adhere to the guidelines while allocating grants to the schemes/programmes. Further, out of the total plan grants of PRIs nearly 45 per cent constitute Central grants. This has to be spent on the Central programmes only. A majority of members of various ZPs of Karnataka who had participated in the training programmes during 1996-98 at the Institute for Social and Economic Change, Bangalore, opined that after meeting the expenditure as per the above guidelines nothing remains for taking new projects/schemes on their own. A study points out that "after earmarking grants as per the guidelines the PRIs are left with about 14 per cent of the plan outlay to plan and implement their own schemes. The extremely low level of discretionary or free outlay is a mockery of the very philosophy underlying the decentralised plan process" (Aziz, 1991: 35). The Report of the State Finance Commission also highlighted this problem and recommended a provision of 10 per cent of the PRIs plan grants as united grant (Government of Karnataka, 1996). The only flexibility the PRIs have is to effect changes in the allocations to the extent of 10 per cent from one scheme to another in the course of the year if need arises.

Gap between the Needs and Resources

The PRIs in the State are facing the most common problem i.e. the mismatch between the needs and resources available. As noted earlier a large number of programmes/schemes have been entrusted to PRIs in the State. Though compared to other States the State has been devolving larger plan grants to PRIs every year, they are finding it difficult to meet the developmental requirements. This aspect will be clear if we analyse the pattern of allocation of money across the sectors over the years. This information is presented in Table 7.6. It can be seen from the table that there are nearly 24 development sectors under PRIs. The allocation pattern indicate that on an average 78 per cent of the total plan grants has gone to 8 sectors such as education, drinking water, employment, rural development programmes etc. and the remaining 22 per cent to the other 16 sectors. For a large number of sectors the grants allocated are very meagre. It was less than one per cent even for the important sectors like minor irrigation, horticulture, cooperation, and sericulture. This implies that the needs of PRIs are more whereas the availability of resources is far less. The resource constraint has tied the hands of PRIs and as a result only nominal allocations were made on several programmes. In contrast to this, in Kerala the share of PRIs in the State's total plan outlay was around 35 to 40 per cent and these grants have been given without pre conditions (John and Chathukulam, 2001: 4)

Gram Sabha

An important issue that needs attention in the context of decentralised planning is working of Gram Sabha (GS). The State PR Act has a provision for GS (Peoples' Assembly) which has to meet at least twice a year. Further, the GS has to be held in every revenue village. Various functions such as review of panchayat finances, action plans, audit report, implementation and monitoring of programmes, identification of beneficiaries etc. have been entrusted to GS. The main intention of this forum is to involve local people in the panchayat activities particularly in the plan formulation and implementation. The panchayat while preparing plans has to get feedback from the citizens with regard to their needs and resource potential in the area. This could be possible only through the GS. This is also the right forum for the panchayat to encourage the public to make contributions for the development purposes. The involvement of people and the non-governmental organisations results in efficiency in the planning and implementation of programmes. Thus, the GS acquires greater importance in the panchayat planning.

Viewed in this context, the working of GS in the State leaves much to be desired. Various studies on the working of GS reveal that they are not regularly meeting and effective also. When the State implemented genuine decentralisation in the year 1987-88, GSs were held regularly in the initial years of 1987-91 (Aziz, 1994: 56). In the second tenure of PRIs, GSs were held only at the GP headquarters and not in every revenue village. On an average, one

Table 7.6: Sectorwise Allocation of Plan Grants by Zilla Panchayats (all the three-tiers) in Karnataka

(Rs. lakh)

*Sector**	*1994-95*	*1995-96*	*1996-97*	*1997-98*	*1998-99*	*Average grant per year*	*Per cent to total*	*Rank*
Primary and Secondary Education	9364.34	13537.68	16637.86	11299.16	15838.09	13335.43	10.73	3
Adult Education	194.25	200.88	204.35	120.71	114.39	166.916	0.13	27
Sports and Youth Services	327.00	324.91	325	412.98	417.97	361.572	0.29	22
Rural Health	3886.50	4084.52	4092.5	3456.01	2812.13	3666.332	2.95	10
Indian System of Medicine	267.00	317.40	343	311.49	247.41	297.26	0.24	24
Family Welfare Programmes	4429.90	5314.91	6111.5	6566.40	7210.71	5926.684	4.77	6
Rural Water Supply	7726.60	11466.77	15508	19226.69	18035.61	14392.73	11.58	2
Welfare of SCs/ STs	4188.87	4643.86	5082.07	6491.36	5798.64	5240.96	4.22	8
Special Component Plan	3654.48	3877.14	4595.54	4980.67	4605.99	4342.764	3.50	9
Welfare of BCM	1325.00	1560.40	1713.5	2007.19	1990.38	1719.294	1.38	16
Welfare of Women and Children	3932.48	4742.93	5247.72	6909.25	8504.33	5867.342	4.72	7
Nutrition	1164.91	3352.26	3389.5	3752.16	3589.47	3049.66	2.45	12
Agriculture	1976.99	1794.12	1837.34	1933.58	1942.63	1896.932	1.53	14
Horticulture	486.02	460.74	483	472.69	469.08	474.306	0.38	19
Animal Husbandry	1775.15	2067.73	2555.00	1748.94	1627.20	1954.804	1.57	13
Fisheries	345.23	386.22	380.77	415.19	409.80	387.442	0.31	21
Forest (Including Soil Conservation)	2112.06	2060.64	2242.47	1417.31	1328.83	1832.262	1.47	15
Co-Operation	297.00	262.76	268.5	238.13	222.88	257.854	0.21	25
RDP-Rural Development Special Programmes	8480.66	8167.81	10089.38	11166.02	10428.14	9666.402	7.78	5

(Contd.)....

Table 7.6: *(Contd.)*

(Rs. lakh)

*Sector**	*1994-95*	*1995-96*	*1996-97*	*1997-98*	*1998-99*	*Average grant per year*	*Per cent to total*	*Rank*
Rural Employment	25865.20	23570.20	22997.5	36976.90	37395.29	29361.02	23.63	1
Other RDPR Programmes	8856.95	11285.61	16235.08	14589.75	14344.76	13062.43	10.51	4
Minor Irrigation	1205.65	1099.96	1157.5	1124.69	1024.13	1122.386	0.90	18
Village and Small Scale Industries	342.57	343.66	349	278.55	351.51	333.058	0.27	23
Sericulture	471.81	443.88	450.5	428.30	408.89	440.676	0.35	20
Roads and Bridges	3664.46	3305.74	3353.5	3776.90	3517.94	3523.708	2.84	11
Secretariat Economic Services	100.00	128.02	75	31.42	125.10	91.908	0.07	28
Tribal Sub Plan	647.53	1027.95	1355.29	1586.49	1660.12	1255.476	1.01	17
Handlooms	172.06	202.69	230.45	237.05	260.93	220.636	0.18	26
Science and								
Technology	**	**	**	18.00	20.70	7.74	0.01	29
Total	97260.67	110031.39	127310.8	141973.98	144703.05	124256	100.00	-

Note : * Some sub-sectors clubbed in the respective main sectors, ** Sector not existed

Source: Government Press, 'Budget Allotment for Zilla Panchayat Plan and Non-Plan' (Various issues), Government of Karnataka.

(Contd.)....

GS meeting was held each year (Bhargava and Raphael, 1994; Aziz, *et al.* 1999). Further wherever GSs were held they were not utilised for constructive and intended purposes. By and large, they were reduced into beneficiary identification meetings. A large number of factors contributed to the dismal functioning of GSs, The most important factors are limited resources of GPs, innumerable demands from the people, lack of leadership, public hostility, non-cooperation of members of other parties, non-participation of local TP and ZP members and officials.

Role of Members

The success of decentralised planning depends upon the active participation of elected representatives and the standing committees concerned. By and large, the standing committee on planning while initiating planning exercise asks the departments concerned to prepare their department's needs along with budget estimates. After receiving this information from the departments the members of standing committee, the President and officers give final shape to the plan. This is the existing procedure in formulating the plans at the ZP and TP levels. It is nothing but sectoral planning which takes place mechanically. The ordinary members are hardly involved in the planning process and they are invited for a meeting where the draft plan has to be approved before forwarding it to the State Planning Department. A large number of ZP members complained that they had been kept in the dark throughout the preparation of plan and that they were invited for a meeting to approve the plan. They said that one full day is hardly sufficient to discuss the important subject of planning (Babu, 1997). However, the members exercise freedom in suggesting location of projects/schemes while preparing action plans in the months of April/May.

Lack of Planning Personnel

Another problem encountered at the TP level is that the State is yet to provide planning personnel to them. The TPs by and large depend upon the ZP for plan preparation. In fact, till 1998-99 the plan grants of TPs were retained at the respective ZPs, they formulated plans and implemented on their behalf. However, this has been reversed from 1999-2000 onwards. Since then the plan grants of TPs have been distributed to them and plans were prepared at the TP level of course with the assistance of ZP planning personnel. Similarly, there is no planning expert at the GP level. The only official i.e. the Secretary has to look after various responsibilities and as such planning is given least importance at the lowest tier of PRIs.

Distribution of Plan Grants

One of the objectives of planning is to reduce the regional disparities. For this the need is to distribute the resources across the panchayats on a set of broad criteria. In this respect the State has adopted 12 criteria as far back as in 1987-88 for distribution of plan grants across the ZPs. Similarly, 6 criteria have been adopted since 1998-99 for distribution of plan grants across the TPs. But the field information reveals that these criteria have not been followed in deciding the shares of each panchayat. For ZPs the State government hikes their shares annually by about 5 per cent to the previous year outlay. At the TP level, the ZPs apply their own method in arriving at the development levels and on this basis distribute the grants and not on the State criteria. At GP level, the State is providing fixed grant uniformly.

Political Instability

The State over the years reduced the tenure of Chairpersons of ZPs and TPs from 5 years to 2.5 years and then to 20 months. At the GP level the tenure of Chairpersons was reduced from 5 years to 2.5 years. The panchayat members themselves by internal understanding further reduced this official tenure to 10 months. This is evident from the election of new Chairpersons to several panchayats immediately after completion of 10 months (Bangalore Rural, Bangalore Urban, Kolar, Bidar, Mandya ZPs etc.). Further, the functionaries could not prepare plans in time resulting in delay in the implementation of schemes and losing crores of rupees in the process especially of Central Government every year. It was said that during 2001-02 the utilisation was 45.75 per cent under EAS, 47.18 per cent under ARWSP, 55.30 per cent under SGSY, and 55.30 per cent under IAY (*Deccan Herald,* 2002: 5). Thus planning is the ultimate victim of political instability. The goings on in the panchayats reminds us of the skepticism expressed by a French Economist on decentralisation in his famous article 'The Dangers of Decentralisation' coming true (Prudhumme, 1995).

Conclusion and Suggestions

The above account of the planning experience at the local level in the State is self-revealing. Though the PRIs have been entrusted with large number of functions and fairly large grants, the kind of planning carried out presently is not fully akin to the visualised decentralised planning. A study on Karnataka's PRIs system pointed out that the decentralised planning is yet to become a reality. Panchayats at the lower levels do not have staff support needed for meaningful plannng. Planning continues to be essentially a top down process (Chandran, 2000: 144).

The decentralisation effort of the State is commendable but still lot more refinement is needed in the system especially to make planning one of bottom up, effective and efficient. First of all, the elected body and the Chairpersons should be accorded their due share of power. The staff working in these bodies should not show disrespect and instead they should cooperate with the non-official members in the interest of people and development.

The PRIs instead of acting as agents of spending for the State and the Central schemes should be allowed to choose their own schemes and priorities. Further, the grants given for development planning is grossly inadequate and it should be enhanced according to the needs. Not only this, they should be allowed to utilise and allocate the grants as per their priorities.

There is need to provide larger grants to GPs as their share in the PRIs total plan grants is just around 13 per cent. This calls for proper allocation of functions between the three tiers.

The grants should be distributed on a broad set of criteria. The existing criteria at the ZP and TP levels have not been applied in reality. The *ad hoc* method followed leads to unequal distribution of resources and thereby accentuating further regional and interpersonal inequalities. Keeping the long term interest and overall development in view, a concise set of criteria needs to be adopted. Alternatively, the criteria suggested by the first SFC after 73rd amendment should be followed.

Gram Sabha the core of the decentralised system needs to be revived and invigorated. Merely bestowing some functions to GS do not serve any purpose. Along with the functions it should be given enforceable powers for its decisions. The local members of TP/ZP should be educated to participate in the GS meetings and they should in turn try to incorporate the demands of the people in their action plans. It is also the right forum to rope in the services of people and non-governmental organisations in their developmental efforts.

One of the advantages of decentralisation is that the programmes/schemes could be implemented in an efficient and cost effective manner. When people and other local organisations participate actively in the plan formulation and implementation it is expected that they would also share the burden of resources by way of cash, kind and labour. The PRIs have to strive to motivate the people to contribute for the developmental activities. But the field studies reveal that the PRIs have a dismal track record in this matter. A study points out that about 95 per cent of the sample citizens reveal that the GP has not asked for contributions. Further, the same citizens expressed that they would contribute if the GP asked for (Babu, 2000). There are instances of mobilising contributions by the local organisatons. Similarly, there are instances where the farmers and the public themselves voluntarily came forward to construct channels, barrages, bridges, roads without waiting for government intervention (Jadar, 2003; Acharya, 2003; Patil, 2003). The PRIs failed miserably in this aspect due to various reasons. The important reasons are political instability, corruption, ineffective functioning of GS, lack of knowledge etc. These negative aspects have to be removed by bringing appropriate policy measures. The panchayats should use the GS forum to motivate the people to contribute to the panchayat works.

To get projects/schemes to their constituencies the members envisage large number of works to be taken up unmindful of availability of resources. Thus, in large cases the panchayats deviate from the set norms and guidelines. For instance, the norms prescribe that at least 50 per cent of the cost of the project has to be earmarked in the first year itself and the project has to be completed in the second or third year by allocating the remaining funds. But the members do not adhere to these norms and the scarce resources have been thinly spread on a large number of projects leading to spillover in the subsequent years. The elected representatives at all the three levels should shun this habit of sharing certain types of grants constituency-wise which affect adversely the creation of assets and infrastructure.

Though the TPs have been in existence since 1994, they are yet to be provided with planning personnel. The plans prepared by TPs are mechanical in nature as they were prepared by departmental and ZP officials. Thus there is need for filling the posts of planning officers at TPs which facilitate the middle tier to have plans prepared by themselves. The GPs also need to be provided with planning experts.

The reduction in the tenure of Chairpersons of PRIs has led to political instability and its impact is felt on planning. Planning is a technical subject and the functionaries need through knowledge about the nature of functions, resources, guidelines etc. For this the executive heads need sufficient time. Thus, the unsavoury developments have to be reversed and efforts should be made to put the panchayats on the right track so that the advantages of local planning are realised.

The most important need is awareness creation among people and capacity building of the local level functionaries. A majority of members are unaware of their total budget amount, the schemes, guidelines, importance of GS etc. Thus, before assigning any task especially of planning and implementation to the newly elected members, it is most essential to impart training to them on a continuous basis.

NOTES AND REFERENCES

Acharya, Keya, Making way for progress, Spectrum, *Deccan Herald,* 7 March, 2003.

Aziz, Abdul, *District Plan Process: The Karnataka Case,* in R.P. Kurulkar, (ed) Seminar Papers on District Planning, 1991, Pune: Ramachandra and Co., 1991.

Aziz, Abdul, *Decentralisation: Mandal Panchayat System in Karnataka*, Hyderabad: National Institute of Rural Development, 1994.

Aziz, Abdul, *et al., Ford-NIRD Untied Grants to Selected Gram Panchayats in Karnataka: A Concurrent Evaluation,* (mimeo), Bangalore: Institute for Social and Economic Change, 1999.

Aziz, Abdul, *et al., Ford Foundation-NIRD Project on Strengthening the Panchayati Raj Institutions in Karnataka: Impact Evaluation Study,* (mimeo), Bangalore: Institute for Social and Economic Change, 2000.

Devendra Babu, M., Decentralised Planning in Karnataka, *The Asian Economic Review,* Vol. XXXIX, (1997) No. 2.

Devendra Babu, M., *Functional and Financial Devolution to PRIs: A Study in Karnataka*, (mimeo), Bangalore: Institute for Social and Economic Change, 1999.

Devendra Babu, M., *Koppa Gram Panchayati* in Abdul Aziz *et al.* 2000, Ford Foundation-NIRD Project on Strengthening the Panchayati Raj Institutions in Karnataka: Impact Evaluation Study, (mimeo), Bangalore: Institute for Social and Economic Change, 2000.

Devendra Babu, M., Governance, Planning and Development: The Case of PRIs in Karnataka, *Indian Journal of Regional Science,* Vol. XXXIII, (2001) No. 2.

Devendra Babu, M., Report of the Karnataka State Finance Commission: Status and Implications, *The Indian Journal of Economics,* Vol. XXXII, (2002) No. 326.

Bhargava, B.S., and C. Raphael, Working of Gram Sabhas in Karnataka: A Study at Micro Level, *Journal of Rural Development,* Vol. 13, (1994) No. 2.

Chandran, T.R. Satish, 'Karnataka', in George Mathew (ed.), *Status of Panchayati Raj in the States and Union Territories of India*, 2000, New Delhi: Concept Publishing Company, 2000.

Cheema, G.S., and D.A. Rondinelli (eds), *Decentralisation and Development: Policy Implementation in Developing Countries,* Beverly Hills, CA: Sage, 1983.

Herald Deccan, "State has not utilised funds for drought relief", *Deccan Herald,* (23 May 2002), Bangalore.

Government of Karnataka, District Governments and Decentralised Planning: Karnataka Shows the Way, Bangalore: Government of Karnataka, 1988.

Government of Karnataka, The Karnataka Panchayati Raj Act, 1993, Bangalore: Government of Karnataka, 1993.

Government of Karnataka, Report of the State Finance Commission Relating to Panchayati Raj Institutions, Bangalore: Government of Karnataka.

Harris, R., Centralisation and Decentralisation in Latin America in G.S. Cheema, and D A Rondinelli (eds), *Decentralisation and Development: Policy Implementation in Developing Countries,* Beverly Hills, CA: Sage, 1983.

Suresh Jadar, M., "Out of muddy waters", Spectrum, *Deccan Herald,* 14 February (2003), Bangalore.

John, M.S., and Jos Chathukulam, *Measuring Decentralisation: The Case of Kerala (India),* in Conference on Panchayati Raj Institutions, Karl Kubel Institute of Development, 28-29 (December 2001), Coimbatore.

Naginahal, R.T., Plan Formulation, in Agriculture Department, Role and Importance of Planning in Agriculture Development, (in Kannada), Government of Karnataka (1995).

Parajalu, Pramod and Smitu Kothari, "Struggling for Autonomy: Lessons from Local Governance", *Development,* Vol. 41, No. 3 (1998).

Patil, Bhimappa, "Collective Success", Spectrum, *Deccan Herald,* 28 March (2003), Bangalore.

Prud'humme, Remy, "The Dangers of Decentralisation" *The World Bank Research Observer,* Vol. 10, No. 2 (1995).

Stiefel, M., and A. Pearse, UNRISD's Popular Participation Programme: An Inquiry into Power, Confilct, and Social Change, *Assignment Children* (59/60) 1982.

8

MICRO LEVEL PLAN IN RAJASTHAN

THE HUNGER PROJECT

THE HUNGER PROJECT'S CONCEPTUALIZATION

The 73rd Constitutional Amendment Act passed in 1992 and the subsequent legal reforms in the Panchayati Raj system in Rajasthan have presented immense opportunities in enhancing the role of these institutions in development of rural areas. Moreover, the provision for reservation of one-third seats for women signifies an extremely progressive step in their empowerment process in a traditionally oppressive and highly discriminatory society.

Yet the gaps between law and implementation remain. THP's own experiences point to four broad 'problematics,'or manifestations of this gap:

(1) *Accountability:* Greater accountability can be achieved if people demand it and there is an effective organization of people. Only the presence of strong pressure groups can instill a sense of accountability, which will then ensure proper use of powers and funds.

(2) *Leadership among people:* In a highly stifling environment where women go through their lives behind *ghoonghats* and caste equations are strongly entrenched, ferreting out true leaders itself is a complex process. Unless conditions nurturing such leadership arc prevalent, those who actually

come to power may lack the vision or the capacity to bring about any concrete development.

(3) *Financial Autonomy:* Panchayats may have intentions but not the means to implement development work in their areas, owing to financial constraints. While this problem is genuine to a certain extent, there is also a tendency by panchayats at the village level to use it as an excuse for inaction. Still, there is scope for fuller utilization of the existing provisions and further legal reforms in this respect, provided there is a mobilization of demand from below.

(4) *Leadership of elected representatives:* The reservation for women in itself does not ensure their voice in a male-dominated society, as elected women leaders often make for 'proxy' representatives. It clearly emerges from the project experience that lack of awareness and information at an individual level poses a serious obstacle to the empowerment process at the societal level. Thus, disseminating information and training of elected representatives becomes an important input in realizing the potential of a favourable legal framework.

The Hunger Project's (THP) Objectives

While THP has, in the past, effectively tried to address the question of leadership among elected women representatives through intensive trainings and workshops, there was limited opportunity to put this acquired knowledge into use. Hence, the project "Mitigating Hunger by Mobilizing Women's Leadership in Panchayati Raj" was envisaged. The project was built on a holistic approach of training elected representatives on the one hand, providing inputs so that they could develop a comprehensive plan for their areas and finally, providing support for implementation of such plans. The objectives of this project were:

- To try to address the problem of food insecurity in rural areas;
- To strengthen the structures of local governance;
- To promote development-oriented leadership among women.

Specifically, the project intended to help people in enlarging their horizon of felt development needs. It also intended to help the Panchayat leadership in developing micro-plans for addressing the livelihood concerns of people. Rather than reduce panchayats to implementing agencies of state and central schemes, the focus was on securing support from the government for the plans developed by the panchayats. The project also specifically targeted women headed panchayats in order to develop the capabilities of the elected women panchayat functionaries.

The Short-term Objectives were:

- Capacity building of elected panchayat functionaries, especially women, to become effective in implementing their roles, by involving them in various training activities;
- Capacity building of women panchayat leaders in the preparation of micro-plans to address the problem of food insecurity and assist them in its implementation;
- To increase awareness among people about various government-sponsored schemes and to facilitate its utilization, with special emphasis on schemes having a direct correlation with food security issues of village families;
- To facilitate formation of various formal and informal groups in the Panchayats to broad-base participation and deliberation over local development issues;
- To document the process of implementation of this project so that the findings could be shared.

Underlying Rationale

The raison d'etre of this project, coinciding with THP's own convictions, was that, to address the problem of hunger, two overarching and interlinked issues must be addressed:

1. Local democracy—ensuring that local people have the resources and the authority to manage programmes to meet their basic needs;
2. Transformation of gender relations—women need to be able to participate as full and equal partners in the process of development and gain a voice in the decisions that affect their lives.

Approach

It was envisaged that the project would be based on credo of "learning by doing", with two basic aims of promoting development-oriented leadership among people who may not have been in leadership positions earlier and to empower people, especially women, by providing them support to use their capabilities.

This would involve:

- Regular training of the elected women leaders to develop their skills required in preparing micro plans;
- Providing a space to put these skills to use through implementation of these plans, imparting skills of budgeting, maintaining accounts, records, reports and documentation and supporting self-help groups and community based organizations in the panchayats so that they become a platform for voicing social issues;
- Providing a monetary contribution to meet some basic aspects of the plan through NGOs on behalf of the panchayats, so that issues unresolved by the state government may also be taken care of.

It was also anticipated that increasing awareness, participation and providing a space to put the knowledge and skills acquired to use - all important components of this project - would automatically ensure that the benefits of this initiative would endure long after its official duration would come to an end.

Potentials

Potential areas of work during the course of this project were identified as follows:

- Enhancing the role of panchayats in pasture land and agriculture development;
- Promotion of self-help groups through training and support in their institutionalization;
- Raising awareness levels among people on the existence of various schemes implemented by the panchayats and

ensuring people's participation in the proper selection of beneficiaries; and

- Mobilizing people's demands to ensure proper delivery of existing schemes and services provided by the government such as primary health care, primary education etc.

Proposed outcome/outputs

The proposed outputs of the project were:

- — Preparation of resource maps and micro plans by each partner panchayat;
- — Implementation of a component of these micro-plans by NGOs on behalf and under the supervision of the panchayats;
- — Creation of community based groups and self-help groups;
- — Training and workshops for the panchayat leaders, SHGs, field workers etc;
- — A process documentation report on each site;
- — Increase in participation of people in various panchayat activities;
- — Increase in utilization of various social security schemes implemented by the panchayat; and
- — Dissemination of the project's learning in a workshop.

The Intended Outcomes of this Project were:

- — Increase in awareness among people about the functioning of the panchayat;
- — Increased ability of the village community to critically appraise their development problems;
- — Increase in skills of panchayat leaders to plan for development of the village and in being to implement these plans;
- — Increase in confidence of panchayat leaders, especially women leaders;
- — Enhancement in status of women panchayat functionaries as able panchayat leaders;
- — Increase in accountability of the panchayat leaders to the village community;

— Increased ability of village community to leverage support from various development agencies of the state; and

— Strengthening of democratic traditions in the village etc.

Sequence of Activities

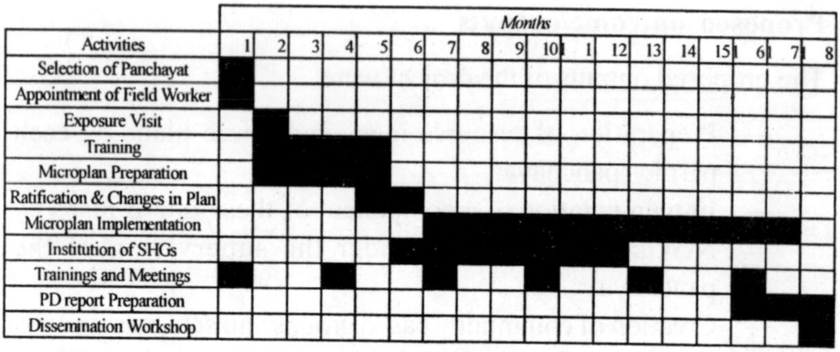

Chart 8.1: Gant Chart of Key Activties

Budget

Table 8.1: Project Budget (per panchayat)

Main Head	*Amount (Rs.)*
Exposure Visit	8000
Trainings and Meetings	50000
Tot on Micropalning	25000
Microplan preparation	35000
Support for Plan Implementation	100000
Salary of Field Worker	108000
Process Documentation	12000
Support Costs of NGOs	36000
Total (per panchayat)	374000

The Starting Point

In May 2002, it was finalized that three non-governmental organizations—Seva Mandir, Udaipur, PEDO, Mada and Urmul Setu Sansthan, Lunkaransar-would participate as partners for the proposed project. In the same month, the panchayat or area of work was arrived at by each of the NGOs through a process of discussion and elimination. Accordingly, the panchayats chosen by the three NGOs were respectively—Alisgarh, Girwa block (Udaipur district), Pal Maodi, Bichiwada block (Dungarpur district) and Makdasar, Lunkaransar block (Bikaner district). Broadly, the guiding criteria for selecting these panchayats were that: it had to be headed by a woman, her family environment (especially her husband) had to be supportive of her participation in this project and the NGO had to have a reasonably good relationship with the panchayat.

The Documentation Report

Need for a Documentation Report

One of the specified objectives of this project was to prepare an on-site process documentation report on the experiences of the three panchayats during the course of the project's implementation. Provided it is done meticulously, process documentation is a rich source of information, vital for understanding the final outcomes of any intervention. Process documentation throws considerable light on many aspects of the plan, which might not have been taken into account while originally visualizing the project. Thus it can prove critical in further planning and refining of existing approaches.

In addition to these reasons, and in the specific context of this project, a consolidated process documentation report was thought of to juxtapose the varied experiences of the three panchayats. It was perceived that this would help in finding common ground, if any, and at the same time sift out specific factors that have taken each of these panchayats in directions as varied as the outcomes reveal.

Objectives

The main objectives of this report are:

- To capture in detail, the processes that went to influence the outcomes at every stage of this project in the three chosen panchayats,
- To recognize and learn from both processes - those leading to positive outcomes and those which were disruptive,
- To understand and analyze the underlying dynamics that

played an imperative role in shaping these results, and

— To try and build a direction for the future based on these crucial learnings.

Outline

This report is organized around four parts. The first three examine in detail the evolutionary processes shaping the outcomes in each of the three panchayats for the duration of this project. In the final section, a comparative critique is presented with an attempt to visualize some critical pointers for the future.

It remains to be mentioned here that this documentation report is based on information provided by the individual NGOs as well as visits to the three panchayats, discussions with panchayat members and residents, key field persons and NGO representatives by the writer of this report. The documentation maintained by the field offices varied both in detail and form, having a direct bearing on the depth of descriptions of each process in this report. Sketchy documentation proved a serious limitation in some cases. This was especially true of Pal Mahodi Panchayat in Dungarpur. Any errors or biases transpiring in this account hence should not be construed as intentional, but the result of scarce information. There may be many positive outcomes, which have also been missed out on, as a result. Secondly, the writer was unable to verify all the information provided in the individual documentations and has based this report accepting them at their face value. The report may hence not be totally free of individual biases.

Alsigarh Panchayat, Udaipur

A Brief Profile

Situated in Girwa Block of Udaipur district, Alsigarh Panchayat is located in a picturesque hilly terrain predominantly inhabited by *adivasis* or scheduled tribes called *Meenas*. A snapshot of the *Panchayat* is provided in the table below:

Table 8.2: Profile of Alsigarh Panchayat

Panchayat Detail	*Description*
Name	Alsigarh
Location	25 kms from Udaipur City, Girwa Block, Udaipur District
Population	5246 (2001 Census)
Number of families*	982
Sex Ratio (female:male)	922:1000
Revenue Villages	Alsigarh, Aad, Popalti
Phallas	*Alsigarh* :Kheriya, Khatiya, Kada, Damliya, Naal, Wada *Aad:* Upla, Kaltiya, Nichala, Malakad *Popalti* : Rohi, Limbda, Bidra, Bhavdi, Hamelghati, Ambavala, Pannakat, Phanda
Number of Wards	13
Number of Wards reserved for Women	4
Major Castes	Meenas: Kharwad, Parki, Rodat
Land Ownership/Type (%)	State Government:25%, Panchayat:6%, Departments:3%, Forests: 42%, Private: 24%
Main Occupations	Agriculture, Livestock, Labour
Agriculture - Main Crops	*Kharif:* Maize, Jowar, Rice *Rabi* : Wheat, Mustard, Channa
Physical Infrastructure	Wells: 226, of which 108 are working.
	Anicuts: 5
	Roads: There are either kucha or pucca roads in most phallas. But they are very inconvinient and in most cases unfit for plying vehicles.
	Electricity: Available in some phallas and very few houses.
Social Infrastructure	Schools: Primary or *shikshakarmi* in most phallas.
	Anganwadis: In some phallas like Kheriya, Damliya Health center: In Bidra, Damliya phallas
Elected Representatives	Sarpanch: Mirabai
	Up-Sarpanch/Ward panch no:11: Veerjiba
	Ward panches (1-13): Punakibai, Kanhaiyalal, Varkibai, Dharam, Homa, Dhanna, Lalu, Baira, Dalu, Chowklibai, Veerji, Rama, Kankudi.

Source: for this table are from an earlier study of Seva Mandir and the microplan.
* does not include Wada phalla.

The Process

As Pratap Mote, the field worker in charge of this project appointed by Seva Mandir, would go on to discover during the course of this project, the complex equations between the panchayat members and the region's 'kingpins' would prove the greatest stumbling block in forming any kind meaningful alliance to take the project's objectives forward. Yet, the process succeeded in a short span to touch people, create visible changes in personalities of women, provide sustainable solutions to livelihood problems and cause a flutter in well-entrenched political equations…

Strategies for Implementation

Preparing the Ground

In the month of May, Pratap visited all the *phallas* in the panchayat and focused on constant interaction and explanation of the project idea to the people. This included:

- Phalla-wise meetings with residents: Documentation of these initial *phalla* meetings revealed the people's varied perceptions and attitudes towards the panchayat's working. It appeared that physical distance from the panchayat headquarters played an important role in the awareness level in different phallas. In Popalti the revenue village situated furthest from Alsigarh, or Naal, a *phalla* in Alsigarh situated deep in the forests, people almost never attended gram sabhas. The women had no knowledge of what it meant and when asked the name of the sarpanch, they mentioned her husband's name.

  Secondly, there was a sense of disillusionment across *phallas,* since many proposals got written at gram sabhas, but few actually materialised on the ground. Pratap also perceived that the people themselves lacked interest, citing excuses for not actively participating in the panchayat's functioning. In some *phallas* (Wada, Khatiya), their interest in THP's project was confined to what economic benefits it would bring them in terms of work, facilities and money. Topics like women leadership, participation and strengthening the Gram Sabha institution did not enthuse them in the least bit, although in few *phallas* (Aad), the women showed better responsiveness.

Finally, people also expressed a lack of unity or trust among themselves and between the functionaries. They also articulated that the sarpanch was constantly under pressure from her husband although she repeatedly tried emerging from his shadow.

Right at the start, the presence of disruptive forces became evident. At an interaction with people in Kheriya *phalla,* a few people started making allegations against *Seva Mandir* and the meeting had to be aborted.

- *Attending meetings of the panchayat body*: There were five meetings concerning the panchayat body in the first two months of the project- the quorum meeting on the 6th, which was called off since only three people showed up, the gram sabha on the 20th, a meeting regarding land allotment and two more quorum meetings in June.

The underlying dynamics of Alsigarh panchayat surfaced quite clearly at these interfaces. Documentation on the gram sabha noted that the sarpanch had little say and it was the sarpanch pati Kalu, at the helm of affairs, along with Dhanraj, the ration dealer in Alsigarh. After the meeting, the ward panches handed in their demands and in the entire process, none of the villagers were involved.

The meeting on land distribution on June 4th further clarified the highly oppressive equations between a few 'powerful' people in the panchayat and the rest and its implications for the project. People from Popalti were conveniently 'left out'. The *patwari,* the *sarpanch-pati,* the ration dealer, the MLA, the SDO and the tehsildar all attended the meeting. When people were asked by the MLA to voice any problems they faced, there was silence, whereas only over the previous month they had poured out a list of woes to Pratap.

Pratap's attempts to present the project idea to the MLA and SDO met with a categorical reaction, "if people of the village want it, then we are also for it, if they don't we'll have to drive you out". One of them alleged that "these organizations only cause trouble, they have 'Delhi connections' etc." Then they turned to the gathering and warned them to think of whether or not they wanted to "keep these people (i.e, the NGO)".

In the quorum meeting that followed next day, a similar show of power was exercised, this time by *sarpanchpati* and the *sachiv*. Decisions to formulate new proposals on development work such as *medbandhi,* tree planting, digging works etc were done without any participation from the women present. Pratap checked the proposal register only to discover that there were items recorded in it, which never really took place in that forum. The meeting ended with a closed door *tête-à-tête* between the sachiv and each ward panch.

By the time of the second quorum meeting in the month, it was evident that Pratap's presence at these gatherings was being resented. The meeting was poorly attended and there were no satisfactory answers to the questions posed by the women ward panch or the sarpanch. The proposals were written entirely by the sachiv, who did not even read them out at the end.

- *Dialogue with the local political representatives and administration:* On the face of it, the sarpanch and her husband appeared co-operative during initial discussions about the project. The reactions of the ward panches were mixed - some showed initiative in moblising people in their wards, while some women panches remained suppressed by their husbands. On the whole, the sachiv was not comfortable with Seva Mandir's presence in the panchayat, although he later shared with Pratap how he had become a victim of the 'system'.

Trainings and Exposure Visits

Frequent trainings and visits to other panchayats was an in-built component of this project. In Alsigarh, these took place in the specified frequency. Following a one-day orientation in Alsigarh itself, a two-day workshop was conducted around mid-June at the Kaya training center. Twenty-nine people including the sarpanch and 10 ward panches participated. The project objectives and process, status of women importance of community based organizations, problem identification, role of panchayat in ensuring livelihoods, presentation of a previous study on Alsigarh panchayat, formation of self-help groups and the powers and responsibilities of Panchayati Raj Institutions were discussed at the training session. This was followed by an exposure visit to PEDO, Mada, in Dungarpur district, where the participants saw for themselves the working of self-help groups (SHGs) in this area.

A three day training on micro-planning was organised in August, for which external resource persons were called. This was followed-up by trainings to review the microplans in October. Other possible livelihood sources like *safed musli* farming, goatery, cattle and dairy farming and natural resource development were introduced to the particpants at this forum. End-October, a review of the work impelmented in all three panchayats under this project was organised in Badgaon, attended by the sarpanches and wars panches from the three locations.

A training took place in November for women SHGs on small scale activities like soap making, grain bank, agarbathi making, washing powder, dholi musli and goat rearing. Information on government schemes, the meaning and importance of savings groups were also discussed. Women were taken to an exposure visit to Prayantna Samiti, an NGO in Salumbar block, Udaipur district, to see the functioning of grain banks that have been operational for the last two years.

In December, a workshop of farmers growing *safed musli* in different blocks of Udaipur took place, where farmers from Alsigarh also participated.

Thus trainings were regularly organised to orient women towards income generating activities, and once taken up, they were given specific knowledge inputs such as on safed musli and marigold farming in the last quarter of this project.

Formation of Committees

As decided in the workshop, ward-level committees were constituted in July. Each committee comprised 6 people—3 men and 3 women including the ward panch. The main role of the committees was to co-ordinate the project within their respective wards, involve people, undertake development work and iron out any hiccups arising in its course. The outcomes of these committees in reality varied greatly with their original purpose and this is discussed in a later section.

Formation of SHGs

The exposure visit to PEDO, Mada gave the impetus to form 6 new SHGs in Alsigarh panchayat in the month of July. The status of SHGs, however, considerably evolved during the subsequent months, and the final outcome will be discussed in a later section (see "The Outcomes").

Film Shows

Appealing to visual aids, film shows were an important part of Seva Mandir's strategy to create awareness in people. Films like *Sanshodhan, Pratiksha and Manthan* were regularly screeend in different *phallas*, which spanned issues relating to women's struggles, health and Panchayati Raj. The impact of this was particularly visible in the Janurary 26th, 2003 gram sabha where women from Bidra, Hamelghati and Ambaghati *phallas* vociferously demanded a school in their area.

Microplanning

Besides dialoging with *phalla* residents on the specific problems in their *phallas*, a questionnaire was filled in to obtain an idea of the various livelihood-related issues faced by the people. Questions relating to landholding, production of various crops, yields, labour obtained, other income, consumption and expenditure were included and information was collected pertaining to a good year and a bad year. Excess of expenditure over income was explained through factors like other income, overstatement of expenses etc.

Subsequent to the August training on microplanning, phalla-wise microplanning was carried out. On an average, around 25 people turned up in each *phalla*. By September, this had been done in all except Wada and Kaltiya *phallas*. The table below gives the format of the microplan while the detailed plan itself and its outcomes are presented in Annexure 1:

From the first round of microplanning where 215 people participated on the whole, the main problem that emerged was that

Table 8.3: Format of the Microplan

1. Panchayat Details
Village names and phallas
Number of wards
Population details
Resources: wells, anicuts, forest land, pastureland
Agriculture: kharif and rabi
Occupation
Facilities: schools, anganwadis, roads, health centre
Problem ranking in each phalla and prioritisation by women and men
Discussion of solutions and people's contribution
2. Ward wise /Phalla wise Microplanning
Number of people who attended the microplanning exercise: men and women
Family and population details
Wells/anicuts etc
Land
Road
School
Dai
Balwadi
Savings groups
Other organisations present in the panchayat
Jobs - govt, private etc
Women's problems
Men's problems
Women's routine
Women's diseases
Expectations/Proposals
3. Future strategy for intervention
Meeting with each ward to finalise what interventions they needed
Study of wards by technical people to find out the most needy among them
Study of the families in each ward
Proper cost estimates
Finalising contribution of people and completion of legal formalities.

Table 8.4: Prioritzation of Needs

Name of the Phalla/Village	*First priority*	*Second Priority*	*Third Priority*
Kheriya	Water		
Katiya	Cattleshed	Water, Health	Labor
Naal	Foodgrain	Water, TBA	Milk
Aad	Water		
Rohi-Limbda	Water, labor		
Bhadavi-Bidra	Water		
Dambliya	Cattleshed	Water	Electricity, Medbandhi
Kada	Labor, Health Centre	Water, Foodgrain, Cattle Hospital	

of water. The table above sets out the priorities defined by the residents of each *phalla:*

According to Pemaram Patel of *Seva Mandir*, difficulty in mobilizing people in certain *phallas* like Kaltiya and Wada, where even the microplanning could not be accomplished, could be attributed to many reasons. For one, there is a fear owing to past experiences that NGOs may turn out to be tricksters. Secondly, he feels that a high degree of corruption prevalent among certain circles within the panchayat implies that such people become indifferent once they realize that there is no scope for making easy money. In places like Naal, factors like low information reach, bitterness towards NGOs and lack of motivation to get organized played an important role.

Implementation

Decision-making Process

Economic Activity

With the main priorities of the panchayat becoming explicit, internal discussions at *Seva Mandir* veered around the view that working in all wards would be problematic. It was felt that a better strategy would be to start with one *phalla.* Among the possible works that could be undertaken, well deepening, grain bank and growing water-saving plants were suggested. It was also decided that the microplans should be presented at the Gram Sabha, and the future course of action be decided with involvement of the people and a meeting of all stakeholders.

For the rest of September, Pratap initiated a series of meetings at Kada, Dambliya, Rohi Limbda, Kheriya, Pannakat and Kaltiya. This was done to elicit solutions from the people for the problems identified by them, to inform and mobilize them for the Gram Sabha to be held on 2nd October .

In these meetings, the overwhelming solution proposed was well-deepening. Many people came forward to get their private wells deepened and costs were estimated. However, the politics of well deepening became all too evident and arguments as to whose well should be deepened became the heated focus. People also expressed dissatisfaction that most of the proposals which had come were from committee members or certain influential people in that *phalla.*

By January, when people had finally zeroed in on which wells would benefit, some glitches still remained. For instance, in Pannakat *phalla,* local enmity between two neighbours Phula and Poonja led to a conflict since the well deepening had been planned on Phula's private land and he feared its misuse once the deepening was over. Some people also felt that this was not worth implementing since every 4-5 people had a well, so deepening would benefit only that many. Finally, the entire idea was abandoned.

Besides well-deepening, in some *phallas* like Dambliya and Kada, women evinced interest in taking up activities like dholi musli farming, vegetable farming soap making and so on.

The interest in *dholi musli* farming also materialised in May, after a training session was organised on how to grow the crop, water and fertiliser usage etc. About 50 women came forward to try this out initially. The training on soap making however, did not see the light of day. According to Pratap, this involved some effort in collecting the *ratanjot* seeds from the forests, which the women were not willing to take. Similar was the case with goat rearing and *agarbathi* making.

The trainings in November on various small scale activities and exposure visits translated on the ground in the form of a grain bank in Aad, under the initiative of the women SHG in this village. The participants' contribution and the rules of the grain bank were clearly set out in a meeting in January.

Even as the protracted discussions on the use of funds went

on, Seva Mandir made simultaneous and continuous efforts to form SHGs, disseminate information on various schemes available at the panchayat and mobilize people to take greater responsibility in the panchayat's affairs. The process of participation - both by panchayat members and the local residents of Alsigarh - over the duration of this project took interesting twists, hitting highs and lows, driven by the underlying dynamics in the villages.

Gram Sabhas

There were five Gram Sabhas held in Alsigarh during the eighteen month period - May 20th, 2002, August 15th, 2002, October 2nd, 2002, January 26th, 2003 and May 1, 2003.

The evidence of non-participation in the Gram Sabha in May 2002 and oppressive behaviour of the sarpanch pati and the ration dealer have already been noted in an earlier section.

In a sense, the Gram Sabha in August was a contrast. Participation showed a marginal rise and the proceedings reflected a higher awareness level among the people and even a certain degree of empowerment. The women, especially, spoke up with confidence on issues like lack of transperancy in the panchayat accounts. Following Seva Mandir's information campaign on PDS, people had also questioned the practices of the ration dealer; indeed a bold step given that he wielded considerable power over the residents.

The high point of this Gram Sabha was an incident concerning Dharam, ward panch of ward number 4. As the Gram Sabha was going on, he started flipping through the pages of the register on which proposals were written down and signatures taken. He noticed that people had been made to sign at the end of a few blank pages. In objection to this, he struck out the blank pages and put his own signature at the end. This act of his created a furore at the meeting, with the sarpanch pati, ration dealer and many others joining in admonishing him for his deed. Not one from the gathering present dared to speak in favour of the ward panch. While a public apology was demanded from him and allegations charged against Seva Mandir "for leading people the wrong way", people agreed in private that the ward panch had done the right thing.

Perhaps the only silver lining was the final outcome of this entire incident - in the next Gram Sabha on October 2nd, signatures were taken only at the end of the meeting.

However, this Gram Sabha reflected disturbing signs in more ways than one. The participation had drastically dropped (there were only around 25 people including officials according to Pratap's documentation), although the sarpanch attributed this to the ongoing *Gowri* festival. The sabha was totally devoid of the flash of courage displayed by Dharam the previous time and the initial signs of confidence expressed by the rest. In this Gram Sabha, people just came, put forth their demands and left; confining any sort of questioning to the minimal. Pratap percieved that there had been some pressure since the last Gram Sabha—the women ward panches did not speak and the sarpanch did not have any specific agenda. The Gram Sabha took place without fulfilling the required quorum, yet no one questioned how and instead mutely signed on the register.

Seva Mandir's Work and Progress on the Project was also Presented at this Gram Sabha

It is significant in this context to note the sarpanchpati's allusion to Seva Mandir's work on this day. Making a comparison in purely monetary terms, he declared that "Seva Mandir cannot do anything with 1 lakh - whereas the panchayat has spent 22 lakh".

The gram sabha on January 26th, 2003 outperformed the one in August both in terms of participation and empowerment levels displayed. There were 350 people at the sabha, as opposed to 50-80 in the previous ones. The various issues discussed included relief works, mid-day meal scheme, *Shiksha Apke Dwar programme,* other government schemes, panchayat savings groups, women's problems, Antyodaya, Annapurna, birth and death registration, Jalgrahan scheme and the progress on the project front. Women were the most vociferous on corruption in relief work schemes, issue of rotational labour, distribution of ration cards under the *Antyodaya* and *Annapurna* and incorrect below poverty line (BPL) list. The highlight of this gram sabha was the confidence with which women belonging to the groups in Hamelghati and Ambaghati demanded that the new Rajiv Gandhi Patshala be opened in their phalla instead of in Limbda, where one already existed. They had even come with a written proposal which they submitted to the gram sachiv. Throughout the Gram Sabha, there were disruptive elements who tried to suppress those articulating their problems or bringing to light corruptive practices, but this did not deter the women from speaking their minds.

The May 1st, 2003 Gram Sabha, attended by about 125 people, lacked the dynamism of the previous gram sabha, and almost established a pattern whereby any gram sabha demonstrating people's awareness was ensued by a one where villagers were passive, showing signs of subjugation. In total contrast to the January gram sabha again, people started leaving by 1.00 p.m whereas proposals were written down by the sachiv till 4.00 p.m, by when only a few remained.

No gram sabha took place on August 15th, 2003. It was said that the idea of having gram sabhas on pre-determined dates, coinciding with an officially declared 'Day' (like Independence Day/ Gandhi Jayanti etc) had been done away with, since the adminsitrative officers had to take part in many functions on such days and hence found it difficult to attend gram sabhas. Another explanation being offered was that, being close to the assembly elections, the government was not keen that gram sabhas took place, lest the public exposed them in a bad light.

Ward Sabhas

Available documentation on participation in Ward Sabhas shows that it remained at a low level with the Sabhas being held many a time without fulfilment of the quorum. This was true throughout the duration of this project. In all the ward sabhas which took place in the month of September, for instance, the participation ranged from as low as 6 to 18. Those on the higher side were joint ward sabhas of at least two wards. Villagers from Naal and Kaltiya *phallas* were as usual, non-participants. This was also the time when the Gowri was going on.

Six months down the line nothing much had visibly changed. Pratap, who had been banned from attending quorum meetings by the Sachiv in February, now had to rely on information doled out by people as to the ward sabha dates. In his documentation, he reports how the *sarpanchpati* and a few ward panches misled him. On March 22nd, he met a wardpanch, Dharma of Popalti, who informed him that there was a ward sabha to take place that day in his village. Only a week ago, Pratap had met the sarpanch, who told him that there were no ward sabhas these days, and they would be organised after Holi. He came to know through Dharma, however, that there had been one on the very day he spoke to the sarpanch, and there were three more scheduled in a span of about 10 days. It was clear that the sarpanch pati and a few others had begun to detest his involvement in the affairs of the panchayat.

When Pratap went to the venue of the ward sabha that day, the *sarpanchpati* and the *sachiv* were surprised to see him. Dhanraj, the ward *panchpati* who was bitter about the Rajiv Gandhi school episode, is reported to have turned to the *sarpanchpati,* his eyes on Pratap, saying, "give me the permission to beat up people who do wrong things".

Despite being a joint ward sabha of all 4 wards in Popalti. There were only 10 people present that day. The ward panches put up their demands without a complete quorum or any participation for that matter.

It was a similar event at the joint ward sabha for wards 4 and 7 in Kheriya. Although people fully agreed with Pratap who explained the objectives of ward sabhas, quorums etc. to those present, his efforts had little impact on improving their capacity to reflect, confront and question. They simply kept mum about the fact that the very ward sabha they were attending did not fulfil the quorum.

Quorum meetings

Meetings of the panchayat body, too, often did not take place due to a lack of a quorum. Ward panches did not come due to many reasons, sometimes they simply did not recieve information as to when or where the meeting would be held. The Sachiv didn't come sometimes if he had to attend other meetings at the *Panchayat Samiti.* The sarpanch occasionally did not make an appearance for no apparent reason, and her husband attended it as her 'proxy'.

Informal talks with ward panches highlighted the problem of lack of unity among them. Subtler equations between the ward panches and the sarpanch (pati), local politicians and the administrative powers - all determined who said what in the meetings and outside them. There were, however, some encouraging signs, too. In a quorum meeting where the topic of discussion centered around opening of a *Samudayik Bhawan* and education centre in the panchayat, the sarpanch pati was not very pleased with the suggestion to use the already existing *Samudayik Bhawan* building in Kaltiya. The reason: it was serving as his son's study and his private storage space. But at the end, it was the people's opinion that prevailed.

Growing resentment towards Pratap's participation in the panchayat activities culminated in a ban on his presence at quorum meetings. In one such meeting in February, the *Sachiv* turned to Pratap and categorically told him that he could not attend the quorum meetings any more. Significantly, none of the ward panches or people present reacted to this.

Other Meetings

Pratap relied on continuous dialogue with people in the phallas throughout the project period to give direction and shape to the project. However, in certain wards, it proved extremely difficult to bring people together. This was especially true of Kaltiya and Naal *phallas.* While Kaltiya people showed no interest right from the start, participation in Naal fizzled out after the microplan was drawn out. People had to be coaxed into attending the meetings and still, everytime, the response was luke-warm. According to Pratap, people did not percieve any direct economic benefits from this project. Secondly, Jalgrahan, which had a stronghold in Naal, seemed to resent Seva Mandir's presence in what they presumed as 'their' area of work. The Jalgrahan leader reportedly told Pratap that he need not come to this *phalla* any more. Since none of the people particularly objected to this, Naal fell out of the project area.

Another reason for the erratic involvement of people was the fact that the drought had taken on horrifying proportions by that time. Relief work proved to be the only succor in this situation and attendance for meetings dwindled once relief works started. Still, it was attempted to organise meetings on dates which were official holidays for relief work. Pratap was told that people did not attend them in spite of this, since these were the only days they got to do their other work or take rest. Those who were not employed on relief work also had an excuse - they were busy thinking of what to do for a livelihood.

In spite of all these difficulties, the women in Popalti and Aad emerged showing positive signs of empowerment by the end of this project. Meetings to discuss the opening of a balwadi or a school were well attended by the women, who also showed much initiative in flagging the issues in the gram sabha and following it up. Moreover, they also resolved conflicts within their wards on issues such as who should run the balwadi and where, without bowing to pressure exerted from the more 'powerful' people. Women in Bidra also reacted on hearing that a balwadi was being planned in Hamelghati (and not in their *phalla*), and reproached themselves to show more unity in the future.

Self-Help Groups (SHGs)

Formation of SHGs was a concious strategy adopted by Seva Mandir to mobilise women at the grassroot level. Although many new SHGs were formed in Alsigarh panchayat consequent to the exposure visit to PEDO, Mada, some of them ran into rough weather, as described below. According to the NGO, this could be the manifestation of pressure from the menfolk, lack of understanding of the potential social impact such SHGs could have, lack of time or commitment to attend meetings regularly especially during the drought months and in some cases, lack of discipline to make regular savings and loan repayments. Some of the problematic groups were:

Pannakat

After repeated meetings to sort out why the savings group in Pannakat was not functioning properly, it was decided to dissolve the group. The women expressed that they did not understand the concept of the SHG properly, they were not saving regularly, did not have the support of their husbands and so on. The earlier experiences with an organisation which had fled away with their money made them even harder to convince. It may be recalled that Pannakat was where the dispute regarding well-deepening had also occurred. The end result was that no work got implemented in this *phalla*, in spite of the efforts put in by women like Homlibai to mobilise the people here.

Bidra

There were hurdles in the working of the SHGs in this *phalla* and Ambaghati but it was difficult to pinpoint the reasons for this. Successive meetings were called to thrash out a solution. There was hope, however, that the SHG would work since this *phalla* had shown good unity from the start.

Rohi-Limbda

In Rohi-Limbda, too, the women had difficulties in comprehending how an SHG works and were not conducting meetings properly. It was decided that some rules of penalty would be fixed if people paid late or did not save. The problem in this *phalla* also concerned the ward panch Chowklibai herself, who was trying to break the group. She claimed that the women were not keen on continuing as a group, and that Seva Mandir had not made any financial contribution on their part. Chowklibai had borrowed Rs. 1000 and returned only an interest of Rs. 60. When Seva Mandir people had pointed out that repayments should be made properly, she resented it. Another reason that she and her husband Dhanraj were bitter about Seva Mandir was due to the fact that women from Bidra had spoken out against setting up a school in her ward. Allegations had also been made in the same Gram Sabha that there were some malpractices in relief work in her ward. Finally, this SHG also had to be closed.

Yet, the formation of SHGs did have some positive imapct, in places where it was well-understood and the women were committed. The January 26th Gram Sabha where SHG women were among those who spoke assertively, stands testimony to this.

An intensive review to understand the problems plauging the SHGs was also conducted in September 2003. This proved useful and since then, the SHGs showed improvement in functioning.

Use of Funds

The economic costs incurred for this project can be summarised in the tables below:

Table 8.5: Budgetted amount and use of funds under the major heads (May 1, 2002—October 31, 2003)

Head	*Budgetted (Rs.)*	*Actual (Rs.)*
Exposure Visit	8000	10083
Training and Meetings	50000	44598
TOT on Microplanning	25000	10725
Preparation of Microplan	35000	1367
Support for Plan Implementation*	100000	47487
Process Documentation	12000	2500
Honorarium for Field Worker	108000	102872
Support Costs for NGO	36000	0
Total	374000	219632

* This amount does not include an estimate of Rs. 86,000 for the proposed construction of a Community Hall in Alsigarh. Thus the total amount spent under this head would actually be to the tune of Rs. 133487

Table 8.6: Detailed use of funds under plan implementation

Sl. Number	*Project*	*Nature of Expenditure*	*Amount incurred (Rs.)*
1	Soap Making	Training	526
2	Flower Cultivation	Training	200
3	Safed Musli Cultivation	Training	656
		Purchase of seeds	43000
		Pesticide & Spray Machine	2000
4	Grain Bank	Foodgrain Drum	500
		Foodgrain	605
5	Community Centre*	Material Cost	86000
Total			133487

*In Progress

Significant aspects in this regard are:

- The funds available were well dispersed among the residents.

- The costs are highly participatory, with equal shares being put in by the people and the NGO. A concious policy of Seva Mandir, this is likely to bring about a higher degree of commitment and responsibility from the people's side.

Dynamics of Interaction

Panchayat and NGO: The choice of Alsigarh for this project was based on earlier associations of the NGO with the sarpanch, who was also the local 'dai' in that area. Besides, Seva Mandir already had a presence in this panchayat, in the field of education and health. However, this relationship evolved considerably in the course of the THP-backed intervention in Alsigarh. Being for the first time, a direct interface with the panchayat and its working, which encouraged people to question the elected representatives and improve their own awareness, it was evident that those who weilded power and misused it, were not happy from the start. Although it appeared that the sarpanch was initially co-operative, her actions often contradicted her words spoken outside her husband's earshot. And in spite of repeated trainings and one-to-one talks, there were few signs of her visibly breaking out of her husband's clutches at least till the end of the project period.

The NGO's relationship with the Ward Panches varied in accordance with their own responsiveness to this project, the panches' perceptions of the NGO and the hold that people 'behind' the panches had over them. In the 'extended' panchayat body, which includes the *patis* of women panches and sarpanch, the NGO was percieved to be a threat to their present domain of power and this often figured as the main reason for resentment. This was only magnified by the panchayat members' equations with 'powerful' people outside this set-up, who acutally called the shots. Finally, there were petty games between the panches, which the NGO found itself in the midst of This also determined whether the ward panch would be supportive or not of the NGO; as the Rajiv Gandhi school episode and Dhanraj's urge to beat up Pratap revealed. Still, a few women panches emerged at the forefront at the end of this period, bringing some concrete changes to their wards.

The panchayat body and other 'leaders': While the ward

panches or the sarpanch derived certain powers by holding these posts, they were also individuals in a village system that followed its own chain of hierarchy, had its nominated headmen and defined fear and respect for certain kind of people. For example, a ward panch may not be in a position to assert himself if the wrongdoer (say, someone who has encorached on common land) turns out to be a person he has borrowed heavily from.

The traditional political equations also played an important role in ascertaining patterns of behaviour among the Ward Panches or between the Sarpanch and the panches. Usually, it would prove difficult to unite ward panches from traditionally rival parties. In Alsigarh, it became apparent that the ration dealer had strong links with the then MLA from the region, and hence commanded authority over the people, including the *sarpanch pati,* the *sachiv* and some of the ward panches. The documentation frequently refers to the subtle pressures exerted by the ration dealer on the people at gram sabhas or his presence everytime at important meetings along with the *sarpanch pati*.

NGO and other 'leaders': Having positioned itself as a project that aimed at raising awareness, leadership among women and assertion of their rights, the NGO itself faced many obstacles from people who saw them as a menace. The manner in which Pratap was slowly but surely distanced from the panchayat's meetings and blocked in whatever way possible from gaining a knowledge of its working, itself showed that there were forces working both within the panchayat and without, to do away with this threat at any cost.

NGO and people: The NGO's involvement of the people in all three villages was considerable and appreciable. In general, people's awareness of the project was high and the field worker had established a good rapport with the people, including the women.

Sarpanch and women: There did not appear to be any special rapport between the sarpanch and other women in the panchayat. The sarpanch's own neighbour, Limbdibai mentioned that no one really trusted her and gave examples of how many panchayat schemes had been misused by the sarpanch's family entirely to their benefit. The sarpanch is also not a member of any of the SHGs formed by Seva Mandir.

The Outcomes

Tangibles

The main tangible outcomes of this project in Alsigarh may be captured in a nutshell as below:

Table 8.7: Tangible Outcomes in Alsigarh Panchayat

Village	*Ward No:*	*Name of Hamlet*	*Implemented Activity*
Alsigarh	1,2,3	Khatiya	Safed Musli Farming Marigold Farming Community Centre (Well Deepening) (Farm Bunding) (NFE Centre)
	4,7	Kheriya	Marigold Farming Safed Musli Farming (Farm Bunding)
	8	Damliya	SHG
	9	Kada	Safed Musli Farming SHG
Aad	5 6	Malakad Upla Aad	Safed Musli Farming Grain Bank SHG Marigold Farming Community Centre
Popalti	10	Rohi & Limbada	SHG (Farm Bunding)
	11		(Farm Bunding)
	12	Bidra, Hamelghati, Ambaghati	SHG Marigold Farming Safed Musli Farming (Farm Bunding) (NFE Centre) (Balwadis)
	13	Pannakat & Fanda	SHG

It is important here to specify two things. There were many activities that were planned but not implemented. This includes soap making, *agarbatti* making, goat rearing and charnot development. The reasons for non-implementation are clearly set out in table 8.9, in the section "Key Observations and Learnings".

Table 8.8: Costs and Benefits at a Glance

Project Description	*Location*	*NGO's Contribution*	*People's Contribution*	*Employment Generated*	*Number of days/labourer*	*Outcome (Current and Long Term)*
Safed Musli Cultivation	Kheriya Khatiya Malakad, Popalti	Rs. 43000	Rs. 43000	51 Women	Self-employment	Women are expected to make between Rs. 2000 and Rs 10,000, depending on the amount sown in the first year. Being a cash crop, this activity can potentially result in large future gains. Assured livelihood means in the long run implies their economic independence with significant effects on empowerment.
Marigold Farming	Kheriya Khatiya, Upla Aad, Amba ghati, Hamel Ghati	Rs. 200 towards training	Rs. 200 (being equal contribution from people) and sourcing of seeds by themselves.	4 groups 42 women in total	self-employmemt	Women have earned as much as Rs. 8000 by selling flowers this year. A crop which requires less investment and hence, a potentially viable long term source of livelihood, with similar implications for empowerment as above.
Grain Bank	Aad	Rs. 500+110 kgs of wheat	500+131.25 kg of com	21 women	n.a	Important step towards ensuring food security in this phalla. Also, likely to be a source of empowerment and organisation as women get together and discuss many issues, manage the bank etc.
Community	Khatiya	Rs. 86000 (cost of material+ karigari's wages)	Labour for *veldari*, digging the foundation, collecting stones and other labour involed	n.a n.a		Current employment generation and building for community activities in the *phalla*.
HGs	Damliya Kada, Upla Aad, Bidra Hamel-ghati Amba-ghati	Training in setting up SHGs, continuous support and sortng out of difficulties in initial slages.	n.a	116 women in table in the 6 groups formed during the project time period	n.a	If run properly, a powerful economic tool in reducing dependence on usurious moneylenders. Potentially, it can inculcate strong financial discipline. On linking with the formal financial sector in future, SHGs can expand the menu of livelihood options available to women. Organisation of women around issues may strengthen their roie as agents of change.

Secondly, while the amount available through THP for plan impementation was mainly used in five areas—*dholi musli* farming, marigold farming, training for soap making, grain bank and building of community centre, Seva Mandir also took separate initiatives in furthering development work in the panchayat during the same period. This included farm bunding funded by Hindustan Zinc Ltd and opening of balwadis and non-formal education centres, marked in the table in parentheses.

The above table clearly sets out the spread and participatory nature of the projects undertaken. It can be noted that:

- The activities undertaken were small-scale and sustaining, with potential of improving the earning capacity and livelihoods of people in the long run.
- Most of the beneficiaries are women, which implies that these activities could prospectively empower them financially—an important step towards emancipation.

Formation of SHGs was an important startegic component of the project. Although the SHGs faced hiccups in functioning (as decribed in section "Implementation"), it is reported that problematic groups have been revived. The status of the SHGs as of the end of this project period may be set out as follows:

Table 8.9: Position of SHGs as of end-October, 2003

Name/Location of SHG	*Number of Members*	*Savings/Member/ Month*	*Total Savings(Rs)*
Kheriya-A	20	20	5380
Kheriya-B	15	10	4550
Kheriya-C	16	10	5826
Khatiya-A	27	20	4804
Khatiya-B	18	20	3898
Mahadev Damliya	20	20	2651
Lakshmi Aad	21	10	3480
Kada	15	20	3100
Bidra Popalti	20	10	1600
Hamelghati Popalti	20	25	6021
Ambaghati Popalti	20	10	2420
Rohi Limbda Popalti		*Stared, but dissolved*	
Pannakat Popalti		*Stared, but dissolved*	
Total	212		43730

Intangibles

Among the intangible outcomes, the following deserve mention:

Increase in awareness: Although this was not uniform throughout the panchayat, information dissemination resulted in visible empowerment among people who chose to be receptive to it. This included both women ward panches and women residents in certain *phallas*. The January 26th Gram Sabha, where women spoke confidently about issues like corruption, or decisions regarding where to open a school, is definitely a manifestation of this.

Leadership: The project provided an opportunity for people to break out of conventional systems and fears. Those who had the courage to 'defy' abused authority, like ward panch Dharam in the August 15th gram sabha, showed all the potential to emerge as a eader. Whether these people continue to fight despite tremendous pressure, however, remains to be seen.

Organisation of women: The formation of SHGs is yet to make a significant impact in tackling social problems in the panchayat. On the other hand, the creation of a grain bank entirely through women's initiative is a pointer to how mobilising women around issues that connect to deeply-felt needs to start with, may work rather effectively.

Questioning dominant behaviour: The entire approach of the NGO which stressed on people's involvement and persistently raising awareness levels has had one very significant impact - that of disturbing people who misuse power. Banning Pratap from attending panchayat meetings or threatening to beat him up, are, in fact, positive signs that people in the wrong were getting antagonized. While in the short run, this might have disrupted the progress of the project, it appears that pursuing such a strategy may lead to much richer long term pay-offs.

Key Observations and Learnings

In the entire process of this project in Alsigarh, certain crucial factors have played a role in its evolution. An understanding of these 'givens' is an important step in comprehending why a process took a certain path, in identifying sources of problems or recognising certain inherent characteristics that brought about positive outcomes:

NGO's approach: Seva Mandir's own approach to its work ensured that, along with training of ward panches and elected representatives of the panchayat, people's participation was given equal importance. Involvement of people at every stage of the project ensured that the entire process was participatory, transpaerant and empowering.

Field workers' motivation: Since one key field worker was made in charge of the project, this implied that much responsibility hinged on that person.The high degree of motivation and perseverance displayed by Pratap certainly went a long way in influencing the positive outcomes of this project. To susbstantiate, Popalti is one village in Alsigarh panchayat which is difficult terrain (it did not have road connectivity until a year ago) and backward in many respects. This village was untouched by any NGO till THP decided to work with the entire panchayat. Any positive developments in this village can thus be definitely attributed to, among other things, the efforts made by the field worker.

Sarpanch's environment: The sarpanch's earlier associations with THP notwithstanding, her immediate environment held sway over her behaviour during this project. It maybe reiterated here that her husband's dominance and the political equations seemed too deeply entrenched for the project to make any visible impact on personality in such a short duration. Her absence at the microplan presentation in Badgaon was evidence to this. Yet, the trainings seemd to have had some impact as she was reasonably well informed about the panchayat schemes and Seva Mandir's work in the panchayat.

Sarpanch's perception of the project: When spoken to in her husband's absence, the sarpanch Meerabai appeared appreciative of Seva Mandir's efforts. The first thing she noted was that "women were earlier not coming to panchayat meetings, now they do and moreover, they speak". In reality, however, it remains difficult to gauge her actual perceptions, since she spoke to the writer of this report in the presence of the Seva Mandir field worker, and in knowledge that whatever she said would go back to THP. The sarpanch pati's perceptions are clear from his comment in the gram sabha—that "Seva Mandir had spent only 1 lakh, while the panchayat had splurged 22 lakh". In fact, this tendency to look at development merely in monetary terms seemed to be so deeply rooted that it prevailed as the predominant mentality across all sections in the panchayat.

Ward members' perceptions: Some ward panches, too, succumbed to this dominamt stream of thought. Some quoted politics as a reason for non-participation (In one of Pratap's meetings with a BJP-affiliated ward panch in Kaltiya phalla, he is quoted to have said that since he was in the opposition, no one would listen to him anyway, if his party won then he could also take part in the project!). In Alsigarh, 4 ward panches (of wards 2,6,12 and 13) are said to be BJP-affiliated while the rest are Congress. A few others, especially women, displayed signs of high receptivity. This is indeed encouraging as it means that providing the right inputs and exposure to certain different ideas can, in itself, work its way through in women's minds. Although the project may not have succeeded in empowering women ward panches in the full sense, it certainly appears to have sowed the seeds.

People's perceptions: People's reactions to a project such as this was as varied as were the reasons. While these have been referred to in different parts of this chapter, it might be worth revisiting them in this section's context. For one, people were, on the whole, more receptive to income generating activities than those which called for organisation around social issues. Even within the former, there was a noticeable preference for individualistic rather (example: well deepening or *dholi musli* farming) than common activity (example: development of pastureland). Secondly, among those who did not wish to participate in this project, two classes of reasons prevailed. One set of them were those who were cynical about the functioning of NGOs in general, and probably justifiably so, since they had not forgotten bitter past experiences. Another set were plain indifferent -they did not percieve any benefits from a project whose main thrust was not economic.

Resistances: The main resistances to this project came in the form of dominant people in the panchayat's environment, who saw its emphasis on increasing people's awareness as a personal threat (Table 8.10 throws more light on this). A second set of resistances,

Table 8.10: Reasons for Non-Implementation of Planned Activities

1. *Kheriya:* Goat rearing training was given, but did not materialise. Since goats had to be taken care of by one person and cannot be kept in one place, it was decided that the women would take this responsibility by turn. In reality, no one came forward.
2. *Khatiya:* For soap making, ratanjoth seeds had to be collected. This plant is available in abundance here. Although training was given, people did not show initiative in collecting these seeds and preferred to buy it from the market. But the seeds are expensive, wiping out any cost advantage, so the idea was abandoned.
3. *Damliya:* People here were unable to undersatnd THP's idea of working with the panchayat. They did not come forward and take responsibilities, nor were the beneficiaries themselves willing to contribute.
4. *Naal:* Microplanning to place but people did not think all this was important and were more concerned with their daily routines. They told the Seva Mandir worker not to come there anymore and waste his time. Another organisation, Jalgrahan, has a stronghold here.
5. *Kada:* Women here were active and willing to participate, obtained the jamabandhi for pastureland developmentbut it turned out that both places they had identified were belanam (this is a land classification which denotes revenue land belonging to the government,usually encroached upon). So it was decided not to work on it. Goat rearing proposals from this phalla were also later withdrawn.
6. *Wada:* Although people initially appeared receptive to the idea, they kept giving dates for preparing the microplan and never turned up. Clearly, they were not interested.
7. *Kaltiya:* Only one woman showed a lot of initiative in trying to organise people here but people seem to lack trust. This belt has an earlier history of one organisation cheating them with false promises of giving work. Hence, a lot of mistrust has creeped up.
8. *Upla:* Grain bank worked out here, but a community center did not. Seva mandir was willing to contribute to material and *karigari* costs and asked people to contribute towards labour, stone and foundation. They were agreeable to this, but were not willing to contribute labour towards taking sand from the road to the actual site of work. Seva Mandir did not have the budget for this either, so this idea was dropped.
9. *Malakad:* Charnot did not materialise since identified area was encroached land.
10. *Rohi-Limbda:* Pastureland was available in this *pahlla* for development, but the ward panch pati of ward no:10 is said to have instructed the patwari not to divulge the *jambandhi* and land records required for this. Repeated efforts to obtain the records came to no avail. The ward panch pati has regularly and openly resisted Seva Mandir's work in this area. The SHG in this phalla also dissolved due to similar reasons.
11. *Pannakat:* A community well was proposed in this *phalla* but a dispute between two neighbours broughtthis effort to naught. Homlibai of this phalla had put in a lot of effort in unifying people here. The SHG here was also dissolved.

from the panchayat's menfolk, resulted from the project's thrust on women empowerment. This was clearly indicated in many instances, including wardpanch Dhanraj's comment that "in 15 years, women from Popalti have never attended gram sabhas, after Sewa Mandir has come, women have been asking questions......... Sewa Mandir should be banned from coming here".

From all these reactions, it was clear that any attempt that questioned the status quo or upset traditionally unchallenged equations would be inevitable if the project objectives had to be met.

Potential Directions—Suggestions from the NGO

The project has reasonably succeeded in creating a momentum among women, who have come forward to implement their learnings in a relatively short period of time. Any future efforts might be channelised in encouraging women who have already shown initiative and mobilising more women in groups. There is also much scope for strengthening bonds beween the sarpanch and the women's groups. So far, there has been no such interaction.

MAHODI PAL PANCHAYAT, DUNGARPUR

A Brief Profile

A snapshot of Mahodi Pal panchayat is provided in the following Table 8.11.

The Process

Bridging the gap between government schemes to ensure food security and employment and people's actual access to it, was PEDO's dominant strategy in meeting the project's objectives. A strategy that might have worked well if the government had been truly responsive, the project ran into rough weather since assurances simply failed to materialise. A deep look at the processes shaping this experiment is inevitable, in order to bring the project back on rails...

Strategies for Implementation

Involvement of ward panches: In the preparatory phase, the NGO worker took part regularly in panchayat meetings during which the

Table 8.11: Profile of Pal Mahodi Panchayat

Panchayat Detail	*Description*
Name	Pal Mahodi
Location	40 kms from Panchayat Samiti H.Q.Bichiwada, 15 kms from Dungarpur city, District Dungarpur
Population	3440
SC Population	3038
Number of families	426
Sex Ratio (female:male)	1019:1000
Number of literates	505
Revenue Villages	Pal Mahodi, Vasuva
Number of Wards	11
Number of Women Ward Panches	5
Major Castes	Adivasis: Katara, Nanoma, Manat, Kharadi, Roth, Kalasua etc.
Total area	1155 hectares
Cultivable area	423 hectares
Main Occupations	Agriculture, Livestock, Labour (Migration to Gujarat)
Agriculture - Main Crops	*Kharif:* Maize, *Urad, Tur, Til, Hamli, Daan, Kodra* *Rabi*: Wheat, Mustard, *Jow, Channa*
Livestock	295 Cows, 14 Bulls, 372 Goats, 97 Hens, 3 Donkeys, 2 Camels
Flora	Sagwan, Timru, Kikar, Bamboo, Hadhod, Kher, Mahua, Mango, Ber, Desi Babool, Peepal, Nilgiri, Khakra, Hitari, Neem, Behda etc.
Physical Infrastructure	No: of Wells:215 (Private), 7(Community) Handpumps: 27 (of which only 6 are functional) River: 1 (Sadri) Canal: 3 Road: Pucca road cuts through the panchayat via Vasuva towards Sasarpur. Kuchcha roads are used to go from one ward to another.
Social infrastructure	Teachers: 6, A.N.M (Nurse): 2, Malaria worker: 1, Ayurvedic Store: 1, Ration Shop:1, NFE Centres:2
Elected Representatives	*Sarpanch*: Heerali Devi/Kachrulal Roth *Upsarpanch/Ward No:1 Panch*: Kodarlal/Marta Roth *Ward Panches (2-11)*: Prabhulal Roth, Kanku Kantilal, Nani Nandkishore, Natha Nanoma, Mani Maganlal, Badi Manath, Jeeva Kharadi, Devli Roth, Jeeva Roth.

objectives of the THP project was explained. The responsibility of doing all the groundwork was assigned to the ward panches. The NGO worker also participated in the 11 ward sabhas held in July 2002. At these fora, the ward panches were informed of their rights and their powers.

Microplanning: A 5-day PRA module was designed in the month of August in order to draw up a detailed microplan of all the wards. For this purpose, a resource group comprising 11 members was constituted within PEDO. 11 committees were also set up in each ward comprising the ward panch and five ward people. In the microplanning exercise which ensued, a total of 37 women and 34 men took part (see Table 8.12 for format of the plan).

Table 8.12: Format of Microplan

1. Panchayat Details
Locational details
Community/Caste details
Economic
Political
Landmark events in the panchayat:1967-2001
Chart of seasonal activities
Details of seasonal activities
Tree planting
Pie diagram: A typical day for women and men
Education
Programmes implemented through the panchayat
Chapati diagram: Departments and their relationship with panchayat
Trainings and livelihood programmes
Village assets
Natural and land resources
Livestock wealth
Population
Various committees at the panchayat level
2. Ward-Wise Details
Name of ward panch
Family and population details
Number of BPL households
Livestock
Water sources
Self-help groups
Social infrastructure
Private and common resources
Geographical details
Condition of water sources
Livelihood/income-generating plans: Private tree planting, strengthening of land and water resources
Map of the ward

Sharing with SHGs: The project idea was also shared with 8 existing savings groups of PEDO situated in and around this panchayat. Information regarding the microplanning process and techniques was given and suggestions solicited on how the plan should come into effect. It was decided that the involvement of women's groups was necessary for taking the project forward. The head and treasurer of the savings groups were asked to attend all panchayat meetings, especially the bi-monthly quorum meetings that took place on 5th and 20th of every month.

Trainings, workshops and exposure visits: Subsequent to the microplanning workshop in August, a training was organised by Seva Mandir at Kaya training center on the recent Panchayati Raj amendments, women's rights and so on. This was followed by presentation of the microplan in October, at a joint session of all three panchayats at Badgaon. In March 2003, a camp was organised by the savings group in Vasuva that clearly set out the nitty-gritties of self-help group formation, functioning and benefits. This included a one-day confidence building workshop for the postholders in these groups. Towards the end of the project period, a field visit to Ghatol, Banswara was organised by PEDO where women from Pal Mahodi got to see vermiculture, flower and vegetable farming, solutions to drinking water and women's health problems and so on. Panchayati Raj members and district level officers from states of U.P. Orissa, Chattisgarh and Andhra Pradesh also paid a visit to Pal Mahodi, during which time the microplan was shared with them.

Use of funds: As per the microplanning exercise, water emerged as the single largest problem throughout the panchayat. Since the support for implementation of Rs. 1 lakh under this project was seen as insufficient for the entire panchayat, it was decided to combine it with the ongoing relief works in the panchayat. The microplan was then discussed with the District Rural Development Authority (DRDA) towards end-2002 and it was agreed upon that the government would contribute 75 per cent of the project component (in the form of wheat) and the NGO would put in the remaining 25 per cent (in cash). Based on this agreement, it was decided to draw up a list of possible community works, each work's detailed plan, cost and requirements. This was presented to the DRDA and it was decided that work would start once the sanctions were received. Eight such works had been enlisted relating to anicut, talawadi, talab, community well deepening etc., costing Rs. 4,81,752 in total.

Implementation Process

Decision-making Process

Economic Activity

According to the documentation available, PEDO met the DRDA officials and the district collector of Dungarpur after the microplanning exercise and obtained their assurances that relief work could be undertaken jointly in a 75:25 (Government : NGO) proportion. The list of works—7 talab deepening and 1 well deepening —was finalised in consultations with the panchayat body. However, till April end, the DRDA did not clear the proposals, despite repeated follow-ups. So starting May 2003, it was decided to go ahead with 2 of the 8 works planned, using the funds available under this project. One concerned the repair of Adunvawali talab in ward no: 2 and the other, the deepening of a well at ward no:7, Gogaraphalla, Vasuava village.

At the ward meeting attended by the writer of this report, the *Sarpanch* and a few ward panches alleged that the decision regarding which well and pond to deepen, once the DRDA idea fizzled out, was not taken in a transparent manner. It seemed that the pond deepening had been earlier decided in another ward, which could not take place since there was a dispute between the residents of that ward. However, the decision to change the ward in which work would be done, was reportedly taken at the sarpanch's house in the presence of a few people, rather than at a quorum meeting. Both from the people's side and the NGO's side, not everyone involved in the project had information regarding this change. This possibly led to apprehensions that it was not a transparent process.

Moreover, it may be noted that the well deepening was done on a well situated on private land which belonged to a relative of a PEDO worker. The well, however, has been declared as a community well, used by people living in that phalla. The writer of this report also had a chance to speak to his neighbour who had been employed on this work. While his wife was totally unaware of the THP project, the neighbour was not clear on how much money he had received for his labour and there was a contradiction between the amount he quoted and the NGO worker claimed was given out. It turned out that there were different rates depending on the depth at which the digging took place and the corresponding difficulty levels. Neither the labourer nor the NGO worker offered this as an explanation to resolve the confusion and this information was finally gleaned from PEDO's accounts department.

Finally, the labour employed for both the works were predominantly men. Thus, as far as work relating to economic activities under this project was concerned, women had a minimal presence—in participation and actual implementation.

Gram Sabhas, Ward Sabhas and Quorum Meetings

Documentation on Ward Sabhas and Gram Sabhas in the project period was extremely sketchy on the part of the NGO. Barring allusions that the NGO participated in these gatherings, there was no detailed description of the proceedings, or sufficient evidence to establish that the NGO had made sustained efforts in mobilising people to attend these sabhas. The quorum meeting witnessed by this report-writer was well attended (there were around 30 people present including 7—8 ward panches) and it was disclosed that these bi-monthly meetings had been taking place quite regularly since 1995.

SHGs

PEDO has a very strong network of SHGs in Pal Mahodi (see Table 8.13). However, it appeared that there was little involvement of the SHG women as far as this project was concerned. Mainly, there seemed to remain a gap between women groups and their active participation in the panchayat; whether it concerned livelihood-related activities or creation of social and political awareness, right through this project period.

In SHG's meeting, some women expressed that although the main post-holders of the group had been asked to attend panchayat meetings, little of what they saw or heard transpired to the ordinary members of the group. For instance, Raju, an SHG member, was

Table 8.13: SHGs in Pal Mahodi Panchayat Initiated by PEDO (Mada)

Name of Group	*Year of Formation*	*No. of Member*	*Savings (till Oct'03)*	*Loans given (till Oct,03*	*Amount Repaid (till Oct'03) Principal*	*Interest*	*Loan O/S (till Oct)*	*Bank Balance*
Bagasira-I	1995	19	41449	17200	10654	932	6546	35135
Bagasira-II	1995	16	24009	15050	6137	737	8913	18237
Andikadayi	1995	20	28754	16200	7121	1280	9079	23001
Mahodi-I	1998	20	28874	24250	4813	1351	19437	14991
Doongriphalla	1999	19	19360	29250	10199	1037	19051	11216
Kutiyapada	1999	19	22382	28150	17999	1413	10151	13314
Vasuva	1999	18	20605	5700	2368	462	3332	19617
Mahodi-II	1999	17	16972	2000	958	358	1042	7300
Uplaphalla-I	1999	17	25942	16000	10903	950	15097	15419
Uplaphalla-II	1999	20	23028	30550	10377	1076	20173	9780
Uplaphalla-III	2000	16	17923	17350	7556	701	9794	9363
Total		201	269298	201700	89085	10297	122615	177373

not aware of any government schemes, did not go for any panchayat meetings and said that those who went did not share what happened in these meetings.

Use of funds

Details of the use of funds are set out in the tables 8.14 and 8.15. Significant aspects in this regard were:

- The funds available under the project were fully utilised under just two works.
- The entire amount came from the NGO, barring a small contribution from the people for the well deepening in the form of own labour towards deepening it further by about 7 feet.
- There were some delays in disbursement of payments towards machine hiring charges and blasting charges for the well deepening, which had led to the misconception voiced by the *sarpanch* that the NGO had 'swallowed' some funds.

Table 8.14: Budgetted amount and use of funds under the major heads* (May 1, 2002—October 31, 2003)

Expenditure Head	*Budgetted (Rs.)*	*Actual (Rs.)*
Exposure Visit	8000	7760
Training and Meetings	50000	27225
TOT on Microplanning	25000	14829
Preparation of Microplan	35000	16402
Support for Plan Implementation	100000	95314
Process Documentation	12000	8022
Honorarium for Field Worker	108000	69216
Support Costs for NGO	36000	21966
Total	374000	260734

*Figures are tentative, based on latest available information from the NGO.

Table 8.15: Detailed use of funds under plan implementation

Sl. No.	*Project*	*Nature of Expenditure*	*Amt. incurred (Rs.)*
1	Talab repair and deepening	Labour payments	40474
		Petrol Expenses	4900
2	Well deepening	Labour payments	19040
		Blasting cost	19700
		Machine hiring charges	11200
Total			95314

Dynamics of Interaction

Panchayat and NGO

The smooth process that the microplanning went through could be taken as a sign that the ward panches took this exercise seriously and were committed. But due to lack of detailed documentation, it is difficult to assess the evolution of the relationship between the panchayat body and the NGO field workers. At the only quorum meeting attended by this report-writer towards the end of the project period, though, there seems to have been some mistrust expressed by the sarpanch and some ward panches about the NGO.

The reason for this again revolves around the tendency to see a project only in its physical and economic aspects. The microplanning had created an expectancy that some work would be undertaken in all the wards. Both the sarpanch and the up-sarpanch were vociferous in their anger and disillusionment that nothing had happened at the end. Similar to the Alsigarh *sarpanch-pati's* emphasis on the scale of spending, here too, the remark made was, "we don't need PEDO or any NGO if it is only for a pittance". The notion that "so much time was wasted in preparing the microplan if nothing came out of it" was also expressed.

NGO and People

Throughout the project, it appears that people's involvement (that is, the ordinary residents of the panchayat) especially after the microplanning phase, was not significant. This was evident from blank responses that it drew from people when asked if they knew or had heard about THP or the specific objectives of this project. The particular involvement of women's groups did not seem substantial neither, given the fact that PEDO has an well-established relationship with these women going far back into the past. The NGO, has, however, tried to create a bridge between the leaders of women's groups in the panchayat and their participation in its political processes.

Plan Outcomes

Tangibles

The two main physical outcomes of this project were the deepening of a well and the repair of a pond in the *panchayat.*

The well, which was originally about 36 feet deep, had been deepened by about 12 feet with full contribution from the project funds and a further 7 feet with contribution of labour from the people. The final depth of the well hence stood at 55 feet after the work was completed. A visit to the well when this report-writer was in Pal Mahodi in September 2003 revealed that the water level, which was overflowing during monsoons, was now down by about 15 feet from the ground level. While the NGO workers believed that this water could be used for irrigation, people living near the well felt otherwise. It was said that the water was not sufficient for irrigation, since the pressure of inflow was still low. They also felt that the water was expected to last until the coming Holi.

Although the pond had been repaired and its dimensions extended before the monsoons, not a drop of water had collected in it. This was explained by the fact that the soil was porous and hence all the water continued to flow through the sides of the pond. The monsoon is expected to have naturally aided the process of sealing these pores and hence it was expected to become functional from the next monsoon. When asked if there had been no way of strengthening the sides and making it non-porous before the monsoon ad begun, it was said that this required a special kind of soil which was not available in the vicinity. To bring it from far would entail a cost which was beyond the budget provided in the project.

Intangibles

The process of microplanning was in itself a well co-ordinated exercise, which resulted in a concise document on the panchayat. It helped both people in the panchayat and the NGO to share information and get to know about all the wards, providing the basis for a comprehensive rather than ad-hoc planning. The microplan has been used as a crucial input in the treatment and desilting of the Dimiya dam catchment area within which the panchayat falls. Secondly, the panchayat has also been chosen as one among 140 others, for a scheme (Sam Vikas) under the Planning Commission, which includes implementation of watershed programmes, agriculture and animal husbandary activities.

According to Mr. Devilal Vyas of PEDO, the project also brought with it exposure of the panchayat to various kinds of people and interfaces between the sarpanch and district officials which had never taken place earlier, thus initiating a process of awareness.

The main focus of this project in Pal Mahodi was to solve the problem of water. The deceptive assurances of the DRDA might have resulted in inordinate delays in the actual start of implementing the project on the livelihoods front. This was also the period when drought was at its peak and hence people were more concerned about where to get their next meal from. Owing to all this, the social objectives of this project might have taken a backseat.

Table 8.16: Costs and Benefits at a Glance

Activity Description	*Location*	*NGO's Contribution*	*People's Contribution*	*Employment Generated*	*Number of Days/Labourer*	*Outcome (Current and Long Term)*
Microplanning	All 9 wards	Rs. 31,231 spent on training and microplan preparation	71 peoples participated in preparing the paln	n.a	n.a	A document for advocacy and planning for future action.
Talab repair	Ward 2	Rs. 45,374	nil	35	20	Yet to be seen. Presently, there is no water although it is hoped that it would fill up with next year's rains.
Well deepening	Ward 7	Rs. 49,940	Undertook deepening by further 7 donating their labour	8-10	32	Greater water availability for residents in this ward. Expected to last till Holi but insufficient for irrigation.

In all, the project outcomes may be summarised as below:

Key Observations and Learnings

NGO's Approach: PEDO's strategy was to leverage the available funds under this project with government funds under its various schemes. However, this might not have paid off due to factors beyond the NGO's control. The feeling that the funds available for plan implementation were "too less" was prevalent in the NGO itself. The excessive focus on the economic component and certain observations on the participatory processes noted earlier in this chapter goes to reflect the NGO's reading into this project, which might be in variance with THP's own conceptualisation.

Field Workers' Motivation: As mentioned in Chapter 2, the motivation of the field worker-in-charge seems to have mattered considerably in the progress of the project. From PEDO, this project was mainly handled by Anjana Vyas and Bharat. Their interfaces with the panchayat remained largely confined to predetermined panchayat or SHG meetings, rather than their own initiative to call for discussions or one-to-one rapport building with the panchayat representatives (This is presumed since no evidence to the contrary is provided in the documentation). This might have been a concious decision given that this panchayat is situated in a hilly terrain, houses are far from each other and women workers find it difficult to work here after dark, even if they may be willing to. On the other hand, this probably led to a lack of thorough knowledge of the field workers of their own area of work. It also seemed that there was some glitches in coordination between the various units of the NGO (that is, field workers, accounts, technical, administrative etc). On the whole, it is questionable if the field workers' own perception of the objectives of this project coincided with THP's.

Panchayat's Perceptions: As far as the panchayat was concerned, the financial assistance provided by this project was insignificant. And since the larger objectives did not carry through, it seems to have passed by without much impact.

People's Perceptions: At the end of these eighteen months, it does not appear that the project has touched the grassroots in any significant way. Mobilisation of women has always been done through formation of self-help groups by PEDO and no particularly innovative effort was taken under the THP project.

Transperancy and Awareness: If one main objective of this project was to create political and social awareness, it might be doubted if anything was specifically done to achieve this. The process of decision-making as described in the chapter clarifies that overall, the project was not broad-based in participation, due to which no significant rise on awareness levels through this project was noticeable.

Potential Directions—Suggestions from the NGO

According to Ramila Vyas of PEDO, one cannot change mindsets in one or two years. She felt that the sarpanch and ward panches needed more training and exposure. And importantly, the field workers needed greater orientation towards GTZ and the project ideology. The use of SHGs in enhancing their livelihoods and independence and ensuring their involvement in the panchayat's political processes also needed to be seriously explored.

MAKDASAR PANCHAYAT, BIKANER

A Brief Profile

Situated about 60-70 kilometres from Bikaner city and 10-20 kilometres from Lunkaransar, Makdasar is a panchayat comprising three villages—Makdasar, Binjarwali and Musalki, divided into 9 wards. Its population roughly amounts to between 3000-4000. The region is characterised by a high adverse sex ratio, this being especially true of Musalki. The sex ratio in this village stands at 909:1000 (female:male) while the average for the state is 922:1000. Agriculture, livestock and labour remain the main livelihood sources. The topography and scarcity of water makes it a difficult terrain for cultivation. Hence, migration by men to the richer regions of neighbouring Punjab is not uncommon.

Makdasar has a heterogeneous caste and religious make-up. While the majority are Hindus, Muslims are also well represented. The caste structure varies from village to village. Thus, while Binjarwali has a predominance of Meghwal, Nayak, Rajput and Brahmin communities, Musalki mainly comprises Rajputs and Jats.

One peculiar characteristic of this panchayat is its political set-up. All the ward panches have been elected to their posts uncontested. Their names are (wards 1-9): Mangilal Kumhar, Ganesh Singh Rajput, Banwarlal Nayak, Rukmadevi Nayak, Narayanidevi, Likhmaram Meghwal, Rupadevi Nai, Poonamram Luhar and Manaram Jat. The sarpanch, Kalavati Sharma was the only one to contest the elections.

The Process

The Makdasar experience exemplifies how one person—a woman can make a big difference to an entire process leading to development of a panchayat. While the process itself meandered along depending on circumstances and sometimes gave the impression of going astray, this could also be construed as having taken on an adaptative and natural course. Until the end, involvement of ward panches remained shrouded in the complexities thrown up by their socio-political environment. But a fine combination of an intelligent sarpanch, NGO support and people's own conceptualisation of their problems ensured that social dimensions were persistently kept in foreground.

Strategies for Implementation

Choosing the panchayat: Makdasar was chosen mainly on the grounds that:

- the sarpanch was a woman,
- the NGO Urmul had a prior and co-operative relationship with the panchayat,
- the sarpanch had a sense of responsibility towards work, and
- her husband was non-interfering.

Motivation to attend Gram Sabhas: The first formal presentation of this project was made at the May 20th Gram Sabha. When Urmul workers had a meeting with sarpanch Kalavati on this, she said it would be difficult to fulfil the quorum. People did not usually attend Gram Sabhas since they were disillusioned with so many proposals being taken down but nothing being implemented on the ground. However, she expressed that if Urmul was willing to help in motivating people from the other two villages (that is,

Binjarwali and Musalki), it may be possible to hold the Gram Sabha.

Consequent to efforts by Urmul workers, the turnout at the Gram Sabha was appreciable. There were totally 180 people present, of which 70 were women. Following the gram sabha's proceedings, Rameshwar of Urmul presented the work of the NGO and Aparna Sahay, then state coordinator, THP spoke of the organisation's work and the project.

Trainings and Exposure visits: On 14th and 15th of July, a training was held in the Rajasar, attended by 9 people from the panchayat—the sarpanch, 6 of the ward panches and two others, besides the Urmul workers. The main idea of this workshop was to inform and clarify the objectives of this project and chart out a future course of action. Present facilities, needs and priorities of each village was also discussed. It was decided that a ward-wise microplanning would be made ready by October, so that it could be presented in the gram sabha. Information about the panchayati raj system and about THP was also given using innovative media like theatre.

In October, the Sarpanch and 7 ward panches also attended a workshop organized by Seva Mandir, Udaipur for the presentation and sharing of the work done till then in all three panchayats. The microplan of ward no: 5 in Makdasar was presented at the meeting. The next day, a visit to Dungarpur to see the success of their programmes (Charagah development) was also organised.

Microplanning: The microplan for ward no: 5 was done on August 24th- 26th. There were 21 participants from the ward, including the ward panch and 6 members from Urmul.

The plan contained the following details:

1. A geographical map of the ward prepared by one of educated boys of the village, containing all the houses, roads, community places etc in the ward. The ward panch had a list of residents which had been made earlier, but after making this detailed map, they realized that some people had been left out.
2. A wealth ranking of all the households in the ward, along with details of each households' wealth/assets etc.
3. From 1 and 2, the following details were obtained:

- Total/male/female population, households by caste.
- Number of *kachcha, pucca* and semi-*pucca* houses
- Cattle wealth of households classified as very poor, poor, middle-income and higher income.
- Means of transporting water from source to house, by the above classification.
- A comparison of people classified as poor according to the microplan and according to the government (BPL and AAY).

4. The ranking was also indicated on each household in the map, along with whether BPL/AAY etc, whether there are undernourished children in the house, and out-of-school children.
5. Main problems of the ward were identified and then prioritized. The biggest problem emerged as "lack of advocacy/pressure on administration/government", the second was lack of employment and lack of information, third was rations and fodder (On this day, there were 15 participants).
6. It was clearly thrashed out as to what the problems were, their details, who were affected and what could be possible solutions.
7. Other details of ward no:5 included in the microplan were:

   - Number of malnourished children, the degree of malnourishment and whether they qualify to be in an *anganwadi,* whether they are enrolled or not.
   - Number of 6-14 age group children not in school.
   - Children in various schooling programmes.
   - The different proposals taken out in the ward so far and whether it had materialized or not.

It was said that the problems that received priority did so because of drought. It was also clarified that Urmul or THP could not solve all these problems, but an understanding could surely develop. THP desired that a microplanning of the entire panchayat be done before the funds under this project were distributed, but the amount was, in any case, too little to be of long standing use if spread across the entire panchayat. So it was decided that a wealth ranking be quickly done and this information be brought to the attention of the administration.

Everyone present—from ward no: 5 and other wards—were agreeable to this. Details of the wealth ranking included total number of truly poor families, how many among them were in the government's BPL list and how many were left out, each family's livestock, land and housing situation.

On 26th, a Ward Sabha was convened and the plan prepared till then was read out. A wealth ranking in the remaining 3 wards of Binjarwali was also done. On 27th, this was attempted in Musalki and Makdasar wards, and it was decided to meet the district collector on some day to present this.

Experiences During Microplanning

When the microplan was going on, many people who were not aware of the overall project right from the start thought that this concerned some list being prepared for the relief works. The fact that the patwari was also simultaneously making a list of people to make cards for obtaining fodder from the depot, reiterated their belief. They all began to say, "why are you doing this only in one ward, all wards are facing similar situation. During drought, every one is poor." It had to be repeatedly communicated that there were shades of poor even in that case—those without a grain of food to eat and so on.

When the map was being prepared, some people were pressurising the map-makers that their sons should be indicated as living in a separate house. The ward panch's husband explained why. People thought that if they were shown separately, they would get more benefits for relief work, which usually followed a 'one job per family' policy. He then retorted, "you people are crooks, when it comes to collecting donations in the village you say you are a joint family, when it concerns relief work, you want to be shown as separate!"

In July 2003, microplanning was carried out in ward no. 9 (that is, the entire village Musalki) on similar lines as ward no. 5. However, the ward panch was not present during this exercise. On being asked why, he said he was not free on the date the microplanning was fixed.

With problems relating to drought becoming overriding concerns, microplanning took a backseat. In August 2003, it was decided to attempt a joint microplanning of ward nos 6,7 and 8 together. The day it was scheduled, the ward panches were not present. The men who came cribbed about how nothing gets done, only proposals keep getting written, how the ward panches are useless and so on. At the end, no microplan was prepared and Urmul decided that they would involve only the women and the ward panches as far as possible. The next day, the same was tried out with women and a problem identification and prioritisation was done. It was decided to schedule a discussion on future course of action based on the identified problems at a later date, but that never really took place.

However, in an frank discussion of women's 'concealed' problems on the same day, they all said that so far, no deep debates had taken place on such issues like discrimination against women, girl education, women's health problems etc. in any ward or Gram Sabha. The Urmul worker pointed out that as long as problems that came forward were only economic in nature, the solutions would remain limited to these, and so would development.

Significanlty, no microplan was carried out till the end of the project period in wards 1, 2, 3 and 4, which covered the entire village Makdasar.

Implementation

Decision-making Process

Initial resistances

For reasons not absolutely clear, the decision of the Panchayat to work in alliance with Urmul for the GTZ project was taken at a separate sitting with the Panchayat body after the Gram Sabha on May 20th was over. This led to misconceptions and allegations by certain 'influential' people right from the start, that the sarpanch had 'sold out' to the NGO. Thus, when Aparna went to Makdasar to take the sarpanch along for a discussion on 'role of media in women empowerment' in Bikaner, there was a lot of pressure on her not to go. Rameshwar of Urmul had to sit down with these influential people and pacify them, after which they cooled down. The main one who had raised objection was one Gaffur Khan, who is also the present up-pradhan.

Economic Activity

In November 2002, by when drought had become a certainity, Urmul and the *panchayat* body came to the consensus that while the original idea was to draw out microplans in all wards systematically and prioritise work, the drought posed certain concerns that called for immediate redress. So the *panchayat* body decided to split the amount of Rs. 1 lakh available under project implementation among the 3 villages depending on its size—Rs. 40,000 to Makdasar and Binjarwali each and Rs. 20,000 for Musalki.

This was communicated in a follow-up meeting of ward panches and residents of Binjarwali. Since lack of livelihood was the most serious problem, the people of Binjarwali proposed that they undertook repair and cleaning of a johad situated to the south-east, on the way to Lunkaransar. Everyone agreed to working on this one, since it would benefit many people if the water would collect in '*kuis*' (or little wells) which the individuals had access to.

The entire nitty-gritties of doing this work was charted out in the meeting. It was decided that the poorest would be employed for this work. A committee was also formed with the ward panches as members, which would be responsible for overseeing the entire work, measurement, payments etc.

In a meeting with the up-sarpanch/ward panch no: 9 in Musalki, he suggested that the amount of Rs. 20,000 could be used for cleaning the *johad*, making a garden in the school and constructing a diggi. He indicated that the panchayat funds may also be combined with the available amount for this purpose. Families who did not have any food to eat in the present drought conditions would definitely be given work. The labourers to be employed would be decided by the people and a committee would be formed amongst whom a mate appointed. Participation of women was also stressed.

People in Makdasar decided to clean the streets, since it would provide immediate employment and at the same time benefit the village from a cleaniness point of view.

Then the question arose—what after these few days of work? It was hoped that the process of wealth ranking carried out across all wards in all villages to exert due pressure on the government, would tackle the employment problem on a large scale. Gradually, government relief work trickled in and Urmul also started bringing relief in its own capacity.

When Ashok Ray of GTZ visited Makdasar and was updated about the people's plan, he expressed his opinion that the government was anyway doing kachcha works and hence the GTZ money should be used for something that is long-lasting and could serve as a model.

As people started getting sufficient relief work, they stopped thinking of the GTZ money. Kalavati also decided that this money should be kept intact for use in some sustaining activity.

By March 2003, the need for a Panchayat Bhawan had become acute. People were not able to access records which remained with the gram sewak, there were unnecessary delays, the sarpanch was unable to answer queries from people and there was no place to hold meetings. Besides, this need had been expressed by the people themselves, as reflected by the fact that 'lack of information' had come out as the top problem in microplanning.

Kalavati's proposal for Panchayat Bhawan got accepted in the MLA quota. But the ward panches were not happy since they wanted the money to be split. So the decision was left to the Gram Sabha.

In the May 2003 Gram Sabha, the proposal got passed, and plans to build a Panchayat Bhawan and resource centre were finalised. The cost of the latter was to be covered by the THP project funds, to the extent possible. In the meanwhile, the government announced that every panchayat must have a library, so it was hoped that the resource centre building would surely come into good use for the people. A committee was formed in Makdasar itself for purchasing material, monitoring etc, under the sarpanch.

In spite of an apparently democratic decision, some of the ward panches still expressed dissatisfaction during a field visit to Makdasar. Although it had been explained that the plan to split the money was an outcome of stressful employment situation which relief works had taken care of, the notion that the sarpanch had kept only her village and her relative's concerns in mind remained.

Anganwadis : Makadasar and Binjarwali

Urmul had been running *anganwadis* in the district's rural areas with the help of ICDS and CARE programme. The *anganwadis* were not run properly for many reasons. The location was usually in someone's house and that led to some problems. The panchayat was not aware of its working, whether truly malnourished children were beneficiaries and so on. In Makdasar panchayat itself, there were three such *anganwadis*—2 in Makdasar village and 1 in Binjarwali. The anganwadi workers would not give proper answers and were not really accountable to the panchayat.

In 2002-03, the second phase of the programme under ICDS (Samekit Poshan Evam Swasthya Karyakram) started. In the new programme, thrust was given to involving the people of the village in monitoring of the anganwadis. Out of 970 *anganwadis* in Bikaner district, 10 per cent were chosen to become 'models' that would set an example for others. Of this proportion, it so happened that two fell within Makdasar panchayat—one anganwadi in Makdasar village and the other one at Binjarwali.

Under this, it was decided to identify the true beneficiaries, chart out a microplan, take the help of health workers, involve the community in looking out for those falling out of the programme net etc.

In Makdasar, the *anganwadi* was run in the worker's house. The house was situated at an inconvenient location and and since she belonged to an upper caste, the scheduled caste children would not go. Hence those enrolled (40 children 0-2 years, 40 children 3-6 years, 9 pregnant and *datri* women, 2 adolescent girls) were not truly needy.

To correct this situation, first a 5-member team each was constituted in both villages. The team was given training, then a map was made and a survey conducted on those enrolled and those left out. Two big problems remained—the location of the anganwadi was still in the house of the worker and secondly, the nurse was not staying in the village or coming regularly.

When Dileep Singh, the field worker from Urmul met the sarpanch on this, they decided to make a representation to the Health Officer and got a room in the health sub-centre. This building was in a dilapidated condition and Urmul helped in getting it fixed. A delegation of Urmul workers and panchayat representatives also met the Health Officer in Bikaner to make it compulsory for the nurse to stay in the village.

In Binjarwali, too there were similar problems: the *anganwadi* was being run in the worker's house and the SC children would not go. Some of the children enrolled were also over-age and some were not malnourished. But here, there was no community place readily available where the anganwadi could be shifted to. On discussing with the sarpanch, she promised that building an *anganwadi* in Binjarwali would be given preference under any government scheme which was available to the panchayat.

Later, when Praneeta of THP, New Delhi, paid a visit to Makdasar, the sarpanch requested that Rs. 60,000 available under the project may be used for building the *anganwadi.* This was accepted and work on it is being undertaken.

Gram Sabhas and Ward Sabhas

The documentation on gram sabhas/ward sabhas is not extensive but a detailed account of the first gram saabha in May 2003 is available. Participation in this gram sabha was reasonably high and it was attended by people from THP as well as a few presspersons.

People from all three villages were present. Many men were surprised at the turn out of women at the gram sabha and started commenting "why have they come".

The agenda for the gram sabha was read out, but since people did not have prior knowledge of it, the actual gram sabha took its own course. The past two years' development works in the panchayat was first presented along with expenditure figures. People were given a chance to question these. When asked about the income side, people were told that all the figures were with the gram sewak. Since the gram sewak was in charge of two panchayats, he was not available at that moment. Thus, although people had a lot of questions they did not get satisfactory answers and were disappointed. In fact, the first signs that people lacked access to information was evident at this gram sabha itself.

Poor Participation: Why?

This *panchayat* faces a terrible water crisis. The water supply is through a pipeline coming from the *nahar*. This supply is very irregular, at most 2-3 days in a month. In fear of complaints during the gram sabha, the supply is usually opened just a day before the gram sabha. So many people do not come for the meeting because they are busy stocking up their water reserves!

The various problems put forth by the people were as follows:

1. In Binjarwali village, the rations under BPL and AAY were not available regularly. It was decided that the ward panch and villagers would meet the ration dealer and demand an explanation, and if the supply would not regularise after that, a complaint may be filed with the district authorities. The impact of this decision was seen within a few days: the dealer began to distribute the rations properly.
2. Makdasar residents said that the food given in schools and the rations being distributed were very poor in quality, some people had even brought a sample to show everyone. The ration dealer defended himself that this is what the government dished out and in fact, he was suffering himself since he was saddled with bad stocks.
3. People from Binjarwali and Musalki presented their drinking water problems. Their problems were age-old and there has been no lasting solution so far. It was again decided to write a letter to the administration.
4. There were a lot of complaints that the nurse was not coming to the panchayat. People said it had to be made compulsory for her to stay here, or they had to complain to the department authorities. No decision was reached on this. Some people broke away from the gram sabha and started holding their private discussions.

Thus, this Gram Sabha clearly established people's needs and certain pointers to the future course the project would take. The project outcomes of a resource centre and *anganwadi* could be viewed in congruence with lack of information and problems regarding the nurse, expressed right at the start of this project in this gram sabha.

Participation at Ward Sabhas, however, appears to be quite low and from conversations with ward panches, it was learnt that quorum meetings also did not take place regularly.The possible reasons for this may become clearer in the section 'Dynamics of Interaction'.

Use of funds

Details regarding the use of funds are set out in the Tables 8.17 and 8.18.

Table 8.17: Budgetted amount and actual use of funds under the major heads (May 1, 2002—October 31, 2003)

Head	*Budgetted (Rs.)*	*Actual (Rs.)*
Exposure Visit	8,000	8188
Training and Meetings	50,000	18187
TOT on Microplanning	25,000	0
Preparation of Microplan	35,000	0
Support for Plan Implementation*	1,00,000	100318
Process Documentation	12,000	0
Honorarium for Field Worker	1,08,000	110552
Support Costs for NGO	36,000	32384
Total	3,74,000	269629

* This amount does not include Rs 60,000 estimated to be incurred on the *anganwadi* under construction in Binjarwali. The funds for this *anganwadi* have been made available by transferring the unused budget for 'Trainings and Meetings' and 'ToT on microplanning' to 'Support for Plan Implementation'.

Table 8.18: Detailed use of funds under plan implementation

Sl. No.	*Project*	*Nature of Expenditure*	*Amount incurred*
1	Library & Resource Centre	Labour payments Material Costs	18540 81778
2	Anganwadi	Labour payments Material Costs	(Actual cost will not be known till work is completed)
Total			100318

Significant aspects of the cost are:

- The funds were put to use in two large works (the resource centre and *anganwadi*) rather than dispersing them over smaller economic activities. Hence the beneficiaries in terms of employment generation was quite small.
- However the nature of the benefits flowing from these two works in the long run is expected to offset the low one-time employment that these works entailed. Significantly, these paybacks would accrue to women and children.
- There were many intangible outcomes of the microplan and the wealth ranking exercises. These are elaborated upon in the section "The Outcomes".

Dynamics of Interaction

Villages: The three villages in Makdasar panchayat were earlier part of a larger panchayat called *Sodwali.* The first sarpanch of the then newly-formed Makdasar panchayat was from village Makdasar. In the following elections, people from Binjarwali, who shared past rivalries with Makdasar due to cattle grazing disputes, decided that no one from Makdasar should become the sarpanch again. The candidate propped up by Binjarwali, was, however, reportedly 'bought up' by powerful people in Makdasar. The alternative candidate they came up with did not find support from Musalki people. Thus the sapranch was again elected from Makdasar, leaving Binjarwali people embittered. Due to these dynamics, it has proved difficult to unite people from these two villages.

Panchayat and local leaders: Within these village-level politics, there seemed many implicit and shifting equations between the ward panches and people in the village. A peculiar feature of Makdasar panchayat may be reiterated here: none of the ward panches, barring the sarpanch herself had to fight elections, they all came to power uncontested. This could also imply that some ward panches were simply props of some more powerful figures behind them. It is also significant that all expect 3-4 ward panches are reasonably well-off, the others being under debt from some moneylender or the other. This also seemed to alter the power equations, with pure political power (of being a ward panch, but not a rich one) taking a beating in front of economic power.

An important case in this point is with regard to an incident in Binjarwali. A woman ward panch, Narayani Devi of ward no: 5, was beaten up by a Rajput boy who strayed into her field with cattle. His violence was in reaction to her justified demand that he moved out of her field. In spite of an FIR being filed, she did not meet justice, since the doctor who treated her was allegedly bribed by the boy's family. She did not find support in anyone in the panchayat; even the sarpanch was unwilling to stand by her.

Narayani Devi belongs to the Nai caste. She is also poor and in debt.

Sarpanch and ward panches: Relationships between sarpanch and ward panches seemed to swing according to changing equations in the larger context. The sarpanch shared a special respect for the up-sarpanch, also the ward panch in Musalki. The ward panches in her own village were divided, depending on who they shared affiliations with. Finally, the ones in Binjarwali were constantly unhappy with Makdasar leaders.

Panchayat and NGO: The NGO shared a good relationship with the sarpanch, who also showed a high degree of receptivity and leadership. However, it appears that working with the panchayat body (the ward panches) in a coherent manner has proved to be rather difficult. According to the NGO worker, this can be attributed to the complex equations between ward panches, people 'behind' them and their own relationships with the sarpanch as discussed above.

NGO and local leaders: Similar to the Alsigarh experience, the NGO had to face resistances from those having a hold over the panchayat. Intially, there was some misunderstanding around the amount of funds available for project implementation and these 'leaders' in turn raised doubts in people's minds when the right amount was later conveyed. Unlike Alsigarh, however, it appears that the NGO worker managed to pacify people like Gaffur Khan by handling them tactfully. However, these powerful people did manage to create some disunity and misconceptions among people with regard to the project.

Sarpanch and women: There was no special relationship visible between the sarpanch and other women in the panchayat. The Narayani Devi case epitomizes how the sarpanch probably put other considerations above the fact that like her, it was a woman who had been meted out with injustice. During a field visit, the sarpanch simply commented that she was not sure whose mistake it was and hence, unable to take a stand on the matter. On the other hand, her perseverance in building a resource centre and *anganwadi* which would go to benefit women, adolescent girls and children goes to show that some fine tuning can bring her closer to other women in the panchayat.

The Outcomes

Tangibles

The two physical outcomes of this project were, the building of a resource center and an *anganwadi.* The resource center is housed a large room adjacent to the Panchayat Bhawan. It is presently being used to store unutilised relief grain received by the people of the panchayat. The idea is to develop the centre into a one-point information stop where people can easily access all details pertaining to their panchayat including use of funds, schemes available, beneficiaries and so on. The center also plans to make available books and reading material that can improve people's knowledge and awareness. The NGO also indicated that adolescent girls will be given preference in running the center.

The anganwadi was still under construction when this report writer made a visit to Makdasar in September. As described earlier, this would hopefully solve the problem of insufficient attention to malnourished children in this village.

Intangibles

Both the tangible outcomes of this project have intagible spillovers, bringing some meaningful solutions to deeply-felt needs of the people themselves.

Microplan: The microplanning in ward no:5 was extremely detailed and informative. It appears that the people present took genuine interest, time and thought to put this plan together. The maps drawn out were also very detailed and pictorially representative of a number of characterisitics of the place. The plan could serve as a model for developing further understanding of all the wards in the panchayat.

Wealth Ranking Exercise: The wealth ranking carried out right at the outset played a crucial role in exerting pressure on the government, that sufficient employment should be made available to the truly deserving people. Its outcome could also be used as a tool to justify demands for opening fodder depots (based on livestock figures), obtaining cheap grain through the PDS, health facilities and arrangements for malnourished children.

Sarpanch's Leadership and Social Justice: In the course of this project, the sarpanch demonstrated appreciable qualities, bringing concrete solutions to the problems voiced by the people. In itself, the shaping of her personality over the project duration can be construed as an intangible positive outcome. The main areas where the sarpanch displayed initiative were;

Relief Works and Area of Work: In the fourth year of drought, there was fear of starvation deaths. Soon after the ward no : 5 microplanning, a wealth ranking of all 3 villages was done. At that time, people said that employment, water and fodder were the biggest problems. When relief works started, the numbers were very low and those really in need were not getting work. At this point, the sarpanch took the initiative of starting work in Binjarwali village when in most panchayats the first work which came went to the village where the panchayat headquarters was located. She did this, in spite of protests from her own village people, because the situation of the poor in Binjarwali was the worst.

Relief Works and Prioritisation: The Government had ordered that BPL families should be given priority during relief work. However, many genuinely poor people were not on the BPL list. In this context, the sarpanch decided that she would go only by the list of truly poor, as was identified in the wealth ranking/microplanning.

The Gram Sewak was not agreeable to this and would only stick to the BPL list. Kalavati then went to the administrative officer at Lunkaransar and insisted that if these people were left out, they would die of starvation. The officer consented that if the BPL families did not object, the sarpanch could go ahead with their identified list.

Balika Shivir: Urmul has been putting up education camps for girls since 1998. The main aim is to bring access to education for girls in remote villages who are usually sent to work at a young age, and increase their participation. This time, a non-residential camp was put up in Makdasar in October 2002. The main objectives were to educate older girls so far left out, responsibilise the panchayat towards girl education, orient the government schools towards female education and make schooling a pleasant experience for girls. A committee was formed for all this. Work done during this period included involvement of the panchayat and government teachers, disseminating information other than that prescribed in books, a one-day visit to Bikaner, a 4-day mela and open discussions. According to Dileep's documentation, the sarpanch showed considerable co-operation; helping to sort out internal and external problems, speaking of the *shivir* at the panchayat meetings, creating a good prapport with the girls and favourable environment in the government school.

After the shivir was over, many of the girls enrolled in government schools, whereas initially they had been full of fears whether it was worthwhile and so on.

The Table 8.19 summarises the outcomes in a nutshell:

Key Observations and Learnings

NGO's Approach: As far as possible, Urmul appears to have taken the project idea to the people and let them decide on how they wanted to proceed. Largely, it was an adaptative approach, taking shape according to the need of the hour, without losing sight of social justice objectives. Ashok Ray's visit to Makdasar also lent the project a direction which might not have been taken otherwise. There were, however, incongruencies in the fact that the main physical work of building a resource center occurred in the village where no one took interest in the microplanning. It is clear that the sarpanch had a key role to play in this.

Field Worker's Initiatives: The main field worker in charge Dileep Singh seemed to share a good rapport with the sarpanch, and probably had a mature and tactful way of handling the power

Table 8.19: Costs and Benefits at a Glance

Activity Description	*Location*	*NGO's Contribution*	*People's Contribution*	*Employment Generated*	*Number of days/labourer*	*Outcome (Current and Long Term)*
Resource Center	Makdasar	Rs. 1,00,318	nil	13	20	Employment generation for people in need, although of the 13, only one belonged to SC and none were women; A resource center cum library building where people can get information and knowledge on various issues relating to panchayats and development; Possible employment for adolescent girls.
Anganwadi	Binjarwali	Rs. 60,000	nil	n.a	n.a	A proper building where children and women can avail *anganwadi* facilities; If run properly, better care for malnourished children and women of this village.
Education Camp for Girls	Makdasar	n.a	n.a	n.a	n.a	59 girls enrolled, of which 40 stayed till the end; Some of them got into regular government schools thereafter.
Drought Relief Work	Makdasar, Binjarwali, Musalki	30% of cost of providing relief work was bome by the NGO, sponsored by CARE	n.a	240	Relief work in different village started on different dates, but lasted approximately between 3-4 months	People in need were given first preference in which the sarpanch played an important role; Of the total employed, 109 were women; The timely relief prevented migration and ensured food security.

games in the panchayat. His initiative in stopping the microplanning and doing a wealth ranking instead, so that some immediate benefits may be brought to people when they desparately needed it, also shows his responsiveness to situations. He also took serious interest in trying to bring justice to the ward panch Narayani Devi.

Sarpanch's Perceptions: The lead role played by her in shaping the outcomes of this project goes to show how the right environment and certain inherent qualities can work wonders with a little training and exposure. Kalavati's determination to do something for the panchayat that would have a lasting impact is appreciable. But presently, she is not totally free of external pressures, and as long as this is true, it is unlikely that she would put her identity as a woman in front of everything else. The fact that Narayani Devi did not get justice at the end, despite the sarpanch being a woman, is a shocking and telling sign of how difficult it is to unshackle well-entrenched social identities.

Ward Panches' Perceptions: Clearly, the ward panches in Makdasar are caught up in their little political games and are victims of socio-economic pressures. The project as such seems to have by-passed them without creating much impression. In the future, more intensive training at this level may yield better results. However, unifying them would prove an uphill task, given that various other people in the village have a strong grip over them.

Focus on Entitlements: A significant aspect of the Makdasar experience was the outcomes of the microplan. In places where it took place, the prioritisation of problems showed an interesting pattern, different from the other two panchayats. Somehow, the thought process of the people had led them to believe that if they knew more, they could solve their problems better. In a sense, this was a refreshing change from the common mind-set that NGOs or any aid should either bring them employment, or something 'free'. The demand for employment was surely present, but this seemed to be driven more out of a distress situation, due to drought.

The general enthusiasm of the people, however, seems to have dissipated by the end of this project. Actively strengthening people's participation across a broader base, is a direction this project failed to take.

Potential Directions—Suggestions from the NGO

According to the field workers, taking this project ahead requires an approach that entails:

- *Working from below:* Strengthening the Gram Sabhas, ward sabhas and committees at the ward level would ensure that people at the top automatically become accountable.
- Dialogue with the 'influential' people of the village, in an attempt to minimise resistances.
- Discussions with people like the teachers and nurse, who could play an important role in mobilising village residents for *ward sabhas* and strenghten participation.
- Developing a deep understanding of the dynamics of the place and each ward panch's case history right at the start, so that it can be taken into account while planning for future action.

ACROSS THE THREE PANCHAYATS—A SYNTHESIS

Having gone over the individual experiences of the panchayats chosen for this project, it is time to put together these learnings and draw directions for the future. This chapter is presented in the form of questions, whose answers hold crucial lessons in a collective understanding of this entire experiment.

How was the Project Conceived by the three NGOs?

Closely tied to this question is the implicit philosophy and work methods of the NGOs themselves. To Seva Mandir, people's participation held the key to achieving the project's objectives implicit in the title: 'mitigating hunger' and 'mobilizing women's leadership'. Significantly, the NGO underscored the participation of women. While it was attempted to involve the panchayat body in the process, equal, if not greater thrust was given to raising awareness at the grassroot level. This explains much of the resistances put up by various entities who felt the threat of an 'enlightened' public.

To PEDO, which has traditionally shared a good relationship with the government, the project objectives were construed as an opportunity to strengthen ties between the panchayat body and other administrative and political links in the chain. Somehow, there was also excessive attention paid to the funds available for implementing physical work in the panchayat. It also remains perplexing why an NGO that strongly believes in a self-help group approach did not make a significant bridge between women groups in the panchayat and their participation in its political processes.

While Urmul strongly believes in mobilization of people on social issues at the ground level, it seems to have adopted a slightly different approach for the sake of this project. Urmul has always given much importance to improving people's access to their entitlements. It appears that this project was taken by the NGO as an opportunity to work from the other side, that is, with the panchayat body from which people could demand their rights in a democratic, political set-up.

Finally, it may be mentioned in the passing that there were also differences discerned in how different layers within the NGO conceptualized the project. Thus, the NGO management may have had a slightly variant view from what the field worker believed, and implemented on the ground.

What were the Styles of Implementation?

Going along the lines of what the project meant to them, each NGO displayed a different way of working. Seva Mandir laid greater emphasis on working at the people's level by stressing on their involvement and participation. All along, there was a strong focus on women. At the same time, it tried to create a stronger institution at the panchayat level. It also encouraged evolution of leadership among individuals, especially women, both in the present panchayat body and outside of it. Work methods were transparent, with little room for suspicion or mistrust among the people about the NGO. Economic activities undertaken during this project were well dispersed among the women panchayat residents. Those who took interest got work; those who were non-responsive were left out. The NGO maintained a good balance between social and economic aspects. The field worker was extremely motivated, and his commitment, evident both from conversations with him and his documentation.

As noted earlier, PEDO banked on government support for

carrying through the project's objectives. Although this did not really pay off at the end, the microplanning was taken quite seriously and further leveraged to obtain some benefits for the panchayat. But on the whole, the NGO's approach was less participatory with certain hiccups becoming evident in the process. Decision-making was not entirely transparent and communication gaps persistently came up, which in turn created misunderstandings that had an impact on the way the project was understood by the people and the panchayat body. The focus of the project here was predominantly economic.

Urmul attempted to work closely with both the panchayat body and the people. However, the NGO had some difficulties in unifying people in some wards, creating a better rapport between the members of the panchayat and working cohesively with the panchayat. But as mentioned earlier, the NGO seems to have let circumstances shape the outcomes, while providing basic directions to those taking initiatives. In a sense, it tried to play a supportive, rather than a lead role in helping the panchayat fulfil its responsibilities.

What was the socio-political Environment in the three Panchayats?

Needless to say, the prevailing environment in each place made a huge difference to the final outcomes. Alsigarh has strong political interests due to its naturally rich endowments. On the face of it, the panchayat exhibits social homogeneity in terms of caste but it is certainly not free of wealth inequalities. It appeared that economic and political power predominantly defined 'oppressor-oppressed' relations here. Another characteristic is the large proportion of daily commuters (mainly men) to Udaipur in search of wage work. This has serious implications in two areas: their interest in the panchayat affairs, and the degree of independence enjoyed by women.

Situated close to the Gujarat border, Maodi Pal is characterized by mass migration to this state even in times when there is no drought. Significantly, only men migrate and women are left behind to take care of land, livestock, old people and children. Rationally speaking, then, many decisions fall in the domain of women. Belonging to Scheduled Tribes, some of their customs are also in favour of women. In this respect, the freedom experienced by the women here may be even greater than in Alsigarh. In many other aspects, such geographical characteristics, layout of fields, land holding, wealth inequalities, caste makeup and so on, the panchayat shared many similarities with Alsigarh.

Makdasar belongs to a different geographical terrain, being situated in the desert district of Bikaner. Unlike the other two panchayats, it is characterized by heterogeneity in castes and religions. Due to this, 'dominant-dominated' caste equations are prevalent, compounded by economic inequalities and political power. Significantly, all the ward panches in this panchayat have been voted to power uncontested, with many underlying affiliations of the ward panches with other powerful people in the panchayat. As described in chapter 4, there is rampant 'politics' between two of the three villages in this panchayat.

What were the Resistances during the Implementation and how did the NGOs Tackle them?

In Alsigarh, obstacles were posed largely from people who had vested interests in keeping people in the dark. Their fears were two-fold - raising general political awareness would threaten their current position as powerful political players and the potential to make 'gains' through corrupt practices. Secondly, empowering women would mean that one day, their dominance over them would be openly questioned.

For Pratap, who was the point of interface of the NGO in this project, it became a question of carrying forth its objectives without entering into existing political equations. By choosing to avoid it, the NGO had to come up with an alternative strategy to unshackle people paralysed so far from an oppressive set-up. The strategy chosen by the NGO was to focus on empowering women, whether at the absolute grassroot or at the panchayat body level, so that their evolution as agents of change may bring about a lasting impact in their lives.

In doing this, Pratap was alienated from the panchayat body to a large extent. Yet, it seems that the NGO's and his stance of concentrating on the women empowerment angle facilitated the basic objective of this project, which was to strengthen the presence of women in the community through their economic independence and social awareness.

From the available documentation and conversations with people, it appears that their unwillingness to come together and take responsibility in solving their own problems itself acted as a deterrent in mobilizing them. The NGO workers' anger and sometimes, despair in this respect is probably, fully justified. In spite of that, it is noteworthy that the field workers slogged in trying to responsibilise people to the extent possible.

Again, due to sparse documentation, it is difficult to judge if there were any significant hurdles faced by the NGO in implementing this project in Pal Maodi. It can be said that the panchayat body worked quite smoothly with the NGO in the initial stages of the project, although there was a 'sour grapes' attitude expressed by the sarpanch and a few ward panches towards the fag end. There was also much 'back-talking' by some ward panches, that the sarpanch had wanted a cut and was put off because she didn't. Since the NGO itself had not really 'disturbed' anybody with its approach, it does not seem to have faced any serious hiccups either. The volte-face by the government which had assured it funds for well-deepening remained its biggest setback.

In Makdasar, the resistances were similar to Alsigarh—one, from people who were feeling fragile from the potential harm this project could do to their clout in the panchayat, and second, the lack of interest amounting to indifference from the people and ward panches of the panchayat. While Urmul was probably able to make some headway in overcoming the former, it fared far worse than Seva Mandir in tackling the latter. This was evident from the fact that microplanning itself took place only in 5 out of 9 wards, and that too, 3 were not in detail. The saving grace in Makdasar, it seems, was the dynamism and leadership displayed by the sarpanch and the resulting outcomes of her determination.

How was the Project Envisaged by the Sarpanches and Why?

An important factor to be taken into consideration with respect to the sarpanches is their domestic as well as external environment. In Alsigarh, the sarpanch failed to break out of her husband's stronghold and remained a victim of people more powerful than her in the political set-up. This environment she faced can hence explain her attitudes and behaviour in this project and the distance she maintained from the NGO. In Pal Maodi, the sarpanch seemed more outspoken but it cannot be ruled out that she was simply reflecting her husband's views. On the whole, she seemed to conceive the project only in economic terms and judged from that angle, she considered it a waste of time.

In Makdasar, the sarpanch's conceptualisation played a key role in taking its objectives ahead. The sarpanch's initiatives and the outcomes go to reflect that she both understood and acted along the underlying philosophy of the project better than the other two.

How Differently did the Panchayat body in the three Panchayats Visualize the Project?

Since the panchayat body comprises many ward panches and the sarpanch, a project such as this is bound to create different reactions in each individual's mind. The understanding of the project, then, has to be looked at individualistically, each being a function of each ward panch's standing in the village's socio-economic ladder, his/her immediate environment, his/her political affiliations and his/her motivations. It is hence difficult and even not prudent to generalize the panchayat body's visualization of the project in each panchayat. What can be said, however, is that depending on the factors described above; each ward panch in all three panchayats acted in a way closer to, indifferently or in direct conflict with the project objectives.

What did this Project mean to the People in the three Panchayats?

In Alsigarh, there were broadly three kinds of people—those who were indifferent to this project and did not want to associate with it; those who, with some motivation, came forward to participate; and a third category whose only aim was to throw cold water on any concrete efforts taken by the NGO and people. The first set of people either conceived the project as "just another NGO gimmick", had suspicions of the NGO's motives having gone through bitter experiences or simply had no desire/did not perceive this project as an opportunity in somehow improving their lives. The second set of people may have had different motivations - either perceived economic benefits; which livelihood activities generated by this project would bring them, or social gains- by realizing that participating in this project would give them exposure and raise their awareness, or both. Finally, people who acted in disrupting the process mainly saw the project as affecting their own position or power in the panchayat in one way or another.

Conversations with people in Pal Maodi reflected that the project had not touched them in any way. Many were not aware of its intentions nor ever heard of THP.

In Makdasar, there was a similar pattern to Alsigarh, but the proportion of people in the first and third categories were probably even higher.

How far was the Project Successful in Mobilising People for Greater Participation in the Panchayats' Processes?

Seva Mandir focused on increasing people's political awareness for a good part of the project, and the gram sabhas of August 15th, 2002 and January 26th, 2003 exemplify the positive outcomes of these efforts. However, the ban on Pratap's participation in ward meetings and the intensification of resistances and pressures on the empowerment process acted, in a way, as breaks on this aspect. In Makdasar, participation appeared to have taken on a direct relationship with the stress factor. This is evident from the fact that everyone was ready for a wealth ranking during the peak of drought, but not so willing to do a microplanning even subsequently. As the level of desperation eased, so did the participative spirit.

What did the Project do for the Women in the Three Panchayats?

Seva Mandir ensured that women were always kept at the center of any activity undertaken in this project. The direct involvement of women in economic activities and in social organization is likely to have a sustained impact on their lives, beyond the short-term benefits. From this point of view, it might be concluded that the outcomes of the project were most favourable for women in Alsigarh.

Women were not the focus of the intervention in Pal Maodi, although the NGO in its own capacity had done much for empowering women in this region. It is this discrepancy that the NGO might want to seriously consider in any future action.

The project presented a good opportunity for women like the sarpanch of Makdasar to take advantage of her cooperative domestic environment in developing inherent leadership qualities. The outcomes of this project are also most likely to be in favour of women in this panchayat. However, in terms of ensuring their social justice and in broad-basing their participation, the panchayat still has a long way to go.

What were the Outcomes? Why were they so Different?

Alsigarh saw a community centre, well-dispersed flower farms and dholi musli farms managed by women, a grain bank and 11 self-help groups run by women. It also saw the emergence of women leaders in the panchayat. Pal Maodi ended up with a deeper well, a semi-repaired pond and a neat-looking microplan of the entire panchayat. Makdasar got a new resource center, a new *anganwadi,* deserving people on the drought relief work, a regular nurse staying at the village and the panchayat's interest in advocating female education.

In all, it might be said that the experiment in Alsigarh came closest to fulfilling the project's objectives. This is in spite of Makdasar being able to produce a dynamic leader who, in her individual capacity, came up with many positive contributions to the general well-being of people in her panchayat. The main justification behind this judgment could be understood by looking at a hypothetical situation—what if Kalavati, with all her positive attributes, had not been the sarpanch of Makdasar? The fact that the benefits in Alsigarh were largely the result of people's efforts, independent of any one person and having long term positive implications for a large number of women, in spite of tough resistances put up from various quarters makes it a commendable achievement.

Where do we go From Here?

It may be rather ambitious to simultaneously address the objectives of 'women empowerment' in a general sense and 'women leadership' in a political framework. This is because the process of political empowerment, in itself, is quite complex. Focusing on women as political leaders introduces a further complication, since being a woman; she has to deal with an additional set of women-centric issues. The objectives of this project then span an intricately woven web of issues that might have been the reason for it to be pulled in different directions. The experience of Alsigarh probably exemplifies this problem to the utmost, since the sarpanch faced both domestic and political pressures—which is likely to be the case among a vast majority of 'elected' women leaders. But the important lesson from Alsigarh is also that, directing greater focus on the women empowerment aspect to shape them up as agents of change would automatically have important bearings on the political awareness aspects for the entire panchayat. It is needless to add that, empowering women holds many many positive implications not just for women but also men and children, indeed for society at large. Hence, in the future, it might be worthwhile considering the following directions:

- Stressing on strengthening relationships between women sarpanches and women self-help groups in the panchayat,
- Studying carefully in which areas a woman sarpanch or ward panches can improve the general well-being of women by improving access to their entitlements and giving a thrust to these. For example, there may be many panchayat or government schemes for women which are currently not reaching them, in which a women leader could play a significant role,
- Giving training and information not only to elected women leaders or people with 'posts' but across the larger women population in the panchayat,
- Specifying use of funds, if any, being provided under the project for plan implementation, that it should be used only in activities that are beneficial to women in a direct, significant and sustaining way,
- Choosing such panchayats in the beginning, where women have an existing favourable environment - for example, villages where the rate of male migration is high.

9

MICRO LEVEL PLANNING AND PANCHAYATS

PRIA

AN OVERVIEW OF MICRO LEVEL PLANNING

Introduction

The concept of micro-level planning, involving people in plan-formulation and implementation is not new. Right from the days of community development Programmes, people's role and participation has been stressed. Yet in practice putting the people in the centre of the planning process has remained a dream. The Eighth Five-Year Plan made an attempt to deal with this shortcoming by recognizing the need to involve people in the process of development through micro level participatory planning. The plan stressed the need for changing the old pattern of development where everything came from the government and people were the passive recipients. This meant that the people must become active and the government should cooperate in the process of development.

This concept of giving power to the people has been given definite shape with the passing of the 73rd Constitutional Amendment Act. It has given formal recognition to the Panchayats at village, block and district levels to function as a government. In addition to this for the first time reservations for women and Dalits have been made so as to enable and encourage their participation in the political and development processes.

. This Amendment allows the people the following functions, authority to the three-tier structure of Panchayats at village, block and district levels so as to enable them to function as institutions of self-governance. With respect to this, Article 243 G of the Constitution of India reads thus: "Subject to the provisions of this Constitution, the legislature of a state may, by law endow the Panchayats with such powers and authority as may be necessary with respect to:

- The preparation of plans of economic development and social justice.
- The implementation of schemes for economic development and social justice including those in relation to matters listed in the Eleventh Schedule.

Planning is now thought of as a "people-driven" activity, in which each of the layers of governance have been given some degree of independence and self-governance, and have to discuss matters with each of their successive layers in order to obtain their share of benefits.

The responsibilities of the Panchayats are many and varied. Many of the leaders and members of these newly constituted Panchayats have entered the political field for the first time and for those who have been struggling with responsibilities for a long time, the idea of planning is brand new. Doubts are being raised as to their ability for taking on these many responsibilities. For the last 50 years and more the people have been dependent on the government for development, can they now plan for their needs? And even if they plan will the government machinery allow them the space to do so? Do the people and Panchayats have the necessary skills and confidence to deal with their responsibilities? Will they be able to collect and analyse information required for planning for different subjects? What about women and Dalits, will they be involved in the decision-making processes? Will the women be allowed to sit with men to discuss priorities and development issues?

Driven by these and many more questions combined with a basic belief in people's capacities, PRIA began its initiative of strengthening the Panchayati Raj Institutions towards the end of 1995 in eight states of India.

PRIA's commitment to strengthening local self-governance in the country is guided by the belief that:

- Panchayati Raj Institutions are institutions of Local Self-Governance and not mere implementers of centrally determined development programmes. They should not be allowed to become the third tier of development administration.
- The "base upwards" comprehensive planning based on the micro planning exercise is to be the basis of self-governance.
- The PRIs encourage the active role of women and other weaker sections of society in decision-making with the aim of enhancing their role, status and leadership.
- The PRIs should be able to use and control local natural and human resources as well as other development resources available within the state and central governments.
- Strengthening the PRIs will require clarity about their roles, systems of governance, accountability, transparency and inter-linkages.

As a strategy for strengthening PRIs, PRIA and the Network of Collaborating Regional Support Organizations initiated participatory base upwards planning processes (micro planning) in some Gram Panchayats spread over seven states of the country, namely, Bihar, Haryana, Himachal Pradesh, Kerala, Madhya Pradesh, Rajasthan and Uttar Pradesh.

The following document is based on the experiences collected and compiled during these participatory planning exercises. An attempt has been made to retain the uniqueness of each experience and yet recognize the fact that given the opportunity people can plan for themselves.

Participatory Base Upwards Planning Initiatives: A Brief Overview

Name of State	*Name of District and Block*	*Name of Gram Panchayat*	*Objectives of Planning*	*Duration of Process*
Bihar March	Muzzaffarpur, Bochaha	Belthi	• To find possible links between the Gram Sabha and Bochaha Rasulpur government welfare schemes • To involve people in analyzing and prioritizing their problems as well as their participation in implementation	March to May 1998
Haryana	Jhajjar, Salhawas	Dhana	• To encourage people's active participation in the decision-making and implementation processes. • To enhance the participation and decision making capacities of women and Dalits. • To promote transparency and accountability with regard to the functioning of the Gram Panchayat and the administration at the Block level	April to October 1997
Himachal Pradesh	Mandi, Sadar	Kehar	• To develop and work out a real model of base upwards planning where people act as their own agents cf development. • To develop a simple and systematic framework for the participatory planning process which can be replicated. • To prepare a plan that is sensitive to and reflective of the needs of women and Dalits.	May 1996 to January 1997
Kerala	Kollam, Sasthamcotta	West Kallada	• To create a model demonstrating the feasibility and effectiveness of the participatory planning process. • To encourage and enable people to use their knowledge and capacities for the development of their village.	July 1995-on-going

Contd......

Name of State	*Name of District and Block*	*Name of Gram Panchayat*	*Objectives of Planning*	Duration of Process
			• To enhance and develop people's capacity to plan according to their needs. • To empower people - especially women and Dalits. • To encourage and enable people's co-operation and participation in the activities and Programmes of PRIs	
Madhya Pradesh	Sehore, Sehore	Jamunia Tank	• To strengthen participation of people at the grassroots level in decision-making processes with the focus on women and Dalits. • To build the capacities of the members of Gram Panchayat so that they may be able to prepare a plan based on their own needs. • To develop and give shape to a concrete model of base upward planning with the Gram Panchayat.	1995
Rajasthan	Ajmer, Jawaza	Naikalan Durgawas Kabra Jawaza	• Specific attention may be paid to Programmes aimed at the rural poor. • Programmes are geared towards the specific needs of the area and its growth potential. • The process of planned rural development may be decentralised. • A closer partnership with the rural population is achieved. • The lowest rungs of the administration may be organised and coordinated.	
Uttar Pradesh	Kushinagar, Kasya	Mathia Madhopur	• To activate Gram Panchayat and Gram Sabha members through their involvement in the planning processes. • To enable people to identify their needs, prioritise them and find appropriate solutions and resources to address those needs. • To prepare a systematic plan based on people's needs and submit it to the administration.	May 1996

THE HARYANA INITIATIVE

PRIA, Haryana began functioning in 1995, as part of PRIA's initiative on strengthening Panchayati Raj Institutions. It began its initiative with 5 districts of Haryana through the training of local voluntary organizations and elected members of Panchayati Raj Institutions. Now its work has spread to 9 districts. However, the main issue is the strengthening of PRIs so that they may become institutions of local self-governance. The following is an account of the process of planning by the people of Dhana, Haryana, facilitated by PRIA.

A Village Called Dhana

In the beginning of the 19th century a man named Todaram came from the village of Jamalpur and established himself in what is now known as Dhana. He is remembered as the founder of Dhana. Today it is one of the 33 villages that make up the Salhawas block in Jhajjar district. It is situated a distance of just 70 kms from the capital city, Delhi, 34 kms from the district headquarters and barely 2 kms from the block, the centre of all Panchayat activities. The nearest railway station and market is just 10 kms away in Kosli, a sub-division of district Rewari.

According to the 1991 census, the village has a total population of 1,416 out of which 753 are males and 663 females. The dominant castes in the village are Jat (922), Jogi (249), Chamar (109), Nai (60), Brahmin (48) and Khati (28).

Dhana is predominantly an agricultural village. Almost 33 per cent of the population is occupied with agriculture, 30 per cent in agriculture and service, 7 per cent in agriculture and small businesses and about 30 per cent are daily wage earners (labour). The standard of living depends upon the land holding and the type of service they are involved in. The major crops in the area are jawar, bajra, wheat and mustard. The village has a high literacy rate of almost 75 per cent and the dropout rate in the schools is almost nil. The men folk spend most of their time discussing politics, playing cards and in agricultural season are found sowing (mostly by tractor). Women are responsible for all the household chores, livestock rearing, and agriculture related activities during harvesting season. There are taboos on women sitting or attending meetings in the village *chopal*.

Their role in the Panchayat affairs is minimal. The situation of the schedule castes in the village is more or less the same, though the caste structure in Haryana is not rigid, i.e. people of various castes inter mingle freely. The power, however, lies with those in control of the major portion of the village resources.

The village of Dhana is divided into seven wards thus there are seven elected ward representatives called "panches" in the Panchayat. The sarpanch of the Gram Panchayat belongs to the dominant Jat caste. Of the seven panches two are women and one a SC male.

The Panchayat has an annual income of about Rs. 8000-9000 from its land that is leased out to the highest bidder every year and from taxes such as "*chulha*" tax, and house tax. The Panchayat also gets grants and funds from the government under various schemes. The Gram Panchayat has one middle school, one anganwadi centre, one fair price shop and the services of a health visitor every week. In addition there is a registered youth club and a registered community based organization.

Initiation in April 1997

Consultation and meetings: Meetings with these Ward Members and the Sarpanch became the starting point of interactions with the people of Dhana. Gradually these meetings extended to meetings with the Gram Sabha members in their houses. Initially the discussions centred on various issues related to their daily lives in the village and politics in the country, in general. Regular meetings were now being organized to discuss people's participation in Gram Panchayat activities, the basic provisions of the Haryana Panchayati Raj Act, power granted to the people, their ability to think and plan for their needs. Many meetings in small groups were organised in all the wards; care was taken to include members of all communities and women as well as schedule caste members were encouraged to share their thoughts and feelings.

While this environment of mutual trust and co-operation was being built in the village, meetings were also being held in the block office. The sarpanch and PRIA representatives met the Block Development and Panchayat Officer, the planning initiative was discussed with him and after that the block office became an integral part of this process.

Ward Meetings Held in May 1997

During the early phases, discussions and meetings between the ward members took place, and this laid the foundation of the planning process. They were further encouraged to have meetings in their own wards concerning the planning process. Elected members contacted the people in all seven wards. These meetings became a platform for not only sharing their problems but also for looking at possible solutions.

PRIA representatives got their first look into the problems faced by the people as well an opportunity to explain the purpose of planning in detail. They were asked two questions. Why would an outside organization be interested in their problems, and what would they get at the end of it? They were told that there were no quick solutions offered, the idea was to look at their own abilities and build on them. The discussions took on a new meaning after this answer was given.

Survey in May 1997

It was decided to do a survey so that the information already available to the people could be organised in an orderly manner. The survey was planned with the help of the *yuva mandal, mahila mandal,* members of Gram Sabha and Ward representatives. Collecting information was the task of the members of the community. Information was collected about caste, gender, the population, occupation, landholding, education, livestock composition, irrigation facilities and garbage disposal facilities.

Ward and Gram Sabha Meetings in June 1997

Ward level meetings were organised to discuss the issues that would be raised in the Gram Sabha meeting. During the process the panches met the people for the first time to listen to their problems. Care was taken to bring women and scheduled caste members to attend these meetings. These groups so far neglected could now share their concerns about land encroachment and lack of electricity in small ward meetings. A Gram Panchayat meeting was called by the sarpanch to discuss the date, time and venue of the meeting. It was also decided that the BDO and Gram Sachiv would be informed of the meeting.

The Gram Sabha meeting was held on 18.06.97 in the sarpanch's *chopal*. The BDO and Gram Sachiv were present at the meeting and could see the people's active participation in a meeting which is usually just a formality in most of the Gram Panchayats in Haryana.

Setting up of a Cutting and Tailoring Centre in Ward No. 3, Gram Panchayat Dhana

The members of ward Nos. 3 and 4 (mainly SC and OBC dominated wards) held meetings once a week to discuss issues that needed immediate attention. In one such meeting the need for a vocational training centre for young girls and women was discussed. Subsequently it was decided that a cutting and tailoring centre would be started in the Dalit chopal. At the meeting the people could discuss fees for training and the arrangements made by the Panchayats in the chopal. This activity gave the people faith in their ability to bring about changes.

Using Pictorial Exercises to know about Available Resources

In the ward level meetings and survey, it was seen that the people had little or no idea as to where a tap or streetlight could be installed for the best results as well as the resources that are available within each ward. For the purpose of involving the people, pictorial exercises in sharing and collecting information regarding available resources was adopted. People sat together and drew a map of their ward - households, lanes, positioning of taps and electricity poles, garbage disposal sites, land holdings and so on. The exercise had two aims, one the people were actually able to draw a map of their ward with the help of discussions and two, the information collected through the survey could be re-checked as well as discussed.

Village Planning Meeting

All the ward plans were prepared and a discussion took place on the difficult issues of land encroachment and garbage disposal. The sarpanch gave the point of view of the Panchayat on the topic of planning and solving the problem of land encroachment. Everyone contributed to the discussion and listed their needs in order of importance. The proceedings of the meeting were duly recorded so that they could be formally passed in the formal Gram Sabha meeting to be held in December 1997.

Sector Specific Plan : Prepared by the Panchayat and Members

Issue	*Activities*	*Time Frame*	*Responsibility*
Link road from the village to the temple	• Project planning, resolution in Gram Sabha and submission to the block office • Part of the planned estimate given by the PWD Minister	March 1997 Oct. 1997	Gram Panchayat and Block Development Office
Free the common ponds from garbage and clean them	• Arrange an alternative place for garbage disposal • Seek the help of public works and Public Health Department	Nov. 1997 to Jul. 1998 Aug. Dec. 1998	Gram Panchayat and Community Gram Panchayat and Public Works and Public Health Department
Drinking water facilities	• Survey done during planning for location • Project planning for two water tanks and taps (14) and submission to block office • Project passed and construction completed	Sep. 1997 to Jan. 1998 March 1998	IVG Members and PRIA representatives Gram Panchayat Gram Panchayat and Block Development Office
Electricity Supply	• A core group is formed for handling the issue of installing transformer • A request for a transformer and 10 poles • Installation of transformer and poles	July 1997 Oct. 1997 Dec. 1997	Gram Panchayat, community members & PRIA representatives Gram Panchayat, core committee and CBO Electric Supply Department, Gram Panchayat and core committee
Women's Development	• Ward wise awareness camps on health issues • Forming of a health committee and its training • Forming a self help group	Oct. 97 to Jan. 98 Nov. 97 to March 98 May-June 1998	Mahila Mandal, Gram Panchayat VIC and PRIA Mahila Mandal, Gram Panchayat, VIC and PRIA

Contd. ....

Contd. ....

Issue	*Activities*	*Time Frame*	*Responsibility*
	• Opening a vocational training centre (cutting and tailoring) • Continued awareness Programmes and activities for women to encourage their participation in decision making processes and leadership	July 1998 Dec. 1998	Yuva Mandal Mahila Mandal, Gram Panchayat and VIC Mahila Mandal, Gram Sabha members and VIC
Garbage disposal on Panchayat land and land encroachment	• Awareness of and environment building through small group discussions • Solution to the encroachment issue through the SDM court	Apr. 1998 Dec. 1998	Gram Panchayat, Gram Sabha Members and VIC, Gram Panchayat, VIC and Courts
Construction of metalled road and drainage facility	• Plan formulated, passed as Gram Sabha resolution and submission to the block office	Sep 1997 Dec. 1997	Gram Sabha members Gram Panchayat, VIC, Committee and Block Development Office
Kutcha Lane (laying of streets with bricks) and drainage facility	• Budget estimation, resolution by Gram Sabha and submission to Block office	Sep. 1997 to Jan 1998	Gram Sabha members, Gram Panchayat, VIC Committee and Block Develop-ment Office
Establishing a Village Information Centre (VIC)	• Agreement of common place for the centre • Formation of a VIC committee to look into the functioning of the centre Nov.-Dec. 1997	Nov.-Dec. 1997 Jan. 1998	Gram Sabha members, Gram Panchayat and anganwadi workers IVG members and Gram Panchayat
Construction of a cremation ground	• Estimate prepared and submitted to Block Development Office • Formation of a Old Peoples Committee for the maintenance of the ground Dec. 1998	Dec. 1998 Dec. 1998	Gram Panchayat and old peoples committee Gram Sabha members and VIC committee

Strengthening the Process of Participatory base Upwards Planning: Some Initiatives

The discussions took into account the steps that went into the process, resulting in a specific plan for the sectors. However, the actual process did not move in an organised manner. There were many processes taking place in the village and outside, at the same time that contributed to the ultimate plan. Some of these processes resulted in initiatives made by the people, while others resulted in plans made by the PRIA team members. All these initiatives are discussed in brief in the following pages so that the reader may be able to understand the process in totality.

Learning to Help Themselves: The Village Information Centre Initiative

During the planning process it became clear that people were not properly informed about issues that come up on a daily basis, how they can be dealt with, where to go and what their rights were etc. The ward meetings, survey and pictorial exercises, discussions about the possible solutions, helped them to come to the conclusion that a Village Information Centre was needed.

A Village Information Centre (VIC) was set up where the Panchayat and the volunteers of Dhana would take up the responsibility of collecting information and distributing it. The centre will provide information on issues ranging from the new Panchayati raj act, employment opportunities, health and sanitation issues, and how people can solve their everyday problems.

The newly constructed "anganwadi centre" building was used as the VIC after the anganwadi timings were over.

Lessons Learnt

The planning process in Dhana has been a learning experience:

— Some members of the Gram Sabha have shown the qualities of community leaders, realising the importance of their role in the development of the village.

— The Panchayat has learnt to function in a more organised way in the general interest of the people.

— The panches have begun to realise that they have a greater role in the functioning of the Panchayat than just passing resolutions.

— The Panchayat and especially the sarpanch have learnt the task of bargaining with the government administration for more resources for the development of the Panchayat.

— On the whole the people and the Panchayat members of Dhana have learnt to be more aware of their own abilities and use the resources (human and others) available within the village.

— The planning process has enhanced and built up people's skills to organise the information available to them that is essential for planning and they now know where to go for more information and resources so that the planning process continues.

Future Directions

The planning and implementation process in Dhana was completed in October 1997. The number of tap connections has increased from 6 to 14 as a result of the community's contribution and Panchayat initiative. Two water tanks have also been constructed, a new transformer has been installed in order to deal with the electricity problem. The people and the Panchayats have adopted the Village Information Centre initiative.

MICRO PLANNING INITIATIVE IN BALAICHA, HARYANA

Micro Planning

Based on our experiences of carrying out participatory bottom-up planning in two Panchayats Dhana and Khetavas in district Jhajjar Haryana, PRIA undertook a similar initiative in District Mahendergarh, Haryana. Inspired by the process, Jan Sewa Kendra, a voluntary organization based in Mahendergarh District took the responsibility of replicating it in their work area. This was seen as a good opportunity for both replication of the earlier participatory model as well as to build the capacities of the local organization undertaking this process in collaboration with PRIA. Village Balaicha was selected for carrying out this process. The reasons for this selection were:

— Firstly that the office of the Voluntary Association (VA) is situated in this Panchayat and apart from sharing a very close relationship with the people of Balaicha, Mr Sripal who is heading the VA showed a keen interest in carrying out a Bottom-up planning exercise in that Panchayat based on the model developed by PRIA.
— Secondly the Sarpanch of this Panchayat is a woman and one of PRIA's objective is to build capacities and enhance leadership skills of women representatives.
— Finally Balaicha not being a "Roadside Panchayat" is cut off and relatively not so developed as others in the State.

This case has been divided into three sections; section 1 describes the Panchayat and its socio- economic status, section 2 gives some insights into the process of participatory bottom-up planning carried out in Balaicha and finally section 3 highlights some of the learnings derived from this exercise and suggestions for further improvement.

Historical Background

It is said that the village Balaicha is about 1000 years old. Earlier on, it was known as Ballabhgarh and ruled over by the Nawab of Jhajjar. The village was situated one kilometre west of the present day Balaicha and was razed to the ground by a fire (ordered by the Nawab of Jhajjar). Even today remains of the old village can be found in and around the area. During those days only two castes Brahmin and Dalits used to inhabit the village. The Ahirs came to the area much later. Elders of the village say that long ago a young girl by the name of Paira had come to the village and given birth to a male child under the Jati tree. Even today the majority of households in the village belong to the "Paira" sub-caste.

Status of Panchayat

The village is divided into seven wards. The main characteristic of the Panchayat is that all the Ward Members and the Sarpanch have been selected unanimously by the people. The procedure is to call a village meeting whereby all those present select there Panchayat members.

Profile of Panchayat Members

Sl. No.	*Name*	*Post*	*Age*	*Caste*	*Education*
1.	Murti Devi	Sarpanch	40	Brahmin	Illiterate
2.	Shri Hukum Singh	Up-Sarpanch	30	Ahir	10th Pass
3.	Ram Pratap	Panch	35	Brahmin	5th Pass
4.	Satnarayan	Panch	50	Brahmin	5th Pass
5.	Jawahar Ram	Panch	40	SC	Illiterate
6.	Smt.Shanti Devi	Panch	48	Brahmin	Illiterate
7.	Smt.Ompeti	Panch	35	Brahmin	Illiterate
8.	Niranjan Lal	Panch	32	SC	8th Pass

The Panchayat has an annual income of 40-45 thousand rupees from its Panchayat land. This income was utilized in the year 1997-98 for boring of a tube well, repairing of hand pumps and payment of electricity bills (Panchayat tube well). Although initially they carried out a lot of developmental work in their area, the irregular visits of the Panchayat Secretary has led to disinterest in carrying out any further work. It has also become extremely difficult in the absence of the secretary for them to get information about the various schemes and provisions available to them. Further some inter-village dynamics arising out of a water dispute in that Panchayat has resulted in less co-operation and involvement of the people in Panchayat activities.

Socio-Economic Profile

The village is spread in an area of about 60 bighas and is dominated by the Brahmin community having a total population of 1041 of which 542 are males and 499 females. The total number of household is 152. Out of this 90 households belong to the Brahmin community and 30 to the Dalit community. Other than this, one household belongs to Jat community and one household belongs to Nai community. The village is located on the Rajasthan border; therefore the terrain

Sectors	*Present Status*
Agriculture	The main occupation of the villagers is agriculture. Mustard and wheat is the predominant crop of the Rabi Season whereas Jawar, Bajra, Guwar are of the Kharif Season. The agricultural yield is low due to the low water table and sandy water available. Most of the farmers are not aware of the latest varieties of different crops and use of modern practices. Only a few progressive farmers are aware of new varieties and used modern practices for high yield. Some families give cultivated land to other farmers for agriculture and in return they take a proportion of the produce.
Animal Resources	Balaicha is rich in animal resources with a good number of cattle, sheep, goat and camel in the village.
Education	The educational status is low in the village. Primary education is higher among the villagers whereas higher education is not easily within the reach of the villagers. The nearest secondary level school is 4 km away. The dropout rate is higher among girls. Low economic status and traditional practices are some of the other factors responsible for this.
Occupation	Occupational status reflects the economic soundness of any village. The villagers' main occupation here is agriculture. The other occupation is daily wage work. Very few villagers are working as government employees. Wage opportunities are not easily accessible to them.
Health	Lack of hospital facility and lack of preventive measures among villagers is responsible for the low health status in the village. Another factor of low health status is the impure water available. The nearest PHC is 10 kms away and without adequate transportation it is less accessible to them. They approach Mahendergarh for the treatment, which is 10 km. away from the village. Lack of frequent transportation will make it costly affair for the poor villagers.
Women	The major burden of the work is carried out by the women. Women are responsible for the household activities, livestock rearing and agricultural related activities during agricultural season. Despite rigid social taboos and traditional practices resulting in their subordinate status, the presence of the Sanjeevani and the VA has helped to bring awareness about women's equal status and empowerment.

is dry and sandy. The water table is very low and the water is salty. Balaicha Gram Panchayat falls under Mahendergarh Block of Mahendergarh District located 8 km away from the district and 35 km away from the district headquarters Narnaul.

The Process

Step 1: Training on PRI

As an initial step, a one-day training for elected representatives and other interested Gram Sabha members of Balaicha was organized which provided an orientation to micro planning and importance of people participation. The training was followed up by individual discussions with the VA, Sarpanch and panches about their role in the process.

Step 2: Panchayat Meeting

As a second step, a Panchayat meeting was called by the VA who took on the role of initiators steering the participants towards developing an understanding about the planning process and the need for their involvement in the same. A decision was taken as to organize ward level meetings, to identify issues of concern and seeking people's participation in planning for development.

Volunteers were sought for the occasion in helping to facilitate the discussion of people in various wards. These volunteers were given prior orientation on people's participation in planning process. The ward meetings also helped in ensuring the participation of the weaker sections.

Step 3: Pictorial Exercise

During the process of small group discussions and meetings it was found that people were unclear about the exact ward boundaries, which demarcated their wards from others in the Panchayat area. It was observed that more than 40 per cent (a large percentage of which were women) of the people did not have a clear understanding of where the ward starts and ends. As a result they were unable to give suggestions or answers to questions like where the taps can be installed or which part of *gali* should be considered first for construction. It became obvious through these discussions that people could actively participate in such a process only if they had a clear picture in their minds about the ward. Thus plans were made to have pictorial exercises in each ward whereby the different groups and individuals living in those wards could come together and map out a picture of their ward along with the existing resources available in the same.

Pictorial Exercises were carried out in two wards, i.e., Ward No.1 and Ward No. 2. In this exercise all the ward members were asked to draw out a map of their ward and identify the problems along with the probable solutions to those problems in the specific wards. For example where water scarcity was identified as a problem, solutions also were found by the group as to where exactly taps need to be installed to ensure equal water supply to all the inhabitants of the ward. The ward level meetings helped the different sections of the community to articulate their needs and problems as they slowly began to get involved in the process.

Step 4: Sector Specific Plan

Based on the issues/problems identified by the villagers during earlier meeting, the sector specific plan was prepared in the presence of Panchayat members, voluntary agency representatives and others at the Jan Sewa Kendra premises.

Issue	*Activity*	*Responsibility*
Agriculture: As agriculture is the main occupation of the villagers most of the peopled showed a keen interest in improving agricultural practices	• To provide training related to new practices in agriculture. • To develop a channel for providing information about availability of seeds and fertilizers	• VA & Panchayat will approach Agriculture Department
Drinking Water: Non-availability of drinking water close to the households • Maintenance • Installation of pumps	• Form a committee and make rules for fees for private connection and of other related things • Available water sources should be repaired by Panchayat and contribution by villagers	• Panchayat and Committee members • VA will help information of Committee • Alternate: Panchayat will coordinate with Water Supply Department for supply of drinking water

Contd...........

Issue	*Activity*	*Responsibility*
Construction of lane and drainage facility	• Plan formulation and selection of site (priority-wise) • Passed resolution and submitted to the concerned authority	• Panchayat and VAs
Lack of employment opportunity for youth	• Identification of target groups • To prepare literate youth for government and non-government jobs and organize awareness camp for various target groups to engage in income generating activities • To organize training for self generating scheme	• VA and active Gram Sabha members
Health: • Lack of awareness about preventive care • Lack of hospital in the village	• To establish Primary Health Centre • To train and streamline the functioning of Anganwadi and Sanjeevini workers • To raise the awareness and capacity of people to initiate self-help activities • To organize health awareness camp	• The Panchayat will facilitate and approach Health Department for establishment of PHC • The VA will coordinate with Health Department in organizing camp and provide training to target group
Education: • High rate of drop out among girl students • Lack of awareness for higher education • Lack of a middle and high school in village	• Panchayat and school teachers will approach concerned department for up-gradation of school • Organize camps to motivate parents for educating girl children	• Panchayat, Parents and Voluntary Group
Electricity: • Non availability of street lighting • Less number of electric poles for proper connection	• Selection of sight for digging of electric poles • Provision for street light at different corner of village by approaching government	• Panchayat and voluntary group members will approach Electricity Department for electric poles.
A common meeting place	• To build Panchayat Ghar • Panchayat should approach Block office for grant of Panchayat Ghar • To ensure peoples contribution in of Panchayat Ghar	• People's contribution for streetlight Panchayat and VAs

Note: Budgeted cost and times has not been mentioned in the format.

Step 5: Gram Sabha Meeting: Village Planning Meeting

In order to share the sector specific plans with the entire village and elicit discussions on it, a Gram Sabha meeting was called by the Panchayat. While the VA and Panchayat representatives went about organizing the meeting, the volunteer group played an equally important role by meeting individual Gram Sabha members and motivating them to participate in the meeting. Focusing the discussion on implementation of the plans various issues were discussed such as the need for active participation of all, bureaucracy and others. Follow-up plans were drawn up based on the issues identified in the planning process and a committee of 12 people was formed (VA representatives, Panchayat representatives and active Gram Sabha members) to take up the issues with the concerned departments. The issues were divided into two-firstly those which came within the ambit of the different government departments and secondly those which could be implemented by the Panchayats with the assistance of the people. It was decided that contributions by the people in both cash and kind would be called for to implement the latter.

Implementation Plan

Issue	*Activity*	*Responsibility*	*Department*
Water	• Electricity connections to ensure proper supply of water. • Installing pipelines and fixing water taps • Building 6 water tanks in selected areas of the Panchayat. • Installing some hand-pumps in selective areas.	Panchayat members. VA representatives and some active individuals	Water Department, Health Department, block office, DRDA, and CAPART
Health	• Getting an ANM • Availability of medicines • Health awareness camps	VA, Panchayat, Sanjeevini and *anganwadi* workers	Health Department, PHC worker at Narnaul and Civil Surgeon Hospital, Narnaul

Contd.........

Issue	*Activity*	*Responsibility*	*Department*
Education	• Awareness camps in the Panchayat on the need for education • Up-gradation of the primary school • Building rooms in the school • Constructing bathrooms for boys and girls in the school • Constructing a water tank in the school premises	Panchayat, village education committee, VA and the school teachers	DPEP, block office, Education Department, Mahendergarh
Common meeting place	• Building a Panchayat Bhavan/ Ghar	Panchayat, IVG members	Block office, DRDA
Sanitation and environment protection	• Building latrines in the Panchayat and creating awareness about its proper use. • Preparation of soak-pit, to create awareness about protecting the environment. • Tree plantation.	VA, Panchayat and active individuals	CAPART, Forest Department
Village Lanes	• Construction of lanes through the village. • Preparation of a proposal for the same. • Eliciting peoples participation for maintenance and contributing their labour during construction period	VA, Panchayat and active individuals	Block office, DRDA
Providing employment opportunities	• Selection beneficiaries on the basis of economic status. • Organizing trainings to impart knowledge and skills to the people. • Constructing a training bhavan	VA	DRDA, agriculture department, IGSS, Delhi and women and child welfare department,Narnaul
Agriculture	• Waste land development. • Availability of seeds and fertilizers, awareness on new agricultural technologies • Awareness about the harvesting two crops in a year for generating more income	VA, Panchayat	Assistant agriculture department, Narnaul
Access to information	• Organizing camps on this issue on a regular basis • Opening a village information centre, preparing a list of information to be acquired • Create awareness on the importance of information	VA, Panchayat	Block and the various departments

Follow-up of Micro Planning in Village Balaicha

As a part of the follow-up several meetings were organized at the Panchayat in which there was active participation of Gram Sabha members, Junior engineers, committee members (set up in the course of the micro planning exercise), Panchayat members, VA and PRIA representatives. In the course of these meetings it was decided (by all present) that the priority issue of water needs to be addressed, as this was a common issue critical to the entire Panchayat. As water tank was the priority issue, a budget estimate meeting was organized on June 24th, 1999.

The overall amount estimated to build this water tank was R.2,29,000 as drawn by the Junior engineer, Panchayat members and the volunteer groups. The amount was discussed and people thought that the estimate was high and felt that the actual cost would be less. Everybody felt that once the process was started it would be easier for them to request other parties like the government, the local MLA and the other two tiers of Panchayats namely Panchayat Samiti and Zila Parishad to contribute towards this end.

The Panchayat offered to give the land, which had been selected by all in the previous meetings as well as Rs. 50,000 from the Panchayat fund to the committee to star their work. The community members all agreed to contribute either by providing the labour or giving approximately Rs. 200 per household for the completion of the project. Volunteer agencies and non-governmental organization also contributed to the kitty, which was around Rs. 50,000 as a, matching amount given by the Panchayat.

Outcome of the Process

- The entire process helped to bring the different sections of the community together and make decisions collectively for the development of the Panchayat. An increased involvement of the marginalized groups was observed as the process moved forward providing an opportunity for their issues and concerns to appear in the emerging plan.
- People's knowledge about their own Panchayat and wards was enhanced enabling them to identify the various issues and find solutions with the available resources. Knowledge

about external resources and opportunities was also increased in the process of planning.

- The participatory bottom-up planning process helped build knowledge, skills, role clarity and solidarity amongst the Panchayat representatives who played a key role in taking the process forward. Prior to this they had no knowledge about their roles and responsibilities and therefore had been unable to actively engage themselves in the development of the Panchayat. The process helped them to recognize the needs of the people and the resources available for fulfilling some of these needs thus bringing them closer to each other as well as the people.

Conclusion

Despite being an extremely time consuming and intensive exercise, the participatory bottom-up planning process was a unique experience for both the people of Balaicha as well as for the facilitators. Bringing together a treasure of knowledge and skills it provided a platform for people's active participation in development. The Balaicha experience also provided valuable insights for replication of this model as a vehicle for enabling good governance vis-à-vis people's participation. This calls for preparation of some modules enabling replication of the process by other players namely the government and non-government organizations committed to people's participation in governance. The final challenge perhaps lies in finding easily replicable models that could enable the Panchayats to carry out this process themselves with or without any external support.

DECENTRALIZED PLANNING—MANDI DISTRICT, HIMACHAL PRADESH

Himachal Pradesh is situated in the north-west corner of India, in the lap of the Himalayan ranges. It is surrounded by Jammu and Kashmir in the north, Uttar Pradesh in the south-east, Haryana in the south and Punjab in the west. In the east it forms India's boundary with Tibet.

The state is almost entirely mountainous with altitudes ranging from 460-6600m above sea level. It has a deeply divided landscape, a complex physical structure and rich vegetation found in mild sub-tropical latitudes. Himachal is drained by a number of rivers, the most important of which are Chenab, Ravi, Beas, Sutlej and Yamuna. Al these rivers are snow-fed and therefore perennial.

Participatory Planning Exercise

Mandi district is found in the central part of Himachal Pradesh. It is one of the twelve districts of the State. The district is mostly hilly. The Balh valley (in the district) is our work area, it is surrounded by mountains on all sides. This is the valley of the River Suketi, a tributary of the Beas. It originates from the town Sundarnagar and terminates at south of the town Mandi. It is a very fertile valley and has a dense concentration of population. This area is covered by 26 Panchayats and is part of the Mandi Sadar block, one of the 10 development blocks of this district.

A Panchayat named Kehar Getting Started

The micro planning exercise was started in the Kehar Panchayat, Mandi Sadar Block, Mandi district. Since the first round of elections to the Panchayat had just been completed in December 1995 (after the new Amendment to the Constitution), the need came up to enable the Panchayat members to handle their new responsibility of making village/Panchayat plans. The exercise of micro planning, began in Kehar Panchayat. Sukhdev Vishwa Premi was the then Pradhan, the chief functionary of the VA, as well as the co-ordinator of the Rural Technology and Development Centre (RTDC), a local organization in this Panchayat. Panchayat elections in Himachal Pradesh had taken place in December 1995 on a non-party basis.

The Panchayat

The Panchayat has six revenue villages—Kehar, Satoh, Bhiura, Rigar, Khiuri and Chawari. There are a total of 11 wards out of which four are represented by women members.

Before 1978, Kehar was a part of the Baggi Panchayat. Kehar is surrounded in the east by the Segli Panchayat, north-east by the Mowiseri Panchayat, in the north by the Sakroha Panchayat and in the west by the Kummi Panchayat. Most of the Panchayat is situated in the plain regions that have been divided by a number of rivulets.

The total area covered by the 6 villages is 1,177 hectares, while the total population is 3,924. Most of the people are engaged in the irrigation of the agricultural area. As a result, there was an increase in the production of cash crops, especially vegetables. In fact, Kehar Panchayat is the largest vegetable growing area in this region.

Micro Planning: An Initiative

Micro planning can be carried out based on the available skills and capability, knowledge base etc. However, the basic design of the planning process will include a study of the state of affairs, identification of problems and priorities and plan formulation. The method may vary from place to place, depending upon the situation and the circumstances.

Steps in Micro Planning

▼

Selection of a Gram Panchayat

▼

Building a Favourable Environment for the People's Participation

▼

Collection of Data and Information

▼

Sharing of the Findings with the People

▼

Community Problem Analysis and Identification of Development Priorities

▼

Identification of Solutions and Strategies

▼

Making of the Panchayat Level Plan

▼

Implementation

The period taken up by the micro planning process was about one year.

The Process

The entire participatory planning exercise has been divided into different phases depending on the type and nature of the work accomplished.

Formation of Village Development Committee

A village level committee was established. The Ward Member of Bhiura was unanimously declared the Chairperson of the Committee. The Committee had a total of 13 members out of which 5 are women. The main tasks or responsibilities of the VDC were:

(a) To formulate a detailed action plan that was technically feasible and economically viable as well as a detailed budget estimate of all the equipment needed, materials required, wages of technical people employed etc. and

(b) Implementation of the action plan.

Phase one (May 1996), involved building an environment through holding workshops with the elected members along with RTDC, meeting of the Gram Panchayat, training work shops for volunteers and ward meetings. These workshops and meetings focused on building a core team that would work directly with the community in the planning process. A total of 22 volunteers were identified in this process from 11 wards and they were provided additional training.

Phase two (June 1996) dealt with understanding the situation in the area through an organized collection of data and information. The focus was on getting community members to think about their individual realities using a combination of data-collection methods. The door-to-door surveys were used to cover 747 households for this process. Information was collected by the volunteers.

Phase three dealt with the sharing of the findings after the survey. This was achieved by organizing workshops/meetings. The exercise helped people to think collectively as a group rather than one person. The focus of these workshops was to get the community members to understand the socio-economic status of the village and its problems.

Phase four (December 1996—March 1997). This appeared to be the most crucial stage for the formulation of a micro-plan. The facilitators (including the Panchayat, volunteer groups and the non-governmental organizations) encouraged the community members through a series of workshops, to analyse problems faced at the individual, village and Panchayat levels and then arrange the first three in order of priority. From the first three it was easy to see what the development needs of the village were and to take some action. Guidance was given so that the people could choose the right methods. It was important for the people to contribute land, labour and money for the development of the village. Resources available locally could also be used. At this stage Village Development Committees (VDCs) were formed in all the six villages of Kehar Panchayat of 15-25 members chosen from voluntary organizations, Gram Sabha members, elected Ward Members, and technical skills from the line department i.e. education, sanitation, lawyers, forest etc. The ratio of women and scheduled caste in the committee was one-third. The development plan could now be put into action, with the panch as the chairperson and help from the JEs.

Plan for Drinking Water in Bhiura

The Problem: Bhiura's water supply comes from the BBMB project at Baggi, the neighbouring Panchayat.

Identification of locally available resources: the potential source of water was at a distance of one km from the village at Baryha. This according to the people could be tapped in order to get a regular supply of water.

Land required for the construction of the storage tank was also identified and the community members provided the labour.

Action Plan

(a) The laying of a pipeline from the source to the village, along the road. A total of 150 pipes were needed to cover a distance of 1 km, each pipe being 20 feet long.

(b) The building of storage tank, and

(c) 3-4 households would be provided with one tap each. At this rate 18-20 taps would be installed.

Phase five (March-April 1997). The responsibility of the process at this stage is that of the communities rather than the facilitators. The Village Development Committees were responsible for formulating plans at the village level and these helped to form a Panchayat plan.

Phase six (1999) the implementation stage began. The year from May 1997 to May 1998 was called the "Frustration period".

In May 1998, a Gram Sabha meeting was organized, budgetary allocations and the people's contribution were discussed in relation to the plans that were made in the 6 villages on the prioritized issues. These issues need to be further prioritized for implementation purposes. In the Kehar Panchayat the two main developmental priorities of the people are:

- Drinking water facilities
- Road construction—both earthen as well as metalled roads.

For the two priorities mentioned above plans were drawn up, technical advice was sought by the VDC and the people's contribution was generated in the final implementation of the plan. In the implementation process the Panchayat adopted an innovative method, to keep a worksheet of the activities involved, delegation of responsibilities, material required and the budget. This determined and ensured the participation and the timely implementation of the plan.

Worksheet on Plan Implementation

Activities	*Responsibilities*	*Facilities*	*Equipment/ materials*	*Service*
Organize and conduct meetings in the village	VDC, staff of RTDC Pradhan, Up-Pradhan and Ward Members	Place (venue) of the meeting	—	—
Organize labour to clear the land	VDC and PRI members, members of Nehru Yuvak Mandal	Temporary shed to store equipment	Equipment to clear the land	Volun-teers
Collection of material, equipment	VDC, PRI members and CBOs, NYK	Temporary shed	People's contribution for material	—

The Community's Contribution: An Achievement in Kehar Panchayat

The people of Rigar have taken up a development activity for their village, that of road construction. This was a major priority of the people as discussed earlier. On the 4th of February it was also decided that the VDC along with some of the villagers would take up the work of widening and repairing of the village road themselves. This road has been in a state of disrepair for a long time and neither the Panchayat nor the government has done anything till now. On the 23rd of February the people started work on the widening and repairing of the village road. A total of 22 local villagers worked in shifts from 10 a.m. to 7 p.m. The Ward Member, members of the VDC and a member of the core team were all involved in the process.

Lessons and Challenges

From the experiences of micro planning in Kehar Panchayat, H.P, involving the community members, CBOs, PRIs etc. many challenges and issues emerged that needed to be handled in an effective manner in order to get the desired result.

- Participatory micro planning and community participation in village development activities is a pioneering project. It is a new approach for villagers who till recently have been totally dependent on the government for all kinds of support. Very few Panchayats have comprehensive development plans, more so a plan that is a result of a participatory process.
- Long gaps between the phases or the various activities can lead to a loss of interest on the part of the volunteers as well as the villagers. Continuity in the programme is necessary for the active involvement of the people as well as building up a better rapport with them.
- Proper channels should be used for giving prior information to the people regarding the date, time and venue of village meetings. This can be achieved by:

    1. Using posters with the venue, date and time written very clearly and put up at ventage points in the village e.g. tea stalls, shops, walls etc.

2. Visiting people's houses, shops and other places and telling them about the meeting, its purpose and the need for people to attend it. This can be achieved by the team of volunteers.

- Social dynamics, especially the caste factor has to be kept in mind while organizing village level meetings. This way the gathering will be well attended and the people will indulge in healthy discussions.

MICRO LEVEL PLANNING: MADHYA PRADESH

The Background

Samarthan is a support organization working on various capacity building initiatives in the state of Madhya Pradesh since 1995. It has been focusing primarily on project planning, monitoring participants, evaluation and keeping records of the process. One of its core activities is the initiative on strengthening Panchayati Raj Institutions in Madhya Pradesh. This includes training of elected representatives, micro planning, awareness generation through educational material preparation and distribution, an ongoing dialogue with the government, building networks of voluntary organizations and research on issues critical to the success of the Panchayati Raj.

Experiences of the Jumunia Tank Gram Panchayat

In 1995, Samarthan began its initiative on strengthening Panchayati Raj Institutions in Madhya Pradesh. After visiting various districts of the state and interacting with local voluntary organizations, elected representatives, government officials and other interested groups and individuals, a Training of Trainers (TOT) programme was organized in January 1996. This programme was aimed at training representatives of voluntary organizations in this programme was Gyan Deep Mandal—a training programme was organized in collaboration with them and Gram Panchayat of Jamunia Tank in Sehore district. As part of its strategy of strengthening Panchayats directly, Samarthan began its micro planning initiatives in two Gram Panchayats of Sehore namely, Jamunia Tank and Raipura. A similar initiative was also begun in the Nayagaon Gram Panchayat of Gwalior district, in collaboration with a local organization.

Jamunia Tank Gram Panchayat

Jamunia Tank Gram Panchayat is located at a distance of about 8 kms away from the Sehore district headquarters and 40 kms from the state capital, Bhopal. This Gram Panchayat is represented by a woman sarpanch belonging to the backward class. The sarpanch is an educated woman with grit and initiative. The Gram Panchayat includes 12 panches representing the twelve wards, 4 of the panches are women.

The village is spread over an area of 1002.16 hectares and is inhabited by 618 males and 541 women. People belonging to the Mewada, Meena, Khali, Rathore, Aggarwal, Pandit, Gosaii, Dalit, Balia, Prajapati, Kumhar, and Tyagi castes live in the village.

The facilities available to the people living in the village include a primary school, telephone exchange and a child care centre. The Gram Panchayat has undertaken various initiatives to enhance these facilities and to provide new facilities to the people such as an adult education programme, construction of low cost latrines, drains and upgradation of school facilities.

Raipura Gram Panchayat

Raipura Gram Panchayat is also a reserved seat for a backward caste sarpanch. This Panchayat is headed by a male sarpanch. The Gram Panchayat is comprises 3 villages namely Raipura, Hasanpura and Jamunia Farm and is represented by 13 panches from the thirteen wards, of which 4 are women. The Sarpanch is educated (matriculate) and belongs to a family owning the largest landholdings in the village. However, he lacks initiative and takes little interest in the affairs of the Panchayat.

The Gram Panchayat is spread over an area of 823.26 hectares and is inhabited by 703 males and 593 women. People belonging to Mewada, Meena, Khali, Kumhar, Prajapati, Pandit, Balia, Rathod and Gosai communities live in this village.

The facilities available to the people include a primary and middle school and a child care centre. The Panchayat has taken some interest in the literacy programme launched by the district authorities, but by and large the Panchayat leadership and the community lacks initiative in the various development Programmes available for their own development.

For the purpose of this document we are only elaborating the experiences of the Jamunia Tank Gram Panchayat.

The Process

Rapport Building and Awareness Generation

In the initial stages all efforts were focused on building a rapport with the people and representatives of the Gram Panchayats. Meetings were held with various groups like the youth and women groups, groups of men were met separately. Orientation Programmes were organized to create an understanding among the Panchayat representatives and the community regarding the roles and responsibilities of the Gram Panchayat members and the role of the Gram Sabha members in the decision-making processes, especially during the planning process.

This phase was most instrumental in determining the future course of planning and capacity building in the community as it enabled the concerns of the people of the community to be brought out in the open. The facilitators such as VAS, NGOs, CBOs were also able to emphasize their neutral positions so as to generate faith and mutual trust.

The Stake-holders Analysis

The rapport-building phase laid bare the complexities of village life, class and caste conflicts, stakes of various groups and individuals in the socio political structure of the village and other socio-economic relationships. It became increasingly clear that the mere strengthening of Gram Panchayat representatives would not result in the resolution of existing problems. Therefore, it was felt that the viewpoints of all groups and individuals should be so presented so as to ensure maximum benefit for all. Efforts were made to bring the women and other marginalized groups into the mainstream of these discussions, to understand their point of view and enable their participation in the decision-making process. To this end, discussions, PRA exercises and focus group discussions were initiated with women's groups and groups of Dalits so that they could analyse their own status in the village polity. This eventually led to problem identification, prioritization and problem solving through their own efforts. The stakeholders were identified and their perceptions analysed so as to enable their incorporation in future strategies. The needs assessment phase enabled each group in the village to analyse their needs and priorities them on the basis of the needs of the community as a whole.

Building Linkages

The process of rapport building with the community and the stake-holders analysis led to the realization that the Gram Panchayat and Gram Sabha needed to build and strengthen their linkages with "out siders" such as the government officials, MP/MLA, community organizations and so on. However, this process is an ongoing process linked to capacities of the people concerned. After undergoing a number of structured capacity building exercises for the Gram Panchayat members and Gram Sabha members, they have begun realizing their own power to negotiate and make the required linkages and trade offs for the desired results.

Capacity Building

The stakeholder analysis and need assessment exercises led to need-based designs of capacity building initiatives. These initiatives were by and large structured training inputs for Gram Panchayat representatives, women and youth groups, village level functionaries such as the Panchayat karmies and KRPs. Sensitization workshops were also held with the media personnel so as to make Panchayats and governance a wider issue. These trainings were followed up with "follow up" initiatives, such as capacity building on specific issues like finances of Panchayats, conducting ward level meetings and mock Gram Sabhas. Capacities of Mahila Mandals and Youth groups have been strengthened so as to enable their functioning as "monitors" of the Gram Panchayat. Gram Sabha members are being encouraged to take an active part in initiatives such as the Total Literacy Campaign, health and environmental awareness building campaigns.

Participatory Planning: Lessons in "Empowerment"

Building confidence—Ongoing capacity building exercises with exposure to the outside world have built the confidence of not only the Gram Panchayat representatives but also the Gram Sabha members. This in turn has increased the people's participation in Gram Sabha meetings and other communities and informal meetings, giving them the confidence to ask for accountability from not only the Gram Panchayat representatives but also the government officials and functionaries.

Power to Negotiate: A Case in Point

The Public Health and Engineer (PHE) department of the district office, Madhya Pradesh implemented a scheme which provided for building of low cost toilets in the rural areas of the state.

The main features of the scheme were:

- It sanctioned construction of 65 toilets in the Panchayat.
- The PHE would provide for 80 per cent of the cost and 20 per cent of the contribution will be made by the community.
- According to the scheme each toilet (construction) would cost Rs. 2,700.
- The PHE would commission the work to an NGO (the contractors had registered themselves as an NGO) and the NGO would construct the toilets (totaling Rs. 2,160). The community would give their contribution in the form of labour and bricks (amounting to a total of Rs. 540) for the implementation of the scheme.

A meeting was called in the village to prepare the list of people who would benefit from the scheme. The list was made on the basis of those below the poverty line and discussions in the meeting. The people chose the site for the construction of the toilets. Very soon the people realized that very low quality material was being used for the construction of the toilets.

These complaints were brought to the notice of the sarpanch who mobilized a group of people to make an inquiry into the matter.

The group checked the quality of the material beign used as well as its market rate. The total amount spent on the material turned out to be an amazing Rs. 1,000 (as against the government demanded of Rs. 2,160). A complaint was lodged against the contractors in the PHE department. The peoples united efforts forced the PHE officials to make an inspection of the toilets constructed in the village. A dialogue was initiated with the contractors and certain conditions were laid down by the community—the contractors had to reconstruct the toilets with better quality material.

The community was united in their ability to negotiate with the PHE department and the contractors and make a proper inquiry into the entire episode. The Gram Panchayat was able to use this opportunity to further negotiate with the PHE department for the installation of a hand pump in the village.

Access to information has given the Gram Panchayat representatives a new confidence to handle the everyday affairs of the Panchayat with ease. It has also enabled them to become accountable without getting defensive or overwhelmed by the people's questions. They have begun sharing the information on government schemes and programmes with the people and encouraging open discussions in Gram Sabha meetings.

The increase in confidence, access to information, ability to discuss and plan for problem resolution has strengthened people's capacity to negotiate with government officials and politicians.

"We" can do it

For years the people of Jamunia Tank had been trying for the upgradation of the village primary school to middle school. The administration was not listening to their requests. With their newly found confidence the people and Gram Panchayat representatives of Jamunia decided to take a tough stand with the administration as the primary school was being run in a building donated by the people of Jamunia. Along with the head master of the primary school they threatened to close down the government school being run in their building and start a private school unless the education department agreed to upgrade the primary school to a middle school. They went with a list of students who were unable to continue their education because of the lack of facilities. Eventually the school was upgraded to class VIII.

Thc people of Jamunia were overjoyed. They were beginning to realize their strengths and use them for the common good.

Increased Participation

The process of planning enabled the people to realize their own capacities as well as lead to an increased awareness through systematic interventions. The simultaneous processes have increased people's participation in formal and informal meetings. Participation of women and Dalits has also increased in meetings and consequently in decision-making. More and more government schemes are being accessed and implemented by the people.

The people of Jamunia had expressed a need for a village drain a number of times but nothing had been done about it. During the planning process this issue was brought up and they planned for the construction of a drain. The estimated budget for the construction of the drain was Rs. 93,000. The community volunteered to contribute Rs. 50,000, which was collected in proportion to their land holdings. Those who could not contribute money agreed to give labour and Rs. 50,000 was sanctioned as the award for people's successful efforts in the Total Literacy Campaign. The people of Jamunia were able to achieve 80 per cent literacy in the age group of 15-35 through their sustained efforts.

Regularization of Meetings

The ongoing planning process has resulted in the regularization of Gram Panchayat and Gram Sabha meetings. Gram Panchayat representatives have started organizing regular ward level meetings so as to keep in touch with people's needs and priorities.

Formation of Community Groups

The people have organized themselves in mahila mandals, youth mandals and pressure groups of different kinds. Their aim is to not only to monitor the functioning of Gram Panchayat but also to give support to the Gram Panchayat in its negotiations with the administration and the politicians.

Establishing Viable Linkages

The process of base upwards planning has helped the Gram Sabha and Gram Panchayat in establishing co-ordination and linkages with the other tiers of the Panchayats, administration and line departments at the district level. These linkages have led to better utilization of available local and government resources. The linkages have also given the sarpanch of Jamunia visibility and consequently the confidence to represent their Gram Panchayat in various block and district level forums.

Efforts Made by the Community

The various programmes have raised the level of awareness among the community members and an understanding has been created

Table 9.1: Fund Generation

Sl. No.	*Heads*	*Funds Received Jamunia Tank Panchayat*	*Funds Generated (Contributions)*
1997-1998		Rs.	Rs.
1.	Best GP Awarded	25,000	
2.	Construction of road, drain	50,000	17,000
3.	Construction of small bridge	25,000	16,000
4.	Saving Award (Mahila Savings Scheme)	15,000	
5.	Construction of temple	4,000	3,00,000
6.	Funds for Mahila Mandal	1,000	
7.	Jawahar Rojgar Yojana	16,000	
8.	Construction of Anganwadi	1,10,000	
9.	Panchayat Department	12,000	
10.	Extra room in school	75,000	
1996-1997			
1.	House for homeless @ 15,000/- per house	75,000	
2.	Jeevan Dhara Well	96,000	
3.	Destitute pension 4 persons @5,000/-	20,000	
4.	Material benefit @300 for 4	1,200	
5.	Tools for artisans @ 2000 for 5 persons	10,000	
6.	Old age pension @ 150 71 persons	10,650	
7.	JRY	4,00,000	

about the powers and the functions of Gram Sabha. Now better coordination is possible with the Panchayats. The community has started coming together to study the situations, plan for their needs and are willing to put these plans into action.

Community Organization

Issues based debates began, with regular interaction, building a good relationship within the community. The interaction took the form of dialogue, focusing on issues and looking for solutions to problems. People were willing to contribute labour and money. The result was good planning and motivating the administration, the Panchayat and the line department.

Whenever a common issue came up, Gram Sabha meetings were held at night rather than the day. The attendance was greater than at the government Gram Sabhas. Debates and discussions took place more freely.

According to the people oriented plan, those involved in the implementation of the plan, have to negotiate, bargain with the related people, organizations, agencies, the line department as well as the government. For example, at the Jamunia Tank Panchayat, the sarpanch demanded 100 toilets from Zanpad but 65 toilets were sanctioned for the people of Jamunia. Construction was started by the contractors (a newly formed NGO of contractors, in keeping with the government order, that toilet constructions will be handed over to a NGO). But the contractors asked for approximately Rs. 1000 per toilet as against Rs. 2160 per toilet (the total amount in the earlier scheme was Rs. 2700, in which government, central/state were to have contributed 80% and 20%). The beneficiaries opposed the bad quality construction. But it had no effect on the contractors. Immediately a Gram Sabha meeting was called at night and it was decided that the people would meet the chief officer of Public Health, engineering department. They took their problem to the C.E.E. of the P.H.E. The C.E.E. decided to go to the village to see the toilet construction. During the visit the C.E.E. said that either all the toilets should be reconstructed or contractors (NGO chief) should face the beneficiaries and satisfy them. The payment would not be made to the NGO till then. The contractors agreed to repair the toilets, and promised the beneficiaries that this kind of work will not be repeated.

Solving the problem of toilet construction helped to build the self-confidence of the villagers. Now the people can deal with their problems regularly. The villagers monitor all these activities, literacy campaign, drainage construction, temple planning, local road construction, the temporary bridge in SC community, the anganwadi building, school functioning, health centre and functioning of cooperative societies.

The change in the people's attitude, their involvement in training, building relationships and creating awareness helped everybody in the village. For example:

In Jamunia the people focused on the school in their village. The funds for the primary school building had been collected, however they wanted the administration/ department and political leaders to build a middle school. Nobody paid attention to the request. The people brought up this problem in their talks with us. On 2.10.96, as suggested by us the people met in the Gram Sabha and discussed the issue. We also helped them to make plans and share the responsibilities with each other. It was decided that the sarpanch and the primary school headmaster would go to the Collector asking for the school to be upgraded till the 6th class. Other panches and well known people took on the responsibility of talking to the parents of children needing to study at the 6th class level (There were 16 boys and 22 girls) The panches convinced the parents to contribute Rs. 20 per child, per month, so that an educated youth within the community could be hired by the Panchayat as a teacher.

The Gram Sabha told the sarpanch to talk to the Collector, if the department did not start 6th class, the donated building would be used as a private school for the children needing the 6th class. After some discussions the Collector inaugurated the 6th class on the 9th of October 1996. This achievement gave the people of the community self-confidence.

MICRO PLANNING EXPERIENCE: UTTAR PRADESH

Sahbhagi Shikshan Kendra is non-governmental organization in the State of Uttar Pradesh. Since 1990 it has dealt with multiple issues of development. It has also been a part of the PRIA network of Collaborating Regional Support Organizations working on the issue of strengthening Panchayati Raj Institutions since 1995. As part of the initiative of strengthening Panchayati Raj Institutions SSK initiated a micro planning in 2 Gram Panchayats of Kasya Block of District Kushinagar in May 1996 in collaboration with the local voluntary development organization, Nari Vikas Sewa Samiti (NVSS), Kasya. This case focuses on the process of micro planning in one Gram Panchayat namely the Mathia Madhopur Gram Panchayat is made up of two villages Mathia and Madhopur and has a population of approximately 2,600. It is located at a distance of 14 km from the Kushinagar district headquarters. The Gram Panchayat is represented by a woman Pradhan belonging to the OBC category. She is a teacher in an inter college of the Kasiya Block. Being educated and aware of the affairs of the Panchayat, her interest and initiative were one of the reasons this Panchayat was chosen to put micro planning into action.

Historical Background

It is said that the village of Mathia Madhopur is about 150 years old. The story is that once a group of people were performing a *pooja* (worship) to a cap, under a tree. The cap was picked up by a fox and carried some distance, the place where the fox dropped the cap eventually became a place of worship and people began to settle around the place. The village was named Mathia Vishambhar Madhopur after the names of Math Singh and Vishambhar Singh.

The Present Status

Today the Mathia hamlet of the Gram Panchayat has 73 homes and the Madhopur hamlets has 194 homes. The total population of the Gram Panchayat is 2,600. The Gram Panchayat is inhabited by people of various castes like the Dhobi, Kshatriya, Brahmin, Koiri, Sharma, Chohan, Dhunia, Nonia, Yadav, Dome, Gupta and Muslims. The Dalits were the last to come and settle in the village, their numbers are small. The total area of the village measures 188 hectares and the land under cultivation is 153.2 hectares. The irrigated area measures 98.2 hectares. The main occupation of the majority of the people and the basis of the village economy are agriculture and related activities. Over the years there has been a change in the lifestyle of the people, however religion still plays an important role in the lives of people.

Making of the Plan

The micro plan for the Gram Panchayat Mathia Madhopur was prepared in a span of 6 days (15.09.97—20.09.97) using Participatory Rural Appraisal (PRA) technique in combination with the belief in participation. The Gram Panchayat, Gram Sabha members, members of SSK and Nari Vikas Sewa Samiti (NVSS) were all involved in the plan that was prepared.

How it All Began?

Once it was decided that the micro planning initiative would be undertaken in Mathia Madhopur, the most important problems had to be studied. A course of action was decided upon:

- Since Gram Panchayat and Gram Sabha meetings were not held regularly, meetings were held for Gram Sabha members along with a few Gram Panchayat members to help them to raise their awareness.
- A more regular contact with the pradhan, led to regular Gram Panchayat meetings. The last day of the month was fixed for these meetings along with the Gram Sabha.
- Issues of concern and common interests began to appear in the discussions during the meetings.
- After the initial groundwork and rapport building with the Gram Panchayat and Gram Sabha members the micro planning initiative was undertaken and completed within a few days.

Gathering of Data and Information

Three methods were used for this purpose: observation, interviews and social mapping.

- *Observation:* Information about the location and the people was collected by simply observing the conditions and the activities performed in a particular place. For example, it was noticed that there were too many potholes filled stagnant water, leading to the breeding of mosquitoes that cause malaria.

- *Interviews:* were held in order to collect data such as people's daily routine, decision-making, health, seasonal changes in food habits, history of the village and so on. Interviews were held separately with men and women. The questions asked of each person were the same, but the answers were different. The questions were about the life styles, eating habits, farming techniques, the seasonal calendar, ceremonies etc. These were recorded.
- *Social Mapping:* provided basic information about a village such as the number of homes, population, caste structure, assets etc. This information can then be used for future planning activities. Once all the information about the Panchayat had been collected a village meeting was called to check that it was genuine.

The Resource Mapping Exercise

The resource mapping exercise is mainly used to collect information about the agricultural practices/ patterns commonly used in the village and availability of natural resources. The people drew a map of the fields and provided information about the crop patterns. There are three categories of land in Mathia Madhopur, Dhoosi, Samtal and Barha. Corn and Arhar (dal) are cultivated on Dhoosi land. All types of crops and vegetables are grown on the Samtal land. Wheat, rice and cane are cultivated on Barha land as they need land that is very fertile. The village has a total of 44 private pumps and bore wells used for irrigation. In Mathia multiple varities of wheat and rice are cultivated, while in Madhopur cane is the major crop and about 65 per cent people are involved in its cultivation.

A team of five members was constituted for Resource Mapping.

The following exercises were taken up:

The first day

- Time Line
- Trend analysis
- Social mapping
- Resource mapping

The second day

- Seasonality
- Institutional linkages
- Health, PRA
- Livelihood analysis

The third day

- Gender analysis
- Transactional walk
- Wealth ranking

Involvement of Women in Decision-Making

In order to understand the status of women in the village it was decided to find out the extent of their involvement in decision-making within the family. For this purpose the women were met first, and then later along with the men. The following visual shows the decisions that are taken by women and men independently and those that are taken by mutual consent:

Other information was obtained with regard to income and expenditure, as well as the educational status of the people in the Panchayats.

Identification of Major Problems

Once the information was collected and presented to the people, they could identify the major problems facing them. These problems have been divided into 6 categories that are, health, education, environment, social taboos, economic conditions and wear and tear of material.

Men and Women

(Mutual decisions)

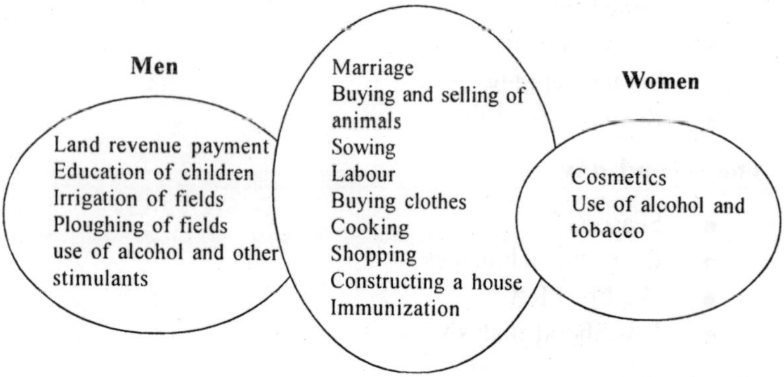

Once the problems were categorized the villagers were asked to distinguish the problems as short term plans and long term plans based on their importance. Women also participated in this process but their participation was not in such numbers as the men. The final short term and long term lists may be seen as follows:

Priority was given to those problems that had been identified, on the basis of the extent to which the issue is prevalent, its seriousness, its effect on the people and the degree to which the people would be willing to participate.

Problems were highlighted in order of importance. The first was illiteracy among women and the need for a siphon. Problems of women and children's health came next, increase in levels of

Short Term	*Long Term*
• Small potholes can be filled with mud by the people • Providing unpolluted drinking water • Women and children's healthcare • Stomach illnesses • Disposal of garbage • Water stagnation • Divided groups	• Low literacy among women • Low wages paid to women • Community toilets • Laying of pipes on the road sides because there is no siphon • Repairing the hand pumps • Building a Panchayat Bhawan • Increasing population level • Low status of women

population and the need for community toilets were placed third, stomach related diseases were placed fourth, polluted water problem was placed fifth, garbage disposal was the sixth priority and women's wages and unemployment were the seventh priority of the people.

Work Plan

The First Year

Once the information was collected, categorized and prioritized, the people of Mathia Madhopur took three years to prepare a plan. During the planning period certain criteria had to be kept in mind, how the problem could be resolved, who would take the responsibility and for which part of the problem. The next question was how much time will be needed and what resources needed to be planned for. What would be the end result of each project undertaken? These criteria were considered before the first plan was prepared on the issue of the low literacy rate among women.

A core group was formed, made up of women and young people, to teach the women to read and write. The Total Literacy Campaign members and the voluntary agencies of the community were responsible for training the group. The materials used were simple and included pictures for easy understanding. The members of the core group and NVSS will follow up by making sure that girl students are enrolling in schools as well as attending them. Meeting the parents on a regular basis will ensure that this happens. The result will be an increased literacy rate among women.

The Importance of a Panchayat Bhawan

The Pradhan, members of the Gram Panchayat and the Gram Sabha identified the lack of a Panchayat Bhawan as a major problem. They wanted the building to be constructed within the first year, as it was impossible to have meetings attended by a large number of people without it. The Panchayat and Gram Sabha members selected the site for the Bhawan. It currently stands in the centre of the village under the peepul tree. The block sanctioned the sum of one lakh for its construction.

The Second Year

The problems related to the health of women and children had been given second priority by the people, they were also able to study the situation in the context of their families. It became clear that many problems related to ill health could also be resolved. The Gram Sabha and Panchayat members were able to form a health committee with the help of a non-government committee. The health committee would look into issues of immunization, nutrition of mother and child, family planning, nursery etc. For this purpose training was organised for the health committee and the ANMs in the area.

The issue of hand pumps and the problem of safe drinking water

As the water table in Mathia Madhopur is very high, the hand pumps can only be installed at a height of 14 feet. As a result, the dirty water stagnating on the roads also seeps into the supply of water feeding the hand pumps. Out of the four 'India Mark' hand pumps that have been installed three are not working, needing repair. Due to impurities in the drinking water incidents of stomach related illnesses in the village are very high. Therefore, the men as well as the women were willing to take action quickly. The storage tanks were cleaned, the length of pipes increased and the existing pipes were repaired. Small groups of people were trained in the use of chlorine tablets, how to boil and strain water for the purpose of purifying it.

The Third Year

Community Toilets

The lack of toilets in the village is a major problem. The people have to use fields and sides of roads to relieve themselves. The drinking water also gets polluted due to this practice. Sites were selected far from the water body areas, funds were generated, the JRY and the community contributed towards this project and for cleanliness plus repair purposes a cleaner was appointed.

Seasonal Unemployment and Low Wages

The problem of seasonal unemployment and low wages paid to women were rated as the last priority of the people. It was hoped that the problem would be resolved in 6 months to 1 year. For this purpose activities like embroidery, knitting, printing and carpet making were looked at. Organizational help was sought in training the women in these skills.

The Gram Panchayat, the people of Mathia Madhopur with support and assistance from a local organization and the SSK took the responsibility of the entire planning process. The process has amply demonstrated that the local people have the capacity to identify and plan for their needs, therefore it is not necessary for planning to be done only by "experts" sitting in state capitals or the centre. The issue of planning is crucial for the success of PRIs and capacities for the same can be developed through trainings and regular support from the administrative machinery at all the three tiers.

MICRO PLANNING INITIATIVE: RAJASTHAN

UNNATI: Organization for Development Education

Based at Ahmedabad, Unnati aims to extend educational support to developmental agencies to promote the perspectives of participatory principles, social justice, gender equality and local self-governance in the process of social development. It provides intensive support to small groups engaged in addressing livelihood issues and facilitating educational processes among the functionaries of NGOs and people's organizations in Gujarat and the desert region of Rajasthan through structured training programmes, informal interactions and distribution of educational materials. Unnati derives inspiration and strength from the association with grassroots groups.

Participatory planning exercise in Rajasthan was carried out in 4 Panchayats of Jawaza block, Ajmer district. These were Naikalan, Durgawas, Kabra and Jawaza. These Panchayats fall under Jawaza Panchayat Samiti. Jawaza is situated about 75 km from the historic city of Ajmer and 23 km from Beawar Tehsil. The profile reveals that the ST and backward communities dominate the caste structure. Though Ajmer district has been declared fully literate, yet the research data of a local NGO reveals that the literacy rate is only 32 per cent, while the female literacy rate is a mere 23 per cent.

The topography is undulating and prone to erosion. The southern part of Jawaza Block has an undulating terrain and very little land that can be cultivated because of high erosion. The region receives a rainfall of 500-750 mm, characterized by variations in quantity, timing and intensity followed by periodic drought.

Agriculture and animal husbandry are the mainstay of the economy. The land is generally barren and unfertile. The people are dependent on the natural resources, but due to increasingly prolonged drought and unfavourable climatic features the people's survival is threatened. Only 33.7 per cent of the cultivable area is irrigated. The agricultural produce is dependent on timely rainfall and is further affected by the size of operational holdings. For a large family, which is dependent on small holdings, given the current state of production, it is difficult to meet the food grain requirement. As a result, people are left with no other option but to migrate to adjacent cities in search of wage employment. Women play a supportive, role to their husbands in agriculture and animal husbandry related activities. They have a very low status in society and are not allowed any communication with men outside their own family. In most cases the *purdah* system is still prevalent.

People do not have access to government health services and other facilities due to remote locations, ignorance and other socio-economic and cultural factors.

The criteria for the selection of these Panchayats is:

- The Rural University Experiment in educational innovations has prepared the base for carrying out planning with the participation of the people. The people have a sense of involvement and understand the value of co-operative effort. They also appreciate the need for long term planning.
- This was the field area of a local grassroots NGO, Magra Mewar Vikas Sansthan (MMVS) who worked in collaboration with Unnati.
- The presence of Artisan Alliance Group and other local NGOs of the weavers and leather workers, who helped in initiating the process with the community and the Panchayats.

How the Process Functioned

Step-1: *Building linkages*

In the initial stages of the project, meetings were held with the Panchayat functionaries of each Panchayat separately. The PRI functionaries were briefed about the project thoroughly in order to avoid suspicion, fear and misunderstanding on their part. During this time the right to information campaign had been launched by Mrs. Aruna Roy on the issue of corruption at the Panchayat level. As a result the Panchayat representatives had some doubts about the micro planning exercise. However, the relationship between the Magra Mewar Vikas Sansthan (MMVS), and the local organization was of great help in overcoming the initial doubts and fears. Later the facilitators also met with the government officials at the block and district level.

Meetings were held with the people of each village to inform them about the Panchayat level planning exercise. The attitude and response of the people was positive. It seemed that the people had no faith in the Panchayat. Separate meetings were held with the women in order to understand their point of view. Like the men, the women too had no expectations from the Panchayats. The majority of the women complained about serious corruption in the Panchayat.

Step-2: *Understanding the background of Panchayat functionaries*

A series of educational programmes were undertaken with the Panchayat members—the purpose was to gain insights for a future course of action.

- About 40 per cent of PRI members of four Panchayats are totally ignorant about the finances, sources of funds for the Panchayats and taxes levied by the Panchayat. Of the women members 80 per cent of them are ignorant about maters related to Panchayat finances.
- Only 5 per cent of the PRI members were aware about the role of the Gram Panchayat.
- Only 10 per cent of the PRI members were aware about their role as people's representatives.

- Not a single member or sarpanch was totally aware of the Panchayati Raj Act.
- Of the PRI members 75 per cent do enquire about the needs and problems of the people and the village.
- Indira Awas Yojana and JRY are the two most popular government schemes.

***Step-3:** Assessing the Needs of the Village*

The needs of the participants were assessed in the four Panchayats. In order to involve different sections of the community, especially the poor, Dalits and the women, separate exercises were undertaken. These were mainly PRA exercises like season based service maps, social maps, wealth and matrix ranking, resource mapping etc. After this a series of meetings were held in each Panchayat to share the information and findings with the people in the presence of the elected representatives. The people were asked to express their opinion/ viewpoints in these meetings. Separate meetings were held with the women to take into account their point of view. From these series of discussions with the community members the main problems faced by the villagers emerged very clearly. These were related to education, health and irrigation. After this the sector specific planning exercise was initiated.

***Step-4:** Sector Specific Planning Exercise-People's Conference*

Based on the "felt needs" of the people, it was seen that importance has to be given to three sectors during the planning phase, namely, primary education, health and irrigation. In order to carry out sector specific planning, "Peoples Conferences" were organized, based on the Future Search Conference methodology. However, this method was modified to make it more suitable for the rural people who are not accustomed to meetings attended by a large number of people.

Micro Planning for Primary Education

A series of meetings with teachers and PRI representatives were undertaken on the issue of the drop out rate and low enrolment. The aim was to undertake a dialogue with all the people concerned, villagers, students, Panchayat members, teachers, school administration and block and district officials of the education department on the above mentioned issues.

The Preparation for the People's Conference

The various categories of the people concerned became very anxious when they were told about the conference. They had doubts that a group made up of very different kinds of people, may not lead to any positive interaction or there might not be any interest in it. In order to remove these doubts and create a positive attitude towards the events, the team met these people individually and also established a personal contact with each one of them.

About 70 people were invited to the meeting. It was ensured that the total number of each category of the stakeholders was not too large so that they could dominate the exercise. It was also determined that the women and weaker sections from the villages were adequately represented. After the selection of the participants, they were contacted personally, the objective of the conference was highlighted and how it is related to their work and development.

Such a conference or meeting cannot be arranged without proper planning. In this case the process of identification of the participants began almost two and a half months prior to the conference.

For this process some prior information about the person is essential. It is important to know something about the person's background and interests, as it is on this basis that the person's interest in the programme can be awakened:

- The participants that were invited to the conference were,
- The Sarpanch and two ward members from each of the four Panchayats,
- Parents (at least 2) from each Panchayat,
- Students (at least 2) from each Panchayat who have studied or have been drop outs from the primary school,
- Teachers of primary schools as well as heads of the primary school unit,
- Education Extension officers from Jawaza Panchayat Samiti,

- District officials like Divisional Commissioner, DEO, Dy. Director of Rajasthan Education Board,
- NGO representatives.

A request was made to the Panchayat Samiti office and the BDO to send official letters to all the sarpanchs and the teachers identified to attend the conference. A letter from the Divisional Commissioner's office was sent to the BDO to extend his co-operation. This official sanction gave legitimacy to the conference.

There was a second meeting with the invitees just before the conference. This was considered important, in order for them to take the conference seriously and speak about their needs and problems as well as the major issues.

Arrangements for the Conference

A three-day conference, residential in nature requires a great deal of attention to practical details. The meeting hall was arranged in a way that made it possible for a large number of participants to interact freely with each other. Board and lodging arrangements were also made at the venue of the conference. The conference was organised at the district headquarters.

The Conference

About 70 participants attended the three-day conference. Participants included the primary stakeholders like the Panchayats representatives, Gram Sabha members and teachers. For each group of participants one person was selected as a facilitator. The facilitator's role was to help the group to interact and hold discussions on the concerned issues. His role was also to help to take down the points of discussion faithfully, for the benefit of the groups that were illiterate.

The Divisional Commissioner chaired the inaugural session. The discussion revolved around issues of primary education, concerns, issues and what needs to be done about them.

The meeting began, with discussions within the groups formed by participants belonging to similar backgrounds. They were able to talk openly about the various issues of concern. Later mixed groups were formed to discuss how to deal with the areas of concern.

These discussions helped in arriving at a proper understanding of the problem without blaming other groups as to being the cause of the problem. Once the cause of the problem was identified, potential solutions and the responsibility for the resolving of the problems emerged. The focus shifted from looking for 'problems in people' to looking at 'problems per sector'. This process resulted in objectivity and a positive approach towards solving the issues.

This positive attitude helped the people to look within themselves and discover their own ability to solve problems. For the first time people felt that their views and opinions had been taken into consideration.

The main issues of concern that emerged from the participants' discussion have been given below:

- Low enrolment
- High drop out rate
- Lack of motivated teachers
- Lack of quality education
- Absence of the minimum level of learning
- Lack of ownership towards education

For each of the 6 identified issues, the participants listed three to four causes. For example the causes of the "lack of quality education" were:

- Corruption in recruitment of teachers;
- Involvement of Panchayat representatives in the affairs of both the schools and teachers;
- Lack of preparation on the part of the teachers.

After this possible solutions were suggested for each of the causes cited for the six areas of concern. This was done in mixed groups:

- Proper recruitment procedures for teachers.
- Teachers to maintain cordial relation with the parents.
- Syllabus should be restructured.

The mixed groups seeking solutions were more effective because they continued with their policy of not blaming each other.

Based on the discussions and the list of suggestions a micro plan was developed for primary education. In this plan, each participating group identified their roles and acknowledged their responsibilities:

- Students will attend their classes regularly, keep their campus looking neat and clean and help their younger siblings to learn.
- Parents will send their wards to school, call at least 4 meetings to find out the problems of the teachers for the smooth running of the schools. They will also help the teachers in getting the basic facilities related to primary education in the village.
- Panchayat representatives will arrange for housing facilities for the teachers, call ward-wise parent meeting, form village committees to monitor school functioning, honour good teachers, establish linkages with concerned government officials to ensure that the teachers are not involved in other government duties.
- Teachers will help to develop an effective learning environment, organise rallies for more enrolment, organise and celebrate major events in schools, develop innovative teaching methods.
- The NGO representatives will provide new learning methods and models by subscribing to newsletters and journals and forwarding them to the teachers.

The Impact of the Conference

After a month and a half of the conference, it was found that the enrolment rate had gone up substantially. The people along with Panchayat members had conducted meetings in many villages and had constituted village education committees. It was praiseworthy to note that in one village, Dhola Dhata I, a village education fund had been formed with about Rs. 2000 to meet the local expenditure of the school. Teachers felt refreshed, full of energy and were more punctual in attending to their duties. The Panchayat started taking an active interest in the education sector. In the village Dhola Dhata II, the Panchayat Durgawas members ensured the attendance of all the boys and girls in the village. In a few cases it was seen that the Panchayat members had solved the problems of the teachers in their area as well.

Micro Planning Used in Rural Health

The second issue taken up for micro planning was rural health services. In the process of implementing PRA it was found that though services of health personnel were available, the rural health facilities were very poor. The worst sufferers were the women and the adolescent girls. There were a large number of unregistered practitioners who were easily available to the people. A community dialogue on the issue was initiated, it was felt that another Peoples' Conference should be organised for the formulation of a micro plan related to the health sector.

The steps taken for this conference were the same as that for primary education. It was organized at the Tehsil headquaters and lasted two days. In this case the District Health Officials and CHMO were asked to give official orders and instructions to all doctors, nurses, ANM, and health workers belonging to the four Panchayats.

The participants were identified in consultation with the community and Panchayat members. Those invited to the conference were:

- Government PHC doctors and health workers
- PRI representatives
- Villagers (male)
- Villagers (female)
- Adolescent girls in the villages
- Traditional practitioners and *dais* (untrained helpers, midwives)

In the initial round of the conference, diseases occurring seasonally were analysed by the participants and the reasons behind the poor condition of rural health were also studied in detail. These were the suggestions given by the participants:

The Doctors and Health Workers

- Doctors and the health staff should not be asked to perform other administrative tasks apart from their duty.

- Health workers, nurses and ANM should sit in the sub-centre instead of attending to cases, individually.
- Voluntary efforts should be promoted in the village.
- Volunteers (male and female) should mobilise people towards using the health facilities available to them.
- Doctors should visit the health sub-centre at least once a month.

The Panchayat Representatives

- Co-operation and co-ordination of PRI members, Panchayat and other participants is essential.
- A village health committee should be formed.
- The committee should act as a pressure group.
- The people should be trained to pay attention to cleanliness and safe drinking water.
- Effective means of communication between the village and PHC, Jawaza must be found.
- There should be a quarterly planning and review by the Panchayat and health committee about the existing situation.

The Task of the Male Villagers

- Forming Health Committees in villages.
- Organising immunization camps in their respective villages.
- Ensuring cleanliness.

The Task of the Female Villagers

- Making sure nurses visit the Panchayats regularly.
- Make women aware of minor diseases and reproductive health concerns.

The Traditional Practitioners and Dais

- Ambulances should be provided for villages in remote areas at subsidised rates.
- The *dais* (midwives) should be provided with essential kits to conduct safe deliveries.
- They should be given a fixed honorarium.

Based on these suggestions, a joint action plan was prepared by all the participants:

The "Joint Action Plan"

- Four Panchayats will constitute a Health Committee by January 1997.
- Meetings will be held so that a village health fund can be organised.
- Villagers and the Panchayats will ensure cleanliness.
- Every participant will use his/her influence to make it possible for children to be immunized.

The Impact of the Conference

In Naikalan and Jawaza Panchayats, meetings were conducted by PRI functionaries with the focus on the issue of health and measures that needed to be taken to ensure cleanliness in the villages. A health committee was formed in Jawaza Panchayat and a donation box for surplus medicine for those who couldn't afford them was placed in the PHC, Jawaza. In Naikalan and few other Panchayats, the doctors have begun to visit the sub-centres regularly, to attend to their duties for the first time.

Micro Planning on the Issue of Irrigation

The area is known for its uncertain and erratic rainfall, deforestation, increasing population, low levels of literacy and the dependence of the majority of the people on minor agricultural activities.

The irrigated area is 33.7 per cent of the net sown area, out of which 86.3 per cent is irrigated by dug wells, and tube wells, the yield of which is again dependent on rainfall and the size of the landholding. Thus, the present irrigation system is inadequate. The Panchayat planning process revealed that there is ample scope within the budget provided for the Panchayat to improve the existing irrigation system.

The Panchayats have enough scope for the creation of a network of facilities for irrigation as well as reviving the denuded natural resources. Government schemes like JRY, Jiwan Dhara, Akal Rahat, EGS etc. provide funds for construction as well as repair of check dams, lakes, wells, anicuts etc. The irrigation network created by the Panchayat under the above mentioned schemes was found to be either defunct or not serving the purpose. The people's opinion regarding selection of sites and the nature of the network were not taken into consideration.

The Process of Correcting the Problems of Irrigation

Group meetings were conducted in each village of three Panchayats, namely Naikalan, Kabra and Jawaza. PRA techniques were used for gathering information. Villagers drew resource maps of the villages locating the present irrigation network as well as its present condition. They were also asked to give their opinion about improving the irrigational facilities in terms of coverage and frequency. Some of the suggestions were construction of new anicut check dams and the digging as well as deepening of wells. These were also mentioned in the resource maps. The entire process was conducted in large community meetings in every village in the presence of PRI functionaries of the respective Panchayats.

The entire information was collected and tabulated by using PRA methods. The purpose was to prepare consolidated irrigation plans priority wise, taking into account the common knowledge of the people. The Sarpanchs of these three Panchayats committed themselves to incorporating this plan in parts in the annual development plan of the Panchayats in relation to the resources available. In every village a group of people were sensitized about the plan of their village and were asked to raise the issues in Gram Sabha meetings.

Foll ow-up Support for Plan Implementation and Some Insights:

- All the Panchayats were exposed to the new techniques and methods, so that they could get the people's consent to address many local level difficulties.
- Insights derived from these sector specific plans has helped the local NGO, MMVS to start new programmes in the region.
- The people began to have faith in the micro planning process.
- All participants to come together.
- Mobilising the disadvantaged and the poor.
- Providing them with an opportunity to interact and share.

- Facilitate sharing of problems and developing action plans for solutions.
- Constant follow-up on action plans.

As a follow-up support, a method was developed so that each group could support and help another group in carrying out participatory planning, thus taking the process beyond the NGO. Group to group linkage was the main follow-up support planned in the process.

MICRO PLANNING INITIATIVES: BIHAR

CENCORED (Centre for Communication Resources Development)

CENCORED based in Patna, Bihar is an active centre for providing training workshops, seminars on various issues from Organizational Development, Panchayati Raj, formal education, self-help groups, micro planning etc. to voluntary organizations, government organizations and grassroots level workers. It provides educational resources, follow-up, evaluation and other support services. The organization's mission has been promoting people centred development with the focus on participation and partnership.

Participatory Planning in Bihar

The participatory planning exercise was carried out in Panchayat Belthi Rasulpur, Bochaha Block, Muzaffarpur District, Bihar. The Panchayat is situated in the north-eastern part of the block at a distance of 12 kms from the block-head quarters and 21 kms from the district headquarters. Situated on the banks of the Bagmati river, this area is prone to floods, and the crops are often affected by them. The Panchayat has 10 villages out of which one is practically uninhabited, with only two houses. The total population of the Panchayat is 6,933, out of which there are 3,687 males and 3,246 females. The Panchayat is largely dominated by the Scheduled Caste, Backward Classes and minority groups i.e. Muslims. There are a total of 1,165 households. The economic condition of the Panchayat is poor. A total of 405 people or (32% of the families of which 20% are SCs) have been identified as living below the poverty line. Most of them are agricultural labourers. They do not have proper housing facilities. Often two or three families live in one thatched house. Under the Indira Awas Yojana scheme of the Central Government 54 houses have been constructed for the homeless. However, out of these 36 are damaged and are not fit for living.

The Panchayat has 7 primary schools and 2 "madrasas". All the school buildings have permanent structures, with two rooms each for the five classes. The total number of enrotted children is 862, out of which 461 (53.5%) are boys and 401 (46.5%) are girls. Around 891 boys and 748 girls do not go to primary school. The Panchayat has a very low literacy rate, only 22 per cent. Female literacy is even lower. Only 150 (8%) adult females out of the 1,733 are literate.

The Bihar Education Project is operational in Muzaffarpur district. But despite all efforts, the Village Education Committees (VECs) are not functioning properly. The VECs exist, but since no meetings have been held, no decisions have been taken regarding the enrolment of students or the development of schools. Moreover, most of the VEC members are not aware of their roles and responsibilities.

Criteria for selecting the Belthi Rasulpur Panchayat:

- The Panchayat is socially and economically backward.
- The majority of the population consists of scheduled caste and religious minority groups.
- The area is prone to floods and waterlogging.
- It has a low literacy rate.
- The Government Programmes are not given priority.

The process of rapport building:

- Rapport building with the people of the Panchayat was facilitated. This was done to create a favourable environment for carrying the planning process forward with people's participation. In order to gain the confidence of the villagers Mahila Gram Sabha, Voter Awareness Campaign, or *Matdata Jagran*, village meetings and cultural activities were organised.

- Another entry point was the identification of veteran leaders and organization of orientation camps for their understanding about the need for micro planning in the context of the new Panchayati Raj.

Key Informants were Identified

An orientation programme was organised for key informants, dealing with the following topics:

- The new Panchayati Raj Act and its objectives.
- The importance of the Gram Sabha.
- The base upwards planning process and the need for participatory planning.
- The objectives of participatory planning.
- The identification of problems and prioritisation.

A training about PRA tools and methodologies was organised for the micro planning team. PRA exercises were carried out in all 9 villages, each divided into 7 clusters. These clusters were: Belthi Rasulpur, Rahsi, Mushhari, Baharampur, Fatehpur and Bazidpur, Bhoraha, Roshi, Chaknuran and Chal Belthi. These orientation camps and PRA training helped in building the confidence level of the villagers and their opinion leaders.

PRA tools were used for data collection. After the collection of base line data, the key informants analysed and prioritised the problems.

The key informants organised a meeting for the purpose of identifying local problems and needs. Some of the main problems identified have been given below:

(1) Roads have been badly damaged by recurring floods, especially in the months of June to September. Most of the roads in the Panchayat area are built in low-Iying areas.
(2) 32 per cent of the families who live below the poverty line do not have proper housing facilities. Most of these families are SCs. Old Indira Awas houses are poorly maintained.
(3) Education, there is low enrolment, especially of backward and Dalit children.

(4) There is caste discrimination amongst students and between teachers and students.
(5) Water accumulates in the school campus during the rainy season.
(6) Non-functional VECs and lack of monitoring.

Village Planning Meetings

On the basis of PRA base line data, a meeting was organised to carry out the planning process along with the community members. Amongst the participants were government officials like Block Development Officers (BDOs) and District Education Officers. Women made up 70 per cent of the total people attending the meeting.

At the beginning of the meeting the facilitator's team familiarised everyone about the qualitative and quantitative information generated during the data collection phase through PRA exercises. After this, representatives of each village presented the particular problems that people are facing, their causes and effects. These problems were noted down and solutions were sought in consultation with the people present. During the plan formulation, the facilitators focused on government welfare and development programmes. The government officials present in the meeting also contributed in the planning process. After listing down the solutions for the various problems, the facilitator introduced a process called "alternative search", wherein the people selected appropriate alternatives according to their needs, capacities, possibilities and government provisions. The participants identified the strategy, activities, assignment of responsibilities and the time schedule for each solution, in each village. An example of one such strategy prepared by the people in a village planning meeting has been given below:

Learning Experiences

The process of participatory planning was a rich learning experience for the CENCORED team. The entry point strategy of the team was appropriate and timely, like organizing Mahila Sabha, *Matdata Jagran* before Lok Sabha elections, organizing meetings in every village and selection of key informers and community opinion leaders. All these activities helped in building a good rapport with the villagers.

Mushari Village Planning Meeting

Problem	Solution	Government	BEP	Community	VOs
Roads 1. Mushari chowk to Boardih (kaccha road) 2. Kaccha road from Nissar Ahmad's house to Boardih	Brick - soling needed Brick - soling needed	BDO statement passed through JRY. This work will get completed in the same year. Will be done the next year	—	—	—
Education Waterlogging in the school campus during the rainy season	Soil filling	—	BEP rep. will put up this issueVEC VEC meeting	Community will pressurize to organize meeting	VO
Housing 60 SC families are living below the poverty line	Benefits of Indira Awas Yojana for the poor	This will be given priority the following year	—	Nisar Ahmad will take part as a group leader. Community members will apply to local MLA/MP for funds	

During all the PRA exercises women's participation rate (especially SC and BC women) was much higher in comparison with the male members of the community. However, very few men and women from the higher castes participated in the planning exercise. Women's active participation can be further enhanced and built upon. Their capacities can be built to attend Gram Sabha meetings, identification of problems and their solutions, community development processes etc.

The micro planning process is a good way of information sharing and conflict resolution

The village planning meetings were more like Gram Sabha meetings. Thus the people got an idea about the Gram Sabha and showed a lot of interest in taking part in it, since it gave them an opportunity to present their needs and possible solutions for community development.

MICRO PLANNING INITIATIVES: KERALA

Sahayi Centre for Collective Learning and Action

Sahayi, was established in 1991 as a support organization with its headquarters in Thiruvananthapuram. The meaning of this word is apt, the ENABLER. Through a variety of support interventions of training, information sharing, skill up-gradation, consultancy, advocacy, networking, research etc. Sahayi seeks to enable the voluntary and other actors in the development field, to clarify their vision, sharpen their skills and hone their capacities for improving the effectiveness of their interventions. It also works with the civil society and local VOs at the local Panchayat level to help them to participate actively in the local governance process.

West Kallada Gram Panchayat

A micro planning exercise for participants was carried out by Sahayi in West Kallada, Kollam district in Kerala. It was a collective attempt of the people of that area to analyse and understand the basic socio-economic-environmental problems and issues of their area and formulate suitable action plans for their solution.

The area selected by the Panchayat for participatory planning is West Kallada, one of the six Panchayat in Sasthamcotta block in Kollam district in Kerala. This Panchayat was formed in 1952. The Panchayat covers an area of 13.36 sq.kms and has a population of 17,522 out of which there are 8,455 women and 8,677 men. There are a total of 9 wards. There are 22.53 per cent Dalits included in the total population. The population density is 1,312 and the total number of households is 3,651. The literacy rate is 92 per cent women's literacy rate being very close to that of the men. The Panchayat is bordered by Sasthamcotta Panchayat in the north, Sasthamcotta and Kizhake Kallada Panchayats in the east, Munrothuruth Panchayat in the south and Thevalakara and Mynagapally Panchayats in the west.

West Kallada was the first capital of the ancient kingdom of Kollam, dating back to the first millennium A.D. Irrigated by the Kallada river on one side and the Sasthamcotta fresh water lake on the other, the Panchayat is blessed with abundant water running through the numerous canals and into the backwaters, fields, ponds, wells of the area. Most of the terrain is believed to have been originally linked to the Arabian Sea, and is 10 metres above M.S.L.

The Criteria used for the Selection of this Panchayat:

- Sahayi had established a rapport with several sections of the community and also with the elected representatives of the Gram Panchayat.
- West Kallada, a not very accessible, under developed village with the backward communities in the majority, was receptive to carrying out the participatory planning exercise
- There was a clear understanding of the socio-economic background of the area.

The Major Issues and Problems of the Area

- The main occupation, of this area traditionally has been paddy cultivation. But socio-environmental changes over time have made half the arable land suitable for growing mixed crops. The excavation of clay from the fields for brick industries, has rendered the land unfit for farming and is a health hazard because of the high acidity in the water that collects in the trenches after the clay has been removed. Excessive clay mining has already damaged the local environment.
- Though nearly total literacy exists, yet there is lack of corresponding social awareness and consciousness regarding the environment, so that the local administration has never been able to tackle the socio-economic problems of the area, mainly chronic unemployment and poverty.
- Caste discrimination, divisions on political party lines, low status and low participation of women, lack of holistic approaches, increasing trends of consumerism and alienation from native culture are serious social factors that stand in the way of the area's total development.

The Process of Orientation and Training

This was a part of the preparatory stage before taking up the data generation exercise. Much importance was attached to this stage and a lot of time and energy was spent on it. A series of orientations and trainings were given to the key participators of the programme, mainly the PRI and NGO representatives and community leaders.

Sahayi in West Kallada was responsible for creating an awareness about the PRI, as early as 31st July, 1995. This included consultations, seminars, and dialogues meant for the members of women's groups and the youth clubs. A total of 20 orientation/ consultation/ training events on Panchayati Raj and participatory planning was held from 31st July 1995 to 18th August 1997. Most of these were organised exclusively for the participants of the programme in West Kallada, while some were common events in which the community members of West Kallada also participated. These awareness generation, skill development and planning exercises covered a vast area of themes related to Panchayati Raj and micro planning and were guided by resource persons from the Sahayi team and outside. Some of these eminent persons were Mr. M.P. Varkey, retired Deputy Director of Panchayats, Prof. T.S.N. Pillai, Dean of Social Work in Sankaracharya University, Kaladi, Dr. G. Antony, Reader, Department of Management, Cochin University.

The most important training intervention of Sahayi was the State Level Training of Trainers (STOT) in January 1996. In which the people of West Kallada participated. It was unique not only in the matter of duration, but also involving participants from all over the state and several eminent resource persons as well as a balanced combination of theory and practice. The main objectives of this training event were:

- To deepen the understanding of the participants about the 73rd Constitutional Amendment and Kerala Panchayati Raj Act, with emphasis on the role of voluntary organizations.
- To facilitate understanding and development of skills related to planning and PRA methods.

The training, with the formal inauguration of the PRI project by one of the state ministers and supplemented by numerous participatory sessions and exercises, including the field testing of PRA methods. The training is remembered by one and all as a landmark of learning, particularly in the area of participatory approaches in planning.

This training influenced the micro planning experiment in West Kallada for the following reasons:

- The state level event was organized in West Kallada Panchayat, giving an opportunity to the people and the local leaders to interact with delegates from all over the state.
- A few of the prominent prospective participants of the micro planning exercise under consideration were present during some of the sessions. Among them were the President and some members of the Panchayat.
- The presence of VIPs including the Minister provided effective publicity for the PRI project and served as a tool of mass education. The treatment of topics was an in depth study, comprehensive, intense and relevant to the realities of the "field". Theory and practice were creatively interwoven.
- It created an opportunity to stay with the local people at their homes and observe the realities of their lives.
- The programme helped in creating a general awareness among the local people on Panchayati Raj and the relevance of grassroots level planning through continuous interaction between the participants and the facilitators.
- Greater enthusiasm was generated among the PRI members and participants by using participatory methods for local level planning.
- The participants, including local leaders/PRI members could understand how PRA methods can be used as a tool for empowering people.
- The STOT was followed by a series of capacity building exercises and trainings aimed at developing the knowledge and skills of the participants in the planning activities. These were mainly:

- Follow-up orientation courses about the PRI .
- Training in the application of PRA and other methods related to participatory planning.
- Training in aspects of leadership and management (as applicable in the field of planning).

Rapport Building

Sahayi's first orientation and awareness programme about the PRI began with its linkage with the people of West Kallada in July, 1995. This was done prior to the formal launching of the PRI programme and before the Panchayat elections, to orient and motivate the people for maximum participation in PRI related activities including the elections. The response of the people was warm and enthusiastic.

The introduction of the PRI programme in August 1995, strengthened the rapport building process with Sasthamcotta Block it was chosen as the venue for the micro planning demonstration/ intervention. West Kallada was one of the Panchayats of the Block.

These Activities were Undertaken During this Phase:

- Contacts were established with government officials, Panchayat functionaries and community based organizations (women's groups and youth clubs).
- Literature in the form of handbills was printed and distributed.
- Important and influential people were met and invited for the inaugural function of the PRI intervention. A minister of the Government of Kerala was present at this function.
- The response of the local people, leaders and officials was positive and encouraging. Several villagers came out that day to watch and participate in the function.

Participatory Data Generation

The data generation is a crucial and important phase of the participatory planning exercise. The data has to be reliable and the people's participation is vital.

In order to help this process a list of the key participants from the Panchayat was prepared. The list included the names of government officials, heads of institutions, local leaders, knowledgeable elders, retired teachers etc. The list was constantly revised to include more persons who could contribute to the data generation process.

Groups of two or three facilitators visited people and held informal discussions, during which time the relevant data was selected. They had prepared a check-list as a guideline for including various socio-economic issues. The data generation was initially focused on two issues, namely, agriculture and animal husbandry. During the discussions one of the team members took down notes, which were then consolidated on reaching the field office.

In addition to dialogues with individuals, focus group discussions were held with groups of women and youth groups. Discussions with mixed groups were also conducted. The "tabulation method" was used to cross-check and verify the information provided by the people. The facilitating team also used the "observation method" for refining the quality of the data and the information generated.

"Resource mapping" was another method used in the process. The purpose was to ensure people's participation for information generation and for providing opportunities for learning.

The data generation process was followed by compilation of the data and sharing the outcome with groups and individuals. This helped in developing the interest of the people and getting them involved in the process.

However, during this phase, some obstacles and limitations had to be dealt with. Just as the Sahayi team had completed the long and difficult process of educating, motivating and empowering the people's representatives with information and skills and was about to initiate the data generation process, the State announced the Peoples Campaign Programme for the Ninth Plan sponsored by the Government of Kerala. The government organised a programme for mass education and training of the resource persons to be followed by participatory data generation and preparation of plans, which had to be done in a short span of time, so that the consolidated plans could be submitted to the Planning Commission.

The Lessons Learnt for Future Planning:

- There was a need for an on-going orientation and training for the community members to keep them actively involved in the Panchayat planning process.

- The realisation of the relevance and importance of micro planning and PRA methods in the planning and implementation of development projects in our country.
- The need for adaptation of methods and procedures. Flexibility, openness of mind, patience etc. become very useful and necessary in such situations.
- The facilitating team needs to be well equipped and properly guided. The team needs training and exposure in this field.

The Problem of the Scarcity of Drinking Water

For the people of Ampalakunnu, a tiny settlement on a hillock in the Ambalavayal Panchayat of Wayanand district in Kerala, the date 7th August 1998 is unforgettable. It is the day on which every person in the settlement forgot their miseries and danced for joy! Water was gushing out from the faucets in their hamlets! It was the day when the decades old problem, scarcity of drinking water was solved in the spirit of community participation.

Ampalakunnu, a hill settlement of the 10th ward of the Ambalavayal Panchayat, inhabited by approximately 100 families, the majority of which were living well below poverty line, has been deprived of safe drinking water for over three decades. A characteristic of the small community was that mostly women were at the head of the groups of poor, widowed or abandoned women. The women had to walk long distances to fetch safe drinking water. When there was a lack of clear water the people used to drink unsafe water, leading to chronic illness and depression. All their appeals and entreaties to the authorities, through the decades, had fallen on deaf ears.

Arshabharat, a local voluntary organization, started its development interventions in 1986, with the introduction of literacy and non-formal education programmes, but till 1994 they were not in a position to seriously attend to the problem of drinking water scarcity.

The participation of the local people in the planning and implementation of development programmes has been a strong point of Arshabharat ever since its establishment as a rural development agency. However, it was because of the insights gained from the participatory training courses of SAHAYI that enabled the Arshabharat team to deepen their understanding and hone up their skills in the field of participatory planning. The core team of the organization had attended a series of participatory trainings, including the PTOT, leadership development, PRA. The insights gained during the training have to be tested against the field realities and supplemented with personal experience.

Arshabharat was fully convinced that the solution of the problem did not depend on the generosity of the government functionaries or the charity of outside agencies, but in the creative unity and participation of the local people, equipped with sound theory and rich practical experience in the area of participatory development. Arshabharat decided to try to mobilize the people and facilitate participatory processes among them for solving their chronic drinking water problem on a sustainable basis:

- The first step they took was to organise awareness sessions on the importance of safe water for the health and hygiene of the families and their overall development.
- This was followed by the formation of a committee to study the problem and plan their course of action. Through meetings and discussions the people were made to accept that no outside agency could help them to solve this problem on a permanent basis. The people had to depend on their collective wisdom and devise their own means to do so. It took some time for the message to sink into the minds of the people. Initially they were passive, but by the third meeting some of the participants asked a question, "Can we can do something"? They suggested that they could perhaps arrange food for the workers, and help to carry materials to the work area.
- Since the settlement was on a hillock, sinking a well in the settlement was ruled out. The alternative was to dig a well in the field at the foot of the hill and pump the water into an overhead tank on top of the hill and distribute it through a pipeline system. The total cost of the entire operations was estimated at Rs. 3,50,000. This also included expenses

related to buying small plots for the well and the overhead tank. But the question was how to generate this amount?

- Thankamma an elderly woman, had some land in the adjacent lowlands/fields. She had many grudges against some of the families, she declared, "No one need entertain dreams of drinking water from my land". M.M. Augustine and his team of activists from the organization were able to overcome this obstacle. Combining humour with wisdom they said: "You want to take revenge on those who have hurt you, don't you? But what sweeter revenge is there than seeing them drink the water taken from your land?" Eventually, the woman was won over and she offered to donate two cents for the construction of the overhead tank. Meanwhile, the local politicians interfered and there was trouble again, caused by Thankamma going back on her promises. This unforeseen hurdle was overcome through a series of community meetings and dialogues.

Now that the problem of the land was resolved, the question of construction and other costs came up. After lengthy meetings with the community, it was decided that Arshabharat would meet the expenses of the well and the tank. The cost of the pump set, pipes, etc. would be met through the voluntary contributions of the people. On this understanding a well was dug in the two cents donated by Thankamma. But after digging to a certain depth the land turned out to be rocky. It was decided to sink another well nearby, which luckily had no rocks and had permanent springs of water. The two wells were then joined together at the bottom, so that the water from one would fill both. Subsequently, the overhead tank was constructed on the top of the hill. But then a fresh problem arose. Through whose land will the pipeline be laid? Nobody was willing to allow the pipelines to be laid on his land. Once again, the Arshabharat team had to swing into action using every bit of wisdom and experience learned in participatory development strategies, trying to convince the people of the need and beauty of sharing for the common good. Finally an agreement was reached and the main pipeline was laid along the property boundaries of two families. The people contributed voluntary labour and part of the costs amounting to Rs. 35,000.

Construction was completed according to schedule and the inauguration of the scheme was celebrated with great rejoicing by one and all. The management and maintenance of the people's drinking water scheme was entrusted to a committee of women, who were doing their work very well. Every month Rs. 5 is collected from each family towards the meetings and the maintenance expenses.

Thus through the people's participation an urgent need of the community has been met. All the families in this hamlet, the most backward ward in the Panchayat, have access to plenty of water, not only for drinking, but also for washing, gardening and the needs their live stock.

It took about two years for the problems to be finally solved, of which one year was spent in education and planning. The participatory methods taught by SAHAYI through the PRA sessions were at the base of the success of this endeavour by Arshabharat.

Breaking Barriers Overcoming Obstacles Through Micro Planning (A Case of 'Labour Force' in Kunnathukal Gram Panchayat in Kerala)

Kerala, a land richly endowed with agricultural resources, has always been and still is primariy an agrarian economy. The state has been held up as an example for successfully carrying out land reforms. The reforms enabled the re-distribution/transfer of land from landlords to tenants and further more the tenants could now claim rights over land for housing sites. The income of the farmers and so also the bargaining power of the labourers increased. At the same time, Kerala was also witnessing a considerable decline in agricultural production and productivity. There was a shift in interest from paddy cultivation to less labour intensive crops like tapioca, rubber, plantain etc. The labour class had also organised itself into powerful trade unions and their strength enabled them to bargain for higher wages. The strong unions formed by the labour class and their improved bargaining powers have strongly contributed to the change of interest to less labour intensive crops. In many ways, the forming of powerful trade unions has succeeded in changing the attitude of the labourers towards the old feudalistic system of the landowner-tenant relationship. However, a new system where a healthy relationship exists between the farmers and the labourers, is awaited.

Kunnathukal, is a Gram Panchayat situated at the southern tip of Kerala. The Panchayat, at the border of Kanyakumari district, has a population of 33,648 and an area of 26.85 sq. km. It has all the features of a larger state as far as the agricultural situation and labour problems go. As in other parts of the state, the Panchayat is dependent on agriculture with paddy once again being the major crop cultivated on the land.

The Agricultural Scenario in Kunnathukal Gram Panchayat

The basic problem of the village as elsewhere, in the agricultural sector, was the decrease in production and productivity in paddy cultivation. The problem took on massive proportions and the solution was nowhere in sight. Statistics revealed that within a span of a decade or so (1980s to 1990s), the Panchayat witnessed a drastic decline in paddy cultivation from 315 ha to a mere 8 ha. The area of cultivable waste-lands increased to around 300 ha. This should be seen against a scenario where more than 80 per cent of the population have land holdings ranging from 10 cents to 5 acres and above. Land owners lost interest in cultivation due to various reasons like high labour costs and subsequent rise in productions costs, acute labour shortage during the harvest season, etc. Besides these, the agricultural sector was facing other problems like marginalizing of agricultural holdings, poor irrigation infrastructure etc. In due course, landowner's either shifted their interest to less labour intensive crops or left their lands fallow. We have seen the situation of the farmers, the situation of the labourers was equally depressing. Whereas the land owners were experiencing acute labour shortage during the brief harvest season, the agricultural labourers were facing severe unemployment during the lean season, resulting in partial employment and poverty, low social status etc.

A Decentralized Planning Process Initiated

Like the rest of Kerala, this tiny village had been living with its problem for many years. There seemed to be no practical solution in sight, given the intense political unionisation of the labour sector. It was in this context that micro planning or decentralised planning initiated through the People's Plan Campaign for the Ninth Plan in Kerala could be applied. The PPC was a concentrated effort of the then ruling LDF government in Kerala, in bringing about democratic decentralisation of the planning and development process. To start with, the government decided to set aside 35 to 40 per cent of the expenditure of the Ninth Five Year Plan towards projects and programmes prepared by the local self-governing institutions. In this new mode of decentralised planning, the district is no longer treated as the basic planning unit. Instead, the planning process begins at the grassroots level with the maximum participation of people together with elected members, non-official experts, volunteers etc. The officials are expected to work alongside with non-officials in the whole process. The campaign thus opened up opportunities and created an enabling environment for the Panchayats to take up innovative and developmental work as per the felt needs and priorities of the local communities.

Thus, with adequate funds coming to the Panchayats for development work, they were enabled to take up comprehensive work in their areas. For this, people were mobilized in large numbers for Gram Sabhas as these provided the forum where the developmental needs and problems could be debated and problems prioritised. Any programme is sustainable only if it is need based, i.e. based on the felt need of the people rather than when the need is imposed on them from the higher levels of government. In the planning stage of every Gram Sabha, the people are divided into groups, sector-wise, like agriculture, animal husbandry etc. to discuss the problems, as they come up. Similarly such Gram Sabhas were conducted in all the wards of Kunnathukal Gram Panchayat too. During these Gram Sabhas, the people in the agricultural sector-wise groups highlighted the problems of labour unemployment, shrinking of areas of paddy cultivation etc.

Analysing the problem and the resources made available through the plan fund, the Panchayat members and the agriculture officer of the line department introduced the concept of a labour bank to the villagers. Consultations were held with the Gram Sabha members regarding the concept, they approved of it.

The Thozhil Sena (Labour Force)

The main purpose of the labour bank or the Thozhil Sena was: to step up production and productivity in the agricultural sector by providing local labour and giving assurance of employment and social status to farm labourers, promising healthier farmer-labourer relations, partial mechanisation in the farm sector to reduce cost of production and physical exertion of farm labourers, social security to labourers etc. As is seen, the purpose of the programme was not just addressing the problem of unemployment. It had a perspective on social justice as well in that the programme went further to enable the growth of healthier farmer/labourer relations. In fact the focus and aim of the programme was that for the farmer, cultivation should not be a great strain.

The Thozhil Sena consists of 300-500 agricultural labourers, whose services are available on demand by the farmers, for the cultivation of crops like paddy, tapioca, coconut, plantain and vegetables. The details of work like labour norms, work time and wage rates are prefixed by a committee at the Panchayat level involving representatives of farmers and labourers. The committee also provides a forum for the farmers and labourers to discuss their needs and problems. The farmers need not haggle over the wage rates any longer. The payment for the work done is made at the Panchayat who will then pay the labourers. Thus the link between the farmers and the labourers is forged at the Panchayat level in such a way that neither side is exploited.

To monitor and supervise the farm operations, farm help societies have been formed at each ward of the Panchayat. This society consists of farmers, members of the Thozhil Sena, neighbourhood groups, agricultural development committee, a key resource person/ a member of the block level expert committee etc. The functioning of the farm help society may be likened to that of a mini agricultural office as it provides all the services of the agricultural office, including dealing with the problems of farmers and labourers, receiving applications for the services of the labour force and other agricultural materials. They also function as a resource centre for providing labour, seeds, fertilizers, agricultural implements etc. Discipline, in the functioning of workers is ensured by the system. If the farmer has any complaints regarding the labourer, he needs to complain to the farm help society, who will deal with the issue. The basic idea being that cultivation should not be a problem to the farmer. This is pertinent when one considers the fact that cultivation was indeed a burden to the farmers, especially with regard to labour.

Moreover, the labourers are assured 20 days employment per month throughout the year, which is a great boon to the labourers. During the lean season, the services of the labour force are used in the service sector like house construction, infrastructure work and when the need arises in other development work, so that they are not unemployed for long periods. With funds being provided to the Panchayats for various activities, the Panchayats are also in a position to assure labourers of employment..

With regard to the budget, the Panchayat reserved the entire amount which it had allocated for the agricultural sector for the implementation of the programme. In the financial year 1999-2000, Rs. 1.55 million from the plan fund and Rs. 0.15 million from the agricultural department fund was set aside for the purpose, thus making a total of Rs. 1.70 million.

The Methodology

The methodology adopted in the whole exercise was a participatory one, where the Panchayat and the agricultural officer took pains to identify and enlist the cooperation of various participants. Various participatory methods were employed in the process. As said elsewhere, the problem was identified and prioritised by the people in the Gram Sabha. Taking the matter further, the Panchayat and the agricultural office held focused group discussions with representatives of important organizations of farmers and labourers in the area, members of the agricultural development society and the task force working on agriculture, to analyse in detail the problems and opportunities in the agricultural sector. Based on this, the concept of a labour force was invented by the Panchayat and the agricultural office.

In order to spread the message of the labour force and the call for people's participation, regular public meetings were convened.

Once the people showed a positive attitude to the concept, the work of putting the concept into action began. Regular programmes were organised for the citizens regarding the concept and the absolute necessity to keep the whole programme free of politics. However, the cooperation of political parties and trade unions in the area was enlisted. At the beginning, extensive consultations were held with the leaders of farmers and labourer's unions, who in turn had discussions with their respective members, and their cooperation was enlisted. Next, the Panchayat and agriculture office members had discussions with the members of the leading political parties in the locality, to ensure their cooperation also. The effort made for the above two steps are commendable, since trade unions and political parties can play a decisive role in making the programme a success.

After a consensus was reached by the high level committee, work details were finalised. As the programme was still at a experimental stage, it was decided to put the concept into operation with a limited number of labourers. The people were asked to select the eligible labourers from each ward, based on previously agreed guidelines. The rest of the labourers were assured that they would be selected in the following years. To provide technical training to the labourers, the Panchayat took the help of Kerala Shastra Sahitya Parishad, the faculty of the Agriculture University and the agriculture officer. A three day intensive training was given to the labour force members on the new concept, the use of new machines and the need for upholding discipline, sincerity and commitment to the new cause.

Obviously, the planning, operation and sustenance of the project was not an easy one. As mentioned earlier, the People's Plan Campaign provided an enabling environment for Panchayats to take up development initiatives. However, this alone could not assure success. It needed people with some control (in this case, the Panchayat) with initiative, with creativity and a vision to make use of the opportunity and take up activities based on the "felt needs" of the people and an awareness of the resources, for the all round development of their village. Above all, it needed the political will, which was provided here by the Panchayat president and the elected members. This proved to be a major factor in handling as delicate an issue as labour and that too with the cooperation of farmers and labourers. Equally significant were the services of the agriculture officer, who was one of the major brains behind the programme. This healthy cooperation and collaboration between the Panchayat and the agricultural officer is praiseworthy, especially at a time, when the Panchayats were at loggerheads with the officials of the line departments.

Promotional Factors

- *The felt need/pressing problem:* The whole exercise was based on the felt need of people especially the farmers and labourers. People were thus in favour of the programme.
- *Participators involvement:* The Panchayat members and the agriculture officer took care to identify and enlist the cooperation of all those people who were directly or indirectly associated with the programme. The inclusion of members of all political parties and farmer and labourers' unions helped in avoiding any obstacles arising from those with vested interests.
- *The formation of people's organizations:* In each ward of the Panchayat, farm help societies were formed which function as mini agriculture offices and provide all the services of the agriculture office. Supervision and management of the whole programme is done by these people's organizations.
- *Work details:* Like labour norms, volume of work, work time and wage rates were fixed only after consultation with representatives of farmers and labourers.
- *Linkage with Panchayat:* The whole operation is managed by the farm help societies and the labour force, the coordination of the labour force activities are the responsibility of the Panchayat and the agriculture office. The Gram Panchayat president and the agriculture officer find representation in all the committees, formed for the programme. This has helped in sustaining the programme and preventing any situation where the labour force/farm help society start functioning parallel to and therefore

undermining Panchayats.

- *Assured employment:* Since the linkage has been maintained with the Panchayat, 20 days employment per month for the labour force members was assured even during the lean season as their service could be utilised in other projects of the Panchayat, such as construction etc.
- *The coordination between the Panchayat and agriculture office:* Without the healthy coordination between the Panchayat and the agriculture office, it would have been difficult to implement a programme of this kind.
- *Political will:* It was the sheer political will which enabled the Government of Kerala to transfer more then one-third of their state budget to local bodies, which in turn motivated the local bodies to take up comprehensive work in their areas. Similarly, it was the political will of the Panchayat president and elected members which paved the way for such an initiative and that too with the cooperation of trade unions and political parties in the local area.

The Challenges Faced

- *The initial doubts of farmers:* The concept of a labour bank was regarded with some doubts and suspicion by the farmers in the initial stages. The fear of unionism is very real in the minds of people, the Panchayat had to deal with this issue as the major challenge. The majority of the farmers feared that the labour force would eventually grow into a labour union. They feared that their applications to the farm help societies requesting services of the labour force could be used as a document by the labourers in later years to claim a portion of their income from the produce. Thus in spite of the fact that local labour was available through the labour force, the farmers continued to depend upon outside labour.

It needed a lot of effort on the part of the Panchayat and the agriculture office to convince the farmers of the potential benefits of the programme. A team of Panchayat members and the agriculture officer had continuous discussions with the farmers. To counter the fear of labourers using their documents against them, the team suggested that they put only their name on the application without their address or signature. The team also detailed the benefits of using up to date machines, lowering the cost of production. For example, the team asked the farmers to pay just Rs. 800 to the agriculture office for harvesting a hectare, the normal rate for which would be Rs. 2000. The few people who took up this option were very happy and the success of the programme paved the way for others to make use of the services of the labour force.

- *Resistance from labourers and vested interests:* An education programme for labourers was required, as some of them were under the impression that they would be paid lower wages in the labour force. The people in general and the labourers in particular were made aware of the broader purpose of the programme, particularly that of assured employment.

The creation of farm help societies provided a check to the siphoning of funds by middlemen and influential people, since in the new set up, all benefits in the agriculture sector can be obtained only through these societies. Naturally, they started attacking the services of the labour force. But by then, the people were convinced enough of the efficacy of the programme not to fall prey to such mischief.

The greatest challenge, however, came when a leading local daily allowed the publication of a series of articles by vested interests against the programme. Despite repeated requests by the Panchayat president to the editor of the newspaper, the articles continued. The Panchayat members, agriculture office, farm help societies and the local people then took a mass decision to boycott that particular newspaper. The boycott continued for two months. A competing local daily took advantage of the situation and tried to increase its own circulation. Realising their folly, the first newspaper sent a team to study the actual facts. After which, a half page article was printed in the newspaper praising the programme. The people from the newspaper began a campaign, going from door to door to regain their leadership.

Outcomes of the Labour Force Experience

An immediate outcome of the whole process was that a healthy partnership developed between the farmers and the labourers. Through the concept of the labour force, a new identity was given to the labourers. It brought in a new culture where the labourers are now assured of continued employment, dignity of labour and work security.

A major outcome of the experience has been the increase in the area under paddy cultivation. Around 60 acres of fallow land have been brought under dry land cultivation and 13 ha of land under paddy cultivation. The cost of production has reduced by 40 per cent due to mechanisation. The interest of the farmers and labourers in agriculture has been revived. Around 1300 farmers have made use of the services of the labour force till now. The major advantage being that the farmers can benefit from the subsidy immediately after the completion of work. Before, they had to shuttle between the government offices with their vouchers. But now they need to approach only the farm help societies for any work to be done. Similarly, those labourers who had kept away from the programme have shown a new interest. There are nearly 400 applications from local labourers to join the force.

Moreover, the labourers were registered under a group insurance scheme worth one lakh rupees. Those labourers who had 150 days of work to their credit were given a festival allowance of Rs. 500 during the Onam festival season. The labour bank provides the workers with credit coupons of various denominations to enable them to buy provisions at a village store, run by the women's self help group 'Samata', formed as part of the initiatives undertaken as part of the People's plan.

The situation now can be contrasted to earlier days when the agricultural labourers had to look for employment in other sectors and outside their village, due to lack of regular employment. They can thus save the additional cost to their living expenses (if they had to work outside the village) and can spend their savings on the family. In addition, the flow of money from the village is checked as local labour is now readily available in the village itself. The money is now circulated in the village itself thus contributing to village development.

The involvement of people in each stage of the process and in the management of the programme has resulted in generating the support of the people in general and the labour force members in particular. They have developed a sense of the "we" feeling. Participation and support of the people were the major factors which enabled the project to overcome all challenges. People are now more aware of the agricultural schemes available and benefits now tend to reach the target group.

With the success of the programme and a revived interest in agriculture, neighbouring Panchayats have started replicating the efforts of the Kunnathukal Panchayat. Various other Panchayats have also requested the services of labour force members.

The Creation of Labour Bank

Perhaps the most positive outcome of the experience has been the creation of a labour bank. In this system, the farmers can avail the services of labourers from the bank on a loan basis, when they do not have enough initial capital to invest. The loan needs to be repaid only after the harvest, in the form of wages with interest at 12.5 per cent.

The Follow up

The Panchayat is now making efforts to conduct a survey of the agricultural land and the practices used by every farmer and storing the same in the computer. The farm help societies are expected to give reports regarding these aspects so that the data can be updated. The major purpose is to provide technical advice to the farmers on modern and scientific practices of farming. For this, efforts are continuing, to identify unemployed students in the area who have undergone vocational higher secondary education to form a core group, so as to provide technical advice to farmers.

II

MICRO PLANNING: "DO-ABLE" (2000-2001)

The learning from the experiences gained in facilitating micro-planning over the years has enabled PRIA and the partners to modify the approach and facilitate micro planning to provide for the maximum participation of women and Dalits, facilitating plans, to be realistic (in terms of time and funds) and enhancing people's ownership by mobilizing people's contribution.

Given below is a brief outline of the states in which the "do-able" micro planning was initiated:

State	*District*	*Block*	*Gram Panchayat*	*Prioritized Issue*	*Total Cost*	*People's Contribution*
Haryana	Fatehabad	Ratia	1 (11 wards)		Rs.1,70,000	Rs.7,925
Himachal Pradesh	Sirmaur	Paonta Sahib	1		Rs.7,00,000	Rs.1,05,000
Madhya Pradesh	Morena, Gwalior, Datia, Tikamgarh, Panna, Sehore & Jhabua	11	16	Toilets well and tube well	Rs.1,83,700	Rs.41,320
Rajasthan	Jaipur Sitapur	Govind-garh	1 (17 wards)	Well, Tank and Hand pumps. Detailed PRA's position was taken up in each ward for drawing up plans	Each ware had its own budget	People's contribution was in the form of labour and kind
Uttar Pradesh		Kasma-nda	1 (5 hamlets)	Various issues in different hamlets	Each hamlet, prepared its own plan with budget	People's contribution was in the form of labour and kind

With the purpose stated above, an experimental "do-able" micro planning module was developed. Different partners in the state in which this experiment was conducted adopted various steps in completing the plans and implementing them within one to two months of the time period, with people's participation and contribution.

The Steps Taken in Preparation of People Centred Plan

Step 1. Elected members underwent an orientation to the concept of micro-planning (focus on economic, environmental and social needs) in a Panchayat meeting of a one-day duration. The role-playing method was also used.

Step 2. Ward/Tola/Muhallah level meetings were held simultaneously, for understanding the concept of micro-plans focusing on economic, social and human development, rather than on infra-structural development. The timing of the meetings were organised to the convenience of the elected members (ward panches) as well as the community. The major issues of the ward were identified in these meetings along with the causes and the probable solutions (Methodology-large group discussions). One or two youths (volunteers) were identified and they facilitated the preparation and implementation of the micro-plan along with the panch. A discussion on the need for contribution in kind or cash from the community was initiated. (This step covered half a day or about two hours in each ward)—the total duration would depend on the number of wards/tolas/muhallas/purvas).

Step 3. The consolidation of the major issues of wards, causes and probable solutions at the Panchayat level was encouraged, and a rough plan was prepared on that basis. The people responsible for preparing the rough plan were the elected members, the Panchayat secretary, ward level volunteers and other Government officials (This took one day.)

Step 4. Preparing the People Centred Plan under the following heads (one day)

- Introduction of Panchayats (a brief description of the location, the terrain and the, socio-economic status—Map of the Panchayat can also be inserted).

- Issues and priorities of wards.
- Consolidation of priorities, probable solutions and appraisal of available resources.
- Plan based on solutions with their implementation and responsibility. Proposed budget with community contribution.
- Conclusion/the way forward.

Step 5. Resolution passed by Ward/Gram Sabha (one day).

Step 6. Getting it typed and making multiple copies (one day).

Step 7. Recording it on a Panchayat board.

Step 8. Submission and follow-up by elected members to the Block Development Office, Block Samiti and District Panchayat Officer, other tiers of PRI (Zila Parishad), MLA, MPs and DPC (Banks/NABARD/SHG etc.).

Some Points were to be Kept in Mind:

- Scale of preparation—Ideally the efforts for a People Centred Plan covers the entire Panchayat or even a ward, but if it is not possible due to various reasons, then to demonstrate the result, a mohala/tola/purva or part of a ward may be considered.
- Linkages with the two higher tiers—In the process of the preparation of the People Centred Plan involving members of the top two tiers was made mandatory as it would help in developing linkages among the three-tiers and mobilizing the resources available to the other two tiers (This can also serve as the basis for further negotiations with other institutions for example DPC).
- Conflicting interest groups—In every Panchayat, there are conflicting interest groups prior to starting the People Centred Plan. Care was taken to involve them as well.
- Generally it was found that soon after the first meeting, elected members, volunteers and government officials were enthusiastic about coming to the ward level meetings. It was important to conduct ward level meetings immediately because of the heightened enthusiasm.

- Secondary Data—Prior to intervention for the People Centred Plan, secondary data was collected. This helped in correlating the problems with probable solutions.
- Initiation of Meetings—All the meetings was initiated by those elected at the ward or Panchayat levels or by the members of the CBOs.
- Learning Materials—Some learning materials were distributed during the meetings in order to promote a better understanding in the community. An easy-to-do People Centred Plan process, with objectives and outcomes was distributed. Special attention was paid to writing this material in a simple, brief and comprehensive manner.
- Media—The media should be contacted prior to the intervention. This helps to replicate the process elsewhere.
- Involving the whole community in the implementation of the plan is of vital importance, the people from the junior most rungs of the community as well as those in more powerful positions have to be involved in the resource mobilization of a People Centred Plan. This way the people are not just acting on orders of people in more influential positions.
- Sustainability—Wherever there is a need-based process in action which could solve at least some problems of the tola, mohalla or purva, the People Centred Plan could be sustained. However, it must be positioned in the Gram/ Ward Sabha and Gram Panchayat processes.
- Distance—The challenge of undertaking People Centred Planning in remote/far flung areas of the block is to be taken up.

Development of a model: The method of doing it may differ from place to place, depending upon the situation and circumstances. PRIA and their partners carried out this experiment in 16 Panchayats in Madhya Pradesh, 2 Panchayats at Haryana, 1 Panchayat each in Himachal Pradesh and Uttar Pradesh they have helped in developing this model.

UTTAR PRADESH

Do-able Micro Planning in Hamirpur Gram Panchayat, Sitapur District, on Rural Infrastructure Development

A proper infrastructure is an essential part of today's activities—consumption, production and distribution. Whenever, the infrastructure fails it very quickly and radically reduces the communities' quality of life and productivity. Conversely, improved infrastructural services enhance welfare, foster economic growth and hence benefit the communities. Providing a sound infrastructure and its services to meet the demands of households and other users is one of the major challenges of social justice and economic development. In the State of Uttar Pradesh (U.P.) a large part of the area is backward and one of the major factors behind this is the lack of a proper infrastructure, especially in rural areas. Regions like rural eastern and central parts of U.P. suffer from a severe lack of infrastructure (both physical and social) and inaccessibility of the community to health centres, schools and markets make the quality of life in these areas.

With this background, keeping in mind the sorry state of the infrastructure in the major parts of the State of U.P., the first and foremost responsibility of any institution, especially the institutions of Local Self-Governance, is to cater to the local issues related to economic development in that area. And if the development, directly or indirectly, is dependent on infrastructure then development of infrastructure, physical as well as social, calls for a heightened focus. Of course, this does not mean that the focus from other developmental issues takes a second place, it is just asking to be looked at urgently.

Why PRCs Undertook Infrastructure Development

As already noted, in rural Uttar Pradesh, one finds a lack of infrastructure like roads, link roads, drainage, hand-pumps, health centres, schools, etc. This has necessarily affected the life of the communities. There are villages, which are in the interior (far from the main roads), land one has to walk or ride a bicycle for about 20 km's to get to the local market or town. There are no health centres nearby, nor proper roads for conveyance and to transport the sick. The households are, in many cases, unable to send their wards to school just because there are no proper roads linking the hamlets to the school. The children have to take routes, which are unsafe where they can be attacked by wild animals. Some times children have been severely injured. These situations call for the immediate attention of the Panchayat.

The community has an important role in the development of the infrastructure, as it is the responsibility both of the individual and the community alike to modify their physical surroundings in order to improve their productivity and protection. On examining the expenses in the financial year 2000-2001 in 15 Gram Panchayats (GPs) of the Kasmanda block of Sitapur district of Uttar Pradesh, it was revealed that more than 90 per cent of the total funds in every Panchayat have been spent on infrastructure alone. However, it is apparent that this amount has not been sufficient for the infrastructural needs of the community. With substantial funds being allocated to cater to the community's need, one has to see that the resources are utilized efficiently and effectively. The urgent needs of the community are properly articulated and the marginalized groups are also given their due share, the Panchayat Resource Centres (PRCs), an informal agency working to make the functioning of the Panchayats more effective, (within the powers which it possesses), is perhaps in the best position to ensure the fulfilment of the above requirement. Hence, the PRCs as facilitators came into the picture to promote (in consultation with Panchayats and the community) effective planning in the development process.

The Process

The process of building the capacities of Panchayats to undertake the development of infrastructure in the rural areas started in the year of 2000. A well thought out strategy was behind the whole idea. The different activities undertaken-information distribution, Gram Sabha mobilisation, and capacity building initiatives, were all focused towards the micro planning processes. Hence, the above activities at the field level were carried out in such a manner that one activity led to another activity and eventually it led to the central activity, that is, the micro planning through which the development of infrastructure was facilitated.

Initially, the capacity building programme emphasised the process of planning at the local level. The information distribution process also gave a focus to the provisions of the Uttar Pradesh Panchayat Raj Institution (UPPRI) Act related to planning at the local level while at the same time attention was paid to providing information to the Panchayat members as well as members of the Gram Sabha on basic issues like quality standards, fixed by the government pertaining to the construction work. Thus, the attempt was mainly to sensitise the community about the significance of the issue of infrastructure as well as the Panchayat members about how to go about addressing the issue. Similarly at the Gram Sabha level also various meetings were conducted to generate a thought process among the community members about the importance of preparing an ex-ante plan before the actual implementation of the activity is carried out. In the micro-planning process the focus was mainly to articulate the need of the different hamlets and bring it to the fore at the Gram Panchayat level. The next step brought the prioritisation issue to the forefront, necessarily the most complicated and the important step in the planning process, as without decisions, which infrastructure development to take up first would be the question. Decisions had to be taken regarding alternative solutions and selecting the one best suited for the problems prioritised. The budgeting part had been attended to earlier, the last being the implementation strategy for the whole plan.

Benefits of the Strategy

One of the major benefits of the strategy decided for the promotion of infrastructure was the building of a favourable environment amongst those in the community involved in planning. A favourable and healthy environment for a particular activity always facilitates the process and it was true here also. When the resources ran short the community came forward and provided support in the form of labour and money. With this kind of community support the implementation becomes easier.

The above process helped us in developing a series of infrastructure plans in a number of Gram Panchayats—Ganeshpur, Kaima, Daudpur, Kaima, Padui, Mahabara, Sabada, Lathia, Ahilaspur, Doth, Antamau, Samaspur Sailwara, etc. to name a few. In all the above Gram Panchayats social as well as physical infrastructure, as per the need of the community, was facilitated by PRCs.

The implementation of the plan for the benefit of the groups that had been marginalized helped in promoting a sense of confidence in the Panchayat and their own abilities to take up the development activities through locally available resources. The example of Ganeshpur, Kasmanda block of Sitapur is one of the cases where people undertook the construction of a school and appointed an educated unemployed young person as a teacher. All this was done with the monetary support and labour supplied by the community members of Ganeshpur, which is mainly inhabited by the scheduled castes. The Gram Panchayat made this endeavour possible. The Panchayat members soon recognised the need of the community for planning and implementation and took up the process of finding the solution finding the solution to the problem.

In Lathia Gram Panchayat, within the same block of Sitapur, the women folk undertook the construction of the link road on their own, with only the moral support of the Panchayat. This action on the part of the women had an encouraging effect on the women in the neighbouring areas of Siddha Ahilaspur Gram Panchayat. With women actively participating in the process of implementation especially where they contributed in terms of labour, it led to a boost to their confidence in that they could also lead such a process if proper support by the community is provided to them.

The overall benefit of the entire process is the advantages that the Panchayat came to recognise, of community participation in the process of micro-planning. It enabled planning in accordance to local needs, knowledge and resources pooled within the community.

The Challenges Faced

Prioritisation of the problems has always been a challenge and this proved to be true in the areas where issues had to be selected. As it is well known, the need of different kinds of infrastructure in different hamlets will arise and to satisfy all of them is difficult keeping in mind the limited resources at hand. Hence, prioritization becomes essential. Prioritization created a lot of tension among the inhabitants of the different hamlets but later a consensus was reached through persuasion and facilitation by the PRCs.

Infrastructure development is one of the most important issues for a Panchayat and care should be taken that it does not become the only one. As the need for infrastructure is predominant in the initial period the Panchayat allocate more resources for it. But the purpose of involving the Panchayat and the community alike in the initial stages, with the help of the PRC, it was hoped, that through the process of discussion, prioritization and planning on an issue, it would contribute to making the concerned committee active and inculcate a sense of ownership among Gram Sabha members and Panchayats. It is expected that if the above development takes place the Panchayat will be able to take up other issues related to social development. PRC's role at this juncture becomes very important, as it has to facilitate the functioning of Panchayats in such a manner that the shift of focus of PRC from the physical infrastructure to social issues is smooth. This is an urgent agenda for the PRCs in the times to come otherwise the Panchayat will become just an implementing agency of government schemes.

The prioritized problems at the Gram Panchayat level are as follows:	
Brick road at Govindpur: Length-1 km: cost	Rs. 1.5 lakh
Brick road at Kusmaura: Length- 300 m: cost	Rs. 30,000
Brick road at Hamirpur: Length-500 m: cost	Rs. 50,000
Installation of handpump at Debiapur: cost	Rs. 50,000
Installation of handpump at Govindpur: cost	Rs. 2,000
Construction of well at Kusmaura: cost	Rs. 5,000
Education problems in Kusmaura and Govindpur	

MADHYA PRADESH
PLANNING FOR DROUGHT RELIEF

Background

It is being increasingly recognized that unless the people are involved in directing and controlling the process of development no real (human) development will take place. And in order for this to happen more powers regarding decision-making, resource allocation, budgeting, etc. need to be given to the villagers. Therefore, the decentralization of governance and development planning is a condition for the realization of hitherto untapped growth potential.

The concept of giving power to the people in order to ensure their involvement and participation in the development of their Panchayat has been given definite shape with the passing of the Constitution (the 73rd Constitutional Amendment Act) in 1993. The Amendment provides power to the Panchayats to prepare plans for social and economic development as well as implement schemes for the same. It also gives space for citizen's participation is still lacking in the planning from the base upward. The main reason being that the capacities of the Panchayats to make plans as well as facilitate people's participation is weak. The question is how can Panchayats facilitate people's participation? How can they be made a part of the planning process? It seems to be a dilemma for the Panchayats as there are no existing examples for them to replicate.

To add this, Madhya Pradesh has been experiencing a drought situation. The Panchayats' attention is on how to tackle this issue. Samarthan, Centre for Development Support, a non-governmental organization for the past 6 years, has been quite active in supporting voluntary initiatives in Madhya Pradesh and Chattisgarh, to promote participatory processes and people-centred development. Giving the issue of drought, priority, Samarthan, in Madhya Pradesh along with the Panchayats facilitated sixteen micro-planning processes with an aim to create a model for future planning initiatives. These initiatives took into consideration people's participation throughout the process. Also the constant involvement of the government and other agencies was insisted upon as it was felt that their presence would provide an impetus to the process of planning from the base upwards.

The Objectives of the Micro Planning Initiative:

- To provide examples of participatory planning in the direction of decentralized governance.
- To find alternatives at the local level to combat the problem of drought.
- Capacity building of Panchayat representatives and Gram Sabha Committee members.

Capacity Building on Micro Planning

A four-day workshop was organized in the month of April 2001, among Panchayati Raj Institutions (PRI) members and the community on micro-planning in order to create a common understanding about planning from the base upwards. Seven community-based organizations along with the local people also took part in the training. As part of the training, on an experimental basis, a village was chosen to put to the test, the steps required for micro-planning. The issue on which the planning was initiated was drought, as the village was experiencing water shortage. The whole process saw a positive participation among the people in planning for water storage systems. Noting the success of the micro planning initiative in addressing issues of drought, Samarthan along with the seven organizations that took part in the training decided to take up the drought issue in the area of its intervention i.e. Madhya Pradesh, through Panchayat Resource Centres (PRCs). The aim was to put forward successful examples of addressing developmental issues through micro-planning. To take up this initiative the whole state was divided into four parts (Bundelkhand, Chambal, Malwa and Mahakauchal). With the seven organizations and Samarthan, micro-planning was implemented in around sixteen Panchayats across seven districts namely Murena, Gwalior, Datia, Tikamgarh, Panna, Sehore and Jhabua.

The Selection of Panchayats

The organizations involved in micro planning selected the Panchayats based on certain criteria. Knowledge of contextual situations—socially, politically and culturally was of paramount importance in the selection process as it helps the people to participate more easily.

The Panchayats that were chosen for micro planning shared the following characteristics:

- The process of micro-planning was initiated in those Panchayats where the organizations have been working for a period of 1-3 years.
- Almost all the Panchayats had a population between 1,500-2,000 people and a proportion of scheduled castes and tribes.
- Among the Panchayats selected half the number were represented by women, the other half by men.
- The basic means of livelihood are agriculture, animal husbandry, milk production and daily labour.

Percentage of Contribution Mobilized for the bottom-up Planning NGOs

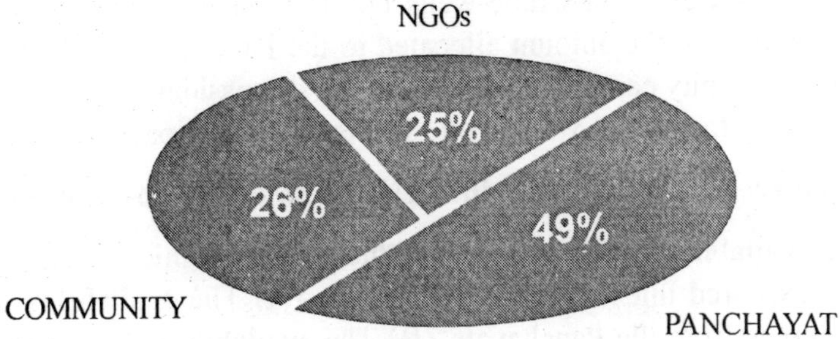

The Process of Micro-Planning

The involvement of people was ensured right at the initial stages of micro-planning. It was decided that to build a common understanding among the people about planning small group discussions could be held with women, Dalits, adivasis, youth members and Panchayat representatives to find out the requirements of various groups. For creating a positive environment, Participatory Rural Appraisal (PRA) was conducted, so that involvement of various sections could be assured. Efforts were made for the involvement of PRI representatives. Street plays were performed to mobilize and inform the people about the process of micro-planning as well as motivate them to attend Gram Sabhas. These steps enabled to build rapport and faith of people in the process of micro-planning. After these stages, a special Gram Sabha was called where discussions were held on:

- Selection of issues,
- Prioritization of issues to be tackled,
- Identification of alternatives to tackling issues,
- Resource mapping,
- Determining the monetary aspect/support, Panchayats, community and organization,
- Division of responsibility,
- Time-frame,
- Monitoring and evaluation.

The PRC and the organization facilitated the discussions along with the Panchayats in taking up the issue of drought, prioritizing activities of putting up hand-pumps, digging wells, widening the depth of existing wells, tanks, tube-wells, etc. The issue of resources was explored as to the amount allocated to the Panchayats, and what the community can generate. During the discussions special care was taken to see that women and Dalits also participated.

Resources being Utilized in the Process of Micro-Planning

The availability of the resources in the process of micro-planning was explored under three broad heads—(A) The availability of resources from the Panchayats, (B) The availability of resources from the community, and (C) resources being given by the organization to fill in the gaps. Overall, the Panchayats gave a total of 49 per cent of the amount and 29 per cent of the contribution being given by the community in the form of labour and cash. Seen above is a pictorial division of the funds procured from the three broad heads.

Achievement in the Process of Micro-Planning

- The recognition by the Panchayat members of the value of people's participation in making the process of planning easier and enabling community mobilization of its resources.
- Increase in the ownership of Gram Sabha members, through the formation of committees at the Gram Sabha level such as the Working Committee, Financial Committee, Monitoring Committee, Stakeholder Committee and

Ad-hoc Committee. The formation of such groups has brought recognition to the Panchayats and has seen an increase in the frequency of visits from various government officials to view the actual implemented plan in the area.

- In the Panchayats of Khari, Behrua, Gherughati and the main Panchayat of Sehore, Dimni, Bhabra and Panna Block there has been 100 per cent contribution from the Panchayats.

Challenges

- The Panchayats being divided on the basis of caste and *mohalla,* the PRC staff had to deal with the challenge of prioritisation. Most of the people were giving more importance to the mohalla level plan rather than a common plan for the whole village. This process was time consuming as it took a lot of persuasion on the part of the PRC and the Sarpanch to convince the people that a common plan would benefit the citizens as a whole.

Lack of cooperation from Panchayat secretaries also made it difficult to elicit information initially from the Panchayats where the micro planning was going to be facilitated. Keeping the government machinery, the secretary involved and informed about the processes soon won their support.

HARYANA

Do-able Micro-Planning Experience in Alika Panchayat, Fatehabad District

Background

PRIA has been working in the Zila of Fatehabad for the last two years. Fatehabad is a newly created zila, it came into being in July 1997. Originally it was part of the Hisar district of Haryana. It consists of five blocks, 231 Panchayats, 104 Panchayat Samitis and 13 Zila Parishads. The most intensive work has been done in the Ratia block.

The Ratia block consists of 61 Gram Panchayats wherein there are 530 ward Panchs and 61 Sarpanchs (20 women Sarpanchs and 174 women panchs). The experiment of micro Planning took place in Alika Gram Panchayat. Alika Gram Panchayat is situated 20 kms from Ratia.

The Process

Step 1: *Selection of the Gram Panchayat:* The Gram Panchayat Alika was chosen on the following grounds, the facilitating organization had already established a rapport with the Sarpanch. The relationship between the Panch (ward members) and the Sarpanch was favourable. The community members had a high regard for the Sarpanch (Bhagwant Rai). Also for the past 10 years the Sarpanchs have hailed from the same family.

Step 2: *A discussion with the Sarpanch of the Selected Panchayat:* A discussion took place with the Sarpanch with regard to what micro-planning is, and why it is beneficial to conduct such a planning with people's participation. This was done prior to taking the issue of micro planning to the people.

Step 3: *Meeting with the Gram Panchayat:* After the initial meeting with the Sarpanch, the Sarpanch of Alika agreed to have a meeting with the rest of the Panchayat members, on 24th June 2001. The issue of micro-planning was taken up for discussion with the members, stressing the need of the people's participation and resource mapping.

Step 4: *Ward Meetings and Prioritization:* In these meetings, information in simple terms about micro planning was given to the community members. The local community based organizations were given an orientation prior to these meetings, for the facilitation process among the community to begin. The discussion among the community members was also focused around the major/pressing issues or concerns that needed to be addressed in their wards or villages. Eleven wards were covered through the facilitation of the panch and the community based organizations. Each ward was asked to pick one major priority.

Prioritized Issues

Ward Members	*Ward Meeting Date*	*Issues*
1 & 2	25th June 2001	Toilets, electricity, drinking water, house construction for the poor, waste management. Priority: Toilets
3 & 5	26th June 2001	Pukka houses, waste management, toilets, upgrading the status of the school, drinking water outlets, electricity, school staffing, pukka roads. Priority: Toilets
4	29th June 2001	Drinking water, drainage system, cement gullies, electricity, staffing in school, library, playground, government shops, internet connections, Panchayat Bhavan. Priority: Cement Gullies
6 & 7	27th June 2001	Electricity polls, drinking water outlets, waste management, pukka houses, toilets, harijan chopal. Priority: Toilets
8 & 9	28th June 2001	Drinking water outlet, waste management, drinking water problem, toilets, electricity connection, staffing for school. Priority: Toilets
10 & 11	29th June 2001	Drinking water, toilets, bus stand, pukka road, school compound, school walls need painting, anganwadi, Daani roads. Priority: Toilets

Step 5: *Finding a solution to the Prioritized Problem:* For this purpose the whole Gram Sabha was collected as ward level meetings brought ward level priorities and each ward wanted their priority to be the focus of attention. It was pointed out that except for ward number 4 all the wards had the issue of toilets as a priority. This was regarded as the top priority after the Gram Sabha meetings as around 80 per cent of the people's houses had no proper toilet facilities. Ward 4 members and the other people were in agreement.

The Implementation Phase

Ten wards of the village convinced one ward to unanimously resolve one of the grave and pressing problems of sanitation. In addition the Panchayats also prepared a joint proposal requesting the administration and the technical wing to prepare an estimate for community toilets. This meeting also decided upon the community's contribution in resolving the problem and encouraged participants to undertake responsibilities to collect the resources.

Two plans were approved as to solving the problem of toilets. One was that if each household had to have a toilet built then 700 toilets had to be constructed. Minimum cost for these toilets was coming to Rs. 3,000 each adding upto 21 lakhs. Seeing that the cost was high the second plan recommended that five toilets be constructed in and around the Gram Panchayats with proper water facilities and flushing. A person would be appointed to look after the sanitation and cleanliness of these toilets. These toilets would be equipped with drinking water for animals and a washing area for women to wash their clothes (a 22 ft long *chabutara*). This latter plan was accepted. The Ward Members and volunteers were asked to collect Rs. 20 from each household.

A community meeting followed the meeting of the invited officials. This meeting apprised the officials about the developments undertaken in relation to do-able micro planning. The community's contribution stood at Rs. 8000 and the Zila Parishad members promised a matching grant of another Rs. 8000 (sourced from EAS Grant). The SDO from the Electricity Department promised to solve the problem of the lack of electric supply to the Village Panchayat. Village members volunteered to take five electric poles and wire from the department and set it up in the Village Panchayat. People volunteered to lend tractors and a trolley and the fuel was paid for by the Panchayat's own income. Another experience with similar processes took place in Jalloli village of Pavitta Sahib block of the Sirmaur district of Himachal Pradesh.

HIMACHAL PRADESH

Do-able Micro-Planning-Process in Jalloli Village Panchayat

Jalloli village located on the main road, connecting Delhi to Shimla, was identified for the do-able micro planning exercise. The Panchayat met with the criteria adopted for conducting the base-upwards planning exercise, with the exception, that it is situated on the main road. The willing co-operation of the Sarpanch and other Panchayat members provided a conducive platform to launch the process, a felt need area with greater likelihood for success, prompted PRIA to choose the Panchayat. The rationale behind selecting this Panchayat was that a successful model of planning might pave the way for replicating the same in other Panchayats with ease.

To begin with, secondary data was collected about the village's composition (caste and class), facilities and resources available in the Panchayat. Following this exercise, the Sarpanch, already familiar with the concept, consented to have a meeting with his other Panchayat members. The meeting focused on orienting the members about the micro-planning concept and seeking their support as well as commitment. Through this meeting, the ward members found a significant meaning added to their role that of assuming leadership roles and spearheading the planning process in their respective wards. In this one meeting alone their doubts and apprehensions were addressed to gain their unconditional support. The Sarpanch was not too confident about the co-operation of certain members of the Panchayat, they were individually contacted by the team members from PRIA. Subsequent to the Panchayat meeting, the ward members organized meetings in their respective wards with the ward people. Once the concept of micro-planning was explained to the people/participants, they were facilitated to discuss their problems and were finally able to prioritize the problems from a whole variety of problems presented.

The women members outnumbered the men in the meetings due to heavy field work carried out by the men in the agricultural season.

Here the unanimous need of the people, more specifically, women was with regard to the village tube well. The drinking water was unfit for consumption and the depth of 100 ft did not meet the requirements of four villages benefiting from the tube well. The system of drinking water was outdated and could not keep up with the increased demand of the growing population. The volunteers estimated that the present requirement could be sufficiently met with an increase in the depth of the tube well to 400 ft.

A Core Committee was constituted drawing volunteers from each ward as well as Panchayat members and retired servicemen. A common meeting of the village was called with representatives from all the wards. This meeting was instrumental in preparing a plan elaborating on tasks, delineating responsibilities, and possible resources for the same. Volunteers estimated the total cost at Rs. 2 lakhs and jointly decided to source Rs. 50,000 from the Panchayat fund, Rs. 20,000 from local contributions and the rest from the government scheme.

10

PLANNING FOR DEVELOPMENT AT GRASSROOTS IN TAMIL NADU

G. PALANITHURAI

Introduction

"Planning" in India is believed by every one to be an exercise that can be done only by top level bureaucrats and technocrats with the direction of the policy-makers for the development of the whole country. The concept of planning as an exercise and process which can be done at the lowest level in the hierarchy of governing structure with the involvement of the people has also been posited to the policy makers ever since India adopted planning as a legitimate government exercise but it did not gain any support (Raj, 1984). Committees were constituted to probe more into the details of the process and as a result reports were submitted (K.V. Sundaram, 1977). In the beginning of 1970s the dominant thought of keeping planning at the top became flexible to some extent as such planning had not yielded the expected results to mitigate the problems of the poor and initiatives at the provincial level that too at the sectoral level were allowed. It went still further in the 1980s with the initiative for planning being undertaken at the district level. The 1990s marked a historic departure from the conventional arrangements to achieve development so as to match globalization of economy and decentralization of powers and planning at grassroots was made mandatory to achieve development and social justice with the participation of the people (K.C. Sivarama Krishnan, 2000). Though globalization gained currency and its operation is in full swing decentralization did not get that much of attention as the stakeholders of decentralization are weak. To make decentralization work an array of support structures have to be created. Against this background, even for planning at grassroots one has to support the grassroots institutions. Though there were sporadic experiences in decentralized planning in the past, implementable strategies and devices could not be gained from all those experiments and experiences. (T.M. Thomas Issac with Richard W.Franke 2000, 21-29). The new initiatives, following the 73rd and the 74th Amendments to the Constitution of India, have to take into cognizance the fact that the top down planning has not addressed the felt needs of the people, has removed people away from governance and participation in development. Development as an activity to be done exclusively by officials resulted in large scale corruption in rural development activities. This too has to be recognized while considering the new option. People were made beneficiaries, the self-respect of the people was jeopardized and people were not regarded as development participants (N. Narayanasamy, M.P. Boraiyan and M.A. Jeyaraju, 2000). It is so not only in India but also in many of the developing countries. Bridging the gap between the people and the government is a difficult task in third world countries. (Common-wealth Foundation, 1999). In this context, planning at the grassroots, initiated through the 73rd and the 74th Amendments to the Constitution of India, has to remove all the above stated obstacles and barriers in the process of development.

The Problem

Though provision has been made in the Constitution for planning initiatives at the grassroots, to what extent steps are being taken at the state level and the Panchayat level to plan for development at the grassroots is a question to be probed. Further at what level initiatives gain momentum and how this can be sustained is yet another question to be clarified.

Objectives and Methodology

This study has the following objectives:

(a) to study the efforts of the State government in strengthening the planning process at the grassroots;

(b) to what extent planning is initiated from below by the Panchayats with the participation of people;

(c) how the planning process is initiated from the grassroots by the Panchayats and with whose support? and

(d) what are the implications of the intervention of the government and other agencies in the planning process at the grassroots?

The above stated objectives could be studied through documentary analysis and process analysis. The government's position on micro-level planning could be evaluated from the steps taken by the government. A process analysis can be made on the initiatives of planning at the grassroots by the Panchayat institutions with the support of development organizations.

Context

To analyze decentralized planning, there are two approaches so far developed. One is historical in nature and the other one is contextual or critical analysis. Through the historical approach, ever since the concept of planning gained currency in India, discussions and deliberations had been conducted as to what alternative strategies have to be evolved to overcome the difficulties of centralized planning (James Manor, 1999). But all the discussions and deliberations were held against the backdrop of centralized planning. The issues and problems were looked at from the perspective of the centre and not from the perspective of the periphery. Macro economic activities through centralized planning did not mitigate the micro-level problems particularly those relating to the basic needs (G. Palanithurai, 2003).

Hence the policy makers were compelled to think of planning units at different levels, namely the district and the block. Yet there was no conscious and deliberate decision to establish planning units below the State level. Even to establish a planning unit at the State level, it took nearly about two decades after independence. Such a kind of rigid centralization had been practiced in Indian politics and administration (Jayati Ghosh, 1998).

But the decentralized planning enunciated at present is totally different and it makes a real breakthrough as it has been incorporated in the Constitution itself. It is not an isolated event that took place in Indian planning. It is a corollary of a worldwide event which pushes the economy to cross the boundaries of the nations and into every segment of the society. Both in economy and polity an overhauling took place by which the paradigm of governance, administration and development has been totally altered (Ajit M. Banarjee and K.A. Chidambaram, 1996; Sofi Ali and Anita Rao, 2000; Olle Tornquist, 1999). A new paradigm has been developed by which new opportunities, which are uncommon, can be harnessed by enhancing the capacity of the stakeholders (International Commission on Peace and Food, 1990). Through this paradigm power is given to the people to determine their destiny (The World Bank, 2003). People have been projected as the major stakeholders and they have to decide their course of action in the process of development (Robert Chambers,1983). In the present context the concept "government" has been redefined. It is not a provider but a facilitator. The government takes a back seat and the community or the user group takes the front to take development initiatives. Thus the concept of government is no more relevant and it is only "governance" which is relevant at present (Rajesh Tandon and Ranjita Mohanty, 2002).

How for the development of the community, activities have to be initiated through a new system of governance created at different levels below the State with the introduction of the Amendments to the Constitution of India. Governance structures have been created at the village level, the block level and the district level, including towns, municipalities and corporations. To activate the people to participate in the development process, powers have been devolved to different levels and the planning mechanism had been incorporated in to the Constitution itself. By doing so the trend of development activities has been altered from "supply driven" to "demand driven" mode (G. Palanithurai, 2000).

The major provisions and basic principles have to be conformed to through an Act at the provincial level. Hence all the states have conformed to the bases of the Constitutional Amendments in State Acts. Tamil Nadu also has passed conformity Act. Enacting a legislation is not a big task in a democracy since it is a representative democracy based on the principle of majority in Parliament and Legislative Assemblies. To pass a legislation the members of the decision-making body have to be managed through the established procedure. The difficult task lies in operationalizing the provisions of the Act which has to take place in the society among the people. In India there are a large number of key provisions in the Constitution which are still not operated effectively because much of social conflict, social discrimination and illiteracy. Hence, the focus should be on the operational part of the legislation. In the Tamil Nadu Panchayat Act due recognition was not given to the District Planning Committee and its responsibilities. The District Planning Committee and its functioning have to be seen and analyzed against the larger backdrop of devolution of powers in Tamil Nadu, because devolution of powers and planning at micro level will alter the existing mode of governance (G.Palanithurai, 2003). To perform the above task the State Government and its leadership should have sufficient will, because this initiative to devolve powers, functions, finance and functionaries will cripple the existing exploitative and corrupt nexus between the ruling elite and the inert bureaucracy. It will mobilize the people for deepening democracy. People's perception has also to be changed as they regard themselves as beneficiaries instead of development participants having lost their self confidence and self respect. Further people have to be conscientized and capacitated. The whole exercise has to be done with the backing of the Central Government.

Perception

To undertake the gigantic and uphill task, normally any leader will pursue a normal course of action. In the Indian context, this new exercise of democratic decentralization starts only from the State Government not from the Central Government. Normally, the term is used in development literature to refer to the transfer of authority to plan, make decisions and manage public functions from the national level to any organization or agency at the sub-national level and down below. Decentralization in India refers to a situation in which lower-ranking units below the State level acquire all powers and responsibilities from the State Government and also sole control over the determination of their goals and targets.

Tamil Nadu's ethnic political culture demanded adequate powers to the State Government since independence. Now these political parties, which are coming to power alternatively, view decentralization as a threat to the power of the State Government. These political parties, namely both the Dravida Munnetra Kazhagam and the All India Anna Dravida Munnetra Kazhagam, forcefully opposed the creation of the three-tier Panchayati Raj System as it would emerge as a countering political force. Hence, they have developed a strategy to keep the Panchayat system a weak instrument while appearing to conform to the major provisions of the 73rd Amendment to the Constitution of India (G. Palanithurai, 1999).

The Panchayat was created through the conformity legislation enacted during the period of the All India Anna Dravida Munnetra Kazhagam. The Act has many retrograde provisions (G. Palanithurai, 1998). The Act has not given any real power to Panchayats. The new Panchayati Raj was operationalized only during the period of the Dravida Munnetra Kazhagam. All the powers given to the Panchayati Raj institutions are supervisory in nature and not of the decision-making kind. The powers given to Panchayats, however meagre, have not been given through Act but through Government Orders. The ruling parties at the State level somehow or other have managed to keep the local bodies in their party fold as the ruling parties have emerged victorious in the local body elections also. As a result most of the local body leaders never raise their voice against the State Government for more power, finance and functionaries to local bodies. Only the lowest units in the system, namely the Gram Panchayats, which are freed from political contest raise their voice against the State Government and demand powers to local bodies. The District Planning Committee was created and it was under placed the Chairmanship of the District Collector. After a prolonged fight he was replaced by the District Panchayat Chairperson.

Elections to District Planning Committee were conducted and now it is in position but no activity is undertaken.

Virtually planning at multi level exists only in concept and theory but not in practice. But the State Planning Commission had prepared a report, guidelines and a training module for multi-level planning (State Planning Commission, 1997). Both leaders and officials had been trained (G. Palanithurai, 2000). The elected representatives elected to the District Planning Committee have taken cognizance of the mandatory functions of the District Planning Committee. But there is no concerted effort to build up this process of planning from below and, as a result, the rural development activities are carried out still in the supply driven mode and people are not involved in the development activities. More than that the felt needs of the people projected through the Gram Sabha are not met, but a variety of activities are being carried out through sectoral departments (G. Palanithurai, 2003).

In order to break the deadlock an exercise was initiated with the intervention of The Hunger Project by which ten Gram Panchayats in Sivagangai District and thirteen Gram Panchayats in Pudukkottai District have been set up as model Panchayats in terms of planning at micro level with the participation of the people who are willing to involve themselves in the preparation of plan for the development of the communities in the Panchayat area. Why these Panchayats in these two districts? The leaders of these Panchayat showed interest in this exercise and volunteered while they were undergoing training. Further these Presidents are supported by the respective District Collectors who have assured that they will extend all possible support and coordination to this exercise.

Initiatives of the Government

By going through the document entitled "Report of the Working Group on Decentralized Planning and Panchayati Raj" prepared by the Planning Commission, 1997 one can infer the poor interest evinced by the Government of Tamil Nadu in all the past experiments. In the 73rd Amendment, while there was a discussion in the Parliament, the two major political parties, namely, the DMK and the AIADMK being in power in Tamil Nadu State alternatively, made a categorical statement that they had not imagined a structure for Panchayat Raj above the Block Panchayats. They wrote letters to the Government of India that the District Panchayat has to be abolished. With both these parties opposed to the district level structure what would have been the fate of the District Panchayat in Tamil Nadu? Further when the District Planning Committee was formed the District Collector was made the Chairperson of the District Planning Committee. After a prolonged fight the District Panchayat President was made the Chairperson of the District Planning Committee. To fulfil the Constitutional obligation, the District Planning Cell with a skeleton staff was created. It has to look after the day to day administration of the District Panchayats. Neither the State Government nor the District Planning Committee took any step with regard to the preparation of the District Development Plan. The State Planning Commission, though it took the initiative it did not have the backing of the State Government. As a result planning at the district level has not seen the light of day.

But organizations and activists engaged in public affairs, seeing the apathy of the State Government in taking the initiative for micro level planning, because interested in taking the initiative. Except in West Bengal and Kerala, micro level planning is the initiative of the development organizations. In this context in Tamil Nadu State The Hunger Project initiated the process of planning at Gram Panchayat level as Gram Sabha has got power to approve the plan document which becomes a legal and legitimate plan document. The Hunger Project has certain objectives namely ending hunger through micro plan mitigating malnutrition, empowering women and children through the micro plan, and working for social development through micro plan, all under women leadership. But The Hunger Project realized the fact that in the context of weak devolution of powers to the local bodies, micro level planning will be a meaningful exercise only when it is done with the partnership of the district administration as the sectoral departments are under the district administration. Since sectoral departments are not under the control of the Panchayati Raj system, for implementing the plans of the Panchayats, the cooperation of the sectoral departments is imperative. Against this background, working with the district administration becomes inevitable. Further, though the State Government is not interested in devolving powers, it is interested in achieving social development. This interest can be exploited to initiate micro level planning. The Hunger Project in Tamil Nadu is taking a major lead in initiating micro-level planning at the Gram Panchayat level. Ten Gram Panchayats in Sivagangai District headed by women have planned and started working on the plan. Following Sivagangai District, in Pudukkottai District, 13 Gram Panchayats have been selected and planning is over. Another 30 Gram Panchayats have been selected for this exercise in Tuticorin District and Dindigul District. Wherever, the district administration is taking initiative, The Hunger Project joins them as partner and initiates micro level planning. Panchayats are selected for this planning on two conditions, namely, the Gram Panchayat leader should have honesty, commitment and capacity and the Gram Panchayat should enjoy the support of the communities without any social and political conflicts. Table 10.1 presents some details of the Panchayats selected for the pilot exercise in Sivagangai District.

Planning Exercise at Phase I

Table 10.1: Model Panchayats for Community Based Micro-Level Planning in Sivagangai District

Sl. No.	*Union*	*Panchayat*	*Name of the Panchayat President*
1.	Kallal	1. Veppangulam 2. Nerpugapatti 3. Kalipuli	Veera Kalaiarasi (SC) A.Pushpam (BC) S.Gandhimathi (SC)* 2.
2.	Thirupathoor	4. Velangudi	A.Alphonsamary (BC)*
3.	Sigampunari	5. Vaduvanpatti 6. Sevalpatti 7. Kozhikudipatti	R.Rakku (SC) S. Poongothai (BC)* Nagajothi (BC)
4.	S. Pudur	8. Urathupatti 9. Manaloor 10. Keelavayal	C.Chinnammal (SC) S.Gomathi (BC) S.Sumathi (MBC)*

* The above Panchayats were included in this pilot exercise only at a later stage as per the suggestion of the District Collector.

A total of 10 Gram Panchayats headed by women were selected in four Unions of Sivagangai District, Tamil Nadu. Out of the 10 Panchayat leaders, 4 belonged to the SC.

Methodology of the Plan Preparation in the First Phase

Before commencing the actual work, an intensive training was organised for three days to build the capacity of the leaders including the men and women who were all committed to this exercise. The training programme was organised from the 27 to the 31 May 2002 in Gandhigram Rural Institute as a fully residential programme. Experts were drawn from different institutions including the government to conduct the training programme (G. Palanithurai, 2002). All the six Gram Panchayat Presidents initially selected wanted to have a common workshop to sensitize the Panchayat Ward Members, community leaders, SHG leaders, members of the youth groups and opinion makers on the importance and the implications of grassroots planning. The lead NGO, Rural Welfare Trust, agreed to help the Panchayats to organise the workshop and do the needful for planning also. The Hunger Council of Tamil Nadu agreed to share some of the responsibilities. As a result on 17 August, 2002, a workshop was organised at Tirupathur for all the six Panchayats and around 210 members from all the Panchayats participated in the programme (G. Palanithurai, 2002). The whole exercise focused on planning at the Gram Panchayat level and the discussion was on the steps to be followed in the planning. It was agreed that the planning exercise would be completed before October 2002 and that the Panchayats and the NGO would take up the responsibility. Further it was decided to identify what could be done by the leaders and the people of the respective Panchayats. What could not be done by the Panchayats would be done by The Hunger Project.

The next step was to collect basic data about the people and their conditions. This could be done by the Panchayats. Before starting the exercise the statutory seven committees had to be constituted so that the number of members in the orbit of governance would be increased. For the data collection a well developed schedule prepared by the State Planning Commission was used. After collecting the data from each village a PRA exercise was carried out with the help of the staff of the Kottayam based NGO Centre for Rural Management (CRM) to assess the needs of the people and to prioritise the needs. This exercise was done extensively and the staff of the CRM prepared a plan. Simultaneously, the representatives of the people in the Panchayats also prepared a plan based on the PRA exercise. Finally both the plans were synthesized and brought out in the form of a document. In the whole process the concept of development was critiqued, the role of the government was criticized and people expressed their willingness to participate in the whole process as the Panchayat leaders provided ample scope for people to participate in the planning exercise. When the document was ready for presentation in any forum for critical evaluation, The Hunger Council of Tamil Nadu organised a development seminar with a set of objectives, namely, of making this document legitimate, to sensitize the government on planning at the grassroots and to motivate other Panchayat Presidents to start this kind of exercise in their Panchayats also. On 26 and 27 October, 2002, the development seminar was organised in Gandhigram Rural Institute, inviting the State Minister for Local Bodies, secretaries, directors, planning officials, experts, representatives from the media, MLAs, community leaders, Panchayat leaders and women and youth groups from the six Gram Panchayats and Women Gram Panchayat Presidents from all over Tamil Nadu numbering around six hundred.

The perspective plan document of the six Gram Panchayats contained a brief history of the Panchayats, details about the former Panchayat Presidents who held office during the pre 73rd Amendment era, basic data about agriculture, source of irrigation, veterinary facilities, land utilization, land ownership, landless families with social background, facilities available in schools, admission in schools, dropouts in schools, status of women and children, energy utilization, non-conventional energy sources, environmental conditions, skills available in the village, housing facilities etc. After projecting all these the document projected the needs and prioritized them. Further it stated how these prioritized needs are to be met (Veerakalaiarasi 2002; A. Pushpam 2002; K. Rakku 2002; V. Nagajothi 2002; C. Chinnammal 2002; and S. Gomathi 2002).

Responsibilities were fixed on individuals and groups to take steps to meet the needs indicated in the plan document. Achievable indicators were fixed to monitor the activities of the Panchayats. It was stated unequivocally that the Panchayat would concentrate on 100 per cent school admission, ensure the normal weight of new born babies, institutional delivery, pre natal and post natal care, malnutrition, family welfare etc. Thus this plan document became a vision document. Responsibility was not fixed on the government alone. Activities were classified and accordingly responsibilities were fixed by which partners were identified for administering development and social justice.

Reactions and Responses to Plan Document

Officials from the State Planning Commission and the Project Office of the District Rural Development Agency of Sivagangai District first examined the document and offered their comments. They found certain deficiencies in the process of data collection. Apart from the basic data all other data were collected through PRA exercises and prioritization was also done through the same exercise. This was not approved of by the officials. The activities envisaged in the plan document could not be carried out under the available schemes of the government. The Panchayats had not identified the individual beneficiaries for the government schemes. While entering the activities in the plan document, the Panchayats had to indicate the source of funding to carry out all the activities. Further they questioned the legitimacy of the plan document in the absence of a planning exercise at the Block level and the District level. On certain issues such as agriculture, veterinary care, non conventional energy and environment, the people in the villages had not consulted the government departments while projecting activities in the plan document. These subjects were highly technical in nature, but the Panchayats had taken the opinion of the people in deciding upon the activities. On the whole it was an expression of cynicism. It is to be noted here that, in the inaugural function, the Minister for Panchayati Raj and Rural Development, Government of Tamil Nadu, showered encomium on the women leaders for their exercise and he said that despite the implementation of a variety of schemes and programmes of the Central and State Governments, people's felt needs could not be met and that this kind of micro level plan would reverse the trend and the felt needs would be met and thereby wasteful expenditure could be avoided. He further said that this kind of exercise would trigger a movement for people's planning. He even appealed that in each district this kind of exercise should be initiated.

Despite the remark of the Minister, the officials recorded their negative remarks about the whole exercise. Following the reaction and response of the officials, some of the experts from the audience came forward to express their opinion. Prominent among them were B.S. Raghavan, retired Chief Secretary of West Bengal and adviser to the FAO, A.K. Venkatasubramanian, retired civil servant specializing in Public Distribution System, Dr. Rajagopalan of the M.S. Swaminathan Foundation, Mr.Vallinayagam, retired Additional Director of Rural Development, and Mr. N.S. Chidambaram, retired Additional Director of Rural Development. First all the experts appreciated the effort expended in taking up this cause and facing all the problems in collecting data and putting them in a plan proposal and getting the approval of the people in the Gram Sabha and the Panchayat Council. It is a plan of the people prepared by the people and not a plan prepared by officials. It is their vision. They have chalked out their activities on the basis of their felt needs. It is true that they have not chalked out activities to implement the schemes of the government and hence there will be a gap between the available schemes and the activities envisaged in the plan document of the Panchayats. The plan document is not a petition prepared by them to get sanction from the government. It is their plan and they seek to be partners in governance to administer development. They have indicated the possibilities to generate employment opportunity with the resources and skills available in their respective Panchayats. Further it is to be noted that social development issues have been projected in the plan document and it is indicated that they will take up the responsibility to achieve sustainable results in development in the social sector. While appreciating the efforts of the Gram Panchayat leaders, they addressed a few questions to the government officials and a few suggestions to the Gram Panchayat leaders.

In fifty years of democratic governance in India, no such document was prepared for village development by the government. Even after the introduction of the 73rd Amendment and the Constitution of the District Planning Committee, no systematic effort was made at the micro level, despite planning officials working at the district level. Having failed miserably in discharging duties and responsibilities at the government level, it was unfair on the part of the officials to criticize the efforts made by the women leaders for their small technical lapses. Further it was characteristic on the part of the officials to denigrate the people's efforts as unscientific. Since the officials have been oriented to act in the supply driven mode of development activities, they look at everything from the supply side and not from the demand side. While evaluating the proposal, officials had looked for proposals for the government schemes and programmes and that was why they were not in a position to suggest ways and means to meet the demands which could not be fulfilled by the government schemes and programmes. The experts said that the officials could have offered their suggestions rather than criticizing the plan. Even the model plan prepared by the officials in some of the villages in Tamil Nadu did not include social development issues. The model plans prepared by the officials have not seen the light of day.

It is a unique exercise in fifty years of governance because every segment of the rural community has been involved in this exercise to make a declaration that their destinies are going to be decided by their efforts only. Now owners have been found for the rural development activities. They have realistically projected their needs as felt by the community without looking into the supply side of it. Hence, it is the responsibility of the officials to help in identifying the institutions to be involved in the process of fulfilling the needs of the people. The existing schemes of the government could be utilized for many of the demands and for some of the demands a slight modification is necessary in implementing the existing government schemes for which the District Collector as Chairman of the DRDA and Inspector of Panchayats can make use of his discretionary powers. Demands which could not be met through government schemes could be taken to various financial institutions for financial support with a viable action proposal prepared by professionals for which the Panchayats have to seek the support of NGOs. It is fortunate that the Rural Welfare Trust is working with all these six Panchayats. The same organization can be involved in preparing such proposals and approaching CAPART, DST, NABARD and other agencies. For the social development issues targeted, achievable and quantifiable indicators have to be fixed. For instance school enrolment of students, birth weight of newly born babies, institutional delivery, reduction of school dropouts, providing safe drinking water supply to all families, ensuring sanitation facilities to all families, eradication of plastics and so on have been identified as activities and responsibilities have also been fixed in the case all the above said activities. The seven statutory committees in the villages have to be activated to involve themselves in all these activities. What the Gram Panchayats now require is partners to carry this task further.

After making these observations the experts again requested the officials directly dealing with planning at the grassroots to give their feedback again. The officials from the State Planning Commission and the District Rural Development Agency informed the audience and more specifically the Panchayat Presidents of the possibility of making use of many of the Central and State Government schemes and programmes to meet many of the issues projected in the plan document. For other issues and demands the nodal agency, the NGO, Rural Welfare Trust, was to prepare and send proposals to NABARD, CAPART and other agencies. Achievable indicators have to be explicitly entrusted to the committees of the Panchayats and their activities have to be monitored every year. This was the assurance given to the Panchayats by the officials.

Finally the Panchayat Presidents concluded their presentation by assuring the officials that they would take up the responsibility to achieve many of the achievable indicators on social development. Further they informed that they would meet all the sectoral departments to seek their help to fulfil all the demands of the people mentioned in the PRA meetings while preparing the plan for the Gram Panchayats. The women leaders, while expressing their gratitude to the officials, explained their struggle to make use of the power devolved to them.

The whole exercise and the presentation of the plan in the development seminar provoked the women leaders assembled in the seminar to think on the social issues highlighted by the women Presidents of the six Gram Panchayats. The women Presidents who assembled in the seminar from all over Tamil Nadu under the banner of the Tamil Nadu Federation of Women Leaders prepared a charter of activities and declared it a charter of activities for the next year. The charter is presented hereunder.

Declaration

We, the elected women representatives who are gathered here at Gandhigram Rural Institute on this 27th day of October 2002, declare that we will address the following issues in the next one year:

1. All the eligible children (girls and boys) will be enrolled in schools.
2. We will strive to remove malnourishment amongst children in the age group of 0-5 years. As elected representatives we shall ensure that no underweight babies are born in our villages. The mothers will be given proper nourishment before and after delivery.
3. Better anti-natal and post-natal care will be provided for all the women in our Panchayats.
4. Any injustice against women in our Panchayats will be dealt with firmly. As a collective we will fight against domestic violence and also any other form of violence against any women in our Panchayat.
5. We will ensure that child labour is abolished in our Panchayats.
6. We will ensure equitable access to and distribution of Panchayat resources among all the people in the Panchayats and guarantee at least the provision of the basic minimum requirements for the poorest. The PDS system will be improved with our intervention.
7. Problems faced by the women Panchayat leaders and women in general will be addressed collectively by making alliance with supportive institutions and organizations.
8. The newly implemented sanitary complexes meant for women will be effectively managed by women's groups with the support of the Panchayats.
9. Our Panchayats will not suffer from lack of drinking water. Everyone will be entitled to safe drinking water.
10. We will ensure that Gram Sabhas take place regularly and more and more people take part in these meetings. We will

ensure that a minimum of 50 per cent of the total women in the Panchayat attend the meetings and that their issues are properly heard.

11. We commit ourselves to the implementation of the 15-point programme prepared by the Tamil Nadu Government and request the state government to devolve necessary powers to the Panchayats and local bodies for the same.

Following the presentation of reports and the declaration of the charter of activities for women Panchayat Presidents, the Pudukkottai District Project Officer, DRDA, representing the Pudukkottai District administration, pleaded that this kind of exercise be undertaken in the whole of Pudukkottai District for which he sought the help of NGOs and Gandhigram Rural Institute. Women leaders from Pudukkottai District who attended the development seminar expressed their willingness to undertake this kind of exercise in their Panchayats. Thus the micro plan exercise done in six Gram Panchayats and the presentation of all the six plans in the development seminar in the presence of the Minister for Panchayati Raj and Rural Development, Government of Tamil Nadu, officials of the State Government, experts in Micro Level Planning and six hundred Gram Panchayat women Presidents created an awareness among the minister, the officials and the local body leaders on the importance of micro level planning and, as a result, the State Planning Commission started the exercise of giving training to the local body leaders on planning exercises to be done at the grassroots.

Analysis of I Phase Efforts

Primarily, though it is a constitutional mandate that the planning exercise has to be initiated at the grassroots, beyond the State Governments and the Central Government producing documents on decentralized planning, nothing has been done on the ground in the 9th and the 10th Plans. These six Panchayats, under the leadership of women, have sensitized the minister and the higher officials to the implications of micro level planning.

Secondly, while carrying out this exercise, it could be seen at what level devolution of powers has taken place in the state as the Panchayats faced problems in getting the support of the sectoral departments. Empirically this proved the extent to which powers have been devolved to the Panchayats.

Thirdly, in the process of interacting with the officials and hearing views of the officials on the plan proposals of the Panchayats, the official attitude to this new dispensation and the exercise has been exposed and they have been sensitized to the legal and social implications of micro level planning.

Fourthly, the other women Presidents have gained confidence that this kind of exercise could be done in their Panchayats also as they heard the methodology adopted in the six Gram Panchayats for planning at the micro level.

Fifthly, social development issues came to the limelight because of the micro plans of the six Gram Panchayats. These six Gram Panchayat leaders gained this insight while they were in self help groups and thereby they quickly grasped the social development issues and fixed achievable indicators for the Panchayats. This kind of exercise motivated the other Panchayat leaders to take up this issue. As a result the women Panchayat leaders published a charter of activities to be undertaken by the Panchayats in the social development sector.

Sixthly, in the recent past people have been mobilized by various agencies for participation in the implementation of various schemes and programmes brought from above. But the position "we govern you receive" has not altered. By undertaking the planning exercise by the people, people's demands and priorities have been prominently projected in the plan document and thereby the old position "we govern you participate" has been replaced by "you govern and you participate".

Seventhly, the six Panchayat Presidents have started negotiations with officials, representatives of the people like MLAs and MPs and NGOs for fulfilling the requirements of the plan. They have developed skills of negotiation.

Eighthly, the hidden potential of the leadership has been exhibited through this process. Class, caste and political organizations have their own roles in the activities of the rural society. While mobilizing all the groups cutting across these differences, the women leaders have exhibited a high decree of democratic leadership. Even the traditional Panchayat leaders have extended their fullest cooperation to the efforts of these Panchayat Presidents.

Ninthly, the conventional mode of looking at issues and demands from the supply mode has been done away with and instead issues are being looked at from the perspective of the people and thereby a sense of ownership has been cultivated among the people for the development of the community.

Tenthly, so far the Panchayats negotiated for schemes and programmes of the government. Now the trend has been reversed and they ask for the government's participation in their schemes and programmes. Petitioners have changed their role to that of negotiators because of this new exercise.

Eleventhly, the Panchayats have started mobilizing partners for their development activities. They have gathered many organizations to their support in implementing their schemes.

Twelfthly, the leaders have built a vision document through this exercise. They have gained rich input on vision building from the training undergone elsewhere by the Presidents. While doing so they are critiquing the very concept of development. They move around the skills and the resources available at their disposal.

Though they are women and, that too, three of them are of the Backward Class and another three are Dalits, their leadership is recognized, appreciated and supported by even traditional Panchayat leaders. The women leaders, by their performance, have won the recognition of the community. Since initiatives are taken jointly by the leaders, the administration becomes transparent and it reduces corruption to the maximum extent. The planning exercise has made the people volunteers in the development initiative.

Summing up of I Phase

Planning at the grassroots for administering development and social justice has long range implications in the paradigm of development. It alters the entire process of development. The roles of the government and the community have been reversed. All the loopholes in the development process in the existing paradigm have been exposed and people have developed a new perspective to look at issues and now plans of activities are chalked out on the basis of their demands and needs as prioritized by the people and not on the basis of the available schemes and programmes of the government. The concept of "we govern you receive" has gone and the new concept "you govern and you participate" has been ushered in. Social development issues have drawn the attention of the people because of this exercise and achievable indicators have been fixed for social development issues and people have taken up the responsibility of achieving the target. People have developed a sense of ownership as this plan document carries the demands of the people as schemes and programmes. Now the government finds itself in a tight spot as to whether this is to be allowed or not. There is no other option except to allow and continue the new practice. Over and above, at the earliest, the entire state has to take the initiative to plan for development from the Gram Panchayat to the District Planning Committee. The new paradigm will gain momentum and it will ultimately end in a movement for decentralized governance for development and social justice.

Exercise in II Phase

Based on the exercise undertaken in Sivagangai District micro-level planning was started in Pudukkottai District. Pudukkottai District offered three advantages for undertaking this exercise. They were: the District Collector is pro-Panchayat and he believes in the potentialities of the Panchayats and the community; the link between Panchayats and the communities is strong; and, the capacity of the leaders is very high as periodical orientations apart from training were given to the Panchayat leaders. As the District Collector invited The Hunger Project, it was decided to work with the Panchayats. The district administration provided office space for The Hunger Project in the District Panchayat office. Thirteen Gram Panchayats were selected from all the 13 Blocks. The main criteria adopted in the selection process is that the Panchayat leader should have commitment and honesty, the link between the leader and the community should be so strong, and there should not be any communal and political conflict between and among the collectivities. By adopting the criteria the following Gram Panchayats were selected in a meeting held in the Collecteroate with the participation of The

Hunger Project staff, the District Collector, the Project Officer, DRDA, of Pudukkottai District. Table 10.2 presents the list of the selected Panchayats.

Table 10.2: Model Panchayats for Community Based Micro Level Planning in Pudukkottai District

Sl. No.	*Name of the Panchayat*	*Panchayat Union*	*Name of the Panchayat President*
1.	Merpanaikadu	Aranthangi	Ms. Bhavani Ilango
2.	Poovalur	Avudayarkoil	Mr. Sarvana Perumal
3.	Melathur	Thiruvarankulam	Mr. Saravanan
4.	Edaiyathimangalam	Manamelkudi	Mr. Arumugam
5.	Elaikadaividuthi	Karambakudi	J. Manjula
6.	Melaputhuvayal	Kunandarkoil	Ms. Dhanalakshmi
7.	Parambur	Annavasal	Mr. Abdulwaheed
8.	Nerinjikudi	Ponnamaravathy	Mr. P. Ramnu
9.	Punalkulam	Gandarvakottai	Mr. Shanmugam
10.	Mookampatti	Pudukkottai	Ms.V. Mangalam
11.	Meenaveli	Viralimalai	Mr. Alagiri
12.	Virachilai	Tirumayam	Ms. Devi
13.	K.Rayavaram	Arimalam	Ms. Rani Sathappan

Out of the 13 Gram Panchayat Presidents 6 are men and 7 are women.

Planning Methodology in II Phase

After getting consent from the Panchayat leaders, the President was asked to constitute the statutory Panchayat committees along with the Panchayat Planning Committee. In all the committees it should be mandatory that women and Dalit representatives should find a place. Panchayat President, Vice-Presidents, Panchayat clerk, committee members, traditional Panchayat leaders, SHG leaders, youth leaders retired officials of the Panchayat areas were drawn for training. A three-day training in planning at the village level was offered. It was a residential training programme and it was conducted in Gandhigram Rural Institute. In the training exercise emphasis was laid on participation of people, especially women and Dalits, and social development issues. Following the training in each Gram

Panchayat a sensitization exercise was conducted to prepare the people for evolving a perspective plan for socio-economic development of the Gram Panchayat area. To change the mindset of the people, this exercise continued till the draft plan was approved in the Gram Sabha. Sensitization was also done on social development issues. When the training was over, responsibilities were fixed as to who and how the needed data have to be collected from both primary and secondary sources. After collecting the data, a neat profile of the village was developed which was termed a development report. After consolidation of the report a Participatory Rural Appraisal for every Panchayat was to be conducted to prioritize the works that were to be undertaken in the Panchayat.

After prioritizing the activities, The Hunger Project staff, with the help of the Panchayat leader and the clerk identified the vulnerable families and gave numbers to the families. A list of the disabled was made for constant monitoring. Schools, *anganwadi,* primary health centre service would be assessed by the staff of The Hunger Project. Thus social development activities became the primary concern of the Panchayat. A manual, listing the activities related to social development to be carried out in the Panchayat area by the Panchayats in partnership with other agencies was supplied to all the Panchayat leaders (activity chart). Malnourished children, pregnant women affected by anemia and poor women affected by diseases would be identified and all the lists would be attached to the plan document. Finally, responsibilities were fixed as to how these prioritized activities were going to be carried out and with whose partnerships. All the needs identified and prioritized through the PRA were to be matched with the schemes and programmes of the Central and State Governments that being operated through sectoral departments. For unmatched issues Panchayats were to seek the help of MLAs and MPs and to get substantial funds from their Local Area Development Fund. The whole plan document was placed before the Gram Sabha for evaluation, suggestion and approval. After getting the approval, with modifications if any, the plan document was to be printed.

The printed plan document would be circulated to all the sectoral departments. The District Collector as Inspector of Panchayats would give necessary instructions to the sectoral department heads to carry out activities in the Panchayats based on their needs. The Panchayats with the help of the Planning Committee and the representative of The Hunger Project should do the follow-up activities.

Lessons Learnt

It is not a State driven planning activity. It is initiated from below. Though it was initiated by the leader of the Panchayat in the process of mobilization, people have been made to participate in the process of preparation of the development plan. Panchayat leaders and the members of various committees have developed negotiating skills in the process of the preparation of the plan. They negotiate with the sectoral departments, MLAs and MPs. Further they negotiate with Union Councillors and District Ward Members to make use of the funds available in the Block and District Panchayats. Since there was no initiative from the State Government and the Central Government for planning from below with the participation of people, these Gram Panchayat leaders took the initiative and followed the guidelines provided by the State Planning Commission for planning at the micro level, especially at Gram Panchayat level. Because of these initiatives, even the State Planning Committee has started doing this exercise in 250 Gram Panchayats throughout Tamil Nadu. It is also not planning but preparing a development report.

While engaged in this exercise it could be visualized at what level devolution of powers has taken place in the State as the Panchayats faced problems in getting the support of the sectoral departments. Empirically this proved the extent to which powers have been devolved to the Panchayats. Further while interacting with officials in the process of plan preparation the attitude of the officials towards planning could be seen. Thanks to this exercise the officials are exposed and sensitized towards planning and social development. The grassroots leaders have exhibited an extraordinary commitment towards communities social development. The micro level plan experience made the Panchayat leaders enhance their capacity and use the full potentiality of leadership. Panchayat Presidents and the people have prepared a plan. Now they have reversed the process of development activities from supply driven to demand driven mode. Realistically speaking the plan is a vision document and the activities listed in the plan document are only their wish list when there is no conducive atmosphere for micro level planning.

Summing up of Phase II

The new dispensation of micro level planning with the participation of the people to administer economic development and social justice envisioned in the Constitution through the 73rd and the 74th Amendments has far reaching implications in the development paradigm in the context of redefining the concept of Government against the backdrop of democratic decentralization of powers and globalization of economy. This new initiative has reversed the process from supply driven to demand driven activities. The old practice of the government providing and the people receiving has been reversed. Now people plan and participate and the government just supports. The whole development exercise moves in a different mode which is totally different from that of the government. People's wishes and vision have been projected as a major set of activities and people have taken up responsibilities.

There is yet another striking feature in the micro level planning process. In all such previous exercises only infrastructural facilities were projected as the major set of activities. But now people have focused more on social development activities because of the continuous sensitization and conscientization programme. This kind of people's initiatives in a few Panchayats has put the Government in a tight spot. As a result the State Planning Commission has taken efforts to prepare a development report in about 250 Gram Panchayat as a pilot project. Thus this new paradigm will gain momentum and it will ultimately end in a movement for decentralized governance for development and social justice.

Integrated Analysis

It has been tested in the process of planning at grassroots that planning is possible even without much power and the cooperation of the government departments. By initiating the process the gap between the Panchayat leaders and the community is bridged. People are mobilized constantly and conscientised on social development activities. Ownership is being developed among the people for many of the development activities. In the process of interaction with Panchayat leaders and officials, Gram Sabha members have established a grip over the Panchayat administration. While the Panchayat Presidents are organizing meetings with various committee members the Panchayat administration becomes transparent and non-corrupt. Planning initiative at the grassroots involves the women's and thereby women's issues have been dealt with. Slowly Panchayat leaders, Ward Members and committee members are sensitized towards gender issues. Committee formation is a process by which women members and representatives from the Dalit community are inducted and their participation in the meetings has created sensitiveness among all towards the issues of Dalits. Panchayat leaders have started bargaining with other representatives of the people namely, MLA, MP, Ward Members of Block Panchayats and District Panchayats. The leaders have developed bargaining capacity to deal with officials. Panchayat leaders have developed a vision for the development of the community. Panchayat leaders and the people have realized the fact that for most of the social development activities money requirement is minimum and that to accomplish the same what is needed is commitment on the part of the Panchayat leaders and the community. The District Collector and his team of officials have shown much interest in Panchayat activities as they have faith in the Panchayat's potential. Along with Panchayats, the officials also claim credit in achieving the target of all development activities. Without the cooperation of the Panchayats and the community, officials cannot achieve the target successfully and hence they now bank on the Panchayats. Further the quality of the works carried out by the Panchayats with the participation of the people is good compared to the work of the contractors. Each and every Panchayat is having a plan document which is regarded as it pride.

By developing a plan document at the village level, indirectly a compulsion has been placed on the sectoral departments to work in the villages with their allocation of resources restricted to the activities indicated in the plan document of the respective Gram Panchayats.

Conclusion

In the given context, however poor devolution of powers, functions and finance in Tamil Nadu, planning at grassroots will compel the government to devolve the same. Administration becomes transparent and involvement of women and Dalits is remarkable in the activities of the communities. Both people and their leaders are sensitive towards the social development issues. Every Village Panchayat has a legitimate vision document which prevents the sectoral developments spending unilaterally. It bridges the gap between the people and the government. The entire State can replicate it.

NOTES AND REFERENCES

Ali, Sofi, and Anita Rao, "Reinventing Public Administration for 21st Century" *The Indian Journal of Public Administration,* Vol. XLVI: No. 2 April-June 2000.

Ajit, M., Banerjee, and K.A. Chidambaram, (eds), *Renewing Governance: Issues and Options,* New Delhi: Tata McGraw Hill Publishing Company, 1996.

Chambers, Rober, *Rural Development: Putting the Last First*, Harlow: Longman Scientific and Technical, 1983.

Chinnammal, C., *Perspective Plan for Development of Urathupatti*, Thirupathur: Grama Iyakkam, 2002.

Ghosh, Jayati, "Development Strategy in India: A Political Economy Perspective" in *Nationalism, Democracy and Development: State and Politics in India* (Eds), Sugata Bose and Ayesha Jalal, New Delhi: Oxford University Press, 1998, pp.165/83.

Gomathy, S., *Perspective Plan for Development of Manalur*, Thirupathur: Grama Iyakkam, 2002.

International Commission on Peace and Food, *Developing Human Resourcefulness: Strategies to eradicate poverty in the 1990's,* Draft Working Paper, California: ICPE, 1989.

James Manor, *The Political Economy of Democratic Decentralization*, Washington DC: The World Bank, 1999, p.1.

Nagajothi, Y., *Perspective Plan for Development of Kozhikudipatti*, Thirupathur: Grama Iyakkam, 2002.

Olle Tornquist, *Politics and Development: A Critical Introduction*, New Delhi: SAGE Publications, 1999.

Palanithurai, G., Development Roles Reversed: People's Initiatives and Governments Participation, (monograph), Gandhigram, Rajiv Gandhi Chair for Panchayati Raj Studies, 2003

Palanithurai, G., *From Participation to Self-Governance: An Agenda for Restructuring Tamil Nadu Panchayat Act 1994,* Gandhigram: Department of Political Science and Development Administration, 1998.

Palanithurai, G., *Grassroots Democracy in Indian Society*, New Delhi: Concept Publishing Company, 2000.

Palanithurai, G., *New Panchayati Raj System at Work: An Evaluation*, New Delhi: Concept Publishing Company, 1999.

Palanithurai, G., *Panchayati Raj System in Tamil Nadu: With Original Act*, New Delhi: Concept Publishing Company, 2003.

Palanithurai, G., Report of the Training Programme on Training of Trainers in Multi Level Planning Conducted for DRDA Officials, Gandhigram: Rajiv Gandhi Chair for Panchayati Raj Studies, 2000.

Palanithurai, G., Report of the Workshop on "Panchayati Raj: Trials and Triumphs", Gandhigram: The Hunger Project, 2003.

Palanithurai, G., Report of the Training on Multilevel Planning, Gandhigram: Tamil Nadu Council for Sustainable Livelihood, 2002.

Palanithurai, G., Report of the Workshop on Multilevel Planning, Gandhigram: Tamil Nadu Council for Sustainable Livelihood, 2002.

Pushpam, Y., Perspective Plan for Development of P. Nerpuhapatti, Thirupathur: Grama Iyakkam, 2002.

Raj, K.N., "Some Thoughts on Decentralization of Development Planning and Implications" keynote paper presented at Seminar on Decentralized Planning and Implementation, Nov, 29-1, Dec, 1984, ISEC, Bangalore.

Rakku, K., Perspective Plan for Development of Vadavanpatti, Thirupathur: Grama Iyakkam, 2002.

Sivaramakrishnan, K.C., *Power to the People?: The Politics and Progress of Decentralization*, New Delhi: Konark Publishers Pvt. Ltd., 2000, pp 95-96.

State Planning Commission, Report of the Working Group on Decentralized Planning and Panchayati Raj, Chennai: Government of Tamil Nadu, 1997.

Sundaram, K.V., *Decentralized Multi Level Planning,* New Delhi: Concept Publishing Company, 1997.

Tandon, Rajesh, and Ranjita Mohanty, *Civil Society and Governance*, New Delhi: Sanskriti, 2002.

The World Bank, World Development Report, 2004: Making Services work for Poor People, Washington DC: The World Bank, 2003.

Thomas Issac, T.M., and Richard W.Franke, *Local Democracy and Development,* New Delhi: Left Word, 2000, pp.16-32.

Veerakalaiarasi, *Perspective Plan for Development of Veppankulam*, Thirupathur: Grama Iyakkam, 2002.

ANNEXURE–1

GRAM PANCHAYAT AND SOCIAL DEVELOPMENT
Activity Chart

INDICATORS

Sl.No.	*Activities*	*Responsibility*	*Outcome*	*Verification*
1.	100% enrolment of eligible children	President, Vice-President, Ward Members, PTA, SHG Members, Youth Clubs, NGO, Retired Officials, Education Committee	Level of literacy increased.	School records
2.	Reduction of Dropouts	President, Vice-President, Ward Members, PTA, SHG Members, Youth Clubs, NGO, Retired Officials	Increase in Educational standard	School records
3.	Ensuring protected Drinking Water Supply to School	President, Vice-President, Ward Members, School Teachers	Improvement of students Health, reduction of ill health of students	Physical verification
4.	Providing toilets to school	President, Vice-President, Ward Members, School Teachers	Increase in health of children	Physical verification
5.	Utilizing the toilets by the school students	President, other members of the Panchayat Council Teachers, PTA, Parents.	Toilet Culture Developed	Physical verification
6.	Cutting the nails of the students every Monday in Balwadi and School	Youth Club, SHG, Panchayat Ward Members, School teachers	Health education, reduction of diseases, improvement of health.	Physical verification
7.	Planting of saplings in the school premises	President, teachers, agriculture departments	Environment awareness eco-development.	Physical verification
8.	Creating a school garden	President, teachers PTA, Youth Clubs, Agriculture Department.	Increase in nutrition as the vegetables are given to noon mean centres	Physical verification

Contd.........

Sl.No.	Activities	Responsibility	Outcome	Verification
9.	Keeping the Balwadi clean and neat	Balwadi teacher, President, Vice-President, Ward Members	Health education, increase in status of health, culture of cleanliness is cultivated	Physical verification
10.	Providing a toilet in the Balwadi	President, Vice President, Ward Members	Education, increase in health status	Physical verification
11.	Bringing a toilet culture among the kids	Balwadi teacher	Health education, increase in health status	Physical verification
12.	Adding vegetables to the noon meal by getting donations and getting the vegetables from the school garden	President, Vice-President, Balwadi teacher, School teachers	Nutritive food for students	Physical verification
13.	Taking steps to prevent the practice of child labour	President, Vice-President, Ward Members, School teachers, PTA, NGO, SHG, Youth club	School enrolment, literacy, HRD	Physical verification
14.	Cleaning over head tanks	OHT operators, under the instruction of panchayat regularly	Health status, productivity	Verifying the records
15.	Creating awareness among the people about the consequence of alcohol and stop brewing and selling the same in the panchayat premises	President, Vice-President, Ward Member, Health Committee, SHG, Youth Club, NGO	Economic status of poor, status of women and children, health of individuals and reduction of social problems	Physical verification
16.	Creating awareness among the people about family welfare	PHC Staff, President, Vice-President, Ward Members, Health Committee, SHG, Youth	Livelihood security ensured.	Verifying the records small family

Contd.........

Sl.No.	Activities	Responsibility	Outcome	Verification
17.	Identify the vulnerable families and ensure food security to them and constantly monitor them with the help of government schemes	President, Vice-President, Ward Members, SHGs	Income generation, reduction of poverty, status of women	Physical verification
18.	Building the skill of the women through training	Presidents, Vice-President, Ward Members, Training Institution, Social Welfare Department at the District Women Development Corporation	Income generation, reduction of poverty, status of women	Physical verification
19.	Establish link between the skilled persons and banking sector for the establishment of business venture by the women	President, Vice-President, Ward Members, Planning Committee Members, NGO, Banks, SHG	Development of rural economy, and increase of status of women	Panchayat profile
20.	Building the skills of the youth through training	President, Vice-President, Ward Members, Training Institutions, NYK	Human Resource Development, Economic Development	NYK Report
21.	Establish link between the skilled persons and Banking sector for the establishment of business venture by the youth	President, Vice-President, Ward Member, Planning Committee Members, NGOs, Banks, NYKs	Development of Rural Economy	Panchayat Profile '
22.	Ensuring proper functioning of PDS	President, Vice-President, Ward Members and SHG Officials of Civil Supply	Food Security	Verifying the BPL List
23.	Prevent open defecation in the villages by creating awareness and constructing toilets in each and every house	President, Vice-President, Ward Members, SHG Youth Club, NGO, Project Staff, TRSP, Retired Employees	Improvement in Health, Sanitation Environment	Physical verification

Contd.........

Sl.No.	*Activities*	*Responsibility*	*Outcome*	*Verification*
24.	Creating awareness about RCH by printing a card and giving it to every family	President, Vice-President, Ward Members, Health Committee, NGO, Staff of PHC	Improvement in women and children, health, economic status	PHC records
25.	Ensure the delivery of services from sub centre and PHC to the people through the schemes available for prenatal and post natal care	PHC Staff, President, Vice-President, Ward Members, SHG, NGO, Health Committee	Increase in health status and economic status	Verifying the PHC records
26.	Creating awareness about growing medicinal plants and make it a business by involving SHG and youth clubs	President, Vice-President, Ward Members, SHG, Planning Committee, Youth Club, NGO, NABARD Bank Staff.	Income generation for women -improvement of rural economy	Physical verification
27.	Creating awareness among the importance of water management	President, Vice-President, Ward Members, Community leaders, Planning Committee Members, NGO	Rational Utilization of Water	Physical verification
28.	Creating a common burial ground in to grave yard in the villages	President, Vice-President, Ward Members, SHG, Youth club	Social justice	Physical verification
29.	Taking steps to manage the solid waste and earn money from it for panchayats	President, Vice-President, Ward Members, Planning Committee, NGO, SHG	Environment development, income generation, better agricultural practices	Panchayat Records
30.	Organise workshop for pregnant women to disseminate the needed information akin to ANC and PNC	PHC Staff, SHG, President and Vice-President	Increase of health awareness, health status, economic status, Reduction of infant mortality and new born babies are in exact weight	Verifying with PHC records

Contd.........

Sl.No.	Activities	Responsibility	Outcome	Verification
31.	Conducting medical camps for poor and school children	President, Vice-President, Ward Member, NGOs, SHG, nearby Rotary and Lions Club	Improved health status	Verifying with PHC Rocords
32.	Make the SHG and Youth clubs to take up Panchayat works instead of employing contractor	President, Vice-President, Ward Members, SHG Youth club, NGO	Employment opportunity, quality of work, reduction of expenditure, local needs	Panchayat Records
33.	Regularly conducting Gram Sabha meetings.	President, Vice-President, Ward Members	Peoples participation, Good Governance	Panchayat Records
34.	Ensuring 60% attendance in Gram Sabha meeting.	President, Vice-President, Ward Members, all eligible members, SHG members, NGOs working in the Panchayats.	Transparency, accountability of panchayats	Panchayat Records
35.	Ensuring Women/Dalit participation 50% of attendance	President, Vice-President, Ward Members, SHG, NGO	Social justice, status of weaker section	Panchayat Records
36.	Information disseminations • Income/Expenditure display • Report on schemes implemented display • List of schemes proposed to be implemented • List of beneficiaries	President and Panchayat Clerk	Transparency, accountability credibility of Panchayat, Better participation	Seeing the Display Board of Panchayat
37.	Participatory decision-making • Opportunities for discussion to all communities • Equal status to all in seating • Developing consensus	President, Ward Members, Community leaders/ retired government officials, school teachers, Planning Committee Members, Dalit Leaders, NGOs and other association members	Achieving communal harmony, evolution of social capital	Verifying the records of Panchayats

Contd.........

Sl.No.	*Activities*	*Responsibility*	*Outcome*	*Verification*
38.	Develop a system of communication to give information about Gram Sabha meeting	President, Clerk, Ward Member, SHG, Youth Clubs, NGOs	Transparency, accountability	Physical verification
39.	Provision of water supply to Dalit hamlets	President and the concerned Ward Members, Committee for water supply	Receiving the services continuously	Physical verification
40.	Removal of untouchability by • Preventing the two tumbler system • Participating in temple festival	President, Ward Members, SHG, Youth Clubs, Community Leaders.	Social justice, Communal harmony	Physical verification
41.	Training to Dalit Youths in skill development and availing THADCO schemes	President, Youth Clubs, NGOs, Education Institutions	Economic development, social justice	Physical verification
42.	Identification of all CPR verifying the status of encroachment details	Panchayat President, Vice-President, Ward Members, Government Officials, Police Department	Environment development social justice, income generation	Verifying Panchayat Records
43.	Removal of encroachments	Panchayat President, Vice-President, (Revenue & Police Department)	Productive use of resources, equity, income generation for Panchayats	Verifying Panchayat Records
44.	Utilizing the Common Properties and developing the same.	Panchayat president, Ward Members, NGO, SHG, Youth groups	Environment development, income generation	Verifying Panchayat Records
45.	100% house tax collection	President, Clerk, Vice-President, Ward Members, SHG, Youth	Financial status of Panchayat more government funds	Verifying Panchayat Records

Contd.........

Sl.No.	Activities	Responsibility	Outcome	Verification
46.	Panchayat functioning as a system	President, Clerk, Vice-President, Ward Members	Accountable	Verifying Panchayat Records
47.	Records maintenance/ transparency	President and Clerk	Good Governance	Verifying Panchayat Records
48.	Preparing a perspective plan through village planning forum	President, Ward Members, Planning Committee, School Leaders, NGO, Youth, SHG	Planned development better use of resources	Verifying Panchayat Records
49.	Formation of Statutory Committees	President	Efficiency of panchayats accountability	Verifying Panchayat Records
51.	Old age, physically and mentally disabled, destitute, orphan and other vulnerable sections	President, Ward Members, SHG, NGO, Government, and Planning Committee	Social security, social harmony	Verifying Panchayat Records

The above projected activities could be carried out easily if the Panchayat meets some key assumption. They are :

Key Assumptions

— Harmony prevails in Panchayat
— Panchayat is perceived as development space.
— Community supports the Panchayats.
— Panchayat leader has got commitment.
— Panchayat leader has vision.
— Panchayat leader has got skill and capacity.
— Panchayat is not leader centric.
— Panchayat is people and system centric.

APPENDIX–1

FOREWORD

In 2002, the process of facilitating the creation of Panchayat level plans commenced in six Panchayats in Sivagangai District. Rural Welfare Trust a local developmental organization was entrusted with the primary responsibility to support the initiative in the district. At a large and well attended development seminar at Gandhigram in October 2002, the Presidents of these six Panchayats presented their plans to a gathering that included the Minister for Rural Development of Tamil Nadu Government, senior bureaucrats from the State as well as district administration, representatives of the media and other elected representatives. Women Presidents headed all six Panchayats. Subsequently, at the suggestion of the district administration four more women headed Panchayats were included taking the total to ten panchayats.

A review of the results of the Plans created, revealed an excessive and undue emphasis on the creation of infrastructure. Had the role of Panchayats been reduced to the equivalent of the Public Works Department? Had the perceptions of the leaders themselves and the expectations from the community created an environment where the success of a representative was measured in terms of fixed assets created? Was the assumption that women representatives would influence the agenda and bring to the fore issues confronting children and women an incorrect one?

These questions and many more were posed before the Panchayat representatives from the ten panchayats of Sivagangai and a process to try and enquire into the reasons for the absence of social developmental issues commenced.

Meanwhile, at the request of the District Administration of Pudukottai District, a decision was taken to take up thirteen Panchayats (seven of which were headed by women) to facilitate the creation of Panchayat plans. It was hoped that based on the learning from Sivagangai: (1) the process at Pudukottai would be streamlined, and (2) that a conscious focus on social developmental issues would be maintained from the outset.

This process document seeks to capture the steps that have been undertaken to facilitate the creation of panchayat level plans. The document highlights the learning, the expectations and the challenges.

Why should Panchayats plan? Basis for the Exercise

It would be pertinent at the outset to clarify the basis and assumptions that have led to this process of facilitating the creation of Panchayat plans:

1. If Panchayats must truly emerge as 'little republics' or institutions of self-governance then their plans must form the basis for their subsequent activities.
2. In a democracy, leadership without a vision is a cruel oxymoron. A plan is an articulation of the vision of elected representatives and residents of a Panchayat. The scheme-based approach to development prevaricates the need for elected representatives at the Panchayat level to possess their own vision.
3. The principle of subsidiarity would necessarily imply that the Gram Panchayats or Village Panchayats are the most appropriate level to decide on the needs and priorities of their citizens. The creation of plans recognizes this.
4. The process of creation of plans can broaden the involvement and engagement of families in the shaping of their own destinies. Plans created in a participatory manner can also lead to greater accountability of representatives as well as transparency in functioning.
5. Panchayat level plans alter the basis of negotiation between representatives elected to the Panchayats and the bureaucracy at subsequent levels.
6. Prioritisation of needs could also lead to activities hitherto ignored being undertaken.
7. The process of planning not just creates a road map for the development of the Panchayat but facilitates a realistic understanding of the financial requirements. It could lead to diverse resource mobilization methods including internal financing by the Panchayats.

The Sivagangai Process—Learning

In the ten Panchayats that were selected for the creation of Panchayat Level Plans the following processes were employed[1]:

- Orientation of elected Panchayat Representatives, SHG leaders, youth and community leaders about the need for creating Panchayat Level plans within the context of Panchayati Raj.
- Workshops on Planning for the future—the steps to be taken and roles and responsibilities.
- Formation of Panchayat level committees[2].
- Capacity Building of Panchayat Presidents.
- Training of Planning Committee members.
- Bench-mark survey.
- Participatory Rural Appraisal to facilitate identification of needs and solutions.
- Regular meetings of the Panchayat level committees.
- Creation of a federation of 10 Panchayats for policy lobbying at the district level and regular meetings.
- Special Gram Sabhas.

A significant amount of time was spent in collecting information. While all of this information could potentially be used, the time spent on collecting information and the absence of a necessary correlation between the information and the emerging needs and priorities, were a matter of concern. The information that was collected included; basic information about the Panchayat, land utilisation—ownership, landless families, irrigation facilities, crops, basic amenities—drinking water, roads, transportation, electricity, community structures, post and telegraph, education- schools and enrolment, health and sanitation—facilities, number of persons with disabilities, women and children- women headed households, widows, deserted, women with disabilities, SHG's, children by age, immunization etc.

1. Not necessarily in the order in which they were undertaken.
2. No statutory role. The committees looked at Agriculture and Irrigation, Basic Needs and Infrastructure, Education, Health Housing and Non-Conventional Energy, Livestock, Income Generation and Small Scale Industries, Women Children and the aged, Arts and Culture.

During the course of the planning process it emerged that while the Panchayats perceived a role in demanding additional resources to fill gaps that existed, for example, inadequate teachers or health staff, they did not perceive a role for themselves in monitoring the quality of the current facilities available in their Panchayats. Partially, the absence of a clear accountability of Panchayat level government functionaries to Panchayats is the reason for this lack of engagement. On the other hand, in their own perceptions of their role, the programme-monitoring function does not find reflection.

When it became apparent that the process of planning itself could have led to issues other than infrastructure requirements being overlooked, a series of discussions were held with the elected representatives to try and identify whether there were other priorities that had not found expression and reflection in the plan. Finally, a breakthrough in the process took place, when two external facilitators—one of whom was an artist—commenced meetings at the Panchayat level. In addition to the elected representatives of the Panchayats, representatives from the nine committees that had been formed, as well as other influential village level leaders were present. A visual depiction of their village as it existed, was created with inputs from the citizens present. This was then posed against their own vision of their Panchayat in the future. The pictures then served as the starting point for the discussion that led to the articulation of new priorities and needs that had hitherto been ignored in the plan. To illustrate the point here are a few examples:

1. The Public Distribution System shop found mention. The problems that were currently encountered in the running of the system were mentioned and in the plan for the future the alterations in the functioning of the Panchayat that were desirable, found articulation.
2. It emerged that in the crèche of one of the villages, no attempt at raising issues of personal cleanliness and hygiene was emphasized. The need for a nail-clipper was identified and a decision taken to purchase one immediately since this did not require any external financing.

Some of the unanticipated benefits from the exercise thus far have been:

(a) The formation of a vibrant collective of the leadership of these ten panchayats at the district level.

(b) The process of creation of the plans led to clarity on some areas that required intervention immediately. In one case, a pond required desiltation. Despite repeated attempts to leverage resources from the administration, no assistance was forthcoming. The Panchayat mobilized community members and desilted the pond earlier this year through voluntary labour.

(c) The Panchayat's own perception of their role has altered.

(d) The attendance in the Gram Sabha's has increased.

This process was undertaken in all ten Gram Panchayats and additions were made to the existing plans. For the past six months these Gram Panchayats have been engaged in trying to leverage assistance for elements of their plans.

THE PROCESS OF PLANNING—PUDUKOTTAI EXPERIENCE

Based on the experiences in Sivagangai there were some clear pitfalls that had to be avoided: (i) It was clear that the process of creation of plans could lead to expectations of the community going up. This had to be sensitively factored into the strategy. (ii) The time taken to formulate the plans had to be reduced as far as possible since a long drawn process could lead to loss of interest and motivation. (iii) A strategic involvement, participation and support of the District Administration was critical to the success and had to be fostered and invested in. (iv) If a choice had to be made between elaborate time consuming processes and rudimentary and yet participatory techniques that could be accomplished in a short span of time then the latter should be preferred. (v) Only information that could be easily accessed and used should be collected. (vi) The objective of the exercise was to facilitate the process of creating a plan. Sophisticated techniques that could not be easily undertaken and owned by community members themselves were to be eschewed. (vii) With external facilitators there would always be the risk that the plan would cease to be the panchayats. The processes should try and reinforce the ownership of the Panchayat rather than alienate them.

Based on the experiences in Pudukottai it is possible to broadly classify the actions and steps to be taken into five categories[3]. The categories and the activities undertaken within each are as follows:

A. Preparatory/Environment Building

1. *Meetings with District administration*—Right at the outset, prior to commence the process of plan creation a meeting with the district administration explaining the objectives of the process and outlining the nature of support required from the administration is necessary. Through, the process of creation of the plans regular meetings with the administration are critical to ensuring their commitment to the process and their interest. In Pudukottai, the administration provided the physical space and basic infrastructure in the District Rural Development Agency (DRDA) for a spearhead team to be located in. Regular meetings and interaction and the commitment of the District Administration to the process, as well as to the Panchayats, ensured that existing schemes and pilots were dovetailed into the thirteen panchayats where the plans were being created.
2. *Identification of Gram Panchayats (GP's)*—Inputs from the administration can aid the process of identifying Gram Panchayats. If the exercise were to be undertaken on a pilot basis in select Panchayats, then it might be prudent to ensure that the geographical spread of the Panchayats across the district be limited to reduce the time as well as recurring costs.
3. *Memorandum with GP's*—Once the GP's are identified, a preliminary discussion with representatives of the Panchayat is necessary outlining the objectives of the planning process and clarifying the respective roles of the facilitating agency and the Gram Panchayat. The GP should subsequently pass a resolution committing its willingness

3. Based on the experience in Pudukottai certain improvements have been added to process.

to create a Panchayat level plan for its Panchayat.

4. *Orientation*—A daylong orientation for GP members, representatives from SHG's, youth groups, and other opinion makers at the village level should be held within the Panchayat. The orientation should emphasise the importance of planning, the steps to be undertaken and the importance of the Panchayat owning the process.
5. *Gram Sabha Meetings*—At the outset the Gram Sabha should be appraised about the activity. There are seven statutory committees that a Gram Panchayat must establish. If these committees have not been established then they must be set-up in consultation with the Gram Sabha. The Appointment Committee does not have any specific relevance to the planning process. However, there is a need to create a Planning Committee to oversee the entire process of creation of the Panchayat Plan. If the number of committees at the Panchayat level is to be kept within a manageable limit the Panchayat Council[4] can take on the responsibilities of the Planning Committee with one co-opted non-elected member from each of the six statutory committees. Periodic updates presented to the Gram Sabha will assist in a broad based participation in the process and ensure that there is constant direction.
6. *Capacity Building*—A five-day workshop for elected representatives of these panchayats - inclusive of council members—can serve as the foundation. The workshop should consist of a vision exercise as well as sessions on planning. Once the planning committee of the Panchayat has been created, a three-day workshop on "Planning for social development" will ensure that the focus of planning does not remain limited to infrastructure creation.
7. *Orientation of Committee Members*—The members of the committees will require orientation and role clarification to take forward the plan creation process.

---

4. Panchayat council consists of the Presidents, Vice-President and the Ward Members.

8. *Interface Between Elected Representatives and the District Administration*—At regular intervals from the inception onwards there should be regular interactions between the elected representatives and the district administrationt[5]. In the long run, this will develop the capacity of the elected representatives to deal with the administration and the interest and commitment of the administration will add value and lend credence to the plan creation exercise.
9. *Exposure*—Organising brief exposure visits to witness innovations undertaken by other Panchayats in the State will enable the Panchayats to 'think out of the box'. The fact that they do not have to limit themselves necessarily to only scheme based activities but they can plan their own interventions will be reinforced.
10. *Ward/Hamlet Level Meetings*—To generate interest amongst all sections, ideally meetings must be held at the ward/hamlet level about the need for plans, the steps to be taken, committees and the roles.
11. *Village Level Officials*—An opportunity for a meeting between members of the statutory committees, the Gram Panchayat and village level officials should be created. This will enable the inputs of village level officials and can facilitate their participation in the plan creation process.

B. Information Collection

12. *Identification of Information Needs*—In consultation with the members of the statutory committees and the Gram Panchayat, an identification of the information that needs to be collected to develop the plan must be undertaken. The sources of the information and the processes by which the information can be verified must be explored. Each committee must take on the responsibility to collect the information pertaining to its area of work.

---

5. Key government officials and elected representatives—District Collector, Project Officer-DRDA, other key officials in DRDA, BDO's Panchayat Union Councillors, District Councillors, MP's and MLA's.

13. *Finalisation of tool to Collect the Information*[6]—The tool to collect the information must be finalized.
14. *Identification and Orientation of Investigators*—The committees might need to enroll additional village level volunteers to assist in the collection of information. An orientation of those undertaking the responsibility to collect the information must be organized to facilitate information collection.
15. *Review of Information and Collation*—Once the information has been received, it should be reviewed with the committee members and investigators if any, to identify gaps and to establish the veracity of the information being collected. Once this step is completed, the information should be compiled and consolidated.
16. *Presentation of Information*—The information that is collected should be presented to the Gram Panchayat and Gram Sabha. An analysis must accompany the presentation of the information. Feedback, comments at both forums are important and will need to be incorporated into the information.

C. Community Based Planning

17. *Hamlet Level Development Conferences*—Comprehensive hamlet level development conferences should be held. At the hamlet level a series of activities need to be undertaken with an emphasis on enhancing the participation of families: (a) Identification of the most vulnerable—Poor families, women headed families, landless families, homeless families, families headed by a person with disability and no other/inadequate wage earners, families headed by the aged and infirm. An attempt must be made to explore the extent of benefits these families receive from existing social security and employment schemes to try and verify the accuracy of the targeting. This information is also useful inasmuch as the Panchayat can use it to monitor the extent of benefits that it is able to make available to the

6. A copy of an improved version of a tool is enclosed in an annexure

most vulnerable on a regular basis. (b) Identification and prioritization of needs—The needs emerging from each hamlet and the priorities should be identified. (c) Solutions, possible costs and a realistic re-prioritisation - For each of the needs that have been identified, potential solutions and the estimated costs should be identified. Once this information is available, it is possible that the hamlet may choose to re-prioritise its needs. (c) Information sharing and review—The Information collected and a brief analysis of it should be shared with the members present at the hamlet meeting since it could aid discussions and assist in identifying needs and priorities.

In the past Venn diagrams, ranking of priorities, resource maps, and wealth ranking have been used as tools. Even in the absence of any PRA technique being utilized, a sensitive and focused facilitator with an inquisitive mind can in a group situation cull out a wide variety of responses and achieve all of the above. The role of the facilitator for the group meetings is absolutely critical.

D. Approval, Ratification and Pre-implementation

18. *Consolidation of Hamlet Plans*—The inputs emerging from the hamlet level meetings need to be consolidated by the committees.
19. *Presentation and Approval of Gram Sabha*—The consolidated plans must be presented to a special Gram Sabha for inputs, comments, feedback and approval. The plan should be finalized only after approval of a special Gram Sabha. The costs for each component and the possibility of internal financing from the community should be definitely discussed. Future operation and maintenance costs of assets and the financial implications must also be raised and planned for.
20. *Panchayat Meeting*—The GP should incorporate the suggestions made by the Gram Sabha and then prepare an action plan with the next steps to be taken and allocate responsibilities for each. The plan should ideally be broken up into realistic annual plans to make it more realistic for

follow-up and monitoring.

21. *Identification of Potential Support Institutions/ Departments*—The Gram Panchayat could try and identify potential sources of support both monetary or otherwise for specific components of the plan. These could include sectoral departments, DRDA, MP-LAD, MLA-LAD, local NGO's, Banks etc.
22. *Proposal Creation*—Several components might require to be converted into specific proposals that are then presented to either sectoral departments or the DRDA for support. Technical details wherever necessary might need to be added to the proposals prior to their acceptance by departments.

E. Implementation, Monitoring and Review

23. The statutory committees and the Gram Sabha must play a key role in the implementation, monitoring and review of the process of transforming the plan into reality. The easiest way to guarantee this is by ensuring the ownership of each of these critical stakeholders in the Plan.

Replicability

Based on the current experiences, for a similar exercise to be replicated across multiple Panchayats the following would be essential ingredients.

(a) *An external Facilitating Agency:* In the absence of a large scale campaign across the state building an environment for the creation of Panchayat plans supported by capacity building of elected representatives and statutory committee members, there is a role for an external facilitator to assist the Panchayats.

(b) *Administrative Interest and Support:* In the districts where plans are to be created there has to be interest and support from the administration. Two key individuals for such an exercise are the District Collector and the Project Officer, District Rural Development Agency.

(c) *Committed Elected Representatives:* The commitment and

interest of elected representatives and other opinion makers is absolutely crucial to the success of a plan creation attempt. In the absence of their support even the existence of the afore mentioned ingredients will prove to be of little use.

Key Learning's

1. At the outset there has to be clarity that mere creation of infrastructure is not development. An emphasis on improving the quality of life of the citizens and a focus on social development is essential.
2. The Panchayats as part of the planning process must not plan only for additional investments, the planning process must also include attempts to monitor and improve the quality of existing services that are being made available in their Panchayats, even if the service providers are employees of the State. Demanding and monitoring the quality of services provided by the State is also an important function that must be performed.
3. Based on entitlements—State Finance Commission Grants- and income trends over the preceding few years from diverse sources, the Panchayats should create a realistic picture of the financial resources that they are likely to have access to. Factoring in even marginal increases by say 10-20 per cent per annum will assist in creating a realistic estimate of the resources that will be potentially available. Planning without any estimation of the total volume of funds that could realistically be leveraged from external or internal resources will lead to exhaustive wish lists that can raise expectations but never be met.

Unanswered Questions

At a macro level if the state is to be considered there are several issues that will require addressing:

1. *Timing*—When should Panchayat plans be created? It would make sense to create these plans within the first six months of a Panchayat being elected. It provides the Panchayat with a realistic time frame to establish its

priorities and seek to meet them. At the outset it would be practical to assume that each newly elected Panchayat might have its own ideas on what needs to be done. To assume that a plan created during one term will necessarily serve, as the basis during the term of a new set of representatives is not realistic.

2. *Relationship and Relevance to District Plans*—What is the relationship of Panchayat Plans to district plans and resource allocations? Unless, a process is introduced whereby the district plans become an aggregation of Panchayat level plans and allocations even to the district are then made available based on the need there is a likelihood of plans remaining pilot initiatives. The process of planning itself by Panchayats in the long run in the absence of support from the State might lose credibility. In the short run, an incentive system whereby Panchayats that create plans as the basis of their developmental interventions are rewarded with united developmental funds or even a dovetailing of existing schemes will lend a fillip to the process.
3. *Single Window*—The current process of allocation is not necessarily need based. More often than not it is supply driven. There are also issues pertaining to the political affiliation of the representatives or their own enterprise that can affect allocations. Needs expressed by Panchayats can be supported by multiple sources—DRDA as well as sectoral departments. Panchayats have to create proposals[7] and then try and leverage support from a source. Ideally, if the Panchayat is an autonomous entity at the district level it should deal with one source. If there are sources of support that lie beyond the district enterprise will prove rewarding.

---

7. Each proposal must consist of the following:
   (a) Basic information about the village.
   (b) Need and Justification for the request.
   (c) Details of the proposal inclusive of availibility of land, basic technical details, costs, contribution from the community if any.
   (d) Information on how the proposal will be executed if sanctioned.

ANNEXURE—1

List of Panchayats

Sivagangai District

Sl. No.	*Name of the Panchayat President*	*Name of the Panchayat*	*Name of the Panchayat Union*
1.	Mrs. Gomathi Sethuraman	Manalur	S. Pudur
2.	Mrs. C. Chinnammal	Orathupatti	S. Pudur
3.	Mrs. A. Alphonsemary	Velankudu	Thirupathur
4.	Mrs. K. SumathiKila	vayal	S. Pudur
5.	Mrs. Y. Nagajothi	Kozhikudipatti	Singampunari
6.	Mrs. V. Poongothai	Sevalpatti	Singampunari
7.	Mrs. K. Rakku	Vadavanpatti	Singampunari
8.	Mrs. VR Kalaiarasi	Veppankulam	Kallal
9.	Mrs. S. Gandhimathi	Kalipuli	Kallal
10.	Mrs. A. Pushpam	P. Nerpugapatti	Kallal

Pudukkottai District

Sl. No.	*Name of the Panchayat President*	*Name of the Panchayat*	*Name of the Panchayat Union*
1.	Vice President (In charge)	Meenaveli	Viralimalai
2.	Mr.A.Arumugam	Edayathimangalm	Manamelkudi
3.	Ms.Rani Sathappan	K.Rayavaram	Arimalam
4.	Ms.V.Mangalam	Mookampatti	Pudukkottai
5.	Mr.P.Shanmugam	Punalkulam	Gandarvakottai
6.	Mr.K.S.Saravanan	Melathur Panchayat	Thiruvarankulam
7.	Mr.P.Ramu	Nerinjikudi	Ponnamaravathy
8.	Ms.T.Dhanalakshmi	Melaputhuvayal	Kunnandarkoil
9.	Ms.Manjula	Elaikadaividuthi	Karambakudi
10.	Mr.Saravana Perumal	Poovalur	Avudayarkoil
11.	Ms.Bhavani Ilango	Merpanaikadu	Aranthangi
12.	Mr.A.Devi	Virachilai	Tirumayam
13.	Mr.Abdul Vahith	Parambalur	Annavasal

ANNEXURE—2

Statutory Committees of Gram Panchayats as per Government Order No. 168 of the Rural Development Department, Government of Tamil Nadu

1. Appointment Committee
2. Welfare Committee
3. Water and Sanitation Committee
4. Public Distribution System Committee
5. Education Committee
6. Works Committee
7. Agricultural Committee

Membership of the Statutory Committees

Appointment Committee

Panchayat President, 2 Panchayat Council members (who will be changed on a rotational basis each year).
Chairperson of the Committee—Gram Panchayat President

Welfare Committee

The Gram Panchayat selects members of the committee. The members of the committee will select a chairperson. Out of 5 members, 3 members are from the Panchayat council, one from a NGO and one social worker. This committee is responsible for the welfare of the women, children, the aged, widows and bonded labourers if any in the Panchayat. The committee shall concentrate on forming SHGs, the abolition of child labour, abolition of illicit liquor, female infanticide and female foeticide, abolition of dowry, abolition of untouchability etc.

Water and Sanitation Committee

The committee shall comprise of 12 members and the Chairperson shall be the Panchayat President. 3 members will be from the Panchayat council, and others shall be drawn from amongst women, SC/ST families of the Panchayat. A third of the membership of this committee should comprise of women.

Public Distribution System Committee

The committee shall consist of a total of 6 members, 3 of whom shall be from the Panchayat Council, 1 social worker and 1 representative of a NGO. The members of the committee shall select the chairperson themselves.

Agricultural Production Committee

There will be a total of 6 members, 3 from the Panchayat council, one from a NGO and one social worker.

Works Committee

Total membership will be 5, of which there will be 3 Panchayat council members, 1 NGO representative and 1 social worker.

Education Committee

1. Panchayat Council members.
2. Citizens
3. Parent Teachers Association members

The Gram Panchayat will issue the appointment for membership to these committees. Unless specified otherwise, the members of each committee shall select a chairperson from amongst themselves. Panchayat council members cannot become members of the more than 3 committees. Each committee (except the appointment committee) should meet once in 2 months to discuss issues. Each committee should submit their report to the Panchayat.

ANNEXURE—3

Information Collected and their Sources

Sl. No.	*Sector*	*Information*	*Sources*
1.	Child Development	Total number of children below 6 years, *Anganwadi* details, Infrastructure facilities Children attendance, Weight, Supplementary food, Main food, General performance of the balwadi teacher, Children's IQ talent, Personal hygiene, Environmental sanitation, Facilities to children mate, play materials, educational materials, uniform etc.	Meeting with anganwadi teacher/ Ayeh, register record in anganwadi, interaction with mothers and personal observation.
2.	Women development	(a) Total self-help groups, Total members, NGOs, Functioning of the SGHs, Loan assistance availed, Training details, Economic activities	NGO, clerk, animators women development corporation office, DRDA, Panchayat Union office
		(b) Pregnant women ANC, PNC, health awareness, small family norms adoption	VHN, anganwadi teacher, NGO
		(c) Number of adolescent girls health status, general awareness	*Anganwadi,* VHN, informal sharing with mothers
3.	Educational Development	Number of primary school, infrastructural details, students number, teacher number, details of extra curricular activities, education standard of the students, scope of the upgradation to next level of school, PTA/VEC function, enrolment of dropouts	Headmaster, teachers, PTA representativ, interview with parents, informal talk with students
4.	Public health	Number of public toilet, individual toilet, drainage, waste management, details of sub-centre, performance of VHN, Performance, PHC, Scope for soak pits	Village Panchayat record, NGO, VHN, SHG members, Personal observation

Contd.........

Sl. No.	*Sector*	*Information*	*Sources*
5.	Basic infrastrucutural facilities (a) Drinking water supply system	OHT/capacity HP availability bore wells, public taps, chlorination, open well, extension of public tap	Village Panchayat OHT operators
	(b) Street lights	Tube light, mercury light, solar lamp, single point light to huts	Village Panchayat OHT operators
	(c) Burial details ground	Facilities like, stage, roof, light, HP, road, passage, encroachment if any	Village Panchayat OHT operators
6.	Road/bridges/ culverts	Details of road and km, gravel road and km, metal road and km, Panchayat road and km, retainint wall, status and what is needed conversion, repair, maintenance, new one needed, where it is needed	Village Panchayat records, clerk, Ward Members, habitation visit spot verification
7.	Other infrastrucutal facilities	Bus shelter, threshing floor, library building, community hall, open theatre, post office building, cooperative institutions, SHG building, TV rooms	Village Panchayat record, habitation visit, SC habitation visit–focus
8.	Public Distribution System	Infrastructure facilities, family cards, ration commodities, non-availability of ration card, AAY scheme beneficiaries	Public Distribution shop records
9.	Agriculture details	Total wet & dry land, other classification of lands, irrigation sources, tanks, cannels, private wells, farmers details, MF, SF, BF,	VAO, Office, records
10.	Village Commons	Tanks, habitation, ponds, with oorain details, extent account if any ownership of tanks (VP/ UP/ PWD) Demand - Repair of tanks, desilting, maintenance of bunds, tree planting, channel maintenance, removal of encroachment	VA office records, Village Panchayat office records

Contd...........

Sl. No.	*Sector*	*Information*	*Sources*
11.	Status of marginalized sector	Total number of physically handicapped, total number of poor widows, poor oldage persons, chronical sick persons, child labour families, bonded labourers, frequently migrant families, affected by flood/ fire and other nature calamities	Village Panchayat records, district disabled rehabilitation office VAO office records, during PRA exercise, Sharing with SHG members
		Poor families eligible for housing	Village Panchayat records, Union Panchayat records
		BPL list families	Village Panchayat records, Union Panchayat records

BIBLIOGRAPHY

Abdul Aziz, *Decentralization: Mandal Panchayat System in Karnataka*, Hyderabad: National Institute of Rural Development, 1994.

Abdul Aziz, *Decentralized Planning: The Karnataka Experiment*, New Delhi: Sage Publications, 1994.

Abdul Aziz, *et al.*, *Ford Foundation—NIRD Project on Strengthening the Panchayati Raj Institutions in Karnataka: Impact Evaluation Study*, (mimeo), Bangalore: Institute of Social and Economic Change, 2000.

Abdul Aziz, *et al.*, *Ford-NIRD United grants to selected Grama Panchayats in Karnataka: A Concurrent Evaluation*, (mimeo), Bangalore: Institute for Social and Economic Change, 1999.

Afsal Mohammed, *Planning Atlas of Medak District, Andhra Pradesh, India*, Hyderabad: The Centre for Economic and Social Studies, 1998. (Revised edition published by Concept Publishing Co. 2004)

Amitab Mukherjee (Ed), *Participatory Rural Appraisal Methods and Applications in Rural Planning*, New Delhi: Vikas Publications, 1995.

Arora, R.K. and Rakesh Hooja (Eds), *Administration of Rural Development*, Jaipur: Arihant, 1996.

Asha Kaushik (Ed), *Democratic Concerns: The Indian Experience*, Jaipur: Aalekh Publications, 1994.

Ashok Mehta Committee, *Report of the Committee on Panchayati Raj Institutions*, New Delhi: Government of India, 1978.

Balwantrai Mehta Committee, *Report of the Team for the Study of Community Projects and National Extension Service*, New Delhi: Government of India, 1958.

Bendavid-Val, A. and Walker, P., (Eds), *Action Oriented Approaches to Regional Development Planning*, New York: Preager, 1975.

Bhargava, B.S. and Raphael., C., "Working of Gram Sabhas in Karnataka: A Study of Micro Level", *Journal of Rural Development*, Vol. 13, No. 2, 1994.

Bhimappa Patil, "Collective Success", *Spectrum - Deccan Herald*, March 28, 2003.

Bhora, O.P., "Decentralization and Devolution of Powers and Functions to Panchayats", *Journal of Rural Development*, Vol. 19, 2000.

Cernea, Michael (Ed), *Putting People First*, Oxford: Oxford University Press, 1991.

Chambers, R., "Project Selection for Poverty Focused Rural Development", *World Development*, Vol. 6., 1978.

Chambers, R., *Rural Appraisal - Rapid, Relaxed and Participatory*, Discussion Paper 3, Sussex: I.D.S., 1992.

Cheema, G.S. and Rondinelli, D.A., (Eds), *Decentralization and Development: Policy Implementations in Developing Countries*, Beverly Hills: Sage Publications, 1983.

Chimanbhai Patel Committee, Report of the National Development Council Committee on Micro Level Planning and Involvement of People at the Grassroots level, New Delhi: Government of India, 1993.

Chitlangi, B.M., "Environment Protection in Rural India Through Panchayat Raj" *Kurukshetra*, Jan-Feb 1997.

Choudhury, R.C. and Raja Kutty, P.S. (Eds), *Fifty Years of Rural Development in India: Retrospect and Prospect*, Vol. 2, Hyderabad: NIRD, 2002.

Clay, E.J. and Schaffer, B.B. (Eds), *Room for Manoeuvre*, London: Heine Man, 1994.

Coork, R. and James Manor, Enhancing and Institutional Performance and democratic decentralization in South Africa, O.D.A., New Delhi: Report copy circulated at a British Council Seminar, 1994.

Cruits, D. and Watson J.R., "Planning that Non-Planners can Do", *Journal of Rural Development*, 1987.

Dantwala, M.L. Committee, Report of Planning Commission's Working Group on Block Level Planning, New Delhi: Government of India, 1978.

Devendra Babu, M., "Decentralized Planning in Karnataka", *The Asian Economic Review*, Vol. XXXIX, No. 2, 1997.

Devendra Babu, M., "Governance, Planning and Development: The case of PRIs in Karnataka", *Indian Journal of Regional Science*, Vol. XXXIII, No. 2, 2001.

Devendra Babu, M., "Report of the Karnataka State Finance Commission: Status and Implications", *The Indian Journal of Economics*, Vol. XXXII, No. 326, 2002.

Devendra Babu, M., Functional and Financial Devolution to PRIs: A Study in Karnataka, (mimeo), Bangalore: Institute for Social and Economic Change, 1999.

Dhawan, K.C., Mittal, J.P. and Bhullar, B.S., "Energy Scenario of Indian Agriculture and its future Requirements", *Energy*, Vol. 18, 1993.

F.A.O., Towards Improved Multi-Level Planning for Agriculture and Rural Development, F.A.O., Economic and Social Development Paper No. 52, 1985.

Gadgil, D.R., *District Development Planning,* Poona: Gokhale Institute of Politics, 1966.

George Jacob (Ed), *Readings in Panchayati Raj*, Hyderabad: NICD, 1967.

George Mathew (Ed), *Status of Panchayati Raj in the States and Union Territories of India - 2000*, New Delhi: Institute of Social Sciences and Concept Publishing Company, 2000.

George Mathew, *Panchayati Raj from Legislation to Movement*, New Delhi: Concept Publishing Co., 1994.

Gittinger, J.P., *Economic Analysis, Agriculture Projects*, New York: John Hopkins, 1982.

Government of India, Agenda paper for the first meeting of the empowered Sub-Committee on Financial Administrative Institutions, held on June 26, 2003, New Delhi: Ministry of Rural Development, 2003.

Government of India, Five Year Plan, Vol. II, Sectoral Policies and Programmes, New Delhi: Centre Planning Commission, 2002.

Government of India, Guidelines for the Formulation of District Plan, New Delhi: Centre Planning Commission, 1969.

Government of India, *Indo-US Workshop on Geographic Information System, Background Papers*, New Delhi: Ministry of Environment and Forests, 1992.

Government of India, *Mid term Appraisal of the Ninth Five Year Plan (1997-2002)*, New Delhi: Centre Planning Commission, 2000.

Government of India, *Report of the task force on Devolution of Powers and functions upon Panchayati Raj Institutions*, New Delhi: Ministry of Rural Development, August 2001.

Government of India, Report of the task force on Panchayati Raj Institutions (PRIs), New Delhi: Centre Planning Commission, 2001.

Government of India, Report of the Working Group on States' resources for thc Tenth Five Year Plan (2002-07) Vol-II, New Delhi: Centre Planning Commission, 2002.

Government of India, The Report of the working group on Decentralized Planning and Panchayati Raj Institutions for the Tenth Five Year Plan (2002-07), New Delhi: Centre Planning Commission, 2001.

Government of Karnataka, District Governments and Decentralized Planning: Karnataka shows the way, Bangalore: Government of Karnataka, 1988.

Government of Karnataka, Report of the State Finance Commission Relating to Panchayati Raj Institutions, Bangalore: Government of Karnataka, 1996.

Government of Karnataka, The Karnataka Panchayat Raj Act, Bangalore: Government of Karnataka, 1993.

Government of Kerala, *Economic Review*, Trivandrum, Government of Kerala, 1996.

Government of Tamil Nadu, Report of the working group on Decentralized Planning and Panchayati Raj, Chennai: State Planning Commission, 1997.

Hanumantha Rao, C.H., "Decentralized Planning: Overview of Experience and Prospects", *Economic and Political Weekly,* Vol. 24, No. 8, 25 February 1989.

Hanumantha Roa, C.H., Committee, Report of Planning Commission's Working group on District Planning, New Delhi: Government of India, 1984.

Hoshiar Singh and Singh, D.P. (Eds), Indian Administration: Current Issues and Problems, Jaipur: Aalekh Publications, 1991.

Inamdar, N.R. and Kshire, K.V., *District Planning in India,* New Delhi: Oxford & IBH, 1986.

Jadar, Suresh, M., "Out of Muddy Waters", *Spectrum - Deccan Herald*, February 14, 2003.

Jain, R.B. (Ed), *Panchayati Raj*, New Delhi: Indian Institute of Public Administration, 1981.

Joshi, B.M., "Evolution and Practice of Decentralized Planning in India", *Indian Journal of Public Administration*, Vol. 35, No.1, 1989.

Jyotiparikh, *Energy Models for 2000 and Beyond*, New Delhi: McGraw-Hill Publishing Company Ltd., 1997.

Kamat, A.R., *Selected Writings and Speeches of D.R. Gadgil on Planning and Development*, New Delhi: Orient Longman, 1973.

Kamta Prasad (Ed), Planning and its Implementation, New Delhi: Indian Institute of Public Administration, 1984.

Kamta Prasad (Ed), *Planning at the Grassroots*, New Delhi: Sterling Publications, 1984.

Kanniappan, P. and Tamil Sevam, T., Proceedings of the Lecture-cum-seminar on Energy from Agricultural residue, *International Journal of Energy Research*, (accepted for Publication), 1993.

Keya Acharya, "Making Way for Progress", *Spectrum-Deccan Herald*, March 7, 2003.

Kuldeep Mathur (Ed), *Panchayati Raj Planning and Democracy*, Bombay: Asia Publishing House, 1996.

Kuldeep Mathur, "Promise of Local Level Planning", *Indian Journal of Public Administration*, Vol. 26, No. 3, 1980.

Kurulkar, R.P. (Ed), *Seminar Papers on District Planning*, Pune: Dastane Ramachandra and Co., 1991.

Maheshwari, R.C., Srivastava, P.K., Tomar, S.S. and Neema, B.P., *Energy Censes and Resource Assessment of Village Islam Nagar in the District of Bhopal*, Bhopal: Central Institute of Agricultural Engineering, 1981.

Mahi Pal, "Decentralized Planning and Panchayati Raj: Report of the Working Group in Tamil Nadu", *Economic and Political Weekly*, March 24, 2001.

Mahi Pal, "Evolution of Decentralized Planning in India", *Kurukshetra*, June, 1997.

Mani, N.D., *Resource Atlas of Dindigul District, Tamil Nadu*, New Delhi: National Informatics Centre, Planning Commission, 1997.

Mani, N.D., Watershed Maps of Athoor Block, Dindigul District, Dindigul: District Rural Development Agency, 1998.

Mathur, P.C. and Rakesh Hooja, *Projects, Planning and Development Administration*, Jaipur: Rawat Publications, 1996.

Mathur, P.C., *The Political Dynamics of Panchayati Raj*, New Delhi: Konark, 1990.

Medhushree Sekhar and Charles Nelson, "Panchayat Reforms in Tamil Nadu—A Perspective", *Journal of Rural Development,* Vol. 17, 1998.

Mishra and Swetha, *Democratic Decentralization in India*, New Delhi: Mittal Publications, 1994.

Misra, R.P. (Ed), *Regional Planning Concepts, Techniques, Policies, Case Studies*, New Delhi: Concept Publishing Co., 1992.

Misra, R.P. and Achyuta, R.N., *Micro Level Rural Planning*, New Delhi: Concept Publishing Co., 1980.

Misra, R.P. and Sundaram, K.V. (Eds), *Rural Area Development*, New Delhi: Sterling Publishers, 1979.

Misra, R.P. and Sunderam, K.V., *Multilevel Planning and Integrated Rural Development*, New Delhi: Heritage Publications, 1980.

Misra, R.P., Urs, D.V. and Nataraj, V.K. (Eds), *Regional Planning and National Development*, New Delhi: Vikas Publications, 1978.

Mundle, S., *District Planning in India*, New Delhi: Indian Institute of Public Administration, 1977.

Naginahal, R.T., Plan Formulation in Agriculture Department, Role and Importance of Planning in Agriculture Development (in Kannada), Government of Karnataka, 1995.

Natraj, V.K., *Non-Finance Factors Impinging on Devolution of Finances*, Chennai: MIDS, 2002.

Oomen, M.A., "Rationalizing Fiscal Federalism vis-à-vis Rural Local Governments", *Panchayati Raj Update*, September 2002.

Palanithurai, G., *Empowering People - Issues and Solution*, New Delhi: Kanishka Publishers and Distributors, 1996.

Paper on "Remote Sensing and GIS", Presented at the Workshop on Introductory Remote Sensing and Geographical Information System, Madras: University of Madras, Department of Geography, 1992.

Peter Smith (Ed), Project Identification in Developing Countries, University of Manchester: Institute of Development Policy and Management, 1978.

Prakasa Rao, V.L.S., *et al*, Working Paper on District Planning Officers Programme, Bangalore: Institute of Social and Economic Change, 1973.

Prodipto Roy and Patil, B.P., *Manual for Block Level Planning*, New Delhi: MacMillan, 1997.

Promod Parajalu and Smitu Kothari, "Struggling for Autonomy: Lessons from Local Governance", *Development*, Vol. 41, No. 3, 1998.

Raghavaiah, V., "District Planning and Administration - The Case for a Unified and Integrated Approach", *Indian Journal of Public Administration*, Vol. 23, No. 4, 1967.

Raghu Vilu, C.V. and Narayana, E.A., "Reforms in Panchayati Raj —A Comparative Analysis of Andhra Pradesh, Karnataka and West Bengal", *Indian Journal of Public Administration*, Vol. 37, No.1, 1991.

Raheena Begum, M., A *Textbook of Foods, Nutrition and Dietics*, New Delhi: Sterling Publishers, 1988.

Raja Sooriamoorthy, C.E., Kanniappan, P. and Ramachandran, T., "Energy Planning and Optimization Model for Rural Development", *International Journal of Energy Research*, Vol. 21, 1997.

Rakesh Hooja and Raju, B.Y., (Eds), *Decentralized Planning in Multilevel Framework*, Jaipur: Rawat Publications, 1993.

Rakesh Hooja, "District as a Planning Unit: Style and Locus", *Indian Journal of Public Administration*, Vol. 19, No. 2, 1973.

Rakesh Hooja, "Issues in Preparing Manpower for Effective Decentralized Planning", *Political Economy Journal of India*, Vol. 3, No. 2, 1994.

Rakesh Hooja, "Planning for Rural Development by Field Staff", *Indian Journal of Public Administration*, Vol. 26, 1980.

Rakesh Hooja, "Project Approach and Development Administration in India", *Prashiasnika*, Vol. 9, 1980.

Rakesh Hooja, "Project Formulation and Planning: Special Problems of Rural Projects and Some Examples of Rajasthan Responses", *Prashiasnika*, Vol. 12, 1983.

Rakesh Hooja, "Project Formulation for Rural Development Administration - A Rajasthan View Point", *Administrative Change*, Vol. 9, 1981.

Rakesh Hooja, "Three Disparate Book on Panchayati Raj Past and Present", *India Book Chronicle*, Vol. 19, No. 8, 1994.

Rakesh Hooja, "Training of Panchayati Raj Functionaries—Some Issues", *Journal of Rural Development*, Vol. 16, No. 4, 1997.

Rakesh Hooja, *Administrative Interventions in Rural Development*, Jaipur: Rawat Publications, 1987.

Rakesh Hooja, *Bibliography on Multilevel and District Planning*, Ujjain: Madhya Pradesh Institute of Social Science Research, 1995.

Rakesh Hooja, *District Planning - Concept Setting and State Level Applications*, Jaipur: Aalekh Publications, 1986.

Ram Reddy, G., (Ed), *Patterns of Panchayati Raj in India*, New Delhi: Macmillan Publications, 1977.

Rao, V.M., "Decentralized Planning - Priority Issues", *Economic and Political Weekly*, Vol. XXIV, No. 25, June 24, 1989.

Remy Prud' Humme, "The Dangers of Decentralization", *The World Bank Research Observer*, Vol. 10, No. 2, 1995.

Santha, E.K., "*Women's Participation in Gram Sabha's in Tamil Nadu*, Chennai Institute of Social Science, 2000.

Saumetra Chaunduri, "Devolution and the Message", *Economic Times*, August 8, 2000.

Sen, L.K, *Readings in Micro Level Planning and Rural Growth Centres*, Hyderabad: NICD, 1972.

Sen, L.K., Integrated Area Development, New Delhi: Government of India, 1972.

Shashi Bala Malik, Satsangi, P.S., Tripathy, S.C. and Balasubramanian, R., "Mathematical Model for Energy Planning of Rural India", *International Journal of Energy Research*, Vol. 18, 1994.

Singh, R.P., Painly J.P., Parikh, J. and Chandra Sen, "Rural Energy and Agricultural Interaction in 2000 A.D. - A study of Uttar Pradesh", *Indian Journal of Agricultural Economics*, 1992.

Singh, S., and Morsh, L., "Optimization of Bio-mass Production in a Village" *Bio Mass and Bio Energy*, Vol. 6, 1994

Singh, S.S. and Mishra, S., *Legislative Framework of Panchayati Raj in India*, New Delhi: Intellectual Publishing House, 1993.

Sinha, C.S. and Kandpal, T.C., "Optimal Mir of Technologies for Rural India - The lighting sector", *International Journal of Energy Research*, Vol. 15, 1991.

Special Number on Decentralization, *Indian Journal of Public Administration*, Vol. 24, No. 3, 1978.

Special Number on Decentralized Planning, *The Administrator*, Vol. 36, No. 3, 1991.

Special Number on District Planning, *Journal of LBS National Academy of Administration*, Vol. 20, No. 1, 1975.

Special Number on Multi Level Planning, *Indian Journal of Public Administration*, Vol. 19, No. 3, 1973.

Special Number on Panchayati Raj, *Journal of Rural Development*, Vol. 36, No. 3, 1991.

Special Number on Panchayati Raj, *Journal of Rural Development*, Vol. 16, No. 4, 1997.

Stiefel, M. and Pearse, A., UNRISD's Popular Participation Programme: An Inquiry into Power, Conflict and Social Change, Assignment Children (59/60), 1982.

Sudesh Sharma, K., *Panchayati Raj in India*, New Delhi: Trimurti, 1976.

Sundaram, K.V. (Ed), *Rural Area Development*, New Delhi: Sterling Publishers, 1979.

Sundaram, K.V., *District Planning in India*, New Delhi: Daya Publications, 1979.

Teddy, *Teri Energy and Data Directory and Year Book*, New Delhi: Tata Energy Research Institute, 1997.

Venugopal Reddy, Y., *Multi Level Planning in India*, New Delhi: Vikas Publications, 1979.

World Bank, Report on Rural Development, Sector Policy Paper, Washington DC: The World Bank, 1975.

Yugandhar, B.N. and Mukherjee, A. (Ed), *Readings in Decentralized Planning*, New Delhi: Concept Publishing Co., 1991.

INDEX